OFFENSIVE AND
DEFENSIVE SECURITY

OFFENSIVE AND DEFENSIVE SECURITY

CONCEPTS, PLANNING, OPERATIONS, AND MANAGEMENT

HARRY I. NIMON, PHD, PMP

LIBRARY OF CONGRESS CONTROL NUMBER:		2013908363
ISBN :	HARDCOVER	978-1-4836-3766-2
	SOFTCOVER	978-1-4836-3765-5
	EBOOK	978-1-4836-3767-9

This book was printed in the United States of America.

Rev. date: 05/15/2013

To order additional copies of this book, contact:
Xlibris Corporation
1-888-795-4274
www.Xlibris.com
Orders@Xlibris.com
131328

CONTENTS

INTRODUCTION AND PURPOSE

SECTION 1: THE BASICS

SECTION 2: THE ENVIRONMENT

SECTION 3: SECURITY PLANNING AND MANAGEMENT

TABLE OF FIGURES

LIST OF TABLES

INTRODUCTION AND PURPOSE

Introduction

Numerous publications exist that examine elements of the security discipline. Few address these elements as a continuum of interrelated functions. None examine the structure of offensive and defensive security in anything other than the domain of international security.[1] This text was written to fill this gap and to support a course in Offensive-Defensive Security, developed for Henley-Putnam University. The course briefly reviews the history of the field of strategic security and its three component parts—protection, intelligence, and counterterrorism—as well as its two distinguishing characteristics: offensive tactics and operations combined with technological innovation.

The course then moves to an in-depth assessment of related security areas that focus on defensive tactics and operations: homeland security, criminal justice, conflict and peace studies, and emergency management. While these fields may appear—at first—to be part of strategic security, this course and the associated text explore the critical differences and the fact that they are also critical elements of industrial, governmental, and military security. This text places an emphasis at an introductory level on both academic and professional distinctions in discussing the structures associated within these domains.

The text is divided into the following key sections:

Section 1: The Basics
Section 2: The Environment
Section 3: Security Planning and Management

Section 1 provides an orientation for the reader to a common frame of reference through information provided in the subsequent chapters. It is not intended to be a single source of all relevant information. Additionally, this book is not intended to be the exhaustive single source for all conditions. Rather,

---

[1]   Lynn-Jones, S.M. 1995. Offense-Defense Theory and Its Critics. *Security Studies*. No 4, Summery 1995. ppg 660-691.

it provides a road map of considerations on how to reach a specific goal in an efficient and informed manner.

Chapter 1, Basic Concepts, delineates the basic ideas, definitions, key learning points, history, and structure of the security profession. It describes the need for a consolidated approach to security operations that integrates the various disciplines necessary to develop and run efficiently. Next, it identifies the concept of offensive and defensive security planning and operations.

Chapter 2, Basic Concepts of Security Elements, describes the following elements of security: physical, personnel, information, financial, and cybersecurity. Understanding of the elements is the primary key to determining how the various pieces of the total environment must work together to ensure success and efficiency. This chapter provides the foundation of this understanding.

Chapter 3, Security Domains, identifies the pieces of the total environment as specific domains. Definitions of the practices, tools, approaches, and tangential considerations serve to introduce the student to the depth of structured understanding necessary to construct a security fortress. The information contained in these first three chapters is not exhaustive. There exists such a wealth of tools, techniques, models, and philosophies that one must first understand the environment one exists within to select the appropriate pieces and the glue necessary to bind them all together into a workable plan.

Section 2, The Environment, examines the world the security professional must inhabit, again, in a generalized manner and, likely, in a way never before considered. This section presents elements of neurology, biology, physics, philosophy, logic, analytics, and finance in a manner unique to the changing paradigm of Offensive-Defensive Security philosophy. The various chapters are labeled as "terrains" to represent the environmental information discussed. Each terrain approaches the referenced topic to clearly represent current thinking and science within each area as critical to the understanding of the total security environment, the how, why, and direct impact to the world of this security paradigm.

Chapter 4, Human Terrain, recognizes that the world is made up of humans. Humans will be performing the security planning, functions, assessments, etc. Humans also make up the majority of the threats against which the security professional must plan for and/or respond to. The chapter examines this terrain in four key parts: definitions of the concepts, the importance of the human condition, human cognition (how humans view themselves, their world, and decide how and when to act), and what is done by humans in the attempt to regulate human cognition for the benefit of the greater whole through laws, culture, and other processes.

This chapter examines current biological theories and knowledge of

- neurological development
- biological processes for memory development and cognition
- development and impacts of language
- introduction to culture, both societal and corporate
- expectation violation, group-think, and Aberdeen theories
- basic aspects of law and regulation

Chapter 5, Cultural Terrain, expands on the aspects of culture, given the depth to which it drives human perceptions, beliefs, and actions. This topic is vast with innumerable theories and conjectures. Yet there is an apparent consensus on the criticality of culture to human behavior and the individual societal acceptance of that behavior. This chapter will also consider theories on the manipulation of cultural dynamics as they relate to both offensive and defensive security.

Chapter 6, Legal Terrain, expands on the introduction to the aspects of law and regulation as they pertain to the generation of security plans and operations. This chapter will not address specific laws and regulations, but rather, it will examine requirements and pitfalls associated with both the application of legal restrictions and individual versus corporate rights and responsibilities.

Chapter 7, Physical Terrain, takes an approach to answer the question: Is security overly focused on the physical environment, and if so, why and should it be? The purpose of this examination is to provide an introduction into the dynamics of a fully integrated security domain. Granted, not all security problems relate to all environments; however, this paradigm of non-interrelationship appears to be changing.

Chapter 8, Cyber Terrain, takes the previous chapter's introductory approach a step further into the environments of information, cyber, and enterprise security. While a significant quantity of material has been written and numerous organizations exist with various information/cybersecurity services for sale, the integration aspects between this environment and the cultural/physical/cognitive domains is limited. The cyber domain examines these aspects with respect to a corporate-author developed model, entitled the Five Pillars of Knowledge, Information, and Data (KID) Management.[2]

Chapter 9, Personnel Terrain, completes the environmental circle by returning to the human element. This chapter examines the aspects of personnel security

---

[2] Van Kuijk, H. J. A. PhD. 2011. Dr. Van Kuijk is an executive VP—IT Solution Management for a major international corporation. His major passion and current objective is, as he states, "the definition and implementation of the digital organization of the future, in which people, business processes, KID, and software systems are integrated seamlessly into an effective and efficient business environment."

in consonance with the human terrain aspect to establish the differences and demonstrate how the two can integrate.

Section 3, Security Planning and Management, incorporates the information of the first two sections and applies the knowledge gained to the planning and management of an integrated security plan. The objective of this section is to use the concepts and processes developed via international agencies, such as the Project Management Institute (PMI), to demonstrate how to create an integrated and manageable enterprise structure and not a one-size-fits-all template.

Chapter 10, Information Evaluation, addresses the preliminary steps taken when preparing to implement and run a security plan.

Chapter Eleven, Security Planning, focuses on the planning processes as defined by PMI. Per their stated charter,

> *Project Management Institute (PMI) is one of the world's largest professional membership associations, with half a million members and credential holders in more than 185 countries. It is a not-for-profit organization that advances the project management profession through globally recognized standards and certifications, collaborative communities, an extensive research program, and professional development opportunities. Our worldwide advocacy makes us the global thought leader in this strategic organizational competency.*[3]

The chapter takes the information presented in the environment section and applies it to the PMI planning process to associate, qualitatively and in an introductory manner, how to use the relationship of the environments when developing an integrated security plan. The reasoning for this approach is to educate the student on the dynamics of organized planning in the face of the variable nature of the human experience, which is increasingly relevant in the security profession.

Chapter 12, Security Management, takes the planning process to its conclusion—that of managing the plan. Management of a plan, under the structure of the PMI internationally validated procedures, is more than simply watching people perform work. It is associating specific data to identifiable and measureable performance metrics that include scheduling, staffing, equipment performance, and financial aspects. The text concludes this process with a discussion on how to use data feedback to systematically change the processes, including the management of the change process itself.

---

[3] Obtained on October 2, 2011, from http://www.pmi.org/en/About-Us/About-Us-What-is-PMI.aspx

Purpose

Conducting a search on the Internet for "the purpose of security" returns thousands of items with a diverse structure of domains. Some, such as from the Department of Homeland Security,[4] define the purpose of security as follows:

    a.   Information sharing and analysis
    b.   Prevention and protection
    c.   Preparedness and response

The United States Army, Regulation 190-13: Physical Security outlines in infinite detail what comprises a physical security program and what specific responsibilities each command and staff level must perform, without defining what the ultimate goals of such a program are beyond being "a component of the force protection program."[5] AR 190-16 expands slightly, stating, "This regulation provides realistic guidance and prescribes uniform physical security policies and procedures for installation access control, aircraft, bulk petroleum assets, and critical communication facilities on Department of Defense (DoD) installations and equipment used by the military services and the Defense Logistics Agency (DLA)."[6]

Regulations on information and personnel security processes provide a better delineation of purpose, such as this excerpt from AR 380-5—Information Security:

> *Establishes the policy for the classification, downgrading, declassification, transmission, transportation, and safeguarding of information requiring protection in the interests of national security.*

---

[4]   Transcribed from information contained within (U.S. Department of Homeland Security, 2012) (U.S. Army, 2000) (Enescu, Vol 6(2), 2011)

[5]   United States Army. 1991. AR 190-13, pg 5, para 2-1

[6]   Op Cit. 1991. AR 190-16, pg 1, para 1-1a

It primarily pertains to classified national security information, now known as classified information, but also addresses controlled unclassified information, to include for official use only and sensitive but unclassified . . . . This regulation contains the minimum Department of the Army (DA) standards for the protection of classified information and material. Such standards may be enhanced but never lessened at command option.[7]

Interestingly, an appropriate definition on the requirement and objective of a security program is found in an article from the journal of *Economics, Management, and Financial Markets* shown in Figure 1: Definition of Security below.[8] This definition is concise and direct. It is the definition used throughout this text.

SECURITY CAN BE IDENTIFIED AS A

PROTECTIVE SERVICE OF

PREVENTION AND CONTROL

Figure 1: Definition of Security

Given this definition, how does the domain of security actually appear? The construction of a visual or other dynamic to represent the reality of a process or flow is a model of that flow. At times, such a representation appears as a graphic having steps and linking arrows or other such optical assists to render the flow visible. Often, it appears as a Venn diagram of interconnected circles depicting a set of actions intersecting at some point, implying separate states that just happen to have some similarities. This is inaccurate. Figure 2 is a more complete depiction

---

[7] Army Regulation 380-5, Information Security. 2000. pg 1, para 1-1.This regulation, as with all Army regulations, establishes responsibilities and minimum processes. At times such regulations also establish minimum performance levels, however, this is generally left to component commands.

[8] Enescu, M., Enescu, Maria., and Sperdea, N. M., The Specifics of Security Management: The Functions of Information Security Required by Organizations. *Journal of Economics, Management, and Financial Markets.* Volume 6(2), 2011, pg 201.

in continuum format.[9] This graphic represents the relationship of various codified requirements as a basis driven by noncorporate and corporate writings leading through to the more intricate requirements of national and global interactions.

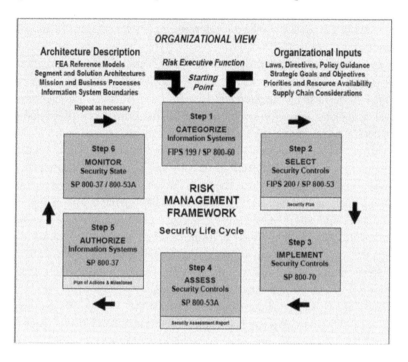

Figure 2: Security Continuum[10]

What this model depicts is a process that begins with an understanding of the requirements, which have been written into a set of minimum standards, process documents, etc., having begun with a firm understanding of the conditions or environment within which the plan and operation must occur. The second step is the integration of the environmental knowledge with the assets, capabilities, costs, and other factors into a development and operational plan. This plan is the basis for a series of projects designed to emplace the plan into the structure of reality. Each project builds upon the previous and adjacent projects to form the whole.

---

[9]   Rybollov Security Model (2009), blog by Security Professional and Carnegie-Mellon University Professor (Smith M., 2009) (Kraut, Vol 3, No 4, Nov 1989) (Agency) Michael Smith and downloaded from http://www.guerilla-ciso.com/archives/1406

[10]   Gikas, C. 2010. A General Comparison of FISMA, HIPAA, ISO 27000 and PCI-DSS Standards. *Information Security Journal: A Global Perspective*, 19:132-141. Pg 135. Taylor & Francis Group, LLC. New York, NY.

As the plan consolidates, integration begins, that of incorporating the security entity into the enterprise as a whole, whether it be a business, government entity, or military operation. The only difference is the scale. This is a vital step in that the act of protection cannot interfere with the process of performing the enterprise function. In fact, it must enhance the enterprise function and assist in ensuring its success.

Many enterprise functions operate within a federation or a community. That federation or community is not necessarily a social or geographic construct. A *federation* is defined by the *Merriam-Webster Dictionary* as "an encompassing political or societal entity formed by uniting smaller or more localized entities as (a) a federal government or (b) a union of organizations." A *community* is defined as "a unified body of individuals having a common interest."[11] Thus, a federation or community may be any specified set or body having common interests. In many business texts, such a group is also known as "stakeholders" and may actually have conflicting goals and objectives while simultaneously having common interests.

The development of a security plan must pay attention to these bodies, as most will have either political or legal standing in the implementation and management of operations. At times, though their goals may seem in conflict, their intentions are comparative and may even be complementary. Chapter 10 specifically addresses the dynamics of this process.

The final two stages of the model incorporate the concept of scale: national and global. The concerns and considerations remain relatively unchanged; however, the intricacies are greatly enhanced. Different political entities incorporate different cultures, behaviors, laws, expectations, languages, and numerous other considerations. What is considered perfectly legal and expected in one entity may be, and often is, illegal in another when the only thing changing is the political boundary. While some international agencies do exist to mitigate such situations, their reach is far from complete and their power to enforce nearly nonexistent.

---

[11]   Merriam-Webster Online Dictionary. 2011.

The Need for Planning and Management

The basic logic for the development of a security plan is simply put: to minimize risk and cost. In all such programs, management seeks to identify and quantify risks with possible solutions. At times, the risks are unknowable; thus, the solution is also unknowable. Figure 3 depicts a situation involving these two organizations.

The figure shows the following information:

a. A crisis event
b. A response generated by the crisis event that was *not* provided an anticipation plan
c. A response generated by the crisis event where the organization established an anticipation plan

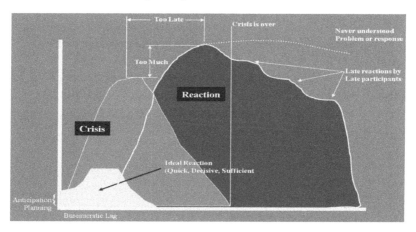

Figure 3: Non-Synergistic Post-Hysterical Reaction/Response Curve

The vertical axis is measured in cost, while the horizontal axis is measured in time.

Examine the graphic in Figure 3. Notice that the crisis initiates and has duration and cost, actually quantified during the events. At some point, with or without intervention, the crisis will end. The first organization had not conducted sufficient due diligence planning to determine that there may be unquantifiable risks associated with the program tasks contracted to them. As such, not only did they not recognize the crisis for what it was, they were not prepared to begin examining it for potential solutions until well into the crisis period. As the organization began to react, costs mounted and did not reach their peak level of effort until the crisis was almost over on its own. Additionally, as other higher-ranking individuals became aware of the situation, they began to micromanage the problem, which increased the duration of the response and subsequent costs well after the crisis had disappeared.

The second organization had performed appropriate due diligence analysis. They realized that there may be unquantifiable risks and established a process for monitoring operations and initiating a "rapid response team," should something unforeseen occur. Thus, not only did they recognize the crisis for what it was almost immediately, they had a team in place to determine and implement an appropriate response. They short-circuited the crisis, as a result, causing it to end much sooner than otherwise would have happened.

Therefore, the reason for planning is to:

a. Identify risks and/or threats,
b. Analyze and prioritize these with respect to cost, opportunity, and assets, also known as performing due diligence,
c. Devise plans and strategies to reduce the likelihood of these situations occurring without a means of identifying and responding to them.

Given the requirements for due diligence and identification of solutions, a means of management of assets, tasks, and operations is also required. Kraut, Pedigo, et al, establish seven key responsibilities for managers:

a. Managing individual performance
b. Instructing subordinates
c. Planning and allocating resources
d. Managing group performance
e. Monitoring the environment
f. Representing one's staff[12]

---

[12] Kraut, A.I., Pedigo, P.R., McKenna, D.D., and Dunnette, M.D., The Role of the Manager: What's Really Important in Different Management Jobs. *The Academy of Management Executives.* Vol 3, No 4, Nov 1989. Pg 286.

Key Learning Points

The approach and purpose of this text include the following key learning points:

a. Define the key elements and environments within which the security plan and operational management activities must occur
b. Familiarize the student with cultural, biological, financial, informational, and legal aspects necessary for the understanding of how these domains influence human behavior; the primary aspect of security planning and operations
c. Familiarize the student with the analytical processes necessary to incorporate the above key points into the structure and culture of the organization or entity to be protected
d. Enable the student to develop an understanding of the need for an integrated approach to security operations
e. Provide a systematic approach for the development of plans and operational metrics for the management of these plans.

The following sections delve into the environments within which the security professional must operate. They are not exhaustive, as this would expand this text beyond usefulness. Nor are they in many cases more than theory, as the sciences involved are still evolving. They are, however, an introduction into a world that welcomes continued exploration to delve into the depths necessary for understanding and development.

SECTION 1

THE BASICS

Chapter 1

BASIC CONCEPTS

Prior to beginning any detailed discussion of any profession, it is necessary and helpful to understand the profession's development history and current structure. Additionally, it is necessary to provide a common frame of reference between the text and the reader by establishing certain basic definitions and positions. This is the objective of this chapter, with the following approach:

a. Provide a structure of the security profession as it will be used in this text
d. Establish a brief history of the profession as a means of associating the reader to the text
e. Define the basic construct or concept of the elements of security
f. Introduce the concepts of both Offensive-Proactive and Defensive-Reactive security
g. Establish a common frame of reference between the reader and the text with some initial assumptions, limitations, and definitions associated with the text
h. Introduce the reader to the planning process by detailing the requirements for planning

The beginning of the text mentions the incorporation of intelligence into the offensive/defensive structure of operations. While this text focuses on the security aspects, the information disclosed can also apply to the intelligence profession. The majority of the text relates to the security profession, with areas specific to intelligence highlighted, when necessary.

Finding a single source structure for the security professional is a difficult task, since there are as many models as there are various elements of security, each focused on those individual elements. One model that appears to come close to an overarching structure of intelligence and security is Confidentiality, Integrity, Availability Triad.[13] The triad appears in Figure 4.

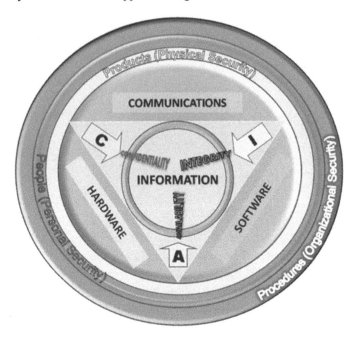

Figure 4: CIA Triad

The CIA triad represents a model for information security where information security itself is the central component supported by all other elements. It does not in turn, however, show how information is critical for the development and support of the other security elements. This model was expanded by Donn Parker with his hexad model, which added three additional elements, but still solely focused on information security.[14]

A somewhat more appropriate model exists in an online publication created by author Simon Holloway, who references a security consulting and contracting company, Vigitrust Limited. The model, shown as Figure 5, depicts the structure as shown in the Bloor Research website.[15]

---

[13] Downloaded on October 4, 2011, from http://en.wikipedia.org/wiki/CIA_triad#Key_concepts

[14] The Parkerian Hexad Model name was actually coined by Michael Kabay and includes the aspects of control, confidentiality, integrity, authenticity, availability and utility. All aspects of an information security program structure.

[15] Downloaded October 4, 2011, from http://www.bloorresearch.com/analysis/11624/security-what-security-p1-p1.html

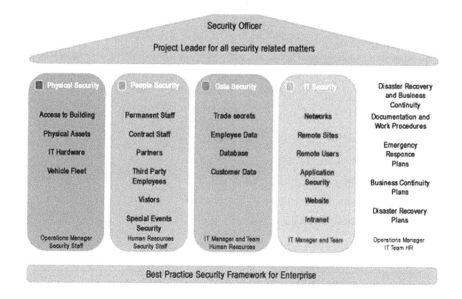

Figure 5: Security Policy Framework[11]

Notice in the model shown in Figure 5 that the organizers at Vigitrust have included disaster recovery and business continuity. This is an interesting inclusion into the realm of security operations. Later chapters will discuss the appropriateness of this addition. The structure of this model shows a base of appropriate best practices critical for any organization. The pillars depict the traditional strengths of the security profession, all under the appropriate set of project/program leads, reporting to the chief security officer. An element not included in this structure, however, is the glue holding all society together: finances. Economic assets are necessary to perform security functions, obtain equipment, hire and retain talent, and provide for the means of ensuring protection of your charges.

Security creates a requirement and set of interactions found in few other professions. While these interactions are not necessarily continuous, they are certainly cyclical. The model is more aptly considered as a construct, as shown in Figure 6. This model approach establishes the basis for this text.

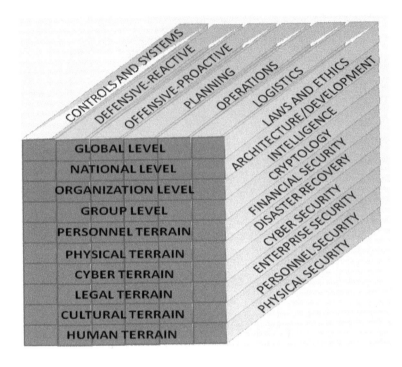

Figure 6: Security Profession Construct

THE HISTORY OF SECURITY

Any search for the history of security on the Internet results in a nearly infinite listing of various sites, few of which actually discuss the origins of the concept of security. Attempting to focus the search by examining the key words of security organizations or *security companies* results in multiple ads for various firms providing monitoring services or the like. There appears to be a wealth of information on cyber or information security processes, firms, etc., as well as additional information on such topics as social security. However, the goal was to ascertain if there existed a history of the development and evolution of what we now term *security*, whether it is a relationship to national, regional, financial, personal, or other factors.

Even prior to beginning this search, the assumption was that such an effort would be too broad for focused results. Therefore, this text only provides a brief examination, focusing on military and societal history.

EARLY HISTORY

From the earliest recorded times, there have been individuals of wealth and power and those seeking to remove that wealth and power from these individuals. It is likely this condition, given the archeological evidence of the mass destruction of prehistoric villages by warfare, existed long prior to recorded history. Per R. Brian Ferguson,

> The earliest persuasive evidence of warfare uncovered so far comes from a graveyard along the Nile River in Sudan. Brought to light during an expedition in the mid-1960s led by Fred Wendorf, an archaeologist at Southern Methodist University in Dallas, Texas, this graveyard, known as Site 117, has been roughly estimated at between 12,000 and 14,000 years old. It contained fifty-nine well-preserved skeletons, twenty-four of which were found in close association with pieces of stone that were interpreted as parts of projectiles. Notably, the people of Site 117 were living in a time of ecological crisis. Increased rainfall had made the Nile waters run wild, and the river dug its way deeply into a gorge. The adjacent flood plain was left high and dry, depriving the inhabitants of the catfish and other marshland staples of their diet. Apart from Site 117, only about a dozen Homo sapiens skeletons 10,000 years old or older, out of hundreds of similar antiquity examined to date, show clear indications of interpersonal violence.[16]

The causes of this violence, per Ferguson, can be examined by observing the current prehistoric tribes of the Amazon basin. The logic is that since many of these tribes have only been recently influenced by modern society and generally retain their prehistoric culture and traditions, they are an appropriate archeological reference source for determining early human behavior. As such, Ferguson noticed that the individuals within specific tribal groups, while they may have difficulties with their other tribal members, generally do not resort to fatal violence. However, when either threatened by a different tribe or faced with shortages in food supplies, mating-age females, or other such society-threatening conditions, they will resort to violent group attacks on neighboring tribes to obtain these needs.

Additionally, there are other tribes that appear to look upon warfare as the means of showing rank and authority within their organization. Societal norms

---

[16]   Ferguson, R.G. The Birth of War. *Natural History,* 00280712, Jul/Aug 2003, Vol. 112, Issue 6. Downloaded on October 6, 2011, from (R.G.) (Walthall, 1980) (Bettinger, Vol 50, No 5, October 2009)

restrict intratribal conflict, possibly due to the need for the tribe as a whole to remain strong enough to deter intertribal aggression. This leaves "warfare" as the only outlet for the achievement of elevation by dominance within a tribal setting. The question arises then of how a society polices and enforces the intra-tribal taboo on violence?

Examination of tribal archeology demonstrates that all tribal societies have authority figures. This use of recognized leaders is a common standard among communities, whether speaking of the early American Indians or the current tribes of the Amazon or the tribes of Afghanistan. John Walthall states in his book,

> The social organization of segmentary tribes was egalitarian in nature. Fried (1960) defines an egalitarian society as one in which there are as many positions of prestige in any age-sex grade as there are persons capable of filling them. While among segmentary tribes certain individuals, such as the official community spokesman, might hold office through ascribed authority (birthright), their distinction and power were slight. Usually, real authority was acquired, at least for brief periods of time, by individuals with special skills.[17]

It stands to reason that such individuals with "special skills" resulting in leadership could, in turn, draw to them other individuals of like mind or desire as followers. These individuals, out of common cause, at least for the duration of the need for the special skill, form a protective barrier against conflict or competition, as long as the leader also provides for the needs of those performing the protective task(s).

It is also logical to conclude that as societies transformed from hunter-gatherer to agrarian, the need for specialized activities grew as well. This conjecture is borne out in further archeological investigation by such authors as Bettinger, Richardson, and Boyd, who concluded that while climate change is a constraint on the development of an agrarian culture, the development of social institutions are dominant.[18]

One of the required social aspects within such societies is the ability to protect oneself and one's associates from the marauders remaining in the land. Segments

[17]   Walthall, J.A. Prehistoric Indians of the Southeast: Archaeolgy [sic] of Alabama and the Middle South. The University of Alabama Press. 1980. pg 110.

[18]   Bettinger, R., Richardson, P., and Boyd, R. Rethinking the Origins of Agriculture: Constraints on the Development of Agriculture. *Current Anthropology*. Vol 50. No 5. October 2009. ppg 627-631. Downloaded on October 6, 2011, from https://ehis.ebscohost.com/eds/pdfviewer/pdfviewer?vid=3&hid=120&sid=b4441d10-f7a5-4634-a170-dad574c126cd%40sessionmgr110

in such texts as the Bible depict situations where, as during the rebuilding of Jerusalem, one half of the available population worked on either rebuilding the walls or supplying those working on fortifications. The other half kept watch for raiders (Nehemiah Chapter 4). For survival, man has always had the need to locate, identify, and classify threats in sufficient time to appropriately respond. The response, at least in the earliest times, would be every male hunter of the tribe obtaining a weapon and rushing out to meet and engage the threat. As noted above, the threat was most often from outside of the family/tribe unit.

However, as these units became more stable, due to the ability to locally grow food and store it for the nongrowth periods, permanent structures became the norm. These rooted communities replaced the temporary tentlike structures found in so many archeological sites. With these permanent building projects came the need for the protection of the structures themselves, given the amount of labor devoted to their construction and their inherent value. The creation of protective walls was the logical response to a long-term defense strategy.

At first, these walls were primarily used to deny access to the compound by wild animals, water (in the event of flooding), and fire. They were only tall enough to permit the defenders to see and defend over them, rather than denying access to other humans. It was not long before the walling structures began to gain a height sufficient to deny human entry while simultaneously permitting their defense. Watchmen were placed to maintain observation on the highest points to provide for early warning. When there was a need to raise alarm, signals were either audible, as in bells, horns, etc.; visible, as in mirrors, flame/smoke, or signal arrows/rockets; or a related combination. As the use of the alarm devices grew, so did the ability to have outposts away from the main compound for even earlier warning.

The problem with this system is that as inhabitants developed specializations, it was illogical to remove them from their areas of training. The need for manpower to perform daily tasks, such as maintaining tools and buildings and obtaining necessary food stores, meant that these specialists could not be spared for fortifications. They could not be long away from their set tasks or risked due to the length of time necessary to replace their learned skills. This was the advent of the need for a professional defender.

One could imagine a leader within one of these compounds discussing the situation with several of the best hunters/fighters who distained the daily work of farming, building, and other such functions. They may reach an agreement where the leadership would provide protection in exchange for the necessities in life. The defenders would risk younger men in the outposts until their skills and experience progressed sufficiently for their elevation to reduced risk and increased rank. The more skilled would be tasked with local protection of the leader and of the compound.

Evolution continues to take its course and the societal compounds flourish into small towns and larger cities, with their leadership becoming more powerful in terms of specie[19] and protective personnel. With such growth, however, comes the additional challenge of individuals that require support but who do not significantly benefit the local society. Whether due to infirmity or even those too lazy or otherwise unwilling to honestly work for their needs, there is a strain added onto the community as a whole. Also, there is the growth of a religious and healer caste, answering the Maslow Hierarchy[20] needs beyond basic survival (see Figure 7) and taking the society even further into the security and welfare dimensions.

The hierarchy, shown below, was established by psychologist Abraham Maslow in his 1943 work, *A Theory of Human Motivation.*[21] Maslow postulated that as humans progressed in societal/evolutionary development, their needs shifted from the physical to the psychological/social. This postulated evolution also allows for the development of virtues and vices, as time stores shift from basic survival to include "free time" for other pursuits.

Figure 7: Maslow's Hierarchy of Needs

---

[19]   The word 'specie' is used here instead of money as this medium of exchange and barter was utilized far longer than such things as gold, silver, or other metals.

[20]   The Maslow Hierarchy of needs depicts a pyramid structure with the more basic needs at the base which, when fulfilled, lead to the higher levels shown. Downloaded on October 7, 2011, from http://psychology.about.com/od/theoriesofpersonality/a/hierarchyneeds.htm

[21]   Maslow, A.H. Psychological Review, Vol 50(4), Jul 1943, 370-396

With such freedom often comes boredom, which can lead to activities against the members of one's own society if not productively channeled. To manage such situations, the leadership began to develop rules of behavior. Obviously, many of these rules were couched for the benefit and protection of the power base and leadership, as it so continues to this day.

This generation of societal rules led to the need for the development of a means of enforcement and punishment. Per Freud, fear of the gods only lasted so long as there were examples of such retribution. This led to the development of a force beholden to and supported by the leadership as their executive arm. To the leadership, it was easiest to combine this law enforcement function with the overall community protection function, thus the creation of an army.

The creation of armies included an additional evolutionary function: intelligence work. Leadership developed a means of finding out what potential competitors were doing to predetermine threats to the power structure. Again, the Bible captures examples of such societal developments:

> *The LORD said to Moses,* [2] *"Send some men to explore the land of Canaan, which I am giving to the Israelites. From each ancestral tribe send one of its leaders."*

> [3] *So at the LORD's command Moses sent them out from the Desert of Paran. All of them were leaders of the Israelites.*

> [17] *When Moses sent them to explore Canaan, he said, "Go up through the Negev and on into the hill country. 18 See what the land is like and whether the people who live there are strong or weak, few or many. 19 What kind of land do they live in? Is it good or bad? What kind of towns do they live in? Are they unwalled or fortified? 20 How is the soil? Is it fertile or poor? Are there trees on it or not? Do your best to bring back some of the fruit of the land." (It was the season for the first ripe grapes.)*

Sun Tzu in *The Art of War* also discusses the use of spies to generate intelligence, listing that there are five kinds of spy: local spies, inside spies, double agents, doomed spies, and surviving spies.[22] Sun Tzu also describes the types of information each spy is to obtain.

a.   Local spies provide information on the battleground.

b.   Inside spies provide information on the competition.

---

[22]   Clavell, J. (ed). Sun Tzu, The Art of War. Delecorte Press. NY, NY. 1983

c. Double agents play both sides.
d. Doomed spies provide misinformation to the competition.
e. Surviving spies provide real-time information on current battles.

The purpose of spies is to simply provide information to protect the leadership and society from enemies/competition. The spy is similar in nature to the watchtowers and outposts identified earlier, just much more extensive in scope. The fortification processes have evolved, with the spy, into both active-offensive and reactive-defensive functions. This will be formally introduced later in this chapter and extensively developed in the remainder of the text.

As technology expanded, so did the activities associated with security. Scouts and spies were subjected to counter-HUMINT (Human Intelligence) activities, such as the shielding of military forces and movement by cavalry (e.g., General J. E. B. Stewart of the Confederate States of America (CSA) as demonstrated in his failed missions during the Battle of Gettysburg in 1863) and the execution of such spies when caught (e.g., Nathan Hale during the Revolutionary War).

During the United States Civil War, General Stewart's mission, as assigned by General R. E. Lee, was as follows:

> If General Hooker's army remains inactive, you can leave two brigades to watch him, and withdraw with the three others, but should he not appear to be moving northward, I think you had better withdraw this side of the mountain to-morrow night, cross at Shepherdstown next day, and move over to Fredericktown. You will, however, be able to judge whether you can pass around their army without hindrance, doing them all the damage you can, and cross the river east of the mountains. In either case, after crossing the river, you must move on and feel the right of Ewell's troops, collecting information, provisions, etc.[23]

Looking again to Sun Tzu, he addressed screening an enemy's scouts and discovering their spies to turn their information against themselves while simultaneously hiding your own capabilities. As technology has developed, this requirement for protection and invasion-penetration of the enemy's systems has changed in scope but not in need. An excellent example is the creation of "invisible writing" and ciphers. Notables such as Caesar, Galileo, and many others

---

[23] Downloaded on October 7, 2011, from http://www.brotherswar.com/Gettysburg-3q.htm and confirmed in Sears, S.W. *Gettysberg*. Houghton Mifflin Company, NY, NY. 2004.

used encryptions to protect important writings from being read by those other than the intended recipient.[24]

The invention of signal flags and lights increased the need for protection from unintended recipients. This led to the development of additional ciphers and the processes used to circumvent them by the enemy. Some of the most notable coding/decoding situations throughout history include the following:

a. The use of telegraph systems to dictate national strategy from the president of the United States to general officers in the field during the U.S. Civil War resulted in both interception by Confederate signal personnel and destruction of the lines during the Battle of Gettysburg in July 1863.

b. The severing of the German transatlantic cables in the North Sea by the British cable ship HMS *Telconia* on the first day of WWI, which forced the Germans to use radios, making interception and decryption easier.[25]

c. U.S. Navy tapping of an underwater communications cable in the Black Sea during the cold war, enabling knowledge of Soviet naval communications.[26]

d. The Enigma Project during WWII, with the British and American interception, decryption, and exploitation of German and Japanese communications.[27]

In addition to the national security and military applications, there are industrial and public security uses of such coding technologies. As stated earlier, early settlement security relied on watchtowers and outposts that communicated using various means of signaling devices. The development of technology only created new means for this emergency and early notification of threats.

For example, the invention of the telegraph enabled various cities a means of early notification and passage of alarms during disasters, such as fires. In

[24] Ancient Rome utilized ciphers to both communicate and store sensitive information. Julius Caesar is known to have a special cipher used to communicate to his generals in the field. Information is contained on this at http://www.bletchleypark.org.uk/edu/yc/codes.rhtm

[25] Young, M.D. Electronic Surveillance in an Era of Modern Technology and Evolving Threats to National Security. *Stanford Law & Policy Review.* Vol 22:1. 2011. ppg 11-39.

[26] Sontag, S., Drew, C., and Roberts, T. *Blind Man's Bluff: The Untold Story of American Submarine Espionage.* Harper-Collins. NY. NY. 1998.

[27] Paterson, M. The Secret War: The Inside Story of the Codemakers and Codebreakers of World War II. David & Charles. Wales, UK. 2007.

1835, a New York City fire destroyed over seven hundred buildings before being extinguished. This devastation may have been limited, with early notification. To address the communications problem, in 1847, the city devised a means of using telegraph wires to pass coded alarms to each individual fire station.[28] This led to the development of the "call box" concept by Dr. W. F. Channing and Moses Farmer of Boston. These call boxes, linked primarily to the fire departments, later expanded to include police stations.

The central monitoring station concept expanded with the 1874 creation of the American District Telegraph Company, enabled by the invention of the telephone. This allowed businesses and private personnel to have immediate access to a security monitoring service. More than twenty companies were in existence by 1887, creating automatic alarm systems for fire and theft protection in the form of heat sensors, access alarms, and even safe and cabinet alarms linked to a central station.[29] This was the beginning of the modern-day security monitoring industry.

It is possible that about the same time as the advent of armies, various leaders began to have a distrust of other leaders within the same domain. As Julius Caesar learned,[30] this distrust was well placed. In response, leaders identified and assigned various superlative fighters as their own personal security detachment. Such individuals, to maintain their loyalty to the leader, were given places of honor and perks not available to anyone, except the highest officers of the realm. They were also held in extreme dishonor should they fail or betray their leader's trust, providing an additional motivation for loyalty.

In Rome, these soldiers were the Praetorian Guard and the individual bodyguards known as "singulares" or "singulares consularis."[31] These individuals not only had the duty of being bodyguards, they were individual confidants of the leader as well as his personal intelligence and espionage group. The only real difference between the singulares and the rest of the military organization is the loyalty path. The military may have its loyalty to the nation-state, a constitution, or other such entity. The singulares owe their allegiance to the individual who has hired them. They do not receive their perks or pay if the leader does not survive, encouraging them to successfully carry out their duties.

In societies such as those that existed in Sparta, Japan, Korea, China, and the like, the singulares were of a higher caste. The best example is the difference

---

[28] Security History; downloaded on October 7, 2011, from http://www.hsmc-ul.com/customer-info/security-history

[29] Ibid.

[30] Julius Caesar was assassinated by members of his own Senate, to include a man he considered his closest friend and ally.

[31] Davies, R.W. Singulares and Roman Britain. *Britannia*. Vol. 7. 1976. ppg 134-144. Downloaded on October 7, 2011, from http://www.jstor.org/pss/525769

between the samurai and the other three tiers of Japanese feudal society. The samurai comprised the warrior and leadership class in one. Their main task in life was the protection of the farmer/fisherman class, followed closely by strict adherence to maintaining the political structure of the emperor and the shogun. Any failure in these two domains resulted in an instantaneous order to conduct *seppuku* or ritual suicide. Per the beliefs of the culture, failure to perform this act left one dishonored, unable to experience rebirth, and cast one outside of any aspect of the general society.

Next in line were the artisans, followed by the lowest caste containing the merchants. There is one very interesting conjecture, however, within the merchant class. There may have been similar protectionist hierarchies from which the ninja and later the Japanese organize crime syndicate derived. While this is only a conjecture at this point of this author, it does seem a possibility. This is in consideration of the unique degree of societal control of the Samurai class and its subsequent removal from power in the eighteenth and nineteenth centuries in favor of the political and merchant classes. The primary cause of this shift may have included the development of technology in weaponry to the point that individual skill with close combat weapons, such as the sword, were displaced by the more easily trained firearm. The European equivalent of this transition replaced the knight with the musket soldier in battle.

In contemporary times, information and its management are at the forefront of security concerns, specifically cybersecurity and the ability to protect not only the physical structures of housing and the machinery of this revolution but also the electronic access to that information. Information is and has always been at least as powerful as a weapon. A weapon simply is the mechanism or tool of delivering force to an opponent to turn their attentions away from attempts to injure or to enact force. Information, however, can ensure that one is strong enough to control situations without the need to resort to the use of the weapon. The true strength is knowledge, whether based upon intelligence or falsely provided to an enemy via disinformation. This domain will be examined in later chapters, specifically Chapter 8, Cyber Terrain.

Chapter 2

BASIC CONCEPT OF SECURITY ELEMENTS

The preceding chapter discussed a very general history of the development of the profession of security. However, it did not specifically define what makes up the profession, even though it touched on many of the elements. This chapter briefly examines each element prior to delineating how it functions and what it must consider in the next section.

PHYSICAL SECURITY

The element of security involving the protection of objects, places, equipment, personnel, and structures is known as physical security. Army Regulation 190-16 defines *physical security* as:

> *. . . policies and procedures for installation access control, aircraft, bulk petroleum assets, and critical communication facilities on Department of Defense (DOD) installations and equipment used by the military services and the Defense Logistics Agency (DLA) . . . and directs that, commanders, directors, supervisors, and officers in charge . . . will protect personnel and property in their commands against trespass, terrorism, sabotage, theft, arson, and other illegal acts.*[32]

The "how" is left up to the individuals on the site after a thorough review of the nature of the threat(s), the available assets, the physical environment

---

[32] US Army. Army Regulation 190-16. Department of Defense 31 May 1991.

conditions, the geographic conditions, and the political and social/cultural environment at the time.

PERSONNEL SECURITY

Often, this element is linked to what is commonly known as information security. *Personnel security* is defined by the military as follows:

> *Policies and procedures to ensure that acceptance and retention of personnel in the Armed Forces and United States Army, acceptance and retention of civilian employees in the Department of Defense (DOD) and Department of the Army (DA), and granting members of the Armed Forces, Army, DA and DOD civilian employees, DA and DOD contractors, and other affiliated persons access to classified information and assignment to sensitive positions are clearly consistent with the interests of national security.[33]*

INFORMATION SECURITY

Information security is defined in a concurrent military regulation as follows:

> *. . . policy for the classification, downgrading, declassification, transmission, transportation, and safeguarding of information requiring protection in the interests of national security. It primarily pertains to classified national security information, now known as classified information, but also addresses controlled unclassified information, to include for official use only and sensitive but unclassified. For the purposes of this regulation, classified national security information, or classified information, is defined as information and/or material that has been determined, pursuant to EO 12958 or any predecessor order, to require protection against unauthorized disclosure and is marked to indicate its classified status when in documentary or readable form.[34]*

In reality, the only real difference between national and corporate/individual requirements is scope. The information security goal is to address problems concerning the inappropriate access to or release of data, information, knowledge, or intelligence that if released could cause damage. Such leaks can and often do result in lost assets, opportunities, money, and lives. The reason personnel and

---

[33]   US Army Regulation 380-67, Department of Defense. 9 September 1988.

[34]   US Army Regulation 380-5. Department of Defense. 29 September 2000.

information security are often linked is that generally, it is through inappropriate and/or inadequate adherence to the first that the second occurs.

FINANCIAL SECURITY

Some professionals may adequately disagree with the inclusion of this element into the security domain and logically so. There is one major reason it is included here: as a consideration of appropriate integration, all things relate to gains or losses, and these always relate to monetary measurements at some point. Generally, financial security is defined as ensuring the value of an organization's assets and structures against monetary loss. For the individual, financial security is defined as ensuring that the individual is sufficiently empowered, via some mechanism, to adequately support their continued satisfaction of needs and wants.

For the purposes of this text, financial security is more in line with the second definition than the first. The concept revolves around the nature and structure of management. All measurements involve monetary value and the mechanisms to ensure that gains are maximized and losses minimized so that the entity, be it individual, industrial, national, or otherwise, can continue to function appropriately. Through the appropriate application of financial security functions, not only can losses be minimized, but opportunities recognized to increase gain.

CYBERSECURITY

There are numerous documents, texts, definitions, and other sources for this element. As with personnel security, cybersecurity requires the integration of multiple elements to be successful. *Cybersecurity* is defined by *Merriam-Webster* as ". . . measures taken to protect a computer or computer system against unauthorized access or attack." However, the U.S. Army Training and Doctrine Command (TRADOC) provides a different perspective, as follows:

> *Commanders seek to retain freedom of action in cyberspace and in the EMS, while denying the same to adversaries at the time and place of their choosing; thereby enabling operational activities in and through cyberspace and consequently the other four domains. CyberOps encompass those actions to gain the advantage, protect that advantage, and place adversaries at a disadvantage in the cyber-electromagnetic contest. CyberOps are not an end to themselves, but rather an integral part of FSO and include activities prevalent in peacetime military engagement, which focus on winning the cyber-electromagnetic contest.*

CyberOps are continuous; engagements occur daily, most often without the commitment of additional forces.[35]

Given this perspective, TRADOC defines cyberspace and CyberOps in the following way:

a. *Cyberspace is defined as "a global domain within the information environment consisting of the interdependent network of information technology infrastructures, including the Internet, telecommunications networks, computer systems, and embedded processors and controllers."*

b. *CyberOps are "the employment of cyber capabilities where the primary purpose is to achieve objectives in or through cyberspace. Such operations include computer network operations and activities to operate and defend the global information grid (GIG)."*[36]

The army appears to be taking an approach in which cyber operations and electronic warfare (EW) operations are integrated. Per Tim Mather, over the past several years, the army has vacillated between a separate command structure for cybersecurity operations and EW to a point where in 2010, the Army Forces Cyber Command (AFORCYBER) is under the operational control of the Intelligence and Security Command (INSCOM) who is responsible for EW operations.[37]

Such a structure places cyber operations into a domain controlled by the definition of Joint Publication 3-13.1, which defines EW as: "Military action involving the use of electromagnetic and directed energy to control the electromagnetic spectrum or to attack the enemy. Electronic warfare consists of three divisions: Electronic Attack (EA), Electronic Protection (EP), and Electronic Warfare Support (EWS)."[38] Figure 8 graphically depicts the structure of EW. This subject will receive more discussion in Section 2, along with the concept of both electronic warfare and information operations in a security environment.

---

[35] US Army TRADOC Pamphlet 525-7-8. Cyberspace Operations Concept Capability Plan 2016-2028. Department of Defense. 22 February 2010. pg iv.

[36] Ibid. pg 6.

[37] Mather, T. Downloaded on October 7, 2011, from https://365.rsaconference.com/blogs/tim-mather/2010/09/29/definition-of-cybersecurity

[38] Joint Publication 3-13.1. Electronic Warfare. Department of Defense. 25 January 2007. pg I-3.

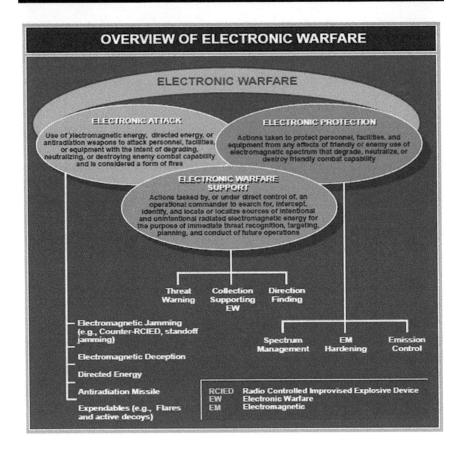

Figure 8: Electronic Warfare—Joint Publication 3-13.1

Business Continuation and Disaster Recovery

The Business Continuity Institute (BCI) defines *business continuation* as "the strategic and tactical capability of the organization to plan for and respond to incidents and business disruptions in order to continue business operations at an acceptable predefined level."[39] Disaster recovery (DR) is an integral portion of any business continuity (BC) plan.

The BCI defines disaster recovery as "the strategies and plans for recovering and restoring the organizations technological infra-structure and capabilities after a serious interruption."[35] This organization states that disaster recovery is only used in respect to information technology and telecommunications. This is

---

[39]   Definition downloaded from the BCI.org glossary of terms. Downloaded on October 8, 2011, from http://www.thebci.org/Glossary.pdf

incorrect, as demonstrated very succinctly on September 11, 2001, when the city of New York and Alexandria, Virginia, implemented specific preestablished and practiced procedures in the event of a major terrorist attack. Disaster recovery is also demonstrated very appropriately in situations such as hurricanes and tornados, let alone earthquakes and large wildfires, such as those that consume vast areas of property in many states on an annual basis.

Figure 9 depicts one particular process for disaster recovery, as obtained from a business continuation agency associated with the United Kingdom (UK) government. This UK government site also provides the following key points:[36]

a. Business continuity and emergency planning are key features of resilience. They are not simply procedures to prepare written policies. They are key corporate management processes. They require an embedded place in the corporate culture of the organizations in which they are undertaken and are the responsibility of senior managers.

b. Business continuation management, or BCM, and emergency planning are processes that must have regard to assessment of risk. However, plans should provide a sound basis for response to unforeseen risks and combinations of risks. For this reason, generic planning is the basis upon which specific plans will be built.

c. Planning should be part of normal business and be led by senior managers.

d. Plans should address the needs of individual organizations and support a combined multiagency response at local, Scotland, or UK levels.

e. Plan development is one aspect of the process, while training and exercising are key features of planning and support for those who use the plans.

f. Plans are only effective if they are current and reviewed regularly to ensure that changes in the environment in which they are set are recognized and that lessons identified from exercises or emergency response are learned and acted upon.

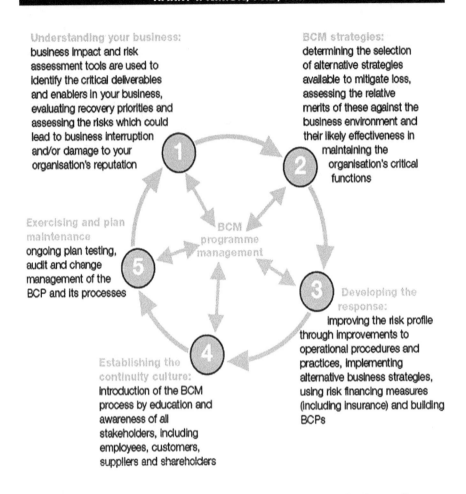

Understanding your business:
business impact and risk assessment tools are used to identify the critical deliverables and enablers in your business, evaluating recovery priorities and assessing the risks which could lead to business interruption and/or damage to your organisation's reputation

BCM strategies:
determining the selection of alternative strategies available to mitigate loss, assessing the relative merits of these against the business environment and their likely effectiveness in maintaining the organisation's critical functions

Exercising and plan maintenance
ongoing plan testing, audit and change management of the BCP and its processes

BCM programme management

Developing the response:
improving the risk profile through improvements to operational procedures and practices, implementing alternative business strategies, using risk financing measures (including insurance) and building BCPs

Establishing the continuity culture:
introduction of the BCM process by education and awareness of all stakeholders, including employees, customers, suppliers and shareholders

Figure 9: Business Continuation Management and Planning Process[40]

Given the information contained in this section, the conclusion that business continuation and disaster recovery are integral to security operations is justified. Organizations that prepare for and practice specific processes are capable of rapid and focused response as well as the ability to continue operations in spite of events that can and often do cause unprepared organizations to falter or succumb to the damage. Thus, the attention necessary to the development and honing of these programs is critical to the entire structure of offensive/defensive security and intelligence.

---

[40] Downloaded on October 8, 2011, from http://www.scotland.gov.uk/Publications/2007/06/12094636/36

Chapter 3

SECURITY DOMAINS

This chapter will expand upon the elements identified in Chapter 2 by delving into the domains within which the security professional must operate. This is not an exhaustive study, as numerous agencies, courses, and consultants having greater depth exist. It does continue, however, with the intent of this text to provide background knowledge of these elements upon which the student will be able to build a career. The security domains used within the elements are as follows:

a. Security management practices
b. Access control systems and methodology
c. Telecommunications and networking security
d. Cryptography
e. Security architecture and models
f. Operations security
i. Application and systems development security
j. Physical security
k. Business continuity and disaster recovery planning
l. Laws, investigation, and ethics

SECURITY MANAGEMENT PROCEDURES

Security management is defined in *Merriam-Webster* as a broad field of management related to asset management, physical security, and human resource safety functions. Security management procedures are the plans, tactics, operations, and policies necessary to ensure the proper functioning of the apparatus established to provide the necessary protection to the desired degree and at the desired cost. A study conducted by Enescu (Maria), Enescu (Marian), and Sperdea quote Charles Sennewald stating,

Sennewald points out that there is a myriad of petty forms of corporate culture that have no specific impact on security's responsibilities. Security can be identified as a protective service of prevention and control. "The security management that understands the reasonableness and logic of providing the broadest possible range of special services moves the security function more closely to the mainstream of the business and makes a more significant contribution to the overall success of the company."[41]

Management establishes a prerequisite of metrics, which in turn provide a quantifiable prerequisite of data. Some authors, as stated in the Enescu et al. article, consider that quantifying security metrics is difficult at best. However, according to Hayden, also cited in the Enescu article and elsewhere, such data is critical (page 203). The first necessary task in security management, therefore, is to understand the problem(s) facing the organization in sufficient detail to develop the appropriate metrics to measure the status and progress of operations to the specified goal.

Step 2 is to break down the problem(s) into pieces that may be defined in terms of a specific set of tasks. In the project management field, this is known as the development of the work breakdown structure (WBS). The goal of this breakdown structure is to create a taxonomy of the threats and risks, along with associated requirements, with the goal of prevention. In some cases, simulation of the model is necessary to determine the extent of the event and effectiveness of proposed solutions.

Step 3 is to decompose the WBS to the point where each task requires the minimum number of individuals possible. This provides the first metric: required assets. These assets may be human, mechanical, electronic, or otherwise. All of these can be applied a financial value, which is easy to track and apply as a metric of progress. The PMI calls this process Earned Value Management (EVM), which will be discussed in greater detail in Chapter 11, Security Planning.

Step 4 is to gather this information into a format that permits analysis against a standard. Some of these standards measure such things as actual cost over time in relationship to estimated/projected cost for the same period. Again, this will be discussed in greater detail in Chapter 11.

Step 5 is to evaluate the information provided by the analysis and use that knowledge to identify and address variations as they develop. To perform this step, the manager must know the possible variations, the possible solutions, and how to implement the correct solution at the appropriate time. Management also

---

[41] Op Cit. pg 201.

involves the hiring, training, and control of necessary personnel, the development of systems and programs for electronic oversight, and the detailed understanding of the budgetary process for expenditure prediction. Again, these are topics for detailed discussion in Chapter 11.

ACCESS CONTROL, SYSTEMS, AND METHODOLOGIES

Access control is generally considered the prevention of unauthorized entry by individuals to facilities, electronic systems, and information. However, there are situations where individuals are authorized access yet should not be permitted to perform a specific function at a specific place or time. Some authors would correctly state such a situation is unauthorized and therefore covered under the basic provision. There is an argument, however, that there may exist conditions within a set circumstance when a normally authorized individual requires restriction to protect the greater good.

An example of this deviation occurred during the early days of World War II. The President of the United States, F. D. Roosevelt, who by law should never be restricted access to any defense information as Commander in Chief, was removed from the distribution list for ULTRA information.[42] The justification for this was a relationship with a woman of unknown loyalty.

A second similar situation occurred with President R. M. Nixon. Immediately prior to his resignation, he was considered by the Joint Chiefs of Staff as a risk to national security and was denied access to certain information and authority.[43] These situations constitute a point of conjecture for authorized individuals having authorized access removed.

A second situation involves access by material to an area where it does not belong. This situation may be deliberate, as in the anthrax letter terrorist activities, or accidental, as in the shipment of radioactive material to a location unprepared to receipt for such materials safely. Various polices, such as contained in Army Regulation 190-16, referenced earlier, specifically address these concerns.

Access control systems range from biological to mechanical to electronic. The organization and type is dependent upon the imagined threat. The major consideration of today's security professional focuses upon electronic access control for counter-cyber operations. This is due to the extensive personal damage available to those impacted by such unauthorized access. However, there also exist such situations as public sustenance supply contamination via natural, industrial,

---

[42] Harris, R. The MAGIC Leak of 1941 and Japanese-American Relations. Pacific Historical Review,

Vol. 50, No. 1 (Feb., 1981), pp. 77-96.

[43] Personal knowledge based upon a position held by the author.

and terrorist actions. Each must be considered and appropriate counteractions developed and applied.

Compaq Computer Corporation experienced one such unintentional access threat of interest. The primary production facilities and headquarters resided in Cypress, Texas, a short distance northwest of Houston. Water supplies for the facility were obtained from a well system known as a municipal utility district (MUD). This groundwater was fairly pure, as far as human consumption was concerned. This benign substance, however, contained a specific type of bacteria, unknown to the MUD authorities, the architects, and others having the responsibility for such planning knowledge.

The bacteria had iron as its only source of nourishment. Normally, such bacteria were of no concern; however, the introduction of iron to the water supply created a situation of concern. Many of the larger pipes contained within the Compaq buildings were made of galvanized steel. The galvanization was in place for the specific purpose of denying the bacteria access to the iron-rich steel. The installed galvanized steel pipe was less expensive than copper and stronger than plastic for the purposes of its use in counterfire systems. The problem revealed itself when many of these major pipes began to spring leaks, as the galvanization was insufficient to stop the bacteria from gaining access to the steel. Several of the leaks breached the access controls of several major research and development laboratories, destroying expensive equipment.

Had Compaq prepared and tested an advanced security process, they could have more swiftly addressed the bacterial issue, saving time and money. Specific access control methodologies include the following:

Biological:
1. Human—guards, officers, counterintelligence personnel, etc.
2. Animal—dogs and other specially trained nonhuman creatures
3. Bacteriological—immunizations, counterbiological organisms
4. Viral—similar to the bacteriological

Chemical:
1. Antibacteriological treatments
2. Antiviral treatments
3. Counterchemical operations
4. Chemical purification operations

Electronic:
1. Cybernetic system controls
2. Card access
3. Passwords

4. Firewalls
5. Other electronic means
6. Cipher systems
7. Scanning systems
8. Ocular scanners
9. Fingerprint scanners
10. Facial/profile scanners
11. Optical/Millimeter wave systems

Physical:
1. Barriers
2. Access denial materials
3. Electronic fences
4. Explosives
5. Other physical systems

TELECOMMUNICATIONS AND NETWORK SYSTEMS

The following taken from a National Institute of Standards and Technology (NIST) report neatly summarizes the requirement for telecommunications and network systems:

> *A report the following year [1990, author] by the President's National Security Telecommunications Advisory Committee (NSTAC) concluded that "until there is confidence that strong, comprehensive security programs are in place, the industry should assume that a motivated and resourceful adversary, in one concerted manipulation of the network software, could degrade at least portions of the PSN and monitor or disrupt the telecommunications serving [government] users.*[44]

The primary issue, per the National Institute of Standards and Testing (NIST) report, is that the debundling of the telecommunications industry and the efforts to standardize technology have resulted in a large quantity of vendors, equipment, technologies, and operating systems impossible to police. Thus, the NIST establishes the following guideline:

---

[44] Kimmins, J., Dinkel, C., and Walters, D. NIST Special Publication 800-13: Telecommunications Security Guidelines for Telecommunications Management Network. US Department of Commerce. Undated. pg 1.

NISTIR 5153, Minimum Security Requirements for Multi-User Operating Systems (MSR), specifies computer-based protection mechanisms for the design, use, and management of information systems. These requirements include technical measures that can be incorporated into multi-user, remote access, resource sharing, and information-sharing computer systems.[45]

Further, the NIST establishes the following impact scope of the threats foreseen:[46]

a. Service denial or disruption—Typically, service disruptions caused by intruders have been brought about by accidental actions rather than malicious attempts.
b. Unauthorized monitoring and disclosure of sensitive information—The current approaches that intruders have used are eavesdropping techniques, network monitoring tools, and intrusions into network databases containing customer information.
c. Unauthorized modification of user or network information and network services—Intruders have changed user service profiles and affected billing and routing. This can result in unreliable service.
d. Fraud—The typical approach is to build upon the previous attacks and masquerade as a legitimate customer to commit fraud related to voice and data services.

Table 1: Telecommunications Threats (NIST) list the likelihood of threats by type, again from the NIST source with the types of attack included in the subsequent listing.[47]

Table 1: Telecommunications Threats (NIST)

Source	Likelihood	Principal Impact
Employees	65 percent	Availability, integrity, privacy
Natural disasters	20 percent	Availability
Hackers	15 percent	Availability, integrity, privacy

The following are the listed types of attack methods:

---

[45] Ibid, pg 4.
[46] Ibid. pg 9
[47] Ibid. pg 10-12

a. Masquerade—An attempt to gain unauthorized access or greater privilege to a system by posing as an authorized user (e.g., using stolen log-on IDs and passwords)

b. Disclosure of information—Data disclosed without authorization, either by deliberate action or by accident

c. Message stream or data modification—Data altered in some meaningful way by reordering, deleting, or modifying it

d. Denial of service—Actions that prevent the network entity from functioning in accordance with its intended purpose. A piece of equipment or entity may be rendered inoperable or forced to operate in a degraded state. Operations that depend on timeliness may be delayed.

e. Traffic analysis—A form of passive attack in which an intruder observes information being transmitted and makes inferences from the calling and called numbers and the frequency and length of the calls

As this publication is an established national standard, compliance is a minimum requirement for American information systems and those foreign systems desiring to link to American systems. Security managers need to be intimately familiar with not only this specific standard but with all similar standards, nationally and internationally, that exist.

CRYPTOGRAPHY

NIST also published standards for cryptography requirements focused primarily on electronic systems. While there are hundreds of sources discussing cryptography in both a military and governmental setting, it is important to realize that cryptography has an even larger role in commercial endeavors, from internet commerce to industrial espionage. The basic NIST standard is FIPS Pub 140-2, dated December 3, 2002.[48]

Cryptography is defined in the NIST publication through the elements it contains, rather than by a specific set of wording. *Webster's* defines cryptography as the enciphering and deciphering of messages in secret code, the computerized encoding and decoding of information. The NIST document lists the following elements of cryptography as a cryptographic algorithm that determines:[49]

---

[48] Available at csrc.nist.gov/publications/ fips/fips140-2/fips1402.pdf.

[49] NIST FIPS 140-2. 3 December 2002. US Department of Commerce. pg 4.

a. The transformation of plaintext data into ciphertext data,
b. The transformation of ciphertext data into plaintext data,
c. A digital signature computed from data,
d. The verification of a digital signature computed from data,
e. An authentication code computed from data,
f. An exchange agreement of a shared secret.

The obvious objective of cybersecurity operations is to prohibit unauthorized access to information that, if released, could damage the owner. As such, it is important to establish these systems and processes and maintain a confidentiality to protect these protocols from inadvertent and unauthorized disclosure. Unauthorized release of these standards could enable an attacker to reverse engineer the process and permit access. Such situations have numerous examples in history, not the least of which is the cracking of the ENIGMA system by the Allies during WWII, as previously referenced in this text.

SECURITY ARCHITECTURE AND MODELS

Security architecture involves the structure of the protection procedures, equipment, processes, etc., inclusive of electronic, physical, human, and cryptographic elements used in the protection of an entity, individual, system, knowledge/information base, structure, domain, area, or nation. There are many models that exist to establish an architecture for these entities. Some examples include:

a. Bell-LaPadula model
b. Biba model
c. Clark and Wilson model
d. Noninterference model
e. State machine model
f. Access matrix model
g. Information flow model

A detailed examination of each of these is not in the scope of this text, but it is suffice to say that there are many more models, each of which conforms to a specific visualization of need and perceived threat. Some models, such as the Bell-LaPadula model, demonstrate simplicity in graphical format yet are extensive when examined via the mathematics associated with the analytical structure.

Each of the above models relates to informational flow and access to that information by individuals/systems at specific levels of security. Other models exist that consider the aspects of physical, personnel, and other security domains.

The point of a model is that it allows visualization of the process enabling analysis of the process for weakness and points of attack. It permits the analyst to portray the flow of process within which the human mind is capable of understanding, as the human mind works in picture and not data bits. Chapter 4, Human Terrain, discusses this aspect in more detail.

There is a significant need to approach the development of a security program in exactly the way a structural architect approaches the design and construction of a building. First, a model of the structure is designed and built from which the architect derives the detailed blueprints for the actual construction work.

Having a model also permits the architect to create a simulation of the reality. Having such a simulation permits multiple interactions with all variables, except one set to a constant. By changing the variable's value, the experiment demonstrates if there is any effect on an outcome. This assumes that the simulation is correctly designed and the variable(s) selected is appropriate to the outcome. Additionally, having such a repeatable simulation, the architect may make hundreds of runs with one or more variable outside of the constraints of a constant to see what the impacts may be.

Stated within the last paragraph is that the simulation is assumed to be correctly designed. This is not always the case. To determine this, the architect performs a sensitivity analysis of the simulation by making several variations to values that should result in either no change in outcome or a significant change. The architect selects the variable and value in such a way that the logical expected outcome change is almost certain.

As an example, the author once participated in the construction of a model to measure the impacts of high-technology electronic systems to a combat unit. To test the sensitivity of the simulation, the author changed the degree of the input value of one high-tech system to make it about as capable as a carrier pigeon. The output showed absolutely no change, indicative of an inappropriately designed simulation.

The objective of such a construct is the determination of domains or modules of the security construct. *Webster* defines a *module* as "a set of standardized parts or independent units that can be used to construct a more complex structure."[50] Identification of such break points, or domains, enables the security manager to determine the following:

a. Logical points of attention for the determination of measurement points
b. Work segmentation points
c. Relationship to other domains
d. Determination of construction order and priority
e. Assignment of appropriate assets at the appropriate time

---

[50] Merriam-Webster Dictionary

Operations Security

Operations security (OPSEC) is defined by the U.S. Army as:

> . . . *a process of identifying critical information and subsequently analyzing friendly actions attendant to military operations and other activities to*
>
> a. *Identify those actions that can be observed by adversary intelligence systems,*
> b. *Determine indicators that hostile intelligence systems might obtain that could be interpreted or pieced together to derive critical information in time to be useful to adversaries,*
> c. *Select and execute measures that eliminate or reduce to an acceptable level the vulnerabilities of friendly actions to adversary exploitation.*[51]

What is interesting is the similarity in this definition to the modules identified in the preceding paragraphs. The primary difference is that OPSEC is designed to examine the security operation in terms of how a threat will be trying to circumvent the processes, as well as what protections are in place.

The army OPSEC regulation echoes this determination as follows:

> *Operations security protects critical information from adversary observation and collection in ways that traditional security programs cannot. While these programs such as information security protect classified information, they cannot prevent all indicators of critical information, especially unclassified indicators, from being revealed. In concise terms, the OPSEC process identifies the critical information of military plans, operations, and supporting activities and the indicators that can reveal it, and then develops measures to eliminate, reduce, or conceal those indicators.*[52]

Military organizations begin this process with a determination of what are known as Essential Elements of Friendly Information (EEFI). EEFI are those pieces of information of which the unauthorized disclosure will cause damage to the operations or organization. EEFI are determined by asking the question: what

---

[51] US Army Regulation 530-1 Operations Security. dtd 19 April 2007. Department of Defense. pg 1.

[52] Ibid

questions will an adversary ask about friendly operations to determine what that operation is and what it has as its objectives/goals? This is the exact opposite of the process used by intelligence personnel to determine what operations an adversary is attempting and likely to perform. The more detail known about friendly plans and operations, the greater the accuracy in the development of EEFI. The greater the accuracy in EEFI development, the more accurate is the knowledge of how the adversary will attempt to collect information against you.

APPLICATION AND SYSTEMS DEVELOPMENT SECURITY

Application and systems development security is actually a subelement of OPSEC. The focus, however, transfers from operations to personnel. Development is primarily intellectual, up until the end item moves from prototype, or low-rate initial production (LRIP), to full production. Once in full production, the end item moves from the lab to the environment, making it much more visible and easier for an enemy intelligence organization or hacker to collect against. The point in denying an adversary the knowledge of the new application or system is the time gained in having an advantage. The adversary or competitor must now react, rather than having a solution ready at the point of end item introduction to the world.

PHYSICAL SECURITY

Physical security involves the efforts, systems, procedures, and processes to protect personnel, hardware, programs, networks, and data from physical circumstances and events that could cause serious losses. These physical circumstances range from human-initiated events to nature-initiated events. Situations associated with improper design in the development and/or construction of the physical item may also contribute to the threat.

One example of improper design that failed to provide physical security occurred on July 17, 1981, in Kansas City, Missouri. An improperly conceived hotel walkway collapsed, killing 114 individuals and injuring 216. Per the National Bureau of Standards investigation, the following cited information was placed into *Wikipedia*[53] and is presented here.

> *On July 17, 1981, approximately 1,600 people gathered in the atrium to participate in and watch a dance competition. Dozens stood on the walkways. At 7:05 PM, the second-level walkway held approximately 40 people with more on the third and an additional 16 to 20 on the*

---

[53]   Wikipedia is generally not considered an appropriate source without conducting further checking into the sources referenced in the specific web page.

fourth level who watched the activities of crowd in the lobby below. The fourth floor bridge was suspended directly over the second floor bridge, with the third floor walkway offset several meters from the others. Construction difficulties resulted in a subtle but flawed design change that doubled the load on the connection between the fourth floor walkway support beams and the tie rods carrying the weight of both walkways. This new design was barely adequate to support the dead load weight of the structure itself, much less the added weight of the spectators. The connection failed and the fourth floor walkway collapsed onto the second floor and both walkways then fell to the lobby floor below, resulting in 111 immediate deaths and 216 injuries. Three additional victims died after being evacuated to hospitals making the total number of deaths 114 people.[54]

In this situation, the physical security failure was in the design of the walkways. This is a situation that appropriate attention to the physical nature of materials and the maximum potential load associated to an appropriate engineering simulation would have detected. This reinforces the necessity for the integration of all aspects of security planning.

BUSINESS CONTINUITY AND DISASTER RECOVERY

As with physical security, a wide variety of initiating conditions may dictate the requirement for business continuity and disaster recovery. While connected, these domains are composed of two supportive elements: knowledge of the risks and their impacts on the business, as well as the ability to construct counteractions for these risks.

Business continuity is defined earlier, as is disaster recovery. The criticality of business continuity, according to Blyth, is as follows: "Companies should be aware that the social fabric of a culture or an area can be quickly undermined by a crisis situation, resulting in unique and challenging risks to commercial organizations, their employees (and families), facilities, and business activities."[55]

---

[54] Wikipedia.com downloaded on October 12, 2011, from http://en.wikipedia.org/wiki/Hyatt_Regency_walkway_collapse citing National Bureau of Standards (May 1982). "Investigation of the Kansas City Hyatt Regency Walkways Collapse". US Department of Commerce. http://fire.nist.gov/bfrlpubs/build82/PDF/b82002.pdf

[55] Blyth, M. (2009). Business Continuity Management: Building an Effective Incident Management Plan. Wiley and Sons, Hoboken, NJ. Pg 2.

LEADERSHIP CONTINUITY AND SUCCESSION

Business continuity is more than simply ensuring the systems and facilities elements of an organization are able to operate, even in the event of major disruptions. It also includes the continuation of the critical leadership and technical personnel. An appropriate example of this concept is the structure of the United States executive leadership.

The United States Constitution provides a definitive progression of leadership and the specific conditions under which this leadership transfers. The Constitution defines the process in two separate locations: Article 2, Section 1, and the Twenty-fifth Amendment. Article 2, Section 1, states, "The Vice President is the direct successor of the President. He or she will become President if the President cannot serve for whatever reason."[56] The Twenty-fifth Amendment provides for the event in which the president is temporarily or permanently disabled or become mentally unstable. Lastly, the Presidential Succession Act of 1947, as amended by the Patriot Act, establishes the following chain of succession for the presidency of the United States of America:

a. Speaker of the House of Representatives
b. President Pro Tempore of the Senate
c. Secretary of State
d. Secretary of the Treasury
e. Secretary of Defense
f. Attorney General
g. Secretary of the Interior
h. Secretary of Agriculture
i. Secretary of Commerce
j. Secretary of Labor
m. Secretary of Health and Human Services
n. Secretary of Housing and Urban Development
o. Secretary of Transportation
p. Secretary of Energy
q. Secretary of Education
r. Secretary of Veterans Affairs
s. Secretary of Homeland Security[57]

---

[56] United States Constitution, Article 2, Section 1.
[57] United States Code, 3 USC 19.

The sole requirement for succession, other than the death or incapacitation of the senior individual in line, is that the next person must be constitutionally eligible to serve as President. That person must be of age and be a native son/daughter, that is to say they must be born within the geographical confines of the territorial United States and of native-born United States citizens.

In corporate society, the criterion for succession is necessarily somewhat more stringent. The individual in line for succession must be sufficiently technically qualified to understand the business, must know the current state of corporate strategy and financial obligation, and must be both accepted by the board of directors in association with the governing policies of the organization and within the boundaries of law.

DISASTER RECOVERY AND INCIDENT MANAGEMENT

Disaster recovery is a reactive situation in that the activities are only initiated in the event of a critical occurrence impacting a specific aspect of a business, organization, or governmental entity. This does not mean that activities are only prepared once a situation transpires, rather the planning takes place long prior to the event to properly prepare, fund, and rehearse the activities.

There are many organizations and agencies with expertise, products, and consultation capability to assist any size and type of organization with their security preparation. Organizations such as the Disaster Recovery Institute International list the following elements of business continuation and disaster recovery.[58]

a. Program initiation and management—Establish the need for a business continuity management (BCM) program, including resilience strategies, recovery objectives, business continuity, operational risk management considerations, and crisis management plans. The prerequisites within this effort include obtaining management support and organizing and managing the formulation of the functions or processes required to construct the BCM framework.

b. Risk evaluation and control—Determine the risks (events or surroundings) that can adversely affect the organization and its resources (examples include people, facilities, technologies) due to business interruption the potential loss of such events can cause and the controls needed to avoid or mitigate the effects of those risks. As an outcome of

---

[58] This listing of elements was obtained from www.drii.org/certification/professionalprac.php

the above, a cost benefit analysis will be required to justify the investment in controls.

c. Business impact analysis—Identify the impacts resulting from business interruptions that can affect the organization, as well as the techniques that can be used to quantify and qualify such impacts. Identify time-critical functions, their recovery priorities, and their interdependencies so that recovery time objectives can be established and approved.

d. Business continuity strategies—Leverage the outcome of the BIA and risk evaluation to develop and recommend business continuity strategies. The basis for these strategies is both the recovery time and point objectives in support of the organization's critical functions.

e. Emergency response operations—Identify an organization's readiness to respond to an emergency in a coordinated, timely, and effective manner. Develop and implement procedures for initial response and stabilization of situations until the arrival of authorities having jurisdiction (if/when).

f. Business continuity plans—Design, develop, and implement business continuity plans that provide continuity and/or recovery as identified by the organization's requirements.

g. Awareness and training programs—Prepare a program to create and maintain corporate awareness and enhance the skills required to develop and implement business continuity management.

h. Business continuity plan exercise, audit, and maintenance—Establish an exercise/testing program which documents plan exercise requirements including the planning, scheduling, facilitation, communications, auditing, and post-review documentation. Establish a maintenance program to keep plans current and relevant. Establish an audit process which will validate compliance with standards, review solutions, verify appropriate levels of maintenance and exercise activities, and validate the plans are current, accurate, and complete.

i. Crisis communications—Develop and document the action plans to facilitate communication of critical continuity information. Coordinate and exercise with stakeholders and the media to ensure clarity during crisis communications.

j. Coordination with external agencies—Establish applicable procedures and policies for coordinating continuity and restoration activities with external agencies (local, regional, national, emergency responders, defense, etc.) while ensuring compliance with applicable statutes and regulations.

Organizations such as the Disaster Recovery Organization offer the professional the ability for training and certification, including continuing education and a historical database of lessons learned. Such organizations also enable professionals to network with other professionals for best practice sharing and consideration. Other such organizations include the Disaster Recovery Journal, the Association of Contingency Planners, and the Business Continuity Institute. There are others as well, and each has similar capabilities and may be focused to a specific industry.

The following table (Table 2) lists some of the risks for consideration when building a business continuation plan. These risks are part of the overall security program plan.

Table 2: Security Risks Table

Man-Made Risks	Natural Risks
Espionage	Floods
Information security breach	Earthquakes
Kidnappings	Pandemics
Hostage/Hijacking issues	Tsunamis
Terrorism	Hurricanes
Power interruptions	Tornados
Traffic incidents	Microbursts
Public complaints/lawsuits	Volcanos
Robberies	Storms
Assaults	Land/mud slides
Disappearances	Building failures
Civil unrest/riots	Lightning strikes
Criminal enforcement agency actions	Wildlife issues
Exit denial	
Sabotage/espionage/hacking	
Bombs/threats	
Fires (arson/accidental)	
Chemical/biological/radiological threats	
Medical emergencies	
Employee issues	
Labor issues	
Repatriations of remains	
Media management/issues	
Equipment failure	
Workplace violence/harassment	
Trespassing	

LAWS, INVESTIGATION, AND ETHICS

Industrial, business, and military organizations have the greatest degree of legislation and regulation in their security planning. Walk into any law library and examine the section on business law. You will be able to count hundreds of texts containing the governance of business. At times, it seems like the greatest monopoly on the face of the earth is the legal profession. Lawyers make the laws via election to political positions. Lawyers interpret the law via evaluations, lawsuits, and arbitrations. Lawyers decide the merits of various arguments by way of serving as the judges and ensuring that only individuals with legal background are permitted as counselors, arbiters, and judges. Finally, lawyers are the ones who decide what the risks of a specific corporation or other entity receive their understanding and interpretation of legislation. These individuals impact the lives of mankind as a whole in today's society.

This is reality and must be both considered and obeyed when dealing with security planning. It is the only aspect of reality that can result in the destruction of lives and organizations, as disobedience of laws and regulations leads to investigation, judicial process, and enforcement. Enforcement may take the form of fines, imprisonment, and restrictions on the scope and breadth of business endeavors. It is, therefore, the professional's responsibility to be familiar with the existence of the need for legal contingency evaluation and compliance. This does not mean expertise, which is what the lawyers are for. It does mean a level of familiarity to permit the professional to both ask the proper questions and to understand the answers received.

Asking the proper questions is the first step in investigation. *Investigation* is defined in *Webster's* as "the act of conducting a formal inquiry or systematic study."[59] Figure 10 below depicts the best process established for the systematic study of an event, situation, or observation. It is known as the scientific method. The scientific method essentially has no formal inventor or beginning. Humans have been using the process since they first were able to ask the question of "why." One of the first individuals to formalize the process was Socrates in ancient Athens. His method of questioning and finding answers is formalized today as the Socratic method, which uses dialectic thinking to seek the truth to a given question.

Many individuals throughout history have sought to relegate the scientific method to the dustbin of time by asserting that their newer method was better, more defined, and modern. Yet when one examines the technique closely, it is

---

[59]   Op cit. Webster's also adds that the inquiry or study must be by close observation and/ or examination.

often found that while the philosophy construct is defined in a different manner, the process remains the same.

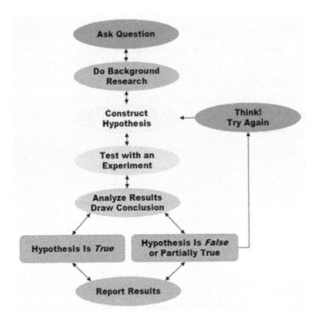

Figure 10: The Scientific Method[60]

Irrespective of the truthfulness or falsity of the hypothesis, the individual should continue to examine the situation in the light of new evidence or observations. Most practitioners of this method perform this step, as they do not accept the simple affirmation of a hypothesis as the creation of a solid fact. Rather, they view the acceptance of the hypothesis merely as a support in the construct of evidence to an applicable theory, which may modify under future investigation and/or discovery.

It is this concept that results in this philosophy expounded upon by Eric Hoffer, "The goal of education is to produce learning, not learned, individuals. For in times of change the learned find themselves equipped to deal with a world that no longer exists."[61] In other words, never stop learning as there is always something more to be learned.

This construct is appropriate in most situations of investigation, a term that brings forth pictures of a law enforcement officer or private investigator. However,

---

[60] Downloaded on October 11, 2011, from http://www.sciencebuddies.org/science-fair-projects/project_scientific_method.shtml

[61] Downloaded on October 11, 2011, from www.**erichoffer**.net/quotes.html

investigation is called for in almost all security situations, both prior to and after an event. An inspection or audit is an investigative process prior to an event. The only difference between a preinvestigation and a post-investigation is the final objective.

Preinvestigative functions examine the organization, facility, etc., for errors, weaknesses, deliberate breaches, suspicious situations, and other factors that indicate incomplete, inadequate, or weakened defenses/procedures. The objective is to discover and fix damaging situations before they become actual loss-producing events. This sort of audit may also bring plans, operations, and equipment to standard compliance due to changes in laws, regulations, or the threat.

Post-investigative functions examine the event. The objective is to discover the what, how, and who of the event in an attempt to recover from the event and/or apprehend for punishment the perpetrator. Understanding what and how enables the security personnel to make appropriate adjustments in both their knowledge base and their procedures to avoid a recurrence. Often, the who is actually an employee. Neil Snyder, a University of Virginia business professor and coauthor of *Reducing Employee Theft* (Quorum Books), asserts that losses just from employee theft have reached an estimated $120 billion a year. This does not include other employee-related crimes such as fraudulent reporting of financial statements.[62] Such situations raise the issue of corporate ethics.

Ethics is defined in *Merriam-Webster* as the discipline dealing with what is good and bad and with moral duty and obligation. To understand this concept, one must further obtain the definition of morality, which is of or relating to principles of right and wrong in behavior or "ethics."[63] The argument appears to be circular. Therefore, what is "ethics"? Richard T. De George of Santa Clara University states,

> *The term "business ethics" is used in a lot of different ways, and the history of business ethics will vary depending on how one conceives of the object under discussion. The history will also vary somewhat on the historian—how he or she sees the subject, what facts he or she seeks to discover or has at hand, and the relative importance the historian gives to those facts.*[64]

---

[62]   Downloaded on October 13, 2011, from http://www.allbusiness.com/human-resources/workplace-health-safety-security/479512-1.html#ixzz1ag2zwZYb

[63]   Op cit.

[64]   Downloaded on October 13, 2011, from http://www.scu.edu/ethics/practicing/focusareas/business/conference/presentations/business-ethics-history.html

Dr. De George believes that corporate ethics has three distinct, yet related connotations, depending upon where the observer/learner decides to give priority to the history of the topic. The first connotation has its roots in academia and the definitions foisted upon the population from these hallowed halls. Academia approaches nearly everything in a philosophical domain, relying upon past and current discourse of learned individuals to assign meaning and structure. This approach is neither inconsequential nor irrelevant. This, however, is only a starting point.

The second connotation Dr. De George establishes is that of media-centric or public definition based upon scandal or the writings of various "experts" in the topic of business ethics. Keep in mind, when considering this avenue of thought, that the objective of a media outlet is to create sufficient outrage to encourage the purchase of their product both now and in follow-ups. Profit is the goal. Media hopes to get this information into public markets as quickly as possible, burying any retractions deep in the pages and at a later date. This is not to say that the reports are necessarily wrong or in some way untruthful at the time. However, it is valuable to assign appropriate value to the author.

Media personnel are trained journalists. *Journalism*, defined by *Webster*, has the following three related elements:

a. Writing designed for publication in a newspaper or magazine
b. Writing characterized by a direct presentation of facts or description of events without an attempt at interpretation
c. Writing designed to appeal to current popular taste or public interest[65]

In none of these definitions does one find the phrase, "with subject matter expertise, education, and/or training in the specific topic being reported." The journalist relies upon others to provide the expertise in the domain within which they report. While this does not mean that the journalist has no knowledge of the topic, it is logical to conclude that what knowledge possessed is neither deep nor current. Thus, the application of an individual's bias is unavoidable, creating inaccuracies either through the omission or inclusion of opinion as data or fact.

The third connotation of Dr. De George is:

> *A sense of business ethics which refers to a movement within business or the movement to explicitly build ethics into the structures of corporations in the form of ethics codes, ethics officers, ethics committees and ethics training. The term, moreover, has been adopted*

---

[65] Op cit.

world-wide, and its meaning in Europe, for instance, is somewhat different from its meaning in the United States.[66]

Basically, corporate ethics in this connotation holds its basis in the primary culture of the corporation. Culture is defined in detail in Chapter 4, Human Terrain. Suffice to state here that corporate culture, as any cultural structure, is a living entity in that the human population therein decides and enforces the dynamics.

While the code of laws and regulations captures certain aspects of ethics and is enforced via various private and public organizations, they are primarily an individual concern. Security planners should therefore examine and process local ethics when establishing and analyzing security threats and operations. This requires knowledge of the biography of the potential threat actors, either specifically or via profiling techniques.

---

[66]   Ibid

Conclusion of Section 1

Section 1 provided an introduction into the history and structure of security planning and operations. It introduced the concepts of offensive-proactive and defensive-reactive security with the objective to:

a. Provide a structure of the security profession as it will be used in this text;

b. Establish a brief history of the profession as a means of associating the reader to the text;

c. Define the basic construct or concept of the elements of security;

d. Introduce the concepts of both offensive-proactive and defensive-reactive security;

e. Establish a common frame of reference between the reader and the text with some initial assumptions, limitations, and definitions associated with the text;

f. Introduce the reader to the planning process through detailing the requirements for planning.

The second section takes these goals into the more involved framework of the environments within which they will exist and have their interactions.

SECTION 2

THE ENVIRONMENT

Introduction

Sun Tzu said that if we know neither ourselves nor our enemies, we shall meet defeat in every battle. Major General Robert H. Scales, Jr., takes this philosophy further, stating in an article for the Naval War College's *Proceedings* magazine, "The type of conflict we are now witnessing in Iraq requires an exceptional ability to understand people, their culture, and their motivation."[67]

The U.S. Army's Field Manual for Operations places the acquisition and use of intelligence about both the enemy and friendly forces at the forefront of all planning. However, the question needs to be asked and answered: How well do we really know ourselves? Do we know what it is that enables us to generate ideas, what determines what information is or is not valuable or valid, which course of action is the appropriate or most efficient? There is, in fact, a professional discipline, or set of disciplines, specifically established for this purpose. It is known as operations research and systems analysis or ORSA.

Individuals within this profession combine the education and attributes of the statistician, the accountant, the cost analyst, the business analyst, the mathematician, the computer programmer, and the philosopher into one unique package. Yet such professionals are still deficient in two major domains: biology and psychology. Biology in that it is impossible to make determinations into human behavior without knowledge of the mechanics of that behavioral process. Psychology, or actually a mixture of psychology and anthropology, is included in the definition as necessary to be able to understand and piece together the processes of biology into the human thought processes.

The security professional, except by individual ability, is deficient in these domains, as it is rare that they receive any reason to become familiar with them. This next section will begin the process of rectifying this deficiency. Borrowing a term from the intelligence profession, the next few chapters will examine the "terrain" within which the security profession must operate and establish a

---

[67] McFate, M. (2005). Anthropology and Counterinsurgency: The Strange Story of their Curious Relationship. *Military Review*. March-April, 2005. Ppg 24-38. Pg 24.

methodology for conducting an Intelligence Preparation of the Battlefield (IPB) of the environments. This section is broken down into the following chapter content:

a. Chapter 4 discusses the human terrain. This chapter briefly discusses what is currently known from the science of the human condition. This is only a piece because the extent of this knowledge is vast, yet in many respects, very limited. What is known identifies clearly how much more there is to learn. It is similar to going to a beach, finding a shell, and knowing its type, then realizing there are thousands more on the same beach . . . of types you do not know.

b. Chapter 5 looks at how humans establish their environments and structures for interaction with each other. We know this process as the development of culture.

c. Chapter 6 expands the cultural aspect with an even briefer discussion of how laws and regulations attempt to justify, direct, and provide feedback to the members of its society.

d. Chapter 7 discusses the physical terrain. The point here is to determine why and if security should be limited to one aspect of its environment or fall within separate domains. Additionally, whether or not it should be considered by how it should integrate into the lives of the culture inhabitants.

e. Chapter 8 does for the cyber terrain what Chapter 7 does for the physical.

f. Chapter 9 closes out this section and links the final domain of the employee/member of society aspect in a more detailed discussion of personnel.

Chapter 4

HUMAN TERRAIN

> The type of conflict we are now witnessing in Iraq requires an exceptional ability to understand people, their culture, and their motivation.
>
> —Major General Robert H. Scales Jr.

DEFINITIONS

This set of definitions clarifies terms considered necessary to establish a common understanding for this chapter.

Expectation violation theory—Expectation violation theory sees communication as the exchange of information that is high in relational content and used to violate the expectations of another. Perception is either positive or negative, depending upon the degree of and type of social interaction between the two people.[68] What this means, in English, is that when an individual feels or believes strongly that something is true or should exist, it does even if it is not real or true.

Computer-mediated communications (CMC)—Computer-mediated communications, which take place through or facilitated by computers, include any communications using computerized networked systems, rather than voice or interpersonal relationships.[69]

---

[68] Burgoon, J. K., & Hale, J. L. (1988). Nonverbal expectancy violations: Model elaboration and application to immediacy behavior. *Communication Monographs, 55,* 58-79.

[69] Ulrich, T. (1999). Computer mediated communications and group decision making. University of Wisconsin, Milwaukee.

Psychotherapy—A process for delving into the human mind to unlock repressed memories and experiences. The basic tenets of psychoanalysis include the following:

a. Human behavior, experience, and cognition are largely determined by irrational drives.

a. Those drives are largely unconscious.

b. Attempts to bring those drives into awareness meet psychological resistance in the form of defense mechanisms.

c. Besides the inherited constitution of personality, one's development is determined by events in early childhood.

d. Conflicts between the conscious view of reality and the unconscious (repressed) material can result in mental disturbances such as neurosis, neurotic traits, anxiety, depression, etc.

e. The liberation from the effects of the unconscious material is achieved through bringing this material into consciousness (e.g., via skilled guidance).

Subconscious/Unconscious—Those areas of the mind which are not accessible by the conscious mind. Theory states that this area of the mind includes repressed feelings, automatic skills, unacknowledged perceptions, thoughts, habits and automatic reactions, complexes, hidden phobias, and desires. Theory also holds that the conscious mind is often controlled by the unconscious and that the unconscious mind is often the site of extensive psychoanalytical processing that the conscious mind cannot manage due to the extreme resource requirements necessary to perform the processing. This is similar to a computer program that runs its process in the background while the user continues to work on other applications, but only weakly so.

Eros—Many individuals believe that Freud used this term to identify the sexual identity of the persona. However, the reality is that in psychology, it is equivalent to "life force."

> *In Plato's work Symposium, Plato argues that Eros is initially felt for a person, but that with contemplation it can become an appreciation for the beauty within that person, or even an appreciation for beauty itself in an ideal sense. As Plato expresses it, Eros can help the soul to "remember" Beauty in its pure form. It follows from this, for Plato, Eros can contribute to an understanding of Truth.*[70]

---

[70] The quote is taken from Wikipedia which references Cobb, William S., "The Symposium" in *The Symposium and the Phaedrus: Plato's Erotic Dialogues*, State Univ of New York Pr (July 1993) as the source.

Freud explains that the psychoanalytic concept of sexual energy is more in line with the Platonic view of Eros, as expressed in the *Symposium*, than with the common use of the word *sex* as related primarily to carnal activity.[71] Thus, the psychological concept is a force that encourages the continuation of the species in a form that is more powerful than self.

Thanatos—Basically, Thanatos is Freud's opposite of Eros. It is the force that is bestial and life taking, enabling the continuation of species over self through the destruction of self. This is not necessarily suicidal, although it does lead to the removal of the individual by removing any inhibitions to danger and self-destruction, particularly in response to extreme stress and/or life-threatening situations. Freud describes it as "a force that is not essential to the life of an organism (unlike an instinct) and tends to denature it or make it behave in ways that are sometimes counter-intuitive."[72]

Id—Freudian subconscious, that aspect of the mind/brain that operates and controls the basic drives and functions of the human.

> *It is the dark, inaccessible part of our personality, what little we know of it we have learned from our study of the Dreamwork and of the construction of neurotic symptoms, and most of that is of a negative character and can be described only as a contrast to the ego. We approach the id with analogies: we call it a chaos, a cauldron full of seething excitations . . . It is filled with energy reaching it from the instincts, but it has no organization, produces no collective will, but only a striving to bring about the satisfaction of the instinctual needs subject to the observance of the pleasure principle.[73]*

Ego—The Freudian term of *ego* is best defined as follows:

> *Ego comprises the organized part of the personality structure that includes defensive, perceptual, intellectual-cognitive, and executive functions. Conscious awareness resides in the ego, although not all of the operations of the ego are conscious. Originally, Freud used the word ego to mean a sense of self, but later revised it to mean a set of psychic functions such as judgment, tolerance, reality testing,*

[71] Freud, S. (1925). "The Resistances to Psycho-Analysis", in *The Collected Papers of Sigmund Freud*, Vol. 5, p.163-74.

[72] Freud, S. (1920) "Beyond the Pleasure Principle" in *On Metapsychology* (Middlesex 1987), pg 275.

[73] Freud, S. (1933). *New Introductory Lectures on Psychoanalysis* (Penguin Freud Library 2) p. 105-6

control, planning, defence [sic], synthesis of information, intellectual functioning, and memory.[74]

This is the active, controllable element of the mind/brain. The ego interfaces directly with the external world and processes the aspects of the inputs to arrive at decisions and/or courses of action.

Superego—The superego is the final Freudian function. "The installation of the super-ego can be described as a successful instance of identification with the parental agency," while as development proceeds, "the super-ego also takes on the influence of those who have stepped into the place of parents—educators, teachers, people chosen as ideal models."[75] Freud establishes this aspect of the human experience as that which determines "right and wrong" as established by genetics, culture, training, and experience.

Catecholamines—A neurological/glandular chemical complex released as a set of molecules that have a catechol nucleus consisting of benzene with two hydroxyl side groups and a side chain amine. They include dopamine, as well as the "fight or flight" hormones adrenaline (a.k.a. epinephrine) and noradrenaline (a.k.a. norepinephrine) released by the adrenal medulla of the adrenal glands in response to stress.

Dopamine—Dopamine plays a major role in the brain system that is responsible for reward-driven learning. Every type of reward that has been studied increases the level of dopamine transmission in the brain. In fact, a variety of highly addictive drugs, including stimulants such as cocaine and methamphetamine, act directly on the dopamine system. There is evidence that people with extraverted (reward-seeking) personality types tend to show higher levels of dopamine activity than people with introverted personalities.

Several important diseases of the nervous system are associated with dysfunctions of the dopamine system. Parkinson's disease, an age-related degenerative condition causing tremor and motor impairment, is caused by loss of dopamine-secreting neurons in the substantia nigra. Schizophrenia is often associated with elevated levels of dopamine activity in the prefrontal cortex. Attention deficit hyperactivity disorder (ADHD) is also believed to be associated with decreased dopamine activity.

Epinephrine—A hormone and a neurotransmitter, epinephrine increases heart rate, constricts blood vessels, dilates air passages, and participates in the fight-or-flight response of the sympathetic nervous system.

---

[74] Snowden, Ruth (2006). Teach Yourself Freud. McGraw-Hill. pp. 105-107.

[75] Ibid, Freud, pg 95-96.

Norepinephrine—This chemical plays a significant role in heart rate, blood pressure, and learning. Experiments have shown that this chemical enhances learning, particularly in high-stress/danger situations. This "learning" is demonstrated in military operations where experienced soldiers, even if only under fire once, react to incoming munitions instantaneously and unconsciously while "green" soldiers remain momentarily frozen and usually end up as casualties. The amygdala controls learning in each section of the brain, engaging the instantaneous reaction centers for self-preservation. When surprised or experiencing initial fear, norepinephrine is the chemical causing the "jolt" felt in one's chest as the heart kicks into high gear in preparation for immediate action.

Neurotransmitter—Figure 117 depicts a neurotransmitter within a neuron. A neurotransmitter is a chemical "soup" that transmits messages from one neuron to another across the synapse. The extensive nature of the composition and densities of the neurotransmitter and the extensive nature of messages passed stand firmly in opposition to the concept of binary code transmission in computers. Computers operate in linear fashion (one step at a time and no others) using binary code (zeros and ones). Refer back to Chapter 4 for more information on this aspect of human terrain.

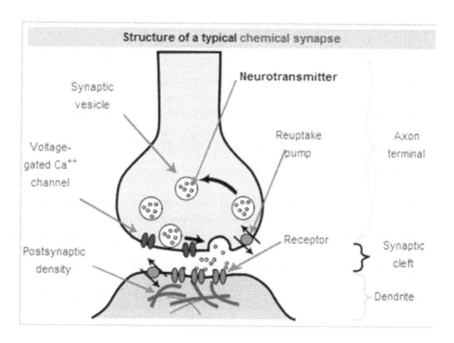

Figure 11: Structure of a Neuron Showing a Neurotransmitter

Cortisol—This chemical is a steroid release that increases the feeling of fear within a human being, as well as most other animals. It also causes increased breathing and enhances oxygen transfer within the body, creating increased transformation of stored energy (i.e., fat) into cell-burning sugars.

Amygdala—An almond-sized neuro-mass located in each hemisphere of the brain, the amygdala is considered to control autonomous action that result from external stimuli based upon both instinctive and learned self-protection behavior.

Axon—One of the multiple "arms" of a neuron responsible for the transmission of neuronic chemical structures between neurons. Experiments show that transmission of specific protein-string constructs is responsible for varied responses in lower life-forms. Similar experimentations in humans are ongoing yet are significantly more complex. This is due to the nature of the human cerebrum, as opposed to the lower life-form cerebellum constructs. To date, there remains no experimentally supported theorem on what this process does or how to produce the level of thought, ideas, and comprehension within the higher life-forms.

IMPORTANCE OF THE HUMAN CONDITION

First, what is meant by the phrase "the human condition"? The philosopher Hannah Arendt provides one definition:

> *Action, the only activity that goes on directly between men . . . corresponds to the human condition of plurality, to the fact that men, not Man, live on the earth and inhabit the world. While all aspects of the human condition are somehow related to politics, this plurality is specifically the condition—not only the conditio sine qua non [inalienable condition], but the conditio per quam [condition through which]—of all political life.*[76]

Political life, per Arendt, establishes the structure of community. Thus, the human condition is comprised of all human experiences in social, cultural, and personal contexts. This leads the process of defining human terrain into the integration of the next few chapters. It is the sum of how human cognition is derived and applied, but what is human cognition?

---

[76]   Arendt, H. Internet Encyclopedia of Philosophy. Downloaded October 14, 2011, from http://www.iep.utm.edu/arendt/#H4

Human Cognition

Any study of human cognition must first recognize that very little is known for fact. There are extensive theories and numerous experimental studies trying to establish what cognition is, how it works, and how it may be understood. Perhaps the key question to further explore the meaning of cognition is, "What is an idea [in terms of how is it constructed in the human mind] and just what is the makeup of the human mind [as opposed to the human brain]?" This is because humans are capable of a vast array of abstract thought and creation, something other creatures are incapable of. This process often segues into interesting and often dangerous directions.

Shiraev and Levy quote J. W. Berry in the following: "Judging from an ethnocentric perspective, one might suggest that the most 'valuable' features for any problem-solving process are analytical, rational skills, and quick reasoning. However, such a view—though prevailing in most contemporary societies—is not universal in all cultures. Some societies may have diverse sets of cognitive values different from the ones highly regarded, for example, in Western societies."[77] Therefore, any discussion of human cognition must also consider the effects of culture on that process. First, however, one must understand the physical dynamics before applying the psychological.

The Mind vs. the Brain

There is a text written by Dr. J. Schwartz and Dr. S. Begley, where the separation of the two, mind vs. brain, is discussed in detail. Dr. Schwartz has conducted extensive research in neuropsychology and the ability of the mind to control brain chemistry. His seminal studies in neuroplasticity include his most recent work involving the role of volition in human neurobiology. Volition is defined as willful intent. The philosophy asserts that humans can, through deliberate and willing thought, change the way their brain works. Because of that, and since an object cannot physically change itself, the two must, under the philosophy, be separate. There is significant conjecture, mathematical analysis, and circumstantial evidence supporting the theory, though no scientific proof exists at this time.

---

[77] Shiraev, E.B., and Levy, D.A., (2010). Cross-Cultural Psychology: Critical Thinking and Contemporary Applications (4th Ed). Allen and Bacon, Boston, MA. Pg. 134.

BRAIN STRUCTURE

The human brain is a jellylike mass of fat and protein weighing approximately three pounds, and it is one of the largest organs in the body (Figure 12). The structure physically turns on itself in such a way as to gain the greatest amount of material in the least amount of space. The brain is divided into the cerebrum and the cerebellum. The cerebrum is the major part of the brain and is divided into two hemispheres, which are further divided into four lobes each.

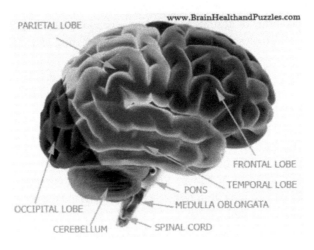

Figure 12: The Human Brain[78]

Each lobe of the human brain has a specific function, which are detailed in the listed sections that follow.[79]

THE HINDBRAIN

Having evolved hundreds of millions of years ago, the hindbrain or the reptilian brain is the oldest part of the human brain. This section of brain anatomy is one humans share with reptiles and is the most primitive. From this section derives our primal instincts and most basic functions such as the instincts of survival, dominance, mating, and the basic functions of respiration, heartbeat. The parts of the hindbrain are the spinal cord, the medulla oblongata, the pons, and the cerebellum. Each is briefly described in the following subsections:

---

[78]   Downloaded from www.brainhealthandpuzzles.com

[79]   Ibid, http://www.brainhealthandpuzzles.com/brain_parts_function.html

THE SPINAL CORD

The spinal cord is constructed of soft tissue neurons that transmit signals from the brain to the body and the body to the brain. It is an extremely complex structure. One known fact is that during gestation, the neurons begin their growth from each end of the structure and meet somewhere in the middle, how is unknown. Additionally, in some situations, as discovered by Dr. Eric Kandel, single neurons once thought to be microscopic single-celled bodies may be several feet and even yards long and remain a single cell.[80] In the human body, various dendrites run as much as 1.5 meters or almost five feet.

A neuron is composed of the cell body, as shown in Figure 13, as well as nucleus, membrane, axons, and synapses. The synapses are the "feelers" of the neuron body, except they never touch. At the end of each synapse is the synapse vesicle that releases a chemical "soup" that is received by the receptors on a neighboring synapse. While an extremely simplistic description, the soup is a complex structure of chemicals. Per Kandel, these chemicals will only enter the neuron body at specific points which cause a chemical reaction within the neuron. It is this reaction that triggers the responses that are the items of memory, reaction, etc.

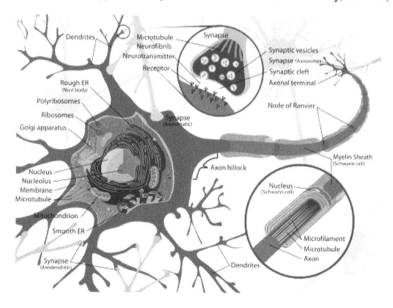

Figure 13: Example Neuron[81]

---

[80]   Kandel E.R., Schwartz, J.H., Jessell, T.M. 2000. *Principles of Neural Science*, 4th ed., McGraw-Hill, New York.

[81]   Image downloaded from Wikipedia.com

The neuron affects other neurons by releasing a neurotransmitter that binds to chemical receptors. The effect upon the target neuron is determined not by the source neuron or by the neurotransmitter, but by the type of receptor that is activated. This is a major difference between the human brain and the computer.

Picture the construct of a computer memory element known as a bit. A bit is a simple on-off switch, thus the construct of the binary codes that run computers. There are only two choices: 0 (off) or 1 (on). With a neuron, the selection is likely unlimited.[82]

Within the neuron, a specific RNA[83] structure may be established that has, as its sole purpose, the creation of a specific protein string. This string, in turn, creates an additional set of neurochemical reactions which, Dr. Kandel postulated, is the source of memory, ideas, and neuroactivity. However, this is theory at this time.

THE MEDULLA OBLONGATA

This neurostructure helps control the body's autonomic functions like respiration, digestion, and heart rate. These are functions that are necessary for continued life and must occur without conscious thought. The medulla oblongata also acts as a relay station for nerve signals going to and from the brain, "switching" signals that do not require conscious thought to the reaction section of the brain. It is also the receptor for what is called the non-sympathetic neuron system. This system is a separate "spinal cord" that terminates the dendrites in the body structures that are not controlled by conscious thought, such as the lungs, heart, stomach, etc. It is also a focus of research into a new neurological construct known as neuroplasticity.

Neuroplasticity is a condition where a section of the brain assumes the neurofunctions of another due to damage or loss of that section. Research shows that this functional transfer may often occur voluntarily or at the "command" of the individual. Their research with individuals suffering from obsessive-compulsive disorder has resulted in individuals, using conscious thought, changed, limited, or cured their disorder.

---

[82] This was learned when the author attended a memory symposium at Baylor University School of Medicine. At this symposium, the author learned that the chemical messages initiated within the neurons are the construct of a set of proteins into a specific chain. This lesson was supported by the research of Dr. Kandel and his associates.

[83] RNA—Ribose-Nucleic Acid which is the messenger within all cells for the construct of not only the cells, but all aspects of the body via the DNA or Deoxyribonucleic Acid.

The Pons

The pons has roles in establishing an individual's level of arousal or consciousness and sleep. It also functions as a relay of sensory information to and from the brain and controls autonomic body functions.

The Cerebellum

The cerebellum deals primarily with movement. It regulates and coordinates movement, posture, and balance. It is also involved in learning movement and enabling the individual to repeatedly perform complex movement functions without extensive conscious thought. A good example of this is the ability to unconsciously move one's feet in rhythm to the percussion beat of a musical number.

The Limbic System

The limbic system, sometimes called the "emotional brain" or "old mammalian brain," is the next brain area to have evolved in the more primitive mammals about 150 million years ago. This is where our emotions reside, where memory begins, and where these two functions combine together to mark behaviors with positive or negative feelings. It's where mostly unconscious value judgments are made. Information going through the limbic system is filed under "agreeable or disagreeable." This system also plays a role in salience—what grabs your attention—as well as spontaneity and creativity. Located in the limbic system are the following:

The Amygdala

Amygdala is Latin for almond, which relates to its shape. The amygdala helps in storing and classifying emotionally charged memories and the automatic responses these memories may trigger, such as sweaty palms, freezing, increased heartbeat/respiration, and stress hormone release. It plays a large role in producing our emotions, especially fear.

Specific mapping processes have shown a difference in the functioning of this element of the brain between men and women. There also appears to be a minor average size difference with the male version being slightly larger. The hypothesis for this is not that the male is more intelligent, rather that the opposite may be true. As the amygdala is responsible for processing sensory input for potential immediate reaction, and as the male, as the hunter/protector, is usually in situations of personal danger in the evolutionary aspects of development, the male, to survive, must react instantaneously to such dangers.

The female, relegated to an evolutionary role of the gatherer/provider/nurturer, is required to be able to observe and recognize things prior to engaging in reaction. The female's amygdala, instead of simply causing reaction, routes sensory input and reaction options to the processing centers of the brain for consideration and thought. Studies have shown that a female's reaction time is slower than a male's for the same stimulus, as the female is placing more thought and consideration to the situation than the male.

THE HIPPOCAMPUS

The hippocampus is all about memory and a little about learning. Its primary role is in memory formation, classifying information, and long-term memory. Like the RAM in your computer, it processes and stores new and temporary memory for long-term storage. It is also involved in interpreting incoming nerve signals and spatial relationships.

THE HYPOTHALAMUS

It should be called the *hyperthalamus* because it does so much. The hypothalamus is linked closely with the pituitary gland to control many of the body's functions. It monitors and controls your circadian rhythms, the human daily sleep/wake cycle. The hypothalamus also controls homeostasis, which makes sure your body is running smoothly, as well as appetite, thirst, and other bodily urges. It also plays a role in emotions, autonomic functions, and motor functions.

THE THALAMUS

The thalamus is *the* relay station in the brain. Sensory, auditory (sound), visual, and somatosensory (from your skin and internal organs) signals are routed through this organ on their way to other parts of the brain for processing. It also plays a function in motor control.

THE NEOCORTEX

The last and most advanced brain area to evolve to date is called the neocortex, also known as the neomammalian or rational brain. Humans share this part of the brain with other higher level mammals, like the primates and dolphins, although in humans, the neocortex is the largest. It takes up two-thirds of the human brain. This is where we find the brain power to develop language, abstract thought, consciousness, and imagination. Let there be no doubt, this is what grants our status on the food chain and allows us to be human.

The neocortex is divided into two hemispheres, right and left. The right side of the brain controls the left side of the body, and vice versa. In addition, the hemispheres are divided in terms of what kind of thought they process or produce. The right being more concerned with the artistic, spatial, and musical. The left hemisphere is more concerned with the colder, linear, rational, and verbal aspects. Located in the neocortex are the following:

THE FRONTAL LOBE

This is the most recent evolutionary addition to the brain. It is the true center for voluntary and personal control in your body. The frontal lobe is responsible for functions such as reasoning, problem solving, judgment, and impulse control. This lobe is the last to fully develop as the individual attains young adulthood. The frontal lobe also manages the higher brain functions which control emotions such as empathy and altruism, motor control, and memory.

THE PARIETAL LOBE

The parietal lobe is involved in processing pain and touch sensation. It is where the somatosensory cortex resides. It is also associated with cognition functions, including calculating the location and speed of objects. This includes movement, orientation, recognition, and speech in association with the frontal lobe. The connections here to the frontal lobe are so intricate that specific sensory factors can stimulate involuntary reactions based upon past events that may have even been forgotten by the individual. This can happen with such dynamic that the individual is often either unaware of the occurrence or cannot control the reaction without significant mental energy.

THE TEMPORAL LOBE

The temporal lobe is involved in auditory sensation and is where the primary auditory cortex resides. On the left hemisphere of the temporal lobe is the Wernicke's area, which controls language recognition. This lobe is also involved in emotion, memory, and speech, as studies have shown that without the creation of language, memory is suppressed. Additionally, memories associated with strong emotions, such as fear, fright, pain, and love, will have a stronger attraction for retrieval than other such memories that are not so connected.

THE OCCIPITAL LOBE

The occipital lobe controls visual sensation and processing. The visual cortex resides here.

Broca's Area

This part of the cortex controls speech, language recognition, and facial nerves.

The Corpus Callosum

This is the neural bridge that connects the two hemispheres to each other, located centrally in brain. An interesting theory concerning the corpus callosum, posited at a lecture of neuropathology at Baylor University in 2005, has the corpus callosum as a critical element for the formation of transition from short-term to long-term memory.

Imagine the brain as a copying machine. One places the document upon the scanner glass—the input sensory unit. The machine takes a photo of the document and immediately processes it to produce the copy. The image, however, is not stored. However, if one inserts a recording device of some kind into the proper receptacle, the image may be retained for future reference. This is the concept of short-term and long-term memory. The same thing happens with a computer. If one does not actively save the material one is using, when the computer is powered down, the information is lost.

The human brain is similar. There is such a large quantity of information being input to the brain continuously, it cannot store all of it. Thus, it stores only those pieces of information it determines as necessary either consciously or subconsciously, depending upon associated events or correlating inputs.

As stated earlier, the current theory is that the brain processes memory via the construction of protein chains. The graphic in Figure 14 shows this at a detail not really necessary for this text yet does show the development of a short-term protein string and is from the Nobel Prize winning neuro-scientist E. R. Kandel. Notice that the cell is producing a string that is then moved into the nucleus as a result of a specific chemical stimulus set, rather than a singular chemical process as once thought.

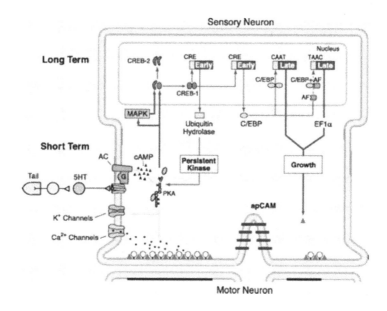

Figure 14: Action of a Single-Type Neuron to Stimulus Producing a Type Memory[84]

This "memory" was observed in the neuron of a specific type of invertebrate shellfish and, when stimulated, repeatedly resulted in the same specific motor function reaction. Kandel explains it this way, "In short-term sensitization (lasting minutes to hours) a single tail shock causes a transient release of serotonin that leads to covalent [a type of chemical bonding such as what changes hydrogen and oxygen into water or H_2O] modification of preexisting proteins."[85] In humans, this process requires significant raw materials to produce the desired "memory," as our processes are so much more complex. It is believed that this raw material derives from the corpus callosum. One interesting aspect to this theory is that there is speculation that the proteins may be disassembled constantly for reuse.

The process of this disassembly is similar to the disassembly of proteins in such diseases as Down syndrome and Alzheimer's. In both of these diseases, neuroproteins are being disassembled at an alarming rate. This is due to the overproduction of a specific enzyme managed by the genetic structure of the twenty-first human chromosome. In Down's syndrome, there is a third chromosome structure within the paired set of the twenty-three human chromosome pairs, instead of only two. Figure 15 depicts this condition in a human male.

---

[84] Kandel, E.R. Science 2 November 2001: Vol. 294 no. 5544 pp. 1030-1038
[85] Ibid

Figure 15: Karyotype of a Human Male Chromosome Structure with Down Syndrome[86]

Note that the chromosomes are strands of DNA. Figure 17, a diagram of the DNA structure, is from the National Institute of Health and depicts one such chromosomal structure. DNA is a structure of paired proteins in a double helix, having a sugar-phosphate backbone of double frame (Figure 17).

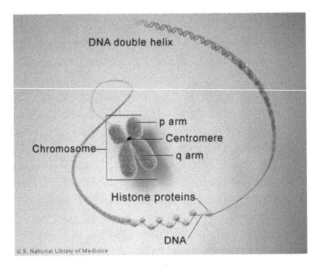

Figure 16: Chromosomal Structure[87]

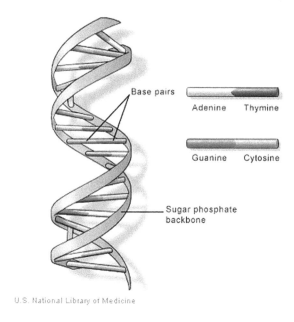

Figure 17: Structure of DNA[88]

Science now knows that:

> *The information in DNA is stored as a code made up of four chemical bases: adenine (A), guanine (G), cytosine (C), and thymine (T). Human DNA consists of about 3 billion bases, and more than 99 percent of those bases are the same in all people. The order or sequence of these bases determines the information available for building and maintaining an organism, similar to the way in which letters of the alphabet appear in a certain order to form words and sentences.*[89]

Various chemical, radiological, or physical situations can break this chain or cause the chain structure to modify or mutate. Just as changing the words of a sentence will change the meaning of the sentence, or even make it totally unreadable, so too with the DNA strand. The difference is that the DNA can and often does replicate the error causing such things as cancer, physical malformations, and even neurological dysfunctions. Chemicals, such as cocaine, LSD, and other hallucinogenic drugs, do such damage to the basic DNA structure, with the resulting changes in behavior and action, even though the individual is already mature.

---

[88]　Downloaded from http://ghr.nlm.nih.gov/handbook/basics/dna
[89]　Ibid

The question then is, to what degree does this knowledge of human neurological structure impact processes for the security and intelligence professional? The answer is contained in the culture subsection.

THE MIND

Any discussion of the mind results in questions and arguments concerning religion, philosophy, dualism, etc. The issue is that there is no definitive proof one way or the other for what the mind, if it is indeed a separate entity within humans, really is. That something exists is really not in question. Research performed by Dr. Duncan MacDougall of Haverhill, Massachusetts, was able to perform several measurements of a human at the moment of death. Taking all physiological factors into consideration, each human lost approximately three quarter ounces of weight at the moment of death. This weight loss did not occur in any other mammal so measured.[90]

In the book *The Mind and the Brain: Neuroplasticity and the Power of Mental Force*, Dr. J. Schwartz uses the mental experiment where a computer is capable of defining the color red and the structure of a rose yet is incapable of appreciating the beauty of a red rose. Dr. Schwartz quotes Nobel-winning physicist Eugene Wigner, saying,

> It is interesting from a psychological-epistemological point of view that, although consciousness is the only phenomenon [sic] for which we have direct evidence, many people deny its reality. The question: "If all that exists is some are some complicated chemical processes in your brain, why do you care what those processes are?" is countered with evasion. One is led to believe that . . . the word "reality" does not have the same meaning for all of us.[91]

Why is this so pervasive within the human psyche? Is it a situation that touches upon our mortality to the point that we shy away from it in fear? Or does it remove the naivety of our belief that we can maintain some modicum of control over our destiny? Because of this sensitivity, this section will examine only some science-related possibilities that are currently only conjecture, with little to no experimental evidence.

---

[90] MacDougall, D. 1907. The Soul: Hypothesis Concerning Soul Substance Together with Experimental Evidence of the Existence of Such Substance. *American Medicine.* April 1907. npn.

[91] Schwartz/Begley. Op cit. pg i.

THE MIND IN PHILOSOPHY

Schwartz concludes his book with the following epiphany of insight:

> *Within the brain, ensembles of neurons represent the world beyond, recording both the perception of our five senses and the world of the mind alone: internally generated imagery produces no less real and measurable a neuronal activation than images of the outside world. But the brain is more than a reflection of our genes. As we saw in Chapter 3, the paltry 35,000 or so genes in the human genome fall woefully short of the task of prescribing the wiring of our 100-Trillion synapse brain. The brain is, therefore, shaped by and etched with the traces of our experiences—the barrage of sensory stimulation, the skills we acquire, the knowledge we store, the patterns our thoughts and attention make. All these and much more, leave their mark.*[92]

Quoting physicist Ian J. Thompson of the University of Surrey, England, "Consciousness, to solve the measurement problem, must initiate the transition from quantum potentialities to definite actualities. It would not have to select which actuality, but merely cause some actuality to be produced."[93] What these two quotes are saying is that, if there is a law of logic that states that a thing that exists—can be measured—must be real. To understand this, it is necessary to have a brief review of the laws of logic as detailed in the following sections on the topic.

A BRIEF REVIEW OF LOGIC

LAW OF DETACHMENT (MODUS PONENS)

The law of detachment states mathematically that if P, then Q. When P is true, then Q is true. A good example of this is taking a college course. The law of detachment is basically an if/then statement. If you get As on your tests, then you will get an A in your course.

---

[92]   Op cit. pg 366.

[93]   Thompson, I.J. 17 October 1990. Quantum Mechanics and Consciousness: A Causal Correspondence Theory. Downloaded from http://www.generativescience.org/ps-papers/qmc1i.pdf

LAW OF THE CONTRAPOSITIVE

This law states that if P leads to Q, then the negative of P leads to the negative of Q. Taking the example from the above, if you get all As on your tests, then you will get an A for the course. You did *not* get all As, so you will NOT get an A for the course.

LAW OF MODUS TOLLENS

Modus tollens states that if the opposite of Q occurs, then it must also imply the opposite of P. So since you did *not* get an A in the course, you must not have gotten all As on your tests.

LAW OF THE SYLLOGISM

First, what is a syllogism? A syllogism is a chain of information. For example, a cat has fur, four legs, and is a member of the genus Felis. Fuzzy has fur, four legs, and is a member of the genus Felis. Therefore, Fuzzy is a cat. In the law of the syllogism, if P leads to Q, and Q leads to Z, then P must also lead to Z. The main rule of this law is that all aspects of the chain *must* be both true and valid for the law to apply.

In logic, truth and validity are separate issues. A statement may be true yet have no relationship to the "rightness" of the issue involved. For example, using the cat syllogism with a minor change, "A cat has fur, four legs, and a tail. Fuzzy has fur, four legs, and a tail. Therefore, Fuzzy must be a cat" is an invalid syllogism. The why of this is that there are many animals that have fur, four legs, and a tail that are *not* cats. In this case, the syllogism has true statements, yet it is incomplete, thus invalid.

LAW OF DISJUNCTIVE INFERENCE

This law is best explained using the following example: Either Sylvia is going to make brownies or she's going to make a pizza. Sylvia is not going to make brownies. Therefore, Sylvia will be making a pizza. An example of where this is not valid is: Suzan is going skiing, or she's going snowboarding. Suzan broke her leg. Therefore, she's going skiing. The relationship between the broken leg and going skiing, even though one usually doesn't ski with a broken leg, has no relationship even though the statement that she broke her leg is likely a fact. The example reads poorly *because* it is a serious flaw in logic. In this example, the flaw is readily apparent. However, in many other situations, it is not, yet it remains as ridiculous.

Take this example. Senator X states that raising taxes on businesses earning over $1m/year will keep the tax burden off the middle class and thus, not raise their taxes. On its face, it appears true, until one actually examines *how* businesses get the money to pay these taxes. They are allowed by law to pass this tax burden to their customers, who are often the middle and lower classes of citizens, thus *creating* a hidden tax to the very people the senator has stated the tax will not touch.

LAW OF DOUBLE NEGATION

This law states that if something is not, not something else, it must be the first something. This sounds a little ridiculous. However, it is often used in math and science. For example, if a hammer is not, not a hammer, it must be a hammer. This is where the existence law comes into effect. If something that does not exist is real, then it must *not, not* be real. Thus, it *must* exist. If something is measurable, and it must be real to be measurable, it must not, not be existent. In quantum physics, this logic has been used to support several hypotheses. If certain things predicted to exist by quantum physics do not, *not* occur, then they *must* actually be occurring, making the predictions valid. If the predictions are valid, then quantum physics must exist.

DE MORGAN'S LAW

De Morgan's laws are used in what is known as Boolean logic. It is mathematically written NOT (P AND Q) = (NOT P) OR (NOT Q), or it may be written NOT (P OR Q) = (NOT P) AND (NOT Q). This is very confusing. The following example clarifies things a bit.

A mortal sin is one that meets

a. this condition *and*
b. this condition *and*
c. this condition

A venial sin is a sin that is not mortal. Thus, a venial sin is one that

a. fails to meet this condition *or*
b. fails to meet this condition *or*
c. fails to meet this condition

The points behind the various laws of logic are generally related to the following statements:

a. A thing cannot be true and false simultaneously.
b. Nothing that is not real can exist. If it is real, it must exist. And if it exists, it must be real (a corollary to this is that for something to be observable, it must exist and thus be real, and if it is not real or does not exist, it cannot be observed).
c. A thing that is real has its own reality irrespective of what humans, through their current level of knowledge, observation ability, or belief, may think it should have, and it may in fact be totally opposite of what humans believe it to be.

Aspect of the Mind to Philosophy

Philosophy establishes that the existence of mankind cannot be defined in purely physical conditions. The primary consideration that leads to this conclusion, from the greatly oversimplified syllogism, is as follows:

a. There are many types of creatures that exist that have brains but which cannot think in the way a human does nor are self-aware.
b. To be able to think and be self-aware must be related to a higher condition in humans than in all other creatures.
c. This condition, since it is *not* part of the physical makeup of other creatures nor do humans exhibit a significant difference, the driving entity must be outside of the normal natural physical state.
d. Therefore, there *must* be something superphysical or supernatural that applies to this condition.

The potential answers to this philosophical question include but are not limited to: a supreme being, a universal consciousness, aliens, blind chance, multiple universes interacting, a gestalt entity, etc. Whatever the belief, it is, in philosophy, exactly that . . . a belief. The belief has its basis in the experiences and ideas of the individuals holding the particular belief. This section does not attempt to confirm or deny any of these beliefs. Also, a full discussion of these philosophies is too extensive to ever be considered for this text.

> **Whatever the belief, it is exactly that . . . a belief . . . based upon the experiences and ideas of the individuals holding their particular belief and is not an element of discussion for this text.**

Several of the major philosophical considerations of "mind" are also the considered major religions. Each involves the belief of an existence outside of the physical. There exist two basic divisions in this structure: monism and dualism.

84

MONISM

Monism establishes that there is only "one" (from the Greek *monas* meaning "one or alone") entity, rather than that entity is one body/mind, one mind, one body separate from the mind, one mind/brain condition, etc. Within this structure, there are numerous schools of thought. These include the following:

a. Physicalism—Everything is physical with nothing being "spiritual."
b. Identity theory—Mental states and brain states are identical. For example, feeling pain is the same as feeling love, that it is a chemical condition within the cortex.
c. Functionalism—The mind has a specific function that needs to be discerned; thus, a mental behavior is caused by a mental state within the brain.
d. Eliminativism—It states that the structure of the brain is built up over a lifetime of events and experiences and is very similar to a functional philosophy known as semiotics.
e. Idealism—It is basically the opposite of the above, in that the physical does *not* exist, only the mental, and all else is illusion.

DUALISM

Dualism is generally separated into three distinct spheres: predicate, property, and substance. The Galilean Library establishes predicate dualism in this manner:

> *Predicate dualism, to begin with, is the claim that more than one predicate is required to make sense of the world. A "predicate" in logic is what we say about the subject of a proposition (see the fourth and tenth parts in our series); thus "Hugo is boring" has "boring" as a predicate. Can the (psychological) experience of being bored be reduced to a physical predicate, such as one explaining in it terms of brain states, say? If not, we have predicate dualism.*[94]

Property dualism states that experience and the law of logic, establishing that nothing unreal exists, means that if we can observe it, and since we exist, the world *must* exist and have associated properties that define it. Any inability to account for "missing" properties are based primarily in either our current level of understanding or technology or the physical conditions wherein we operate limits our ability to observe them. A fantastic example of this is the zero (0).

---

[94] The Galilean Library; http://www.galilean-library.org/manuscript.php?postid=43792

Until approximately two thousand years ago, the zero did not exist, making the advanced forms of mathematics impossible. It was through Brahmagupta's book *Brahma Sphuta Siddhanta* that the Arabs came to know of Indian astronomy. The famous king Khalif Abbasid Al Mansoor (712-775) founded Baghdad, which is situated on the banks of the Tigris, and made it a center of learning. The king invited a scholar of Ujjain by the name of Kanka in AD 770. Kanka used the *Brahma Sphuta Siddhanta* to explain the Hindu system of arithmetic and astronomy.[95] Thus, most of modern science was unknown until this event, supporting the construct of property dualism.

Substance dualism takes property dualism one further step. If something has discernible properties, it must have existence. If it has existence, it must also have reality, even if we cannot yet measure or observe its physical nature or location. This may be one of the strongest philosophical arguments for the existence of "mind," rather than simply that we have a brain that encompasses all activities and actions through some, as yet, unknown process of chemical interaction. It is also the argument that leads to the next scientific definitions of the mind—quantum physics.

THE MIND IN SCIENCE

Thompson, Schwartz, and many other independent researchers have stated the following concerning quantum physics and the existence of the mind:

> *The problem of the relation between mind and body is well known as a difficult "world knot." Over the centuries various monistic and dualistic theories have been proposed, and the subject has had renewed interest as we try to assimilate the implications of quantum physics. These implications may make us reexamine our views of brains and bodies, but it is still not clear what consequences they have for our understanding of minds.[96]*

What is quantum physics? First, understand what a quantum is. A quantum is defined as the smallest amount of or discrete quantity of energy that can exist independently, particularly as electromagnetic energy. Quantum physics is then,

> *Necessary to understand the properties of solids, atoms, nuclei, subnuclear particles and light. In order to understand these natural*

---

95   Downloaded from http://www.math.sfu.ca/histmath/India/7thCenturyAD/brahmagupta. html

96   Op cit, pg 1.

phenomena, quantum principles have required fundamental changes in how humans view nature. To many philosophers (Einstein included), the conflict between the fundamental probabilistic features of quantum mechanics and older assumptions about determinism provided a cognitive shock that was even more unsettling that the revised views of space and time brought by special relativity.

The word quantum refers to discreteness, i.e., the existence of individual "lumps" as opposed to a continuum. In Newtonian physics, all quantities are allowed to be continuous. For instance, particles can have any momentum and light can have any frequency. A quantum is a discrete packet of energy, charge, or any other quantity.[97]

There are many aspects and new concepts associating the physics of quantum mechanics. They define aspects in nature that, at one time, required a leap of faith to believe that they not only existed but were also definable in a term set that did not relegate them to the sole domain of some "god." Note, this is *not* to state that God (capital G) does not exist. It simply means that man's understanding of the nature of reality is taking a huge leap forward. However, what does this have to do with the mind?

Quantum physics is exhibiting the uncanny habit of proving previously considered inane theories of how the universe acts as being, in fact, accurate. One such theory is that the universe is somehow interconnected. Prior to the opening of quantum theory and Einstein, it was believed that distance and time were realities . . . that for something very far away to influence another something locally, there must be an intervening substance, and it would take time for that far item to cause its impact locally. Certain things, however, did not add up, specifically the transmission of light.

Light is simply energy composed of radiation within the electromagnetic spectrum at differing frequencies. Light itself is composed of both particles (photons) and waves (light energy). Herein lies the problem. There are stars, and stars are extremely far away, yet we can see them.

For the human eye to observe and record an event, a certain level of energy must impact the rods and cones within the eye and be converted to neural energy that is transmitted along the optic nerve to the brain. There it is processed into a visual sensory input. A "particle" of light cannot do this, only an energy wave can, and it takes a certain quantity of energy to appropriately stimulate the neurons of the eye. However, a wave *must* have a transmission medium to carry it. Consider

---

[97]   http://www.pa.msu.edu/courses/2000fall/PHY232/lectures/quantum/quantum_def.html

sound, which is also a wave of energy. Sound must have some medium, air, water, etc., to transmit it, or it does not travel. Sound does not travel in space because there is insufficient density to transmit that wave.

However, a particle does not need a medium to transmit. A particle generally has size, weight, mass, and other properties that allow it to transit space without an intervening medium. Thus, the light that we "see" from a star is transmitted as a particle; however, we can see it. Thus, it *must* be a wave. Nobel lariat Max Planck discovered through his experimentation that light is both a particle *and* a wave simultaneously.[98] Einstein's relativity theory confirmed this. Quantum physics is the science that has developed to study this conundrum.

Quantum physics has had other serious discoveries. Again, taking the light issue as our example, a photon was once thought to be a subatomic-sized particle. It is now known through measurements that a single photon can actually be hundreds of miles in diameter, accounting for the human ability to "see" stars. Such a large particle creates sufficient energy through its broad dispersion to stimulate *all* of the neurons of the eye, providing sufficient energy to transmit the signal of sight to the brain. Ever wonder why a photographic plate needs hours of exposure to capture a star photo, yet your eye can see it instantaneously? It is the amount of light available to the plate and to your eye and the amount of energy dispersion versus focus. This is also why a human eye can see and appreciate the large harvest moon in all its orange glory, while a photograph of the same moon at the same time is a standard-sized white lit moon.

Another related quantum aspect is the concept of what is known as "locality." Locality is the aspect of requiring a medium for wave functions to transmit through a specific area of space in a specific time period. This creates what is known as a Doppler effect. As an object moves toward a person, the frequency of the sound or light wave increases to a higher level, having more energy to do so, and decreases while moving away yet stays constant for the person traveling *with* the energy producer. In subatomic physics, this effect essentially disappears and the transmission of interaction, irrespective of the distance, is instantaneous. Thus, time and space have no effect on quantum particles and, in a sense, do not exist.

> **Ever wonder why the thoughts of one person can affect the thoughts of another person even though separated by time and distance? Or when that person is in a crowd?**

---

[98] Planck, M. http://www.nobelprize.org/nobel_prizes/physics/laureates/1918/planck-lecture.html

Quantum physics postulates, and has experimentally proven, that any two associated subatomic particles that once had a relationship will, if the state of one is changed, reflect an instantaneous similar effect on the other, even if the other particle exists on the other end of the universe. There is even one idea yet to be generated into an experimental hypothesis, let alone a theory, that *ideas* may actually be both energy and particle, enabling ideas, or memes, to be transmitted from person to person in a form similar to a virus or photon.[99] It is an idea that may be worth pursuing. The result is the use of the mind, the brain, and whatever else we have for a specific purpose: decision making. There are two basic theories of note on decision making.

PSYCHONEUROLOGICAL ELEMENTS

As stated earlier, the study of the human brain versus the human mind, or more clearly the physical brain versus the processes of thought, is a domain of research that covers many centuries. It has gained extensive scientific study only since the early nineteenth century with the advent of psychology and psychoanalysis. The primary gains have only been since 1996, with the development of a theory on the relationship between the human brain, mind, and quantum physics called neuroplasticity.

The science formed because of research into brain-mapping techniques made possible through the development of the positron emission tomography (PET) scan and magnetic resonance imagining (MRI) technologies. Scientists learned there is much more to the brain than simply the complex webbing of neurons and the passing of electrochemical signals. Scientists, such as Schwartz and Begley, began to decipher complex interactions and research results, confirming that: " . . . there is a very real difference between understanding the physiological mechanisms of perception and having a conscious perceptual experience."[100] Schwartz indicated it is possible to understand the pathways and electrochemical processes associated with the brain perceiving a stimulus and quite a different thing to be able to imply meaning to that stimulus.

A camera is capable of taking a stimulus (light) and transmitting that stimulus through a complex pathway of lenses and, in the case of digital cameras, electrical circuitry to produce an image for retention. The brain does the same thing. The eye takes in light and transmits the impulses to various nerve centers where the image is stored. However, the camera can never understand, or experience, the beauty of

---

[99] Aunger, R. (2002). *The Electric MEME, a New Theory on How We Think.* The Free Press. New York, NY.

[100] Schwartz & Begley, ob cit. pg 29

a bright red apple or a golden sunset. The brain does understand and appreciate these events.[101]

Scientists at the University of California Los Angeles and other organizations have found that various subchemical and often subatomic functions are critical in the formulation of behavioral skills. After these functions establish, they become the basis for obsessive behaviors and are changeable through conscious interaction. In 1995, the concept of subatomic neurological function became more than theory. Schwartz provided detailed data concerning research into such mental disorders as dyslexia and obsessive-compulsive disorder that led one researcher, Merzenich, to coin the term "learning-based representational catastrophe"[102] to describe how humans, through their experiences and interpretations, establish detailed neurological pathways to specific behaviors.

Although many scientists do not accept neuroplasticity, research evidence is expanding to the point that other studies are striving to determine ways to use knowledge of the science to cure various neurological and psychological problems. A potential conclusion, given neuroplasticity research, is that the brain and the mind, even in the face of evidence to the contrary, will respond with a behavior appropriate to the expected elements of a situation rather than with the actual elements.[103]

COLLABORATIVE DECISION MAKING

Collaborative decision making involves the unification of information and process between all elements of a deciding authority. The authority's participation is essential in the successful implementation of the decision.[104] Without authoritative participation, the decision may not be completed or may be completed with inappropriate results. In a CMC or virtual environment, the receivers of electronic communications are free to interpret the communications without providing nonverbal feedback to the sender—in other words, the sender cannot read the body language of the receiver. Therefore, the message is changed by the receiver to something more acceptable to what they expect to receive, instead of what was actually transmitted. Garbage in, and any resulting decision is adversely affected.

---

[101]   Ibid

[102]   Ibid, pg 218.

[103]   Ibid

[104]   Bridgland & Watro, 1987; Buchanan & Kock, 2000; Higgins, 2003; Pidd et al., 2003; Ryan, 2002; Thomas, 2003; Warner & Wroblewski, 2004.

Fault-Tolerant Decision Making

Brown (2004) determined that strategies of distributed decision making derive from social choice theory (see Table 2) to create a balance between organizational complexity and uncertainty. Although group decision support systems include options for making human collective choices, their design requires optimal rules such as laws, ethical standards, and other factors that make human interaction mandatory. This interaction establishes the basis for cognitive process misunderstandings.

Such misunderstandings within the cognitive process create additional areas of uncertainty, leaving the individual more reliant upon their own expectations and personal preferences of action. Conditions of high stress, such as those of combat or anticultural activities, may cause a breakdown of the rules, laws, and processes identified by Brown, increasing the reliance of the individual with their own expectations and preferences of action.[105]

Theories of Decision Making

There are multiple theories on the structure of decision making. Table 2 contains a listing of these theories with short definitions that provide a basis of understanding and introduction. Understanding how decisions may be constructed might provide an advantage in the analysis of threat and determination of counteraction procedures. This knowledge becomes a tool in the arsenal of the educated officer. Decision making also exhibits itself in the structures of society and may in fact be driven by such structures.

Table 3: Description of Decision Making and Cognition Theories

Theory	Description of theory
Cognitive dissonance	Decisions using approaches which reduce individual discomfort
Consistence theory	Decisions made given the degree to which it satisfies internal alignment to other factors
Commitment	A link between a previous public stand, forcing a decision path

---

[105] Brown, M. (2004, June 15-17). *Rapid knowledge formation in an information rich environment.* Paper presented at the DODCRTS Symposium, San Diego, CA. Retrieved September 12, 2004, from http://www.dodccrp.org/events/2004/ CCRTS_ San_Diego/CD/foreword.htm

Theory	Description of theory
Certainty effect	The link between the level of impact of a decision and the probability of the decision's direct influence on the impact
Confirmation bias	The ability to obtain external support for a particular decision
Scarcity principle	Humans anticipate regret and so want what is scarce for personal satisfaction
Sunk-cost effect	The degree to which a decision path is maintained is in proportion to the amount of previous decisions in that direction
Augmentation principle	Decisions are based upon previous similar correct decisions
Bounded rationality	The use of limited logic in decisions
Explanatory coherence	Simple, explainable hypotheses
Filter theory	The use of personal biases to filter information and options to an acceptable conclusion
Multiattribute choice	Use of various theories simultaneously or in structured progression
Mere exposure theory	Personal exposure to various issues generates acceptance
Perceptual contrast effect	Use of comparisons for determination
Involvement	Desire for increased information being directly related to personal involvement prior to decision making
Social choice theory	Decisions are made based upon what society considers appropriate

EXPECTATIONS AND COMMUNICATIONS

Expectations are established norms, processes, and beliefs of an event yet to occur. Although the aspect of expectation in communications appears superficially to be a dichotomy, the future event derives from an analysis of clues, inputs, sensorial attributes, and other factors that stimulate memories and other conscious and subconscious drivers.[106] These drivers provide *fillers* for informational gaps that allow an individual to prepare for action based upon the perceived need for that action.[107] The question remains whether expectations exist as a normative aspect of society and, if not met, could these expectations create negative values. If they do create negative social values, are these values predictable and usable as aspects of risk assessment?

SOCIAL CONDITION OF HUMANS

Social norms as the basis of communications and expectation development. People are social animals reared and developed within the confines of society.[108] People establish themselves as an element of society and conform to the social and normative strictures inherent therein. Society and the necessary communications of a societal organization result from a lifetime of learning expected, acceptable, and unacceptable standards of interaction.

As cited by Allot (2001), researchers[109] have studied the innate character of language or communications as the basis for the creation of society. Dating back to the fifth century BCE, Plato used the structure of language to comment upon patterns of thought, societal dynamics, and relationships in ancient Greece. Plato specifically developed dialectic dialogue and showed the importance of defining each matter under consideration, concluding that matter's definition before effectively applying the matter and its logic to any given communication.[110]

Since Plato's time, the application of scientific methodologies has considered the nuances of language, spoken and unspoken, on the human process of cognition (Gadanho & Custodio, 2002; Sherman, 1975). Allot (2001), quoting De Saussure, examined the nature of language as deriving from society. Allot posited that the nature, structure, and acceptability of a particular social construct

---

[106]   Campo, S., Cameron, K. A., Broussard, D., & Frazier, M. S. (2002, November 11). *Social norms and expectancy violation theories: Assessing the effectiveness of health communication campaigns.* Poster session presented at the annual meeting of the American Public Health Association, Ithaca, NY.

[107]   Burgoon, J. K. (2000). Mindfulness and interpersonal communication. *Journal of Social Issues,* 105-128. Retrieved October 1, 2004, from www.findarticles.com/p/articles/mi_m0342/is_1_56/ai_63716504

[108]   Darwin, 1965; Dickson et al., 2004; Kincaid, 1987

[109]   Such as Levins (1570), Butler (1634), Flint (1740), and De Saussure (1916)

[110]   Sherman, D. (1975). *Noun-verb stress alternation: An example of the lexical diffusion of sound change in the English language.* Pittsburgh: University of Pennsylvania. Retrieved March 14, 2005, from http://www.ling.upenn.edu/~beatrice/300/pdf/sherman75.pdf

create the language rather than the language creating the society. Several authors (Buchanan & Kock, 2000; Burgoon et al., 2000; Burgoon, Hunsaker, & Dawson, 1994; Burgoon & Ruffner, 1978; Kincaid, 1987) echoed the concept that social norms and idiosyncrasies through the use of language affect cognitive, affective, and conative components of human thought. Burgoon and Hale (1998) noted the following:

> *According to the expectancy violation model, expectancies may include cognitive, affective, and conative components and are primarily a function of (1) social norms and (2) known idiosyncrasies of the other. With unknown others, the expectations are identical to the societal norms and standards for the particular type of communicator, relationship, and situation. That is, they include judgments of what behaviors are possible, feasible, appropriate, and typical for a particular setting, purpose, and set of participants.*[111]

In a study published in 2002 at the 130th Annual Meeting of the American Public Health Association, Campo et al. (2002) reported the link between social norms and expectancy violation. Their work demonstrated that socially developed expectations create inaccurate perceptions when required information is not present. These violations cause misconceptions of correct attitude or behavior, leading to incorrect attitude changes in the participants.

The information from Campo et al.'s study points to the powerful effect social norms have on behavior. This behavioral change effect links to and derives from the instinctual desire of humans for acceptance and social membership. Communities establish the processes and forms for human interaction that are forces in a human's physical, mental, cognitive, and emotional architecture.

The role of society in human cognition. Allot (2001) in *The Physical Foundation of Language* aimed "to contest the view of language, which became rigid orthodoxy for the most part of this century and of which De Saussure was posthumously the most influential exponent, that it [language] is a social and essentially arbitrary construct."[112] Burgoon et al. (1994), Burgoon and Ruffner (1978), and Kincaid (1987) echoed this concept. Burgoon and Hale (1988) noted,

---

[111] Burgoon, J. K., & Hale, J. L. (1988). Nonverbal expectancy violations: Model elaboration and application to immediacy behavior. *Communication Monographs, 55*, 58-79. pg 60.

[112] Allot, R. (2001). *The physical foundation of language.* Hebworth, UK: Able. Retrieved on June 10, 2005, from http://www.percepp.demon.co.uk/hypothesis.htm. pg 2.

> *According to the expectancy violations model, expectancies may include cognitive, affective, and conative components and are primarily a function of (1) social norms and (2) known idiosyncrasies of the other. With unknown others, the expectations are identical to the societal norms and standards for the particular type of communicator, relationship, and situation. That is, they include judgments of what behaviors are possible, feasible, appropriate, and typical for a particular setting, purpose, and set of participants (cf. Kreckel, 1981).*[113]

Campo also reported the existence of expectancy violation in social communications. Campo's study identified violations of perceived social norms for the various participants as linked to the participant's expectation of what an expert should and would communicate. The participants, based upon this violation, immediately began to moderate their behavior to match what their new expectations of behavior were, irrespective of how that behavior conflicted with their personal standards of correct behavior in like situations.[114]

The information from the study above supports the opinions concerning the effect social norms have on behavior. The effect links to and derives from the structure of the human desire for acceptance and social membership. In other words, humans will adjust themselves to the cultural processes and forms that are the force of human physical, mental, cognitive, and emotional architecture.

Expectations as guides to communication. Given the relationship of society to communications, the relationship of the development of communicative processes and societal mores provides humans with a set of expected interactions and inputs. Humans use these expectations to establish relationships, structures, and processes to assess the communications, irrespective of their form, and formulate conclusions regarding the meaning of that communication, resulting in a decision. In the absence of sufficient external stimuli or information, the brain delves into memory to supply appropriate patches from similar past events.[115] Therefore, it is also reasonable to conclude that the absence of expected or required data results in some reaction or effect to the cognitive processes leading to the formulation of a potentially faulty decision.

Principal to this concept and the establishment of communications expectations is the work of Burgoon and Hale (1988). Specifically, "the [nonverbal

---

[113] Burgoon, op cit. pg 60.

[114] Campo et al. op cit.

[115] Burgoon, J. K., & Hale, J. L. (1988). Nonverbal expectancy violations: Model elaboration and application to immediacy behavior. *Communication Monographs, 55,* 58-79.

expectations violations model] posits that people hold expectations about the nonverbal behaviors of others."[116] Burgoon and Hale assert that such expectations, when violated, are triggers within the brain to previously stored data, reinforcing the absent data to such a degree that the individual believes it to be present. Whether this data is applicable to the situation at hand or not, the brain uses it to reach a conclusion, decision, or course of action. Mulder (2000) and Donath (2004) support the concept of the modularization of human communications with a majority of communication occurring in a nonverbal format.

Nature of communications as a cognitive process: Conscious versus subconscious processes, nonverbals, and decision making. This next element of the study seeks to determine the processes involved in communications and the subsequent decision making processes within the human brain. Specifically, the study design focused on data to see if these processes are voluntary, autonomic, or a combination of both. Research into this domain is recent. The tools to enable such research have only existed since approximately 1998 within the introduction of neuropsychology and neurosurgery (Schwartz & Begley, 2005).

The structure of the human mind, in particular mental processes for all human beings, indicates the extent to which external, nonverbal communications influence mental activity and decision making.[117] Zaltman noted the limits of language and the importance of not confusing verbal communications with the process of thinking or thought. There are many facets to what comprises thought. These include domains outside or beyond simple speech.[118] Such mental aspects as emotion, memory of scents, tastes, and visual stimuli incorporate themselves into the thought process. People think not simply in words, but in pictures, feelings, and other factors. The process of thinking involves the creation of complex protein structures within the brain that stimulate the various neurological centers into performing the functions culled by the protein inputs discussed earlier (Baylor Medical School, 2004; Schwartz & Begley, 2005).

---

[116] Ibid. pg 60.

[117] Zaltman, G. (2005). How customers think: essential insights into the mind of the market. Boston: Harvard Business School Press.

[118] Mahoney and Yoogalingam also reported that their studies demonstrated a significant amount of what an individual obtains as communications originates not with audio inputs, rather that visual and olfactory inputs. Mahoney, M. (2003, January 13). The subconscious mind of the consumer (and how to reach it). *Harvard Business School Weekly Publication.* Retrieved March 14, 2005, from http://www.olsonzaltman.com/oza/NEWS/WorkingKnowledge.htm and Yoogalingam, R. (2003). *Applications of evolutionary algorithms and simulation to decision making under uncertainty.* Retrieved January 8, 2005, from http://www.schulich.yorku.ca/ssb-extra/phd.nsf/0/3751c20e40c86f4c85256b200072e586?OpenDocument

Zaltman (2005) noted that a consumer is motivated not so much by the tangible elements of a product or service, but by their own subconscious, and potentially the emotional aspects expected from the use of the product or service. The research conducted by Zaltman and others (McClure et al., 2004; Reynolds et al., 1982) provides significant support for the conclusion that language plays only a minimal role in understanding and using the social cues governing interpersonal relationships and therefore decision making. A researched example of unconscious communications effect, reported by the Baylor College of Medicine, involved a blind taste test of Coke and Pepsi drinkers, comparing the two products.[119] In the blind test, the participants are not given the identity of the products prior to making their comparison conclusions.

In the McClure test, majority of the pretest participants stated that they preferred Pepsi and did select Pepsi during the blind test. In the second test where the participants were first shown the labels but the contents were not what the labels identified (e.g. Coke was in a Pepsi can), 75 percent preferred the product labeled as Coke. During the testing, the researchers conducted brain scans, mapping the neurological patterns of the participants. During the viewing of the can labels, the scans revealed significant brain activity with the Coke label and significantly less activity for the Pepsi label, opposite of the scan results during the tasting portion of the tests. This led the researchers to the following conclusion:

> There's a huge effect of the Coke label on brain activity related to the control of actions, the dredging up of memories and self-image. The mere red-and-white image of Coke made the hippocampus, our brain's vault of memories, and the dorsolateral prefrontal cortex, which is responsible for many of our higher human brain functions like working memory and what is called executive function or control of behavior, light up. The point, says Montague, is that "there is a response in the

---

[119] This additional research was conducted by McClure, S. M., Li, J., Tomlin, D., Cypert, K. S., Montague, L. M., & Montague, R. P. (2004). Neural correlates of behavioral preference for culturally familiar drinks. *Neuron, 44,* 379-387. Retrieved March 14, 2005, from http://www.hnl.bcm.tmc.edu/articles/Read/McClureLi2004.pdf and Reynolds, R. A., Koper, R. J., & Burgoon, M. (1982). The effects of communication context, source credibility and message valence as predictors of perceived compliance-gaining message appropriateness and social influence. *Communication: The Journal of the Communication Association of the Pacific, 11, 58-77.* Retrieved November 18, 2004, from the ProQuest database.

brain which leads to a behavioral effect." And, curiously, it has nothing to do with conscious preference.[120]

Allot (2001) supports the concepts considered by neuroplasticity research. His hypothesis relates speech, gesture, and perception and treats phonetic symbolism as a manifestation of the natural foundation of language in the functioning of the human body and brain. Allot (2001) further notes that the brain integrates the construct of language and nonverbals as an automatic and necessary function, without which the higher process of the human cortex dysfunctions to some degree. Therefore, language is a voluntary function or neurological movement. The way humans can expand upon and create new meanings for words are indicative of the nature of the human psyche. To be able to perform this function, the brain must have links with other parts of the brain rather than exist segmented into specific processing domains. Allot concludes the following:

> *Thus, the "wiring" of the human brain extends to areas within which other types of neurological processing are occurring. This creates a need for order relationship similar to that of a computer's hard drive memory. The brain catalogues the pathways so that stored information is retrievable. At times, it accesses and incorporates information, physical protein strings, which create a new element of information or knowledge that did not previously exist as a stored entity. Thus other aspects such as movement, perception, and expectation affect speech and vice versa.*[121]

The aspect of interconnectivity of neural processes supports the assertion that humans rely on numerous elements and aspects of their senses in making decisions. Various studies contend with the above statement, with varying degrees of acceptance. In a book review in *Communication Education*, Comadena (1990) examined the relationship of nonverbal communications in multiple studies. The purpose of the review was to determine if the differences in defining the meaning of various nonverbal cues by different individuals was a matter of symbolic behavior or a result of cultural or other factors. The primary issue involves the aspect of intent: whether the communicator deliberately uses nonverbal cues to enhance communications or if the use is purely an unconscious element of process

---

[120] McClure, S. M., Li, J., Tomlin, D., Cypert, K. S., Montague, L. M., & Montague, R. P. (2004). Neural correlates of behavioral preference for culturally familiar drinks. *Neuron, 44*, 379-387. Retrieved March 14, 2005, from http://www.hnl.bcm.tmc.edu/articles/Read/McClureLi2004.pdf. pg 384.

[121] Allot. Op cit.

of communications. If it is intentional, expectation is no longer significant as a factor in miscommunications. If unintentional, expectation increases in importance as the use and interpretation of the nonverbal cues are no longer a conscious activity (Comadena).[122]

Donath, in a seminar on body language without the body, discussed that the physical body is embedded with social cues used in communications that include gait, race, gender, hairstyle, gesture, position, motion, scent, inflection, etc. Donath stated, "The premise that I am working from is that social cues are really essential to have any kind of very vibrant society that is mediated."[123] In *Being Real*, Donath noted that nonverbal cues carry complex meanings and that the rise of CMC as a primary medium for information exchange has silenced this major mode of communications. Computer-mediated communication has not silenced the need to receive the nonverbal inputs, as again, the need for these inputs is wired into humans from before birth.

Buchanan and Kock wrote that human beings are social creatures, irrespective of the environment within which they exist. The absence of a social condition results in severe dysfunction and insanity. As social creatures, humans establish conditions of behavior. These conditions reinforce themselves through the creation of expectations deeply rooted in the subconscious. Violations of these expectations represent a threat to the foundation of being and require voluntary or involuntary adjustment. In a stress environment, such adjustments may result in negative deviations from the desired course.[124]

MANIPULATION OF HUMAN COGNITION

At first, one might state that activities to manipulate the human mind are unethical and should be illegal. This is until one realizes that this influence already occurs on an hourly basis, both positively and negatively. There are indeed some aspects of human manipulation that are deemed illegal in various countries

---

[122]   Comadena, M. A. (1990). Book reviews. [Review of the books Nonverbal communications: The unspoken dialogue; Nonverbal communications: Studies and applications (2nd ed.); and The nonverbal communication reader]. Communication Education, 38, 161.

[123]   Donath, J. (2004). Being real. In K. Goldberg (Ed.), *The robot in the garden: Telerobotics and telepistemology in the age of the Internet*. Boston: Massachusetts Institute of Technology Press. Retrieved on October 19, 2005, from http://duplox. wz-berlin.de/docs/panel/judith.html.

[124]   Buchanan, J., & Kock, N. (2000). *Information overload: A decision making perspective* (MCDM2000). Retrieved February 18, 2005, from http://www.mngt.waikato.ac.nz/ depts/mnss/john/iomcdm2000_1.pdf

and even internationally. The admonishment against "brainwashing" by the Geneva Convention is one excellent example.[125] While the admonishment is not specific, it does apply that "the right to physical, moral, and intellectual integrity" be maintained. According to the referenced CRS report to Congress, certain processes are in fact legal and others may be approved by the highest levels of the command structure, given critical need, but which cannot permanently damage or change the mental condition of the individual.[126] Table 4 contains a listing of these techniques.

Cognitive manipulation, as stated, occurs constantly in both positive/active and negative/reactive situations. Here are some examples.

ADVERTISEMENTS

Every time an individual views an advertisement, it is an attempt to manipulate the individual into performing an action: the purchase of a product, the support of a political position or candidate, a donation to a charity, and many others. As with the soda example referenced previously, this cognitive manipulation may be audio, visual, olfactory (scent), or even using expectation theory (e.g., pulling a situation into active memory to generate a specific response). The message may actually, and often is, hidden within the structure of the advertisement, as well as uniquely obvious. The target of the behavior has not yet usually performed the behavior; thus, this type of manipulation is positive/active. Such actions may also be to stop an individual considering a specific behavior, such as the "Drink-Drive-Go to Jail'" ads targeted not against individuals currently drunk (they likely no longer

---

[125] COMMENTARY ON THE GENEVA CONVENTIONS OF 1949 201 (Pictet, ed. 1960)[hereinafter ICRC COMMENTARY II]. The ICRC Commentary defined the rights as follows: The right of respect for the person . . . covers all the rights of the individual . . . which are inseparable from the human being by the very fact of his existence and his mental and physical powers; it includes . . . the right to physical, moral and intellectual integrity—an essential attribute of the human person. The right to physical integrity involves the prohibition of acts impairing individual life or health. Respect for intellectual integrity means respect for all the moral values which form part of man's heritage, and applies to the whole complex structure of convictions, conceptions and aspirations peculiar to each individual. Individual persons' names or photographs, or aspects of their private lives must not be given publicity. The right to personal liberty, and in particular, the right to move about freely, can naturally be made subject in war time to certain restrictions made necessary by circumstances.

[126] Elsea, J. K. CRS RL32567 Lawfulness of Interrogation Techniques under the Geneva Conventions. September 8, 2004.

have any cognition to recognize the advertisement) but rather those considering tonight's party.

Table 4: Geneva Convention Allowed Interrogation Techniques

Approved Approaches for all Detainees	Requires Commanding General Approval
Direct	Change of scenery—down
Incentive/removal	Diet manipulation
Emotional love/hate	Environment manipulation
Fear—up harsh/mild	Sleep adjustment
Reduced fear	Isolation
Pride and ego—up/down	Presence of military working dogs
Futility	Sensory deprivation
"We know all"	Stress positions
Establish your identity	Removal of clothing
Repetition	Removal of all comfort/religious items
File/dossier	Forced grooming
Rapid fire (questioning)	Use of near-death scenarios (e.g., water boarding or other nonfatal yet potentially critical situations to convince the detainee of imminent death)
Silence	Use of near-critical potential injury scenarios

COGNITIVE BEHAVIOR THERAPY

Have you ever been to a psychiatrist/psychologist? If so, you experienced cognitive manipulation. This manipulation takes the form of conversation, group interaction (establishing a peer/culture relationship within the group structure associated with the desired behavior), and in some cases, medicinal interventions. The entire process is to remove an undesirable behavior and replace it with a desirable behavior.

TELEVISION/MOVIES/MASS MEDIA/GAMING

There is no more pervasive and potentially insidious method of mass cognitive manipulation than the field of entertainment. Numerous studies on the impacts of these domains on various individuals show both highly positive and highly negative effects. For example, in New South Wales, Australia, campaigns using television, radio, and print media were conducted over three summers, aiming to increase the use of sun protection measures among children under twelve years. While the full results were inconclusive, there was strong evidence of short-term behavior modification while the campaign was being aired.[127]

CORPORATE QUALITY MANAGEMENT/IMPROVEMENT PROGRAMS

One of the most pervasive and yet least effective methods of cognitive manipulation are publicity posters, slogans, and advertising. One sees such items in behavioral improvement consulting sites, change books, and other locations. Dr. W. E. Deming, foremost authority on quality improvement and management, states, "Eliminate Slogans, Exhortations, and Targets for the Work Force."[128] Specifically, Deming stated,

> Posters that explain to everyone on the job what the management is doing month by month to (for example) purchase better quality of incoming materials from fewer suppliers, better maintenance, or to provide better training, or statistical aids and better supervision to improve quality and productivity, not by working harder but by working smarter, would be a totally different story: they would boost morale. People would then understand that the management is taking some responsibility for hang-ups and defects, and is trying to remove obstacles.

Basically, individuals ignore such posters unless the material is specifically engineered to appeal to the subconscious mind as explained earlier. Individuals remember positive information, which is both interesting and true, longer than slogans and platitudes.

CULTURAL/PEER PRESSURE

Chapter 5 contains a detailed examination of the intricacies of culture and the effects culture has on human behavior. The use of the knowledge of what a target population/individual holds as culturally important is a strong method for

---

[127] Smith, B.J, Ferguson, C., McKenzie, J. Bauman, A., and Vita, P. Impacts from repeated mass media campaigns to promote sun protection in Australia. *Oxford Journals: Health Promotion International.* Volume 17, Issue 1. Pp 51-60.

[128] Deming, W.E. *Deming's 14 Points for Management.* Downloaded from http://www.stat.auckland.ac.nz/~mullins/quality/Deming.pdf

cognitive manipulation, both positive/proactive and negative/reactive. The reason for this is the information on neural development presented in Chapter 4.

Two structured theories are considered key elements to this condition: cognitive dissonance and expectation violation theory. The first, cognitive dissonance, also involves the Abilene paradox and groupthink. Each of these corollaries, dissonance and expectation violation, appear to establish dynamics of participation and decision making in group domains, thus necessitating the individual's inclusion into a domain, group, or culture.

Cognitive dissonance behavior and belief are in conflict with each other. A person begins not only to anticipate that others will behave in a particular fashion but also to assign evaluations, or values, to these actions.[129] Breaking this link to the group or making the target believe that the group consensus is other than their current belief results in confusion, expectation violation, and cognitive dissonance to which the individual subconsciously now needs to rectify to the "new" norm.

LEGALITIES ASSOCIATED WITH HUMAN COGNITION

Stanford University conducted a cognition study in 1971, which provides results that give a powerful example of why activities associated with human cognition are so tightly legislated. The following from the abstract of an evaluation of this experiment clearly demonstrates the problem.

> *Research was conducted recently (August 14-21, 1971) in which subjects assumed the roles of "prisoner" or "guard" for an extended period of time within an experimentally devised mock prison setting on the Stanford University campus. The projected two week study had to be prematurely terminated when it became apparent that many of the "prisoners" were in serious distress and many of the "guards" were*

---

[129] Specific discussion of these concepts is extensively researched by numerous experimenters, psychologists, and cognitive researchers such as Burgoon and Cooper. The Abilene Paradox establishes that a group of people will collectively decide on a course of action that is counter to the preferences of any of the individuals in the group due to a common breakdown of group communication in which each member mistakenly believes that their own preferences are counter to the group's and, therefore, do not raise objections. Group-think is similar in that it happens when the desire for harmony in a decision-making group overrides a realistic appraisal of alternatives. Group members try to minimize conflict and reach a consensus decision without critical evaluation of alternative ideas or viewpoints. Mcavoy, J.; Butler, T. (2006). "Resisting the change to user stories: a trip to Abilene". *International Journal of Information Systems and Change Management* 1 (1): 48-61.

behaving in ways which brutalized and degraded their fellow subjects. In addition, the emerging reality of this role-playing situation was sufficiently compelling to influence virtually all those who operated within it to behave in ways appropriate to its demand characteristics, but inappropriate to their usual life roles and values; this included the research staff, faculty observers, a priest, lawyer, ex-convict, and relatives and friends of the subjects who visited the prison on several occasions (for details see Zimbardo, Banks, Haney and Jaffe, 1973; Haney, Banks and Zimbardo, 1973). This research represents one of the most extreme experimental demonstrations of the power of situational determinants in both shaping behaviour and predominating over personality, attitudes and individual values.[130]

Every organization that conducts human research is required by law to perform a review to determine the risk to the subjects known as an Internal Review Board (IRB). The following, from the Handbook for the Protection of Human Subjects in Research,[131] gives the minimum standards for control of any activity involving human cognition experimentation. International law establishes additional requirements by such codices as the Nuremburg Articles and the Geneva Convention.

The Department of Health and Human Services (DHHS) regulations are codified at Title 45 Part 46 of the Code of Federal Regulations (CFR). These regulations became final in January 1981 and were revised in 1983 and 1991. The 1991 revision involved the adoption of the Federal Policy for the Protection of Human Subjects. Generally referred to as the Common Rule, *it is designed to make uniform the human subject protection system in all relevant agencies and departments. The Common Rule covers research supported by the Departments of Agriculture, Energy, Commerce, HUD, Justice, Defense, Education, Veterans Affairs, Transportation, and HHS, as well as that supported by NSF, NASA, EPA, AID, Social Security Administration, CIA, and Consumer Product Safety Commission. The Food and Drug Administration (FDA) has a separate set of regulations governing human subject research codified in 21 Part 56 of the Code*

---

[130]　Zimbardo, P.G. 1972. On the Ethics of Intervention in Human Psychological Research: With Special Reference to the Stanford Prison Experiment. *Cognition 2(2), pp.* 243-256. Pg 1.

[131]　Oklahoma State University. 2008. http://compliance.vpr.okstate.edu/irb/documents/ IRB_Guide.pdf

of Federal Regulations, which governs Institutional Review Boards, and in 21 Part 50 of the Code of Federal Regulations, which deals with informed consent.

The basic IRB requirements and the requirements for informed consent are the same between the two sets of regulations. Differences center on applicability. The Common Rule is based on federal funding of research. The federal Office of Human Research Protections (OHRP) monitors and promotes compliance with the Common Rule. OHRP is located under the Office of Public Health and Science within the Office of the Secretary of HHS. The FDA regulations are based primarily on use of FDA-regulated products, drugs, or biologics. The FDA has primary responsibility for regulating the use of drugs and medical devices in experiments. The OHRP regulates the compliance of institutions with the Common Rule through assurances. A Federal-wide Assurance (FWA) is an agreement between OHRP and the institution and is approved for three-year intervals. Oklahoma State University has negotiated a FWA that states OSU's commitment to follow the regulations governing human subjects in research supported by HHS and all federal agencies under the Common Rule.[132]

The domain of activity is the major difference between security and intelligence operations vs. cognitive research. Cognitive research takes place in academic and/or laboratory settings. Intelligence and security operations happen within the "real world." As such, a subject's permission is not obtainable or desirable, as it would alert the subject/target to the operation. Additionally, per the previously cited congressional report, it is not really a factor beyond the limits of international agreements. The key is for the security/intelligence officer to obtain legal advice prior to initiating any operations and then to monitor and positively control the operations once initiated.

---

[132]   Ibid. pp 2-3.

Chapter 5

CULTURAL TERRAIN

CULTURE AND PERSONALITY

Human cognition, as seen in the previous chapter, is a process that remains scientifically undefined and not well understood. In order for an investigator to understand cognition, they must first be able to define and track the mechanics of an idea. Given the structure of the brain, particularly the processes that are observable for the brain and the mind and an individual's behavior patterns, researchers can ascertain and measure other items such as culture and personality.

Culture is the sum total of the human experience within a specific domain. It defines acceptable behavior, social structure, ethics, and societal norms/mores and may even be an environmental driver for the development of an individual's personality. As such, one may ask if understanding culture, language, and the nonverbal stimuli associated with society as the driver for personality and behavior is available for use in predictive and/or reactive situations. It is this question that many researchers are now labeling human terrain analysis, using this concept as the key for implementing human terrain teams within the various military services.

> **Human social requirements lead to the development of cultures. Cultures drive both language and behavior; thus, they may be utilized for behavior analysis and prediction processes.**

Shiraev and Levy define culture in the following manner:[133]

---

[133]   Shiraev and Levy, op cit. pp 3-4.

Culture as a set of attitudes, behaviors, and symbols shared by a large group of people and usually communicated from one generation to the next. Attitudes include beliefs (political, ideological, religious, moral, etc.), values, general knowledge (empirical and theoretical), opinions, superstitions, and stereotypes. Behaviors include a wide variety of norms, roles, customs, traditions, habits, practices, and fashions. Symbols represent things or ideas, the meaning of which is bestowed on them by people. A symbol may have the form of a material object, a color, a sound, a slogan, a building, or anything else.

Cultures can be described as having both explicit and implicit characteristics. Explicit characteristics of culture are the set of observable acts regularly found in this culture. These are overt customs, observable practices, and typical behavioral responses . . . Implicit characteristics refer to the organizing principles that are inferred to lie behind these regularities on the basis of consistent patterns of explicit culture. For example, grammar that controls speech, rules of address, hidden norms of bargaining, or particular behavioral expectations in a standard situation . . .

As stated in Chapter 4, human beings are social creatures irrespective of the environment within which they exist. The absence of a social condition results in severe dysfunction and insanity. As social creatures, humans establish conditions of behavior. These conditions reinforce themselves through the creation of expectations deeply rooted in the subconscious. Consider the following: Humans, as with other social creatures, establish groupings and cling to these groupings as the source of nourishment, both physical and emotional. Without this nourishment, humans will withdraw psychologically from the physical world and create their own world mentally. Recent studies, however, have concluded that this effect is exaggerated and inaccurate.[134]

Research into the field of isolation led to the development of efforts to determine the effects of sensory deprivation on humans based upon reports and

---

[134] Glancy, G.D. and Murrey, E.L. The Psychiatric Aspects of Solitary Confinement. *Victims and Offenders,* 1:361-368, 2006. Pp 361-367. In this paper, the authors state, "It is probably fair to conclude from the data that in general there is little evidence to conclude that the majority of the prison population kept in SC for a variety of reasons experience negative mental health effects. However, there may be individuals made vulnerable through their pre-existing personality organization or mental disorder or perhaps through their individual circumstances who do suffer from mental health effects."

documents captured from Nazi Germany following the war and reports that the Russians were investigating and using these techniques in Korea against UN soldiers.[135] Sensory deprivation is a technique where individuals are placed into an environment where sight, sound, touch, and taste are denied to the subject. Even short periods resulted in severe dissolution of cognition.

> *For instance, Maitland Baldwin, an American neurosurgeon who had studied under Hebb, once placed an army volunteer in an isolation box for forty hours with disastrous consequences for the man's mental health. Baldwin, who worked at the National Institute of Mental Health in the U.S., concluded that anything more than six days of sensory deprivation would "almost certainly cause irreparable damage."[136]*

As discussed in Chapter 2 and Chapter 4, the human brain changes. This again is called neuroplasticity. Research into sensory deprivation is exhibiting neuroplastic results. Figure 18 depicts this effect when an individual's brain is MRI mapped. The first individual (a) is a deaf-blind subject, while the second (b) is both sighted and hearing. Note the differences in the areas of the brain activated given the similar stimulation.

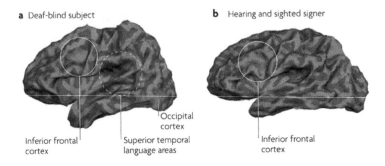

Figure 18: Crossmodal Neuroplasticity in Dual Sensory Loss[137]

---

135 Rosner, C. ISOLATION. *Canada's History*, 2010, Vol. 90, Issue 4. This paper discusses extensive research conducted by Dr. John P. Zubek into the field of sensory deprivation and brain washing, leading to his suicide in 1974.

136 Ibid. http://ehis.ebscohost.com/eds/detail?sid=57e4fb27-4e78-4386-b69f-84d2e1490f 6f%40sessionmgr115&vid=3&hid=124&bdata=JnNpdGU9ZWRzLWxpdmU%3d#db =f5h&AN=55397389

137 Merabet, L.B. and Pascual-Leone, A. Neural reorganization following sensory loss: the opportunity of change. *Reviews*. January 2010, Volume 11 Harvard Medical School, Boston, Massachusetts. Pp 44-52. Photo is from page 48.

The purpose of this discourse is to further reinforce the knowledge of the student that there is more to behavior than choice. It is the creation of an environment. This environment does more than establish a behavioral preference. It drives the genetic development of personality.

PERSONALITY

What is personality? Expectations, being a major element of both cognition and an individual's basic psychological makeup, are therefore elements of personality.[138] Psychologists use personality as a means of determination of behavior and use various processes for the codification of individual personality. Key among these psychologists is Carl Jung.

DR. CARL JUNG AND PREFERENCES[139]

Jung developed a personality typology used as a central element of his theory. Jung believed that every human possesses preferences. Humans simply have an inclination for one over another. Following is a discussion concerning the distinction between Jung's attitudes, introversion, and extraversion, synopsized from the cited text. People with a preference for introversion feel more comfortable in their internal world of thoughts, feelings, fantasies, dreams, and so on, while those with a preference for extraversion feel more comfortable in the external world of things and people and activities.

Introvert and *extravert* have become commonly used words to describe behaviors such as shyness and sociability, partially because introverts tend to be shy and extraverts tend to be sociable. Jung intended for them to refer more to whether the individual (ego) is more often faced toward the persona and outer reality or toward the collective unconscious and its archetypes. In that sense, the introvert is somewhat more mature than the extravert.

---

[138] Buchanan, J., & Kock, N. (2000). *Information overload: A decision making perspective* (MCDM2000). Retrieved February 18, 2005, from http://www.mngt.waikato.ac.nz/depts/mnss/john/iomcdm2000_1.pdf

[139] Jung, C. J., Adler, G., & Hull, R. F. C. (1968). *The archetypes and collective unconscious (Collected Works of C.J. Jung, Vol. 9, Part 1)*. Princeton, NJ: Princeton University Press.

Jungian Functions[140]

Whether one's preference is introvert or extravert, we all need to deal with both the inner and outer world. In addition, each person has preferred ways of dealing with the preference. Jung suggests there are four basic ways or functions: sensing, thinking, intuition, and feeling.

Sensing, the first function, involves obtaining information by means of sight, touch, smell, and so forth. A sensing person generally succeeds at looking and listening and acts involved in generally getting to know the world. Jung called this one of the irrational functions, meaning it involves perception rather than judging of information.

The second function is thinking. Thinking means evaluating information or ideas rationally and logically. Jung called this a rational function, meaning it involves decision making or judging rather than simple intake of information. These are cognitive skills.

The third function is intuition. Intuition works outside of the usual conscious or cognitive processes. It is irrational or perceptual, like sensing, but comes from the complex integration of large amounts of information rather than simple seeing or hearing. Jung said it was like seeing around corners. Recent studies in neuroplasticity tend to combine deeper quantum-level theories to this function.[141]

The last function is feeling. Feeling, like thinking, is a matter of evaluating information. This time, the individual evaluates through a process of weighing one's overall emotional response. Jung labels this a rational function.

Each individual has a superior or dominant function. This function is a preferential function, which has the greatest degree of development. Additionally, each individual has a secondary function used in support of the superior function. A tertiary function, which is only slightly less developed and generally residing in the subconscious, and an inferior function also exist. These functions are poorly developed and so unconscious that their existence is often denied in oneself.

Jung's work, referred to as typology, is the study of human differences. Jung's psychological typologies are not based on set descriptions that real people must fit into, but on basic elements which, when combined together, can be used to describe the differences among people. A typology is the label placed on a group of characteristics or types. Types are a bridge between the universal and the particular.

---

[140]   Amerman, L. (2008). *The structure of Jungian psychology*. Houston, TX: MindStretch.
[141]   Schwartz and Begley, Op cit.

INTROVERSION AND EXTRAVERSION

The extravert is someone whose energy and attention directs outward to the people and things in the world (Jung, Adler, and Hull, 1968). These objects are decisive in the adaptation to the world the individual makes and the actions they take. For the extravert, the external world is real and something to which one must adapt. The individual's inner world is less real and a secondary influence on conduct.

In contrast, the introvert's energy and attention direct inwardly (Jung, Adler, and Hull, 1968). The inner world is the real world to which one must adapt and determines behavior. The introvert strives to protect this inner world from too strong an influence from the outer world. This outer world is less real and of less influence. Extraversion and introversion form a pair of opposite basic attitudes to life. Each of us is both extraverted and introverted, for we relate both to the world around us and the world within, but we tend to favor one attitude over the other.

THINKING AND FEELING

As with all Jungian functions, thinking and feeling are both equally valid (Jung, Adler, and Hull, 1968). A person with a thinking preference will make decisions impersonally on the basis of logical consequences. A person with a feeling preference will rely largely on feelings to make a decision primarily based on personal or social values.

Feeling people take their expectations about people or things into themselves and have confidence in their judgments. People with a feeling typology preference might state that they like something because it has a right feeling, causing others with a thinking preference typology to feel frustration (Amerman, 2008). What the individual with a thinking preference does not know is that the individual with a feeling preference has put a subject person or situation inside on a special feeling scale. From this internal scale, the feeling typology person derives a judgment or conclusion.

The individual with the thinking preference expects that all judgments are preceded by the kind of analysis where things are divided, compared, and then reconnected in a considered final judgment (Amerman, 2008). If thinking compares one thought with another in order to advance to a new idea, feeling weighs the situation and compares it to others. However, feeling cannot spell out exactly where the final decision of like or dislike derives because feeling is more holistic than thinking (Amerman, 2008; Jung, Adler, and Hull, 1968).

Sensing and Intuition

The next set of preferences is sensing and intuition, which Jung referred to as irrational functions because they do not depend on logic (Jung, Adler, and Hull, 1968). Each is a way of perceiving simply what is: sensation sees what is in the external world, and intuition sees (or "picks up") what is in the inner world. Sensing is in the present. It is physical, the use of the five human senses. Sensation is concrete as opposed to abstract. Intuition on the other hand is a hunch, a way of sniffing out possibilities. It focuses on the future.

Personality in the Creation of Culture

Personality and culture were first linked during the 1930s when the Advisory Committee on Personality and Culture (1930-1934) was established to examine if any relationship existed.[142] The concept is that one establishes and reinforces the other. There may even be a genetic aspect, in that a natural selection process may exist where individuals that do not adhere to the accepted structure of the community are rejected by that community and therefore do not remain to breed into the community their particular traits. There is also some thought that this "natural selection" process exists within subgroupings of corporations, military units, etc., as those individuals who either do not or refuse to conform to the group are either removed or remove themselves from the environment.

One specific researcher, Robert McCrae, states, "Culture and the human mind are deeply interdependent, because they co-evolved. Personality traits were a preexisting feature of the primate mind and must have left an imprint on forms of culture."[143]

Theories of Cultural Development

Table 5 lists a few of the more accepted theories of cultural development. There is a significant number more that either modify or take an opposite view of any number of other theories. [144]

---

[142] Bryson, D. Personality and culture, the Social Science Research Council, and liberal social engineering: The Advisory Committee on Personality and Culture, 1930-1934. Journal of the History of the Behavioral Sciences; Fall 2009, Vol. 45 Issue 4, p355-386, 32p

[143] McCrae, R. Personality Profiles of Cultures: Patterns of Ethos. *European Journal of Personality.* Eur. J. Pers. 23: 205-227 (2009). Pg 205.

[144] This table was constructed from a variety of sources by the author.

Table 5: Examples of Various Sociocultural Theories

Theory	Description
Critical Theory	Critical theory refers to a style of Marxist theory with a tendency to engage with non-Marxist influences (for instance the work of Friedrich Nietzsche and Sigmund Freud)
Marxist Theory	Marxist sociology is significantly concerned, but not limited to, the relations between society and economics
Postcolonialism	Postcolonialism comprises a set of theories found amongst anthropology, architecture, philosophy, film, political science, human geography, sociology, feminism, religious and theological studies, and literature to move beyond the evils of colonialism
Structuralism	A specific domain of culture may be understood by means of a structure—modelled on language—that is distinct both from the organizations of reality and those of ideas or the imagination
Psychoanalytic	Processes of the human mind and psyche manage and control cultural development (Freud)
Semiotics	Linked closely to linguistics in that symbols establish the structure of language and, thereby, society
Cultural anthropology	Humans acquire culture through the learning processes of peer/elder observation and instruction
Identity Theory	A family of views on the relationship between mind and body, Type Identity theories hold that at least some types (or kinds, or classes) of mental states are, as a matter of contingent fact, literally identical with some types (or kinds, or classes) of brain states.

TEAM DYNAMICS

The structural model of team collaboration (see Figure 17), taken from a white paper by Warner and Wroblewski (2004), illustrates the primary factors affecting teams in the analysis and decision-making process. Of note are the dynamics of syntax, structured and unstructured definitions (e.g., I think I know what you said, but do you know that what you said is what I think?), cultural dynamics (both native and coalition force dynamics), and the structure of the organization in the decision-making process. Each stage of the model provides a mechanism for analysis and, through analysis, planning. Although the structural model of team collaboration is not the only possible model, it provides a concept for consideration and comparison.

Each stage of the team collaboration structural model establishes domains of cognitive processes. By understanding these processes, it should be possible to institute specific metrics and design them into exercise stimulators to drive evaluation of the team. Some of this will, of necessity, use the survey or Delphi-style approaches,[145] which require specific game pauses to collect the data at the point of event. Experimental controls are also a necessity. Primary to the design of a simulation are the following: the metacognitive process, which is the method the team uses to develop agreements and understanding of the

---

[145] Delphi is a process of structured investigation where questionnaires are used in a repeated fashion to arrive at consensus or agreement on a specific problem, question, or concern.

overall goal, the team mental vision of the associated issues and problems, the communication procedures of this vision to include definition at each level, and the specific problem-solving process. This simulation design procedure must include both the human and the machine processes (Figure 19).

A team can be, in microcosm,[146] a cultural dynamic representation. A team may also be a level of cultural abstraction with which a security or intelligence officer is likely to confront in the planning processes rather than one at a more macro-level such as a tribe, region, state, or nation. This is likely true even when examining broad political and/or religious movements, as individuals tend to migrate to those other members who approximate their own outlooks and beliefs most closely.

---

[146] Microcosm is a term used to describe a small representation of a larger system. For example, the comparison of New York City as a 'microcosm' of the world at large.

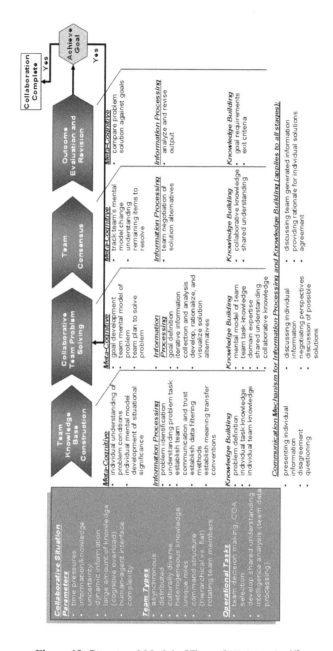

Figure 19: Structural Model of Team Collaboration[147]

---

[147] Note. From The Cognitive Processes Used in Team Collaboration during Asynchronous, Distributed Decision making, by N. Warner and E. Wroblewski, 2004, San Diego, CA: DODCRTS Symposium. Copyright 2004 by N. Warner

PSYCHOLOGY AND CULTURE

The previous subsections addressed the relationship of personality to culture. However, there is more to culture and the human terrain elements than simply the physical and personality aspects. There is also the cognitive or the psychological. The American Psychological Association defines psychology as

> *the study of the mind and behavior—from the functions of the brain to the actions of nations, from child development to care for the aged. In every conceivable setting from scientific research centers to mental health care service, "the understanding of behavior" is the enterprise of psychologists.*[148]

> **Psychology is the study of the mind and behavior—from the functions of the brain to the actions of nations, from child development to care for the aged.**

It is doubtful that one can separate psychology from culture or determine which has the greater influence on the other. There is, however, a vast body of literature on the topic focused into various domains. Primary domains for this text concern criminal psychology, the psychology of terrorism, the psychology of need satisfaction (relating to both work performance and the aspects of employees who turn on their employers), and deviance.

There are some, per Lehman, Chiu, and Schaller, who posit that culture arose out of the psychological need for a buffer against the anxiety (specifically the "existential" anxiety) resulting from knowledge that we are mortal. That a culture allows for the belief that there is some form of immortality after death, which allows us to "continue" even if only in the memory of the cultural body.[149] Such a belief applies to specific needs within the hierarchy, allowing a society to achieve higher levels of physical and cognitive activity once they are no longer anxious about their baser concerns, such as shelter, sustenance, and morality.

The important aspect of psychology to this text is how it relates to the determination of threat and what to do about a specific threat. This is not an easy answer, although there are some who attempt to consider it as such, particularly in television law enforcement shows. A review of the literature on the psychology

---

[148] www.apa.org/support/about/apa/psychology.aspx#answer

[149] Lehman, D. R., Chiu, C., and Schaller, M. Psychology and Culture. *Annual Review Psychology*. 2004. 55:689-714. Pg 691.

of terrorism, for example, will run the gamut of the possibility of creating a psychological profile to enable the prediction of subjects/individuals open to terrorist recruitment, all the way to where Wednesday Addams said of homicidal maniacs in the movie *Addams Family* that they (the terrorist) look just like everyone else.[150] Reviewing the footnoted source, one finds the total range of profile types, from uneducated-poor-abused to highly educated-rich-pampered, male to female, narcissist to psychopath to visionary to political to fanatical and everything in between.

> **Woman to Wednesday Addams in the movie *Addams Family*:**
> **"And what are you dressed up as this Halloween?"**
> **Wednesday: "I'm a psychopath. They look just like everybody else."**

While there are genuine profiles that will fit certain types of psychological threat behaviors, most are invisible until a specific action occurs. A personal theory on this is that most change happens so gradually that it remains unnoticed by the individuals close enough to the perspective perpetrator, who may have the knowledge of the change, that the change is unnoticed. Consider the adage of how to cook a frog. If the water is cold when the frog is added, it will stay in the water until it is too late. If the water is heated first, the frog leaps out.

This is not to state that there is no value in psychological evaluation, quite the contrary. Appropriate psychological profiling and periodic evaluation is quite useful in both determining situations of increasing stress to determine root causes prior to eruption and damage. Imagine, for instance, a situation concerning an individual who, by his military rank, should have been an exemplary soldier. However, the individual fails to perform and repeatedly transfers between several teams due to his belligerence and unproductiveness. Rather than passing this individual along or simply removing them from employment, a new commander decides to have a discussion to determine the root cause.

In the discussion, the manager learns of a significant family situation that the individual previously raised to an earlier manager, resulting in only ridicule. Lack of action by this official left the employee with little hope for assistance and resolution of the situation. Recognizing the situation in full, the new manager obtains agreement from the employee on a plan of resolution, arranging the necessary administrative actions and obtaining agreement from the employee.

---

[150] An excellent compilation of studies on the psychology of terrorism is contained in the Defense Technology Information Center (DTIC) entitled Psychology of Terrorism by the University of South Florida, Randy Borum, Director. http://www.dtic.mil/cgi-bin/GetTRDoc?AD=ADA494527&Location=U2&doc=GetTRDoc.pdf

When the situation resolves, the manager achieves both resolution of the situation and the retention of a valuable employee—valuable as a person, but also in the investment the organization made of several hundred thousand dollars to originally acquire and train the staff member. The employee not only achieved a higher level of performance than before the problem, the action raised the loyalty and morale of the entire team. Thus, the performance of periodic non-obtrusive psychological evaluations can lead to security benefits, as well as offset potential pitfalls.[151]

Following are a few examples of psychological theories of crime gathered together by the University of California, San Diego.[152]

Psychological theories of crime begin with the view that individual differences in behavior may make some people more predisposed to committing criminal acts. These differences may arise from personality characteristics, biological factors, or social interactions.

PSYCHOANALYTIC THEORY

According to Sigmund Freud (1856-1939), who is credited with the development of psychoanalytic theory, all humans have natural drives and urges repressed in the unconscious. Furthermore, all humans have criminal tendencies. Through the process of socialization, however, these tendencies are curbed by the development of inner controls that are learned through childhood experience. Freud hypothesized that the most common element that contributed to criminal behavior was faulty identification by a child with her or his parents. The improperly socialized child may develop a personality disturbance that causes her or him to direct antisocial impulses inward or outward. The child who directs them outward becomes a criminal, and the child that directs them inward becomes a neurotic.[153]

References [sic]

Freud, S. (1961). The Complete Works of Sigmund Freud (Vol. 19). London: Hogarth.

---

[151] By 'non-obtrusive' the author means that there need not be more than an external observation of the group rather than formal psychological examination.

[152] Downloaded from http://psy2.ucsd.edu/~hflowe/psych.htm and last updated December 11, 1996.

[153] Freud, S. (1961). The Complete Works of Sigmund Freud (Vol. 19). London: Hogarth.

COGNITIVE DEVELOPMENT THEORY

According to this approach, criminal behavior results from the way in which people organize their thoughts about morality and the law. In 1958, Lawrence Kohlberg, a developmental psychologist, formulated a theory concerning the development of moral reasoning. He posited that there are three levels of moral reasoning, each consisting of two stages. During middle childhood, children are at the first level of moral development. At this level, the preconventional level, moral reasoning is based on obedience and avoiding punishment. The second level, the conventional level of moral development, is reached at the end of middle childhood. The moral reasoning of individuals at this level is based on the expectations that their family and significant others have for them. Kohlberg found that the transition to the third level, the postconventional level of moral development, usually occurs during early adulthood. At this level, individuals are able to go beyond social conventions. They value the laws of the social system; however, they are open to acting as agents of change to improve the existing law and order. People who do not progress through the stages may become arrested in their moral development, and consequently become delinquents.

References [sic]

Cole, M. & Cole S. R. (1993). The development of children. New York: W.H. Freeman and Company.

Kohlberg, L. (1976). Moral stages and moralization: The cognitive-developmental approach to socialization. In J. Lickona, Moral development behavior: Theory, research, and social issues. New York: Harper & Row.

LEARNING THEORY

Learning theory is based upon the principles of behavioral psychology. Behavioral psychology posits that a person's behavior is learned and maintained by its consequences, or reward value. These consequences may be external reinforcement that occurs as a direct result of their behavior (e.g., money, social status, and goods), vicarious reinforcement that occurs by observing the behavior of others (e.g., observing others who are being reinforced as a result of their behavior), and self-regulatory mechanisms (e.g., people responding to their

119

behavior). According to learning theorists, deviant behavior can be eliminated or modified by taking away the reward value of the behavior. Hans J. Eysenck, a psychologist that related principles of behavioral psychology to biology, postulated that by way of classical conditioning, operant conditioning, and modeling people learn moral preferences. Classical conditioning refers to the learning process that occurs as a result of pairing a reliable stimulus with a response. Eysenck believes, for example, that over time a child who is consistently punished for inappropriate behavior will develop an unpleasant physiological and emotional response whenever they consider committing the inappropriate behavior. The anxiety and guilt that arise from this conditioning process result in the development of a conscience. He hypothesizes, however, that there is wide variability among people in their physiological processes, which either increase or decrease their susceptibility to conditioning and adequate socialization.

*References [*sic*]*

Bandura, Albert (1973). Aggression: A social learning analysis. Engle-wood Cliffs, NJ: Prentice Hall.

Eysenck, H.J. (1964). Crime and Personality. Boston: Houghton Mifflin.

Eysenck, H.J., & Gudjonsson, G.H. (1989). The causes and cures of criminality. Contemporary Psychology, 36, 575-577.

INTELLIGENCE AND CRIME

James Q. Wilson's and Richard J. Herrnstein's Constitutional-Learning Theory integrates biology and social learning in order to explain the potential causes of criminality. They argue that criminal and noncriminal behavior have gains and losses. If the gains that result from committing the crime (e.g., money) outweigh the losses (e.g., being punished), then the person will commit the criminal act. Additionally, they maintain that time discounting and equity are two other variables that play an important role in criminality. Time discounting refers to the immediate rewards that result from committing the crime vis-a-vis the punishment that may result from committing the crime, or the time that it would take to earn the reward by noncriminal means. Because people differ in their ability to delay gratification, some persons may be more prone to committing criminal acts than others. Moreover, judgments of equity may result in the commission of a criminal act. The gains associated with committing the crime may help to restore a person's feelings of being treated unjustly by society. Wilson and Herrnstein hypothesize that there are certain constitutional factors (such as intelligence and variations is physiological arousal) that determine how a person weighs the gains and losses associated with committing a criminal act. According to Wilson and Herrnstein, physiological arousal determines the ease in which people are classically conditioned; therefore, people who are unable to associate negative feelings with committing crime will not be deterred from committing criminal acts. In addition, they argue that impulsive, poorly socialized children of low intelligence are at the greatest risk of becoming criminals. However, they have only demonstrated that low intelligence and crime occur together frequently; they have not demonstrated that low intelligence is the cause of crime.

References [sic]

Wilson, J.Q. & Herrnstein, R. (1985). Crime and Human Nature. New York: Simon and Schuster.

Wrightsman, L.S., Nietzel, M.T., & Fortune, W.H. (1994). Psychology and the Legal System. Belmont: Brooks Cole Publishing Company.

PERVASIVENESS OF THE CULTURE DYNAMIC

The primary reason for culture is psychophysical. Our brains are constructed over the millennia to depend upon others of our similar construction (e.g., stature, race, concepts, etc.) for basic survival. We fear to be alone. However, what is meant by the pervasiveness of the culture dynamic? The condition of being pervasive is a condition of growth, often uncontrolled growth. It means that something is of sufficient strength to expand without external stimulation or support. This subsection examines why this is so, as well as why it is important to the security/intelligence professional.

An interesting and eerily apt photograph (Figure 20) depicts this principle.[154] The obvious purpose of the photo is to demonstrate that individuals, when alone, will go through extreme measures to end this isolation.

---

[154] Obtained on December 22, 2011, from http://www.cultureeveryday.com/culture/the-1-reason-why-culture-matters

Figure 20: "I'm Lonely . . ."

A study performed at Stanford University partially explains this human need for community:

> Culture influences action *[emphasis added]* not by providing the ultimate values toward which action is oriented, but by shaping a repertoire or "tool kit" of habits, skills, and styles from which people construct "strategies of action." Two models of cultural influence are developed, for settled and unsettled cultural periods. In settled periods, culture independently influences action, but only by providing resources from which people can construct diverse lines of action. In unsettled cultural periods, explicit ideologies directly govern action, but structural opportunities for action determine which among competing ideologies survive in the long run.[155]

Culture provides the tool set of action. What is this toolset, other than the structure of individual nature, knowledge, personality, and in other words, life? It shapes the individual potentially more than the individual in turn shapes the culture. History demonstrates that culture does change, but this is usually due to leadership. However, cultural changes are not peaceful, as humans resist alteration. The following are some of the reasons humans tend to oppose change:[156]

a. When the reason for the change is unclear. Ambiguity—whether it is about costs, equipment, jobs—can trigger negative reactions among users.

---

[155] Swidler, A. Culture in Action: Symbols and Strategies. *American Sociological Review*, 1986. Vol. 51 (April:273.-286). Pp 273.

[156] This listing was obtained from a study performed for the US Department of Transportation displayed at http://www4.uwm.edu/cuts/bench/change.htm#resist and is only one of many such lists.

b. When the proposed users have not been consulted about the change and it is offered to them as an accomplished fact

c. When the change threatens to modify established patterns of working relationships between people

d. When communication about the change—timetables, personnel, monies, etc.—has not been sufficient

e. When the benefits and rewards for making the change are not seen as adequate for the trouble involved

f. When the change threatens jobs, power, or status in an organization

History demonstrates that when a culture is no longer supported by a population and the leadership resists popular moves to adjust to perceived needs, the society seizes control and forces the change usually via a violent revolution. However, when a minority group seeks to impose change in an accepted culture, an even more violent revolution is required. Thus, from a historical perspective, culture is resistant to modification as long as the group is present. Individuals, however, do not. Yet this does not fully explain the pervasiveness of cultural influences in the human psyche.

Cultures do not simply begin, they evolve. Note that the main reason for resistance to change from the list above is fear. It is fear of the unknown, of the lack of information, or of the threatened loss of security and sustenance, either through job loss or supply challenges. There is a point at which the individuals making up the society begin to move toward a solution generally espoused by a savior-type individual or group, even if this group is anarchistic. Something is better than the uncertainty of nothing. As an example, consider the dynamics of both the Russian and the German anti-Weimar Revolutions in the early 1900s. Neither society wanted to institute such cultural changes as would lead to a major global war, yet they accepted the change and violently strove for the change to occur.

Max Weber stated,[157]

> Not ideas, but material and ideal interests, directly govern men's conduct. Yet very frequently the "world images" that have been created by "ideas" have, like switchmen, determined the tracks along which action has been pushed by the dynamic of interest.

However, current sociology examines only contemporary societies. Archeology and anthropology examine historical and ancient societies and cultures, and there are many. As far back as human existence is traced, there is

---

[157] Weber, M., Gerth, H.H., and Turner, B.S. (1948). *Max Weber: Essays in Sociology*. Routledge, Oxford, England. Pp 63.

evidence of some form of society or grouping. Scientists also have looked at groupings in primate organizations, both human and nonhuman. This raises the question of the origin of culture. A powerful statement by the president of the American Social Review provides an explanation:

> *Human society emerged over 6 million years of humanoid evolution. During this time group size steadily increased, and to maintain group cohesion human beings gradually evolved a well-developed social intelligence based on the differentiation and refinement of emotions. The neurological structures for emotional expression are part of the primitive brain and developed long before the cognitive equipment for rational intelligence evolved. Indeed, full rationality came rather late in human evolution, and it has only been within the last 100 years that the social conditions emerged for a mass culture based on rationality.*[158]

This is a firm statement that the origin of the need for culture and society is genetic. Being genetic, the need is passed with each birth. This need being passed, the child spends the first years of its life learning language, place, and culture. This learning, per Chapter 4, is hardwired into the neurons of the human brain. As such, cultural influences are pervasive. Given this premise and the previously discussed facts of human cognitive dissonance and manipulation, culture may likewise be manipulated to achieve specific results.

What does this mean for the security and intelligence professional? It means that there are two choices available to them. First, the professional may be well educated in the aspects of human and cultural terrain and use this knowledge to achieve their desired ends. Or alternatively, they may be ignorant of the aspects and dynamics of human and cultural terrain, with the same effects Sun Tzu warned against (shown in the box below).

> **Given the facts of the genetic origin of the need for culture and society and the ability to manipulate human cognition, it is logical to conclude that culture and society may be manipulated for positive and negative effects. This means the security and intelligence profession may either learn of human and cultural terrain or fail to learn with the same effects Sun Tzu warned against. "If you know neither yourself, nor your enemy, you are a fool and shall meet defeat in every battle." (Sun Tzu, *The Art of War*)**

---

[158] Massey, D.S., A Brief History of Human Society: The Origin and Role of Emotion in Social Life. *American Sociological Review.* 2002, VOL. 67 (FEBRUARY: 1-29). Pg 1.

Chapter 6

LEGAL TERRAIN

CONSIDERATIONS

The legal profession is one of the most necessary yet monopolistic professions in the world today. It matters little whether the structure is U.S. constitutional law, state law, Sharia law, Talmudic law, parliamentary law, or whatever. Laws are made by individuals who studied in the intricacies of the profession, enacted by individuals appointed or elected to a governing body, adjudicated by other such professionals appointed or elected to the judiciary, and enforced in civil situations by other members of this profession. The common thread is appointed or elected.

One of the great gurus of quality management, Dr. W. E. Deming, is well known for stating that an organization receives what it measures. If a company measures how many vials of a particular medicine are produced, but not the quality of the medicine itself, it may find thousands of vials being shipped with nothing in them but water. This was the case in a particular story on Soviet manufacturing and has been an issue with some products from other nations entering the United States as well. Another example involves a society measuring how many law cases move through the court system rather than the accuracy of the findings or the impact on the victim. Such a system will attain a level of revolving-door justice. Speed of docket clearance is the objective, even if it places a known criminal back on the streets before the officer finishes the report.

To establish a complete structure of the legal terrain requires a depth beyond the scope of this text. There are numerous texts in publication, as well as appropriate courses discussing this discipline in greater depth. One particularly appropriate chapter on the history of the American legal system is contained in

Curtis and McBride's Proactive Security Administration.[159] This source also provides appropriate summations of the history of the American legal system, as it is supposed to work when politics and vote fishing are not involved or when elected officials decide to forego their oaths of office and become selective in which laws they will enforce for political expediency's sake.

Therefore, this chapter examines the legal terrain in a slightly different format than is generally considered. Rather than approaching this minefield as a historical or legalistic reiteration of laws, this text will examine this terrain with respect to the psychological and cognitive expectations perspective laws establish within a cultural enclave. The objective is to establish in the mind of the security/intelligence professional a means of examining this terrain for use in positive/proactive and negative/reactive planning.

Two powerful statements made by Curtis and McBride are:[160]

> *The legal basis for private sector security typically is not in a federal or state constitution or statute although some exceptions exist . . . and . . . in the absence of a statutory or regulatory basis for security, however, the legal basis for private sector security services is derived from the common law right of private citizens and businesses to defend themselves and protect their property (Post and Kingsbury, 1977).*

The law is a tool. It is a tool that is bidirectional. It protects the rights and functions of the individual and the organization while also limiting what the individual and the organization can do. The law is often abused by individuals and organizations in their attempts to impose their will on others for whatever individual or political purpose may seem appropriate at that time.

The law is also a risk that needs to be considered, understood within the boundaries of current decisions and applications, and planned for in both offensive and defensive conditions. It can and often is more than a simple situation of arrest, trial, and adjudication. There are individuals from various backgrounds working tirelessly through the system to ensure, not protection and justice, but individual and party agendas.

---

[159] Curtis, G.E. and McBride, R.B. (2011). *Proactive Security Administration.* Prentice-Hall, Upper Saddle River, NJ.

[160] Ibid. pg 27.

> An example that comes to mind originated on a syndicated television show, *Law and Order*. In the show, an individual had committed a crime of robbery where a bystander was murdered. Two of the three thieves were later found dead. The third thief worked a plea bargain with the DA, not knowing they would soon find the second thief's body, so he was not able to be prosecuted for the first thief's murder or the bystander's. However, the DA was able to bring a murder conviction for the second thief by *not* stating he knew before making the plea deal that the second thief had been found. He didn't lie or withhold information as that would have been perjury. He simply answered the defense attorney's questions, and she did not ask the correct questions.

One of the more interesting of these situations involves tort[161] law, a decision on an injury case (the basic meaning of "tort") focused on the established facts of the cause of an injury and who was the primary cause at fault for the conditions leading to the injury. However, an issue had developed where individuals and companies at fault were avoiding penalty through various means, such as bankruptcy.

The courts began an official criterion not of who is at fault but rather who can best cover the financial loss in the situation. This precedent established the "deep pockets" process known today. Many companies simply have their legal and insurance departments settle with a complainant rather than fighting the case in court. This is because it is less costly in terms of actual cash and adverse publicity. The logic involves the aspects of basic economics, who ultimately pays in an injury case is often the general population, creating a "tax" that ensures no one party is seriously impoverished.[162]

---

[161] There are several types of law; criminal, Constitutional, civil, probate, and tort are examples. Refer to a dictionary for the definitions of these various types of law.

[162] With conservatively estimated annual direct costs of $180 billion, or 1.8 percent of GDP, the United States tort system is the most expensive in the world, more than double the average cost of other industrialized nations. Whereas an efficient tort system has a potentially important role to play in ensuring that firms have proper incentives to produce safe products, poorly designed policies can mistakenly impose excessive costs on society through forgone production of public and private goods and services. To the extent that tort claims are economically excessive, they act like a tax on individuals and firms. White House Council of Economic Advisors, (2002). http://www.policyalmanac.org/economic/archive/torts.shtml

The simile of a minefield applies well to legal terrain. In warfare, ground forces will use implanted explosive devices to alert them to the presence of an enemy. The devices can also channel an enemy into an area where they are at a tactical disadvantage and/or deny advantageous positions to an enemy when the friendly force is of insufficient size or power to defend the area directly. In creating these fields, designers draw up detailed schematics of the layout and distribute them to appropriate individuals to avoid friendly casualties and/or damage. They plan pathways through these fields and show them to friendly forces so that they can both safely transit the field, enabling them to place defensive fires in these unprotected zones. Failure to take these planning precautions can and will cause inappropriate and unnecessary consequences. The law is no different.

One needs not be an expert in the law to use it in this strategic manner. One does need to understand the goals and requirements that an assessment of the various security/intelligence issues raise, such as which laws apply, how they apply, and the potential outcomes of the various situations if engaged. If the projected outcome of an engaged situation is detrimental to the organization, the security official needs to construct a plan to anticipate and address these conditions. This plan should consider, model, and codify points and methods of departure to disengage. Where the outcome of engagement is beneficial to the organization, the security plan should include conditions and metrics to determine the appropriate steps and points that will entrap the threat in the appropriate minefield.

An excellent document for continued research into various federal statutes is the CRS report to Congress—General Management Laws: A Compendium dated May 19, 2004. This report is periodically updated and searchable on the Internet for CRS reports with the above title and no date. This report applies to this text, in that it lays out the legal minefield through which the security/intelligence professional must pass.

> The compendium includes more than 90 separate entries that describe general management laws for the executive branch of the federal government. The entries in the compendium are organized into the following seven functional categories: (1) Information and Regulatory Management; (2) Strategic Planning, Performance Measurement, and Program Evaluation; (3) Financial Management, Budget, and Accounting; (4) Organization; (5) Procurement and Real Property Management; (6) Intergovernmental Relations Management; and (7) Human Resources Management and Ethics. These categories include many laws and topics, including the Freedom of Information Act (FOIA, section I.E.), Privacy Act (I.F.), Federal Advisory Committee Act (FACA, I.G.), National Environmental Policy Act (NEPA, I.L.), Data Quality Act (I.O.; increasingly known as the Information Quality Act

(IQA)), Inspector General Act (II.A.), Government Performance and Results Act (II.B.), Balanced Budget and Emergency Deficit Control Act (III.D.), Budget Enforcement Act (III.E.), Government Corporation Control Act (IV.A.), Davis-Bacon Act (V.F.), Unfunded Mandates Reform Act (UMRA, VI.C.), Hatch Act (VII.A.(5) and VII.A.(29)), Ethics in Government Act (VII.B.), Federal Tort Claims Act (VII.E.), and issues like information security (section I), improper payments (section III), services acquisition and contracting (section V), and federal employees and civil service laws (e.g., the National Security Personnel System at the Department of Defense, and the Department of Homeland Security personnel system (section VII.A)).[163]

As is seen in this introduction, there are at least ninety separate entries that relate specifically to how the government is supposed to do business. It is likely that each individual state has a similar number, with counties and localities adding to this riotous sound. Additional rules, regulations, statutes, and laws are added with each new day and each new court decision, making this an evolving area of study.

THEORIES OF THE LEGAL DIMENSION[164]

Legal theories, as with the laws themselves, are numerous and actually have some of their beginnings in sixteenth century Europe. It was at this time that various philosophical individuals began to truly question the "divine right" of a certain family of individuals to rule over the general population. The renaissance of this period initiated with an increase in general literacy. With literacy came a more rapid means of spreading ideas and education, which encouraged individualism rather than groupthink. As time continued, the questions and questioners continued to grow. The questions began to change from one of the truth of divine right, to the right of self-governance based not on a ruling body but rather on the will of the people. Karl Harter addresses this evolution in his study *Security and "Gute Policey" in Early Modern Europe: Concepts, Laws, and Instruments.*[165] In his study, Harter examines the,

---

[163]   Brass, C.T. (Updated May 19, 2004). CRS Report to Congress (Order Code RL30795). General Management Laws: A Compendium.

[164]   The word, dimension, here is defined as an area of concern or professional domain.

[165]   Specifically, Sicherheit und "Gute Policey" im frühneuzeitlichen Europa: Konzepte Gesetze und Instrumente. Translated and published in English in Historical Social Research, Vol. 35-2010-No. 4, 41-65.

Development of "security" as a leading category and main field of state activity in the Early Modern Era was closely interconnected with the concept of "Gute Policey" and the increasing body of police ordinances. Within Early Modern administrative law as well as in the theoretical discourses of the administrative sciences, "security" became a crucial objective of the well-ordered police state and thus succeeded "peace" and "unity" as a leading category. In this respect, the growing importance of security indicates the "secularization" of authoritarian regulatory policy. In parallel to this, administrative law was characterized by the differentiation between "internal" and "social" security. Whereas the former focused on exterior security threats, for example mobile marginal groups, the latter manifested itself in scopes such as "poor relief," the "health sector" and measures dealing with risks and hazards including bad harvests, epidemic plagues, fire hazards and natural disasters.[166]

This concept actually is the start of the term "polizei" or police. Harter continues, "The contemporary notion of police is the result of a lengthy process in which the concept and notion of 'policy' was narrowed to an executive agency primarily dealing with the maintenance of 'internal security.'"[167] He concludes, stating,

Hence, the police ordinances as well as the theoretical discourses of Policeywissenschaft (police and administrative sciences) allow us in the following to analyse the intentions and aims of "security" which were to be established and maintained by police ordinances, as well as the more specific security regulations and the concrete fields of administration in which security was considered to be the primary purpose.[168]

From this beginning derives the current concept of security. These concepts are protection, enforcement, and maintenance of order. However, what is it that constitutes "order"? As aptly demonstrated throughout history, the concept of order is linked diametrically with the preservation of the current ruling entity. The structure of this preservation is demonstrated in the graphic below (Figure 21).

---

[166]   Ibid, pg 41.

[167]   Ibid. pg 42. On the history of *gute Policey* as a whole and its notion in particular, see: Härter 2010; Iseli 2009; Nitschke 1992; Raeff 1983.

[168]   Ibid. pg 43.

The United States Code, which contains all U.S. laws, currently has over fifty titles in a number of volumes. That number of volumes changes constantly. The laws covering the rules, regulations, and procedures for only bankruptcy (Title 11, USC) spans more than twenty volumes. Per one unreviewed source, since the start of 2000, Congress has created at least 452 new crimes. So the total number of federal crimes as of the end of 2007 exceeds 4,450. Ninety-one of the 452 were contained in new laws that created 279 new crimes, and the remaining are found in amendments to existing laws. The total of 452 new crimes breaks down by year as follows: 65 for 2000, 28 for 2001, 82 for 2002, 51 for 2003, 48 for 2004, 13 for 2005, 145 for 2006, and 20 for 2007.[169] This listing does *not* include state, county, municipality, and other location laws.[170]

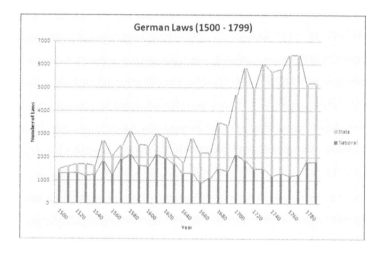

Figure 21: Police Regulations—Europe—1500 to 1799[171]

The situation in developing specific theories of law falls into the same demographic as social theory in general. They are legion. The structure of legal theories revolves around economics, sociocultural, and behavior modification.

---

[169]   http://wiki.answers.com/Q/How_many_laws_are_there_in_the_United_States#ixzz1cE6vJVaz any wiki source is unregulated, thus 'unreviewed" and must be considered inaccurate. It is used here as for example purposes only and should not be further cited.

[170]

[171]   Ibid. pg 48. Per the source, the information is taken from the regulations of 7 imperial cities and 10 territories from various areas of Imperial Germany/Austrian-Hungarian Empire era.

Discussion of each area provides insight to the concepts of thought that drive current activities in law and regulatory development.

Sociocultural/Neo-Sociocultural

> *There are many interesting arguments to be found in the social norms jurisprudence that has been developed over the past decade or so, and it is not at all surprising that this jurisprudence should have made such a splash in the American law schools. Some of it, however, generates more bewilderment than enlightenment. Social norms theorists sometimes seem to make light of difficult issues such as how such norms are internalized, how and why they change, how they may differ contextually (think, for example, of how social norms relating to use of the roads can vary as between cities and rural areas), and why—especially when the socially inappropriate behavior[sic] which is the focus of a social norm is also the subject of a legal norm—such norms ought to be considered especially significant for jurisprudential purposes.*[172]

The concept of sociocultural jurisprudence revolves around the codification of what society believes to be appropriate behavior. The question is always who is the purveyor of the beliefs of society? The society generally decides the source of the purveyor is one common school or source of origin, whether a dictator, king, congress, parliament, etc. The population determines and establishes the structure through their support for those individuals or groups elected or appointed over them.

A second school is one of power. Individuals with significant resources can gain authority based upon their ability to satisfy the needs of others often without taking a visible leadership role. This is in exchange for willing subjugation. The surrendering of this freedom of action to that authority requires at the most loyalty and at the least obedience to the rules established by that authority. While this authority is often a dictator or other singular leader, it may also be organizations such as religious or economic structures which "own" the leadership and/or subjects via coercion.

The theory also establishes that there are limits to this authority. Robert Scott writes,

---

[172] Duxbury, N. Signalling [sic] and Social Norms. *Oxford Journal of Legal Studies*, Vol. 21, No. 4 (2001), pp. 719-736. Pp 722-723.

The law influences the behavior of its citizens in various ways. Well understood are the direct effects of legal rules. By imposing sanctions or granting subsidies, the law either expands or contracts the horizon of opportunity within which the individuals can satisfy their preferences.[173]

This is the basic goal of jurisprudence in the ideal sense. Mankind, however, is less than ideal.

This is where the power aspect of the socioeconomic theory arises. There are those that, for want of better explanation, desire the world to be something they envision. Because they envision it, and either have or believe they have the power to create it, they use the law as a justifiable means of achieving this vision. This is not that different from the concept of divine right of the monarchy. Such a process is in play in many areas of the world today, especially in those areas considered democratic or "people ruled." Here, the "people" are seen as both insufficiently educated and often societally incapable of knowing how to live their own lives. Examples include the Third Reich, the Soviet Union, China, and many others.

Given these beliefs and attitudes, these groups assume it is the duty of those with these positions to enforce their will upon the great unwashed masses. These are the elitists who, by virtue of their supposed or self-proclaimed greater knowledge, position, and/or feelings of "rightness," establish themselves as both above the general population and the guiding principles of law. To this group of individuals, guiding principles such as constitutions, etc. are barriers that should be removed rather than guiding principles to be protected and enforced. This condition often leads to the second basic theory—economics.

ECONOMIC THEORY OF LAW

The White House economic advisors wrote,

The similarity between inefficient tort litigation and taxes suggests that the economic costs of the tort liability system may be better understood by pursuing the analogy between the expected costs arising from the tort system and taxes on firms. As with a tax, it is possible to examine the question of who bears the incidence of—that is, who pays for—excessive tort costs. An important lesson in the economics of taxation is that people pay taxes; firms are legal entities that can bear no real burden. Put differently, the burden of any tax depends not

---

[173] Scott, R.E. The Limits of Behavioral Theories of Law and Social Norms. 86 Va. L. Rev. 1603 (2000).

on who writes the check (the legal liability), which may be the firm, but
rather on the market outcomes that shift the cost to workers, consumers
or owners of capital.[174]

Harry S. Truman is rumored to have stated, "I am constantly amazed that the same people who scoff at gypsies and fortunetellers, believe economists and weathermen." This might also be put, "I am constantly amazed that the same politicians and activists who rail against a supposed inequity of taxation between the 'rich' and the 'poor,' are, themselves rich and ignore the fact that the common individual is the ultimate taxpayer irrespective of upon whom the taxes are levied." The condition where a levied tax falls upon a specific group that actually bears the burden paying the tax is called the "tax incidence."

Irrespective of the desires of various organizations and activists, at the end of the day, it is the general population who bears the burden of any tax. They bear this burden through higher prices, less available work due to loss of demand, payments for those who cannot or will not provide for their own support, etc. This is fact, not fantasy as many researchers and economists admit. For example, Harvard economist N. Gregory Mankiw offers the following statement regarding who actually bears the burden of the corporate income tax in society:

> *But before deciding that the corporate income tax is a good way for the*
> *government to raise revenue, we should consider who bears the burden*
> *of the corporate tax. This is a difficult question on which economists*
> *disagree, but one thing is certain: People pay all taxes. When the*
> *government levies a tax on a corporation, the corporation is more like*
> *a tax collector than a taxpayer. The burden of the tax ultimately falls on*
> *people—the owners, customers, or workers of the corporation.*[175]

Why is this important to individuals within jurisprudence boundaries? As with most things political, it influences their perceptions and actions. Establishing a tax incidence or prevalence enables political motivation for such things as perceived inequities in wealth generation, advancement potentialities, and voting bloc structures. Linking these situations to the ability to manipulate information, known as propagandizing, enhances perceived and actual power. Establishing this within a stakeholder environment creates what is known in military circles as a combat multiplier.

---

[174] White House. Op cit.

[175] Mankiw, N.G. (2009). *Principles of Economics: 6th Edition*. Centgage Learning Products. Mason, Oh. Quote downloaded from http://www.taxfoundation.org/blog/show/1467.html

A combat multiplier, per Field Manual 101-5-1 Operational Terms and Graphics, is defined as

> *supporting and subsidiary means that significantly increase the relative combat strength (power) of a force while actual force ratios remain constant. Examples of combat multipliers are economizing in one area to mass in another, leadership, unit morale, surprise, deception, battlefield information, camouflage, electronic warfare, psychological operations, terrain reinforcement, smoke, and indirect fires.*[176]

Multipliers exist in nonmilitary situations as well. Information is a primary multiplier in that the individual or organization that controls that information is capable of releasing it in ways and times advantageous to their goals. A major example of this is the global marketplace. The objective of this marketplace is to make a commodity or service of greater value at the point of release or transfer of ownership than at the point of creation or acquisition. There is a corollary to this principle—to make a commodity or service of lesser value upon reacquisition than at sale. This is known as "shorting."

In shorting, an individual sells something of value with the promise of repurchasing it at a later established date. The requirement of the seller is to ensure that the value of the sold item does indeed decrease in value. Thus, the seller retains a portion of the initial transaction as profit, while the buyer loses out on the gamble. While the process of shorting is legal, there are times when individuals manipulate conditions through the release of propaganda, insider information, or lying at the outset that forces the value to fall artificially. This manipulation is internationally illegal and difficult to both prove and prosecute.

While shorting is a subject for a course on economics, the value in this situation is the demonstration of the impact of propaganda on global conditions. Such an economic "shorting" situation occurred in 1997 and again in 2007 and may in fact be happening now in the United States. The first event involved the Hong Kong market currency trading, while the more recent event was targeting the British pound. In both situations, only significant action by the governments involved saved the market from total collapse.[177] The goal was not money, but power. The demonstrated power may result in governmental reluctance to pursue action where the power broker does not want that action to continue.

---

[176] US Army FM 101-5-1. (1997). *Operational Terms and Graphics.* Pg 1-31.

[177] An excellent article on this situation is found at http://www.thestandard.com.hk/news_detail.asp?pp_cat=1&art_id=48335&sid=14350285&con_type=1 where reporter Amy Nip has shown how even experts in this area are unable to totally control such situations.

Once again, it is the people who end up paying the penalty. Governments must, to prop up their markets and/or economies in such a situation, expend financial resources. These resources are not under the ownership of the government from the perspective of their ability to generate it independent of their populations. Thus, it is the population which is the "tax incident" in this situation.

Given these facts, governments must ensure a ready supply of revenue, and this revenue can only originate in the taxpayer. The only legal and acceptable means of obtaining this revenue is through taxation. And tax laws and regulations can and are changed with increasing regularity, irrespective of the burden it places on the population, until that population reaches a point of open resistance. This leads to the final environment: behavior modification.

BEHAVIOR MODIFICATION THEORY IN LAW

The concept of using the law to modify behavior is an established fact. It is the objective of criminal law and a goal of civil law. Criminal law establishes various penalties for not following the specific law or regulation. These penalties range from requirements for community service to financial penalties, to the loss of individual freedoms and rights through imprisonment and/or loss of civil allowances, such as voting and licenses of various types.

Over the decades, the concept of modifying behavior through law has evolved into a similar theory of social rehabilitation as the primary goal of jurisprudence. However, many studies demonstrate that the success rate for rehabilitation simply does not justify the costs, as stated by Ness and Strong (1997).

> *The concept of restorative justice acknowledges that the criminal justice system has not been effective in reducing crime, that prisons make offenders worse rather than rehabilitating or deterring them, and that victims are dissatisfied with their treatment by the criminal justice system. Restorative justice is based on a new pattern of thinking that emphasizes informal justice, restitution, victims, reconciliation, and social justice. Restorative justice focuses on the harmful effects of crime and actively involves both offenders and victims in reparation and rehabilitation.*[178]

There are many issues associated with the system of rehabilitation and its corollaries. Not the least of which is fear on the part of the victims in being

---

[178] Ness, D.V. and Strong, K.H. (1997). *Restoring Justice*. Anderson Publishing Co. Cincinnati, Oh. Pg. Abstract. https://www.ncjrs.gov/App/Publications/abstract. aspx?ID=165803

reintroduced to the individual(s) who has so seriously and negatively impacted their lives. Andre Normandeau and Carol Laprairie, writing in the *Canadian Journal of Criminology*, state two substantial arguments concerning the above:

> *(a) if restorative justice is not to affect all aspects of the state justice system, are the evils of the state system appropriate for some offenders but not for others; which offenders are most suitable for restorative justice; which offenders, victims and communities will have access to restorative justice; what will be the relationship between restorative and criminal justice processes; and which are appropriate justice functions for the state and which are appropriate justice functions for the community.*

> *(b) if restorative justice is to affect all aspects of the state system, how will offenders and victims, who may be eligible for restorative justice but who have "bad attitudes" and little potential for rehabilitation, be dealt with; how will dangerous offenders be dealt with; how will restorative justice reintegrate and transform those individuals who are often the most problem for a criminal justice system but who are also the most isolated and marginalized members of society; and, will restorative justice processes be able to satisfy collective expectations of justice, as well as the needs of specific parties.*[179]

History is rife with attempts to modify human behavior, some successful, some not so successful. For example, the United States attempted a national-level effort to lead its population from the evils of alcohol by enacting the Eighteenth Amendment to the U.S. Constitution. This amendment stated:[180]

> Section 1. *After one year from the ratification of this article the manufacture, sale, or transportation of intoxicating liquors within, the importation thereof into, or the exportation thereof from the United States and all territory subject to the jurisdiction thereof for beverage purposes is hereby prohibited.*

> Section 2. *The Congress and the several States shall have concurrent power to enforce this article by appropriate legislation.*

---

[179] Normandeau, A. and Laprairie, C. Restoring Justice (A Book Review). *Canadian Journal of Criminology*. Jul 98, vol. 40 Issue 3. P342-345. Pg 343. Downloaded from http://ehis.ebscohost.com Accession 24258834.

[180] http://www.gpoaccess.gov/constitution/pdf/con029.pdf

Section 3. *This article shall be inoperative unless it shall have been ratified as an amendment to the Constitution by the legislatures of the several States, as provided in the Constitution, within seven years from the date of the submission hereof to the States by the Congress.*

The amendment was an abject failure, as demonstrated by the history of the time—complete with the success of various bootlegging gangs and organized crime syndicates—and the passing of the Twenty-First Amendment repealing the Eighteenth Amendment.

Similar attempts at behavior modification have met with at least civil disobedience (e.g., speed laws), if not outright rejection (e.g., the various race and antiwar riots of the sixties and seventies). Other attempts have been geared to pushing a specific agenda of a minority, such as the trans-fat laws of New York City and extensive smoking bans across the country.[181] In some situations, the government has increased taxation, with mixed success, to modify individual behavior. This often results in a similar situation of bootlegging of items, such as liquor and cigarettes, rather than the desired modification in behavior.

PERVASIVENESS OF THE LEGAL DOMAIN

As with the human and cultural terrain examinations, it is important to look at the drivers and issues behind the spread of the use of regulations and other codified means of establishing security. The most appropriate issue pertaining to this terrain is habit and the associated individual justifications.

There is a logical fallacy labeled *argumentum ad populum*, Latin for, "If people believe it, it must be true." A good example of this fallacy appears in the statement, "In a court of law, the jury votes by majority. Therefore, the jury will always make the correct decision." This logic ignores the simple fact that there are other variables and drivers in play. As demonstrated in Chapter 4, Human Terrain, personal preference, bias, expectation, and peer pressure all factor into the situation.

---

[181] The trans-fat ban in New York was enacted on December 5, 2006, as an amendment to a City Health Board regulation; not a specific city ordnance or law. The specific citation in the law contained at http://news.findlaw.com/wp/docs/transfat/nyctransfatlaw.html cites medical studies showing that heart disease is a leading cause of death in New Yorkers, 1/3 of which are under the age of 75; meaning 2/3rds are OVER that age. The projected (but not provable) improvement in the survival rate of heart disease is 6%. Arguments against the ban appear to be significant and based primarily on limited government issues and positions.

In the case of public law and regulation, a possible syllogism is, "Laws are made to protect us and most people believe that the law is good. Therefore, this law must also be good." Humans are raised to generally respect authority, at least in theory. Authority is present in the government, the enforcement arms of that government, and the implied threat of force where the average citizen will have no recourse against the government. The adage "You can't fight city hall" is an excellent example of this.

Take the example of community activism and the numbers of individuals associated with any particular event. They are generally a minority and often are gathered together more out of curiosity than commitment. Yet where there is commitment, social change can occur as long as the government assumes the position of a servitor of the people. History again demonstrates that this is not always the case, that there are situations where the people are in the right, yet government acts to protect itself rather than serve the population.

During the Great Depression, for example, volunteers were lured into the military with the promise of a bonus payment for their service. This bonus was to be paid in 1945. The impoverished veterans, however, petitioned Congress and the president for early payment to ease their situations. This was denied by antiveteran groups, fearing/believing that such a payment would bankrupt the nation, which led forty-five thousand veterans to march on Washington in 1932. The veterans set up camps to peacefully demonstrate for the payment; however, Congress and President Hoover feared the initiation of riots and revolution. Brigadier Douglas MacArthur was ordered to clear the camps nonviolently yet exceeded his orders and ordered the employment of bayonets, tanks, and tear gas against the unarmed veterans.

The antiveteran policies of denying contracted payments and other economic aid continued until Labor Day 1935, when a massive hurricane slammed into the Florida Keys. This storm demolished a veteran's work camp that had not been evacuated due to governmental inaction, resulting in over 250 vet and civilian deaths. This incident prompted Congress to override recently elected President Roosevelt's veto and pay the bonuses in 1936. Later, as WWII came to an end, Congress feared a similar economic and riotous antigovernment situation and, bowing to public pressure, created the G.I. Bill of Rights. This is a case where the people demonstrated their power to the elite (the president and Congress), forcing an overdue and promised consideration.[182]

People generally trust the law and the authority figures associated with it. When in trouble, it is always a police officer or some other uniformed agent that is

---

[182] Information for the Bonus Army is contained in numerous locations on the web. Some of the information for the above was obtained from http://www.military.com/ NewContent/0,13190,111104_BonusArmy,00.html.

sought for action and/or protection. It is the concept of fairness, the satisfaction of Maslow's hierarchical level of the need for security, that our culture embeds into our psyches from an early age. You can see the reverse of this trust in countries where the police abuse their power of authority against citizens. This is why situations of improper behavior by the police and other uniformed members of government authority are universally criticized and feared. The uniform and/or badge of authority are strong symbols of motivation to the conditions that make society function.

MANIPULATION OF LEGAL DYNAMICS

Anderson and Jackson, writing in *The Independent Review*, quote Paul Rosenzweig's statement concerning changes in the dynamics of the law since the nation's founding:

> To [the] fundamental changes in the nature of criminal liability one must also add significant changes in the subject matter of criminal law. At its inception, criminal law was directed at conduct that society recognized as inherently wrongful and, in some sense, immoral. These acts were wrongs in and of themselves (malum in se), such as murder, rape, and robbery. In recent times the reach of the criminal law has been expanded so that it now addresses conduct that is wrongful not because of its intrinsic nature but because it is a prohibited wrong (malum prohibitum)—that is, a wrong created by a legislative body to serve some perceived public good. These essentially regulatory crimes have come to be known as "public welfare" offenses.[183]

This section, however, concerns positive manipulation of the law for the benefit of the organization involved in security and/or intelligence planning. It is not intended to be a compendium of how to get around specific laws, as this would enter an area of questionable ethics. Rather, the goal here is to show how sufficient planning and "soft power" events/actions can achieve desired security goals, both legally and peacefully.

For instance, in the U.S. on October 30, 2011, it snowed approximately twenty-four inches on several northern cities, which were also experiencing a

---

[183] Anderson, W.L. and Jackson, C.E. (2004). Law as a Weapon: How RICO Subverts Liberty and the True Purpose of Law. *The Independent Review, v. IX, n. 1,* Summer 2004, ISSN 1086-1653, Copyright © 2004, pp. 85-97. Quote from page 85. Downloaded from http://www.independent.org/pdf/tir/tir_09_1_4_anderson.pdf

series of growing civil disobedience demonstrations against various financial institutions at that time.

The groups were rumored to be funded by several anarchistic political interest organizations for the sole purpose of causing disruptions. The police, using city ordinances against open fires and dangerous explosive containers, confiscated a large number of propane tanks and heaters from the crowds a day prior to the scheduled weather system's arrival. The end result was a very cold, very wet crowd that disbursed without incident as the weather turned, ending at least temporarily and maybe for the entire winter the threat of further violence.

Anderson and Jackson focus on this type of activity concerning the RICO law, stating,

> Rather than naming organizations, Congress phrased the statute in language that Fischel describes as "vague" and "almost meaningless," which, he argues, "requires prosecutors to exercise maximum caution to prevent the law from being misused in ways that Congress never intended" (1995, 123). Unfortunately, U.S. prosecutors came to recognize that the law's very vagueness made it a splendid weapon to attack individuals and firms that presented inviting targets even though they might not have broken the law in any straightforward way.[184]

American society is simultaneously concerned with peace, freedom, and security from the loss of liberty and yet also desirous of handicapping the very organizations tasked with the maintenance of these attributes. A *Los Angeles Times* editorial quoted in the Anderson and Jackson article states that for a law to be a "good" law, it must be clear, addresses a specific and clearly defined form of illicit conduct, and prescribes a remedy or punishment proportionate to the damage done by the offense. Failing this, the editorial states, the law is enacted not for justice but for convenience of the state.[185] Yet another recent editorial decries attempts by sanitation officials and police to halt Occupy Wall Street protestors from using public walkways and parks as a sewer, admonishing them to take their biological needs "into the lobby of Goldman Sachs."[186] The editorial posits the concept that a law that denies the right of an individual to express civil disobedience even to the limit of such disgusting acts is unconstitutional and immoral.

Police and military organizations manipulate the law for positive benefits often in situations such as interrogation. Table 4, as shown earlier, provides a

---

[184]   Ibid. pg 91.

[185]   Ibid. pg 95.

[186]   Occupy Wall Street: When basic biological needs are criminalized. *Opinion LA.* October 24, 2011.

listing of techniques used in military interrogation that are not permitted in police interrogations. Under the auspices of the Fifth Amendment, a person cannot be compelled to be a witness against himself. However, until about the turn of the nineteenth century to the twentieth century, physical abuse was a common tactic to obtain information and confessions.

Then in the early 1900s, the Supreme Court began taking a dim view of such situations reaching its apex in Miranda v. Arizona in 1966. This case created both the Miranda warnings and limited severely the tactics investigators may use in interrogations. According to some research, however, as much as 55 percent of criminal confessions happen during police interrogations obtained through the use of astute psychological observation and pressure. Allowable techniques include such things as the color, shape, and furnishings of the interrogation room and positioning the suspect in a corner where one officer is nonverbally communicating resentment, disbelief, and hostility, while the other is nonverbally communicating openness, willingness to listen, and easiness.[187]

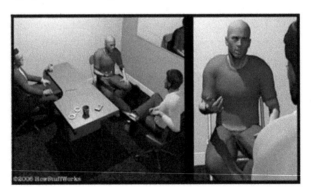

Figure 22: Example of Interrogation Room and Positions[188]

Notice the positioning of individuals in Figure 22. The suspect in the red T-Shirt is backed into a corner with no way to move and is totally enclosed by the walls, desk, and interrogator number 1 in the blue sweater. The suspect's chair is a metal/plastic chair with no padding, straight backed, and without lumbar

---

[187] Non-verbal communications are those where an individual's body position, location with respect to another, facial expressions, and other actions that do not include speech unconsciously communicate a message to the observing individual. The ability to observe these conditions in another provides a powerful advantage as any individual in a stress situation is nearly unable to hide these queues. An excellent text in this respect is "Let Me Hear Your Body Talk" by Janet Hargrave.

[188] Photo obtained from http://people.howstuffworks.com/police-interrogation1.htm

support, specifically selected for discomfort. It is a chair one finds in many fast food establishments, as they want the space to be vacated as quickly as possible for other customers.

Interrogator number 1, the "good" cop, sits with his leg crossed and facing the suspect. His arms are not crossed, and his posture is at ease and open. The space between himself and the suspect is open but leaves no possible pathway out of the situation for the suspect. Interrogator number 1's chair is a cushioned full-backed chair to maximize comfort for long periods. It likely has a lumbar support to enable lower back comfort and maintenance of energy for the interrogator.

Interrogator number 2, the "bad" cop, has a similar chair. Notice, however, he is dressed formally and is sitting erect with his hands on his knees. This is a position of power and conveys authority and suspicion. He also is placing a barrier between himself and the suspect to increase the suspect's unease and distrust of obtaining any support or help from interrogator number 2, leaving his only hope of "escape" through the path of interrogator number 1.

During this period, both interrogators will fire questions at the suspect to first start him talking. Once talking, it is psychologically difficult in stress situations to stop. Secondly, they will ask seemingly random and unconnected questions. This tactic, particularly under stress, causes the brain to access different sections and sets up confusion in the mind of the suspect.

A psychological aspect of the subconscious mind is that it will, once faced with a question or problem, continue to work the problem until a result has been reached. Once reached, it reveals the result irrespective of time and place. This is why individuals will sometimes sit upright in the middle of the night with an answer to a problem they were unaware they were even thinking of. It is during these situations information may be unintentionally released that the interrogator may latch onto to further confuse the suspect into additional revelations and ultimately, a confession.

Security officers face a more difficult situation in that the "suspects" are usually employees, or worse, *not* employees. These security officers do not have the authority of a law enforcement individual, but similar capabilities do exist. Keep in mind that the threat of engagement of civilian or military law enforcement officials often conveys a message of severe escalation of events to a point leading to judicial action most individuals wish to avoid. Therefore, the not-present authority figure becomes the bad guy, while the security official becomes the good guy in the mind of the individual being questioned. In fact, this can be to a point of greater fear of the missing official than if they were present.

Take, for example, a good suspense film sequence of events. The lighting, music, body language, and other factors of the actor(s) on the screen all convey one thought: uncertainty. This queues the observer's brain into trying to solve the problem of just what is the threat, engaging their imagination, which is always worse than the reality. When the actual threat appears, the mind thinks, "Oh, that isn't so bad." This is why it is always best to not show "the monster" to heighten suspense or fear in the audience. In an interrogation, the suspect is the audience.

An example from a movie of some time back had a suspect being questioned by two interrogators in a back room. The one actor was playing the good guy to the suspect, keeping the other interrogator from going to get his "tools." The suspect, though nervous, was refusing to cooperate. Finally, the good guy gave up and told the other to get his tools, to which the second interrogator said he would be right back "with the salt and vinegar."

Immediately, the suspect started crying out questions about what was going to happen with the salt and vinegar, to which the second man said, "You'll see . . . it never fails." The suspect relented and surrendered the desired information. As the two interrogators were leaving the suspect to the local police, the good one turns to the other and asks, "What is the salt and vinegar for?" The second replies, "I have no idea . . . but it does always work."

There are no laws that prohibit officers from lying to a suspect.

> "John, what is the salt and vinegar for?"
> "I have no idea, Tom, but it always works!"

There are laws against physical and psychological coercion. It is not psychological coercion, however, when the suspect draws the wrong conclusions from information presented to their detriment. There is also no law that prohibits an educated officer from using their intelligence, training, and senses to analyze the information being presented to them, using it to cause confusion, uncertainty, or fear in the minds of suspects. Especially as these individuals may be attempting to perform acts against the protected entity or organization.

Sun Tzu has many excellent principles that apply both to warfare and psychology. Here are a few favorites that point back to this area of interrogative manipulation:

The supreme art of war is to subdue the enemy without fighting.

Victorious warriors win first and then go to war, while defeated warriors go to war first and then seek to win.

Appear weak when you are strong, and strong when you are weak.

All warfare is based on deception.

When an enemy is strong, avoid them. If of high morale, depress them. Seem humble to fill them with conceit. If at ease, exhaust them.

If united, separate them. Attack their weaknesses. Emerge to their surprise.[189]

IMPLICATIONS TO SECURITY PLANNING AND OPERATIONS

The obvious lesson from this chapter is to know the law, or at the very least, know who to talk to about the law and both its limitations and opportunities. Be creative in the application of the law to various situations. Legally use publicity, disinformation, and all of the tools in your arsenal to ensure that you have identified all of the potential threats. This way, you can understand and plan for what can and may happen, even if only insofar as knowing what steps you will take to identify a solution, should an event occur for which previous situations have not prepared you.

Know that in any situation, there has been an error made that either you or your adversary may exploit. Look for it because no human or plan is perfect. Be creative in your application of the planning, training, and resourcing processes. The law allows more things than it prohibits, simply because by writing the law, it leaves whatever is unstated as legal.

---

[189] Sun Tzu. Op cit.

Chapter 7

Physical Terrain

Definitions and Considerations

The aspects of physical terrain are likely the most discussed and documented terrain considered by the security/intelligence officer. It is likely also the easiest, as the physical environment is highly visible, as long as one is looking. The security planner should ask, What is the physical aspect to security, and how is it usable in both a positive/proactive and negative/reactive manner? What are the boundaries of what is being termed the physical terrain?

Physical terrain encompasses everything real and tangible, with the exception of the human element. It involves geography, hydrology, horticulture, wildlife, subterranean features, weather, as well as astronomical, architectural, and aeronautical aspects. It is what is termed in the military as Intelligence Preparation of the Battlefield (IPB).

U.S. Army Field Manual (FM) 2-0, Intelligence defines the physical domain as

> *a composite of the conditions, circumstances, and influences that affect the employment of capabilities and bear on the decisions of the commander (JP 3-0). An operational environment encompasses physical areas and factors of the air, land, maritime, and space domains. It also includes all enemy, adversary, friendly, and neutral systems that may affect the conduct of a specific operation.*[190]

The function of intelligence analysis is to facilitate understanding of this environment. Additionally, how the conditions discovered support military force

---

[190]   US Army FM 2-0—Intelligence. 23 March 2010. Pg 1-1.

generation, operational/situational understanding, and information superiority in constantly changing and evolving conditions. However, as Douglas MacEachin, former Deputy Director of Intelligence for the Central Intelligence Agency, states in a forward to Richards J. Heuer's book *Psychology of Intelligence Analysis*,

> *I doubt that any veteran intelligence officer will be able to read this book without recalling cases in which the mental processes described by Heuer have had an adverse impact on the quality of analysis. How many times have we encountered situations in which completely plausible premises, based on solid expertise, have been used to construct a logically valid forecast—with virtually unanimous agreement—that turned out to be dead wrong? In how many of these instances have we determined, with hindsight, that the problem was not in the logic but in the fact that one of the premises—however plausible it seemed at the time—was incorrect? In how many of these instances have we been forced to admit that the erroneous premise was not empirically based but rather a conclusion developed from its own model (sometimes called an assumption)?*
>
> *And in how many cases was it determined after the fact that information had been available which should have provided a basis for questioning one or more premises, and that a change of the relevant premise(s) would have changed the analytic model and pointed to a different outcome?*[191]

While the aspect of human cognition was discussed fully in Chapter 4, it is necessary to remind the student of the seriousness and pervasiveness of this factor, even at the highest levels of security/intelligence analysis. This is especially true of situations involving the physical terrain and our human penchant for making the determination that, since we would not attempt or be physically able to navigate a physical barrier, no one else could do so. Many individuals, from Hannibal to Alexander to Howe to Idi Amin to Eisenhower to Saddam, have learned this to their regret.

Army Field Manual 2-01.3 defines IPB as

> *a systematic process of analyzing and visualizing the portions of the mission variables of threat/adversary, terrain, weather, and civil considerations in a specific area of interest and for a specific mission.*

---

[191]   Heuer, R.J. (1999). *Psychology of Intelligence Analysis.* Center for the Study of Intelligence, Central Intelligence Agency. Washington, D.C. Pg 'x'.

> *By applying intelligence preparation of the battlefield/battlespace, commanders gain the information necessary to selectively apply and maximize operational effectiveness at critical points in time and space.*[192]

This process also includes what is known as site exploitation, which FM 3-90.15 defines as

> *systematically searching for and collecting information, material, and persons from a designated location and analyzing them to answer information requirements, facilitate subsequent operations, or support criminal prosecution. Site exploitation (SE) contributes to exploitation, defined as taking full advantage of any information that has come to hand for tactical, operational, or strategic purposes (JP 1-02). A site, in general, is a location that potentially contains valuable information. Site exploitation operations doctrine describes a systematic and comprehensive approach to obtaining information of value from a site for exploitation.*[193]

IPB is designed to consider the following aspects of the environment:

Political—*Describes the distribution of responsibility and power at all levels of governance or cooperation*

Military/Law Enforcement—*Explores the military capabilities of all relevant actors in a given operational environment/battlespace environment*

Economic—*Encompasses individual behaviors and aggregate phenomena related to the production, distribution, and consumption of resources*

Social—*Describes the cultural, religious, and ethnic makeup within an operational environment/battlespace environment*

Information—*Describes the nature, scope, characteristics, and effects of individuals, organizations, and systems that collect, process, disseminate, or act on information*

---

[192]   US Army FM 2-01.3 *Intelligence Preparation of the Battlefield*. 15 October 2009. Pg 1-1.
[193]   US Army FM 3-90.15 Site Exploitation. 8 July 2010. Pg 1-1.

Infrastructure—*Is composed of the basic facilities, services, and installations needed for the functioning of a community or society*

Physical Environment—*Defines the physical circumstances and conditions that influence the execution of operations throughout the domains of air, land, sea, and space*

Time—*Influences military operations within an operational environment/battlespace environment in terms of the decision cycles, tempo, and planning horizons*[194]

While described in military terminology, the conditions, requirements, and constructs are the same for security operations. Examination of military physical security manuals demonstrates this succinctly. These manuals include the aspects of site exploitation, and a composite picture of the processes associated with analyzing the physical domain emerges.

The task is to evaluate the presented information in conjunction with the four basic types of threat: traditional, irregular, catastrophic, and disruptive. The type of operation involved determines the set(s) associated with these four basic threat domains. Understanding the threat domains identifies the physical nature of the threat against which the physical terrain is compared for strengths, weaknesses, and opportunities, or what in business is known as a SWOT[195] analysis.

POLITICAL EVALUATION

All human activities have political considerations as a primary element. While the word immediately calls to mind the activities of the government, a better definition of politics is competition between competing interest groups or individuals for power and leadership. Politics is the herd instinct depicted in humankind. Individuals and groups use information, favors, bribes, peer pressure, and other means to obtain visible or secret advantages over other groups, usually to advance personal agendas at a cost to the competing groups. Having knowledge of this information enables the analyst to understand the motives and reasons for actions that might otherwise seem innocuous.

An example, contained in an article in *Military History* magazine by Jeffrey Record, evaluates the actions of the Japanese in starting WWII in the Pacific. The Japanese, knowing that there was no possible way for victory, pulled the United

---

[194] IPB. Op cit. pg 1-9

[195] SWOT is a business analysis term standing for Strengths, Weaknesses, Opportunities, and Threats.

States into war with them by attacking Pearl Harbor. Many analysts simply mirror image their own concepts and biases to say that the Japanese government had simply become mentally unstable. Mr. Record posits that Japan, faced with unacceptable competing alternatives due to their culture and psychology, believed there was no alternative. Record states, "One finds not a thoughtless rush to national suicide, but rather a prolonged, agonizing debate between two repugnant alternatives."[196]

This is not saying that the politicians of the U.S. did not see these alternatives, as many theorists have postulated. Instead, they may have viewed their invulnerability as absolute to the point that any enemy would not dare launch a preemptive strike against any U.S. interests so close to home. Roosevelt and his advisors may have expected the attack to fall on the Philippines or Guam, but not Hawaii, given the steps taken to plan for a Japanese war.

Many articles and studies review analysis from the perspective of the effects of politics on the evaluators and their conclusions, and this is a factual perspective.[197] However, the analyst must also examine the standings, desires, objectives, and actions of stakeholders to ascertain the known, suspected, and assumed elements in their desires. Knowing this, as well as the same information for one's own organization, fulfills Sun Tzu's admonition to know both yourself and your enemy.

MILITARY/LAW ENFORCEMENT RESOURCES

In military intelligence analysis, it is vital to know what resources a potential enemy has available and how it can and may be used. It is even more vital to know the same information of allies and your own forces, as well as civilian entities. One may believe such knowledge is unnecessary in civilian situations, which is a faulty assumption. Not only does it violate Sun Tzu's dictates, it violates common sense.

There are few organizations with the resources in their security divisions to respond to a potential event, let alone several simultaneously. Such a force would be prohibitively expensive for an event that may never happen. Therefore,

---

[196] Record, J. The Mystery of Pearl Harbor: Why Did Japan Attack the United States Pacific Fleet and Start a War It Could Not Win. *Military History*. Vol 28. No 5. January 2012. Ppg 28-38. Record states the alternatives were a) economic ruin and capitulation to a U.S. diplomatic diktat that Japan quit China, or b) war with a much more powerful and strategically invulnerable enemy. (pg 30).

[197] See Markiewicz, A. The political context of evaluation: what does this mean for independence and objectivity? Evaluation Journal of Australasia, Vol 8, No 2. 2008, pp 35-41.

the organization should and must rely upon external resources as a pool of responders available when needed. As events may escalate beyond local and even regional control, such as Hurricane Katrina, state and national resources need to be considered in the planning process. Along with this, there is the need to understand and accept prioritization in such situations. Knowledge of where, how, and how much becomes critical as the emergency escalates.

The how of such an evaluation, as with the political evaluation, requires detailed research into numbers, type and quantity of equipment, projected need for type and quantity of equipment, and ability to both access the area with the needed equipment and the will to use it.

As a director for a major computer manufacturer, one professional had the task of evaluating and planning for both disaster recovery and business continuation from the information technology (IT) perspective. The evaluation demonstrated that the primary threat was severe gulf weather in the form of a major tropical storm or hurricane.

This professional examined routes, terrain, drainage, potential damage kinds and quantities, as well as the response capability of the city, county, and state. The result of the analysis was daunting. In fact, it was learned that the emergency shelters for response equipment of the county was insufficient to withstand a Category 2 hurricane, which was proven a few years later with a powerful tropical storm that remained over the area for several days. The equipment flooded and was unavailable in the quantities needed for rapid and sufficient response.

Additionally, power supplies, fuel, and highway access were expected to be cut. Because the area was a high point geographically, it was considered that wildlife would flee to the campus, which they did, requiring protection for emergency stay-behind personnel. As local law enforcement and National Guard troops would be unavailable, it was vital that this protection be on hand and the stay-behind personnel trained in its use. Thus, an on-site armory was established, along with sufficient supplies of fuel, food, water, and generator for a two-week period maintained in fresh condition.

ECONOMIC EVALUATION

There is no city in the entire world more than seven days away from potential starvation and riot in the event of a situation that cuts off supplies. If water and fuel also are cut off, the problem becomes more severe. During Hurricane Ike, the city of Houston, Texas, suffered electricity outages that lasted for as long as three weeks. The priorities for restoration were as follows: hospitals and emergency centers, water supply centers, transportation and supply hubs, food distribution centers, then residential areas. The restoration of transportation and supply hubs also impacted most major economic centers that handled fuel distribution, as over one million automobiles were stranded on the emergency evacuation highways due to overcrowding that led to vehicles running out of fuel.

As an example of an economic evaluation, consider the situation generated in the Middle East by the so-called Arab Spring.[198] The region is destabilized. Using Egypt as an example, it is easy to see the most vulnerable and economically destabilizing areas. The most vital resources of this desert country are water and food. These supplies are located and transported along the Nile River, where there is a large lake held by the High Nile Dam. The only food region is immediately in the flood plain of the Nile River. Additionally, the majority of the country's electrical power generation is obtained from the hydroelectric plant at the High Nile Dam. A group seizing control of such a facility could create economic blackmail for an entire country. This in turn could create a blockage through mining or other activity at the southern end of the Suez Canal, potentially leading to an economic blackmail for all of Europe.

By considering the economic drivers of a given area or organization, a security planner can identify key target areas and best arrange for potential threats.

SOCIAL EVALUATION

When performing a societal evaluation, security planners should consider certain questions. What is a society willing to accept? Where is that society, from the perspective of the micro to the macro levels? What are the society's structures capable of performing in both positive and negative terms? How does one establish what these norms are without invading privacy or performing investigative acts that may be either expensive and/or illegal? What level of action is appropriate for the situation against which the professional is to plan? Can the professional make a determination of the changes that may occur in stressful or extreme conditions or to the legal/cultural environments?

The U.S. Department of Commerce (USDC) decided to ask these questions in 1994, creating the principles and guidelines for social impact assessment in the USA. This document was updated in 2004. Within the document, the USDC examines social impacts under the National Environmental Policy Act of 1970. The primary purpose of the study was to preemptively determine the impact to the lives of the populace for certain changes to laws, regulations, policies, and other environmental changes prior to actually taking action.

Under this guideline, the term "social impact" is defined as follows:

---

[198] The Arab Spring was an event occurring from 2011-2013 where a series of revolts sprung up across north Africa and the Middle East resulting in the collapse of the governments of Libya, Egypt, and Syria to a populist movement.

The consequences to human populations of any public or private actions-that alter the ways in which people live, work, play, relate to one another, organize to meet their needs and generally cope as members of society. The term also includes cultural impacts involving changes to the norms, values, and beliefs that guide and rationalize their cognition of themselves and their society.[199]

Within the guidelines is an excellent summary of the principles and their related guidelines for conducting a social impact assessment shown in Figure 23.

This social impact evaluation may be conducted in a variety of ways. The guidelines above contain a detailed description of the types of items to investigate for each of the associated principles. They also caution, however, that the very act of investigation will result in changes to the environment, as will the various stages of implementation of the proposed changes. As such, this is a continuous process that requires periodic reevaluation.

The U.S. government performs an analysis of this type in a detail exceeding that of most businesses. The first thing the professional needs to do, however, in coordination with the appropriate legal, environmental, and executive leadership of their organization, is perform a detailed SWOT analysis. SWOT stands for strengths, weaknesses, opportunities, and threats (see Figure 24). The analysis is simply a listing of the various aspects within each of these domains organized to encompass their relationships and provide a means to consider the potential join impacts.

---

[199]   US Dept of Commerce. Impact Assessment and Project Appraisal. September 2003. *US principles and guidelines for SIA.* Pg 231. Available at http://www.nmfs.noaa.gov/ sfa/reg_svcs/social%20guid&pri.pdf

Achieve extensive understanding of local and regional settings to be affected by the action or policy
- Identify and describe interested and affected stakeholders and other parties
- Develop baseline information (profiles) of local and regional communities

Focus on key elements of the human environment
- Identify the key social and cultural issues related to the action or policy from the community and stakeholder profiles
- Select social and cultural variables which measure and explain the issues identified

Identify research methods, assumptions and significance
- Research methods should be holistic in scope; i.e. they should describe all aspects of social impacts related to the action or policy
- Research methods must describe cumulative social effects related to the action or policy
- Ensure that methods and assumptions are transparent and replicable
- Select forms and levels of data collection analysis which are appropriate to the significance of the action or policy

Provide quality information for use in decision-making
- Collect qualitative and quantitative social, economic and cultural data sufficient to usefully describe and analyze all reasonable alternatives to the action
- Ensure that the data collection methods and forms of analysis are scientifically robust
- Ensure the integrity of collected data

Ensure that any environmental justice issues are fully described and analyzed
- Ensure that research methods, data, and analysis consider underrepresented and vulnerable stakeholders and populations
- Consider the distribution all impacts (whether social, economic, air quality, noise, or potential health effects) to different social groups (including ethnic/racial and income groups)

Undertake evaluation/monitoring and mitigation
- Establish mechanisms for evaluation and monitoring of the action, policy or program
- Where mitigation of impacts may be required, provide a mechanism and plan for assuring effective mitigation takes place
- Identify data gaps and plan for filling these data needs|

Figure 23: Principles and Guidelines for Social Impact Assessment[200]

---

[200]   Ibid. pg 233.

SWOT ANALYSIS

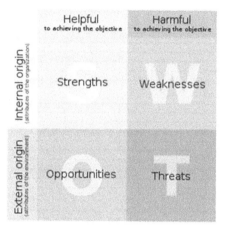

Figure 24: SWOT Diagram

The first step of the analysis is to identify and define the desired end state(s) of the item, topic, or situation under consideration. Using SWOT, the security planner can determine the attainability of the end state(s). If not, then the planner must reexamine and redefine the end state(s). Note: *It is the end state(s) that requires reexamination, not the standards against which they are measured.*

Once the planner identifies an appropriate set of end states as achievable, the next step is to examine the social impacts using a matrix of variables, such as those contained in Figure 25. The planner identifies the specific variables by determining what aspect(s) the team might consider, usually in a Delphi process.

Social impact assessment variables*	General planning, policy development preliminary assessment	Detailed planning, funding & impact assessment	Construction implement	Operation/ maintenance	Decommission/ abandonment
Population change					
Population size density & change					
Ethnic & racial comp. & distribution					
Relocating people					
Influx & outflows of temporaries					
Presence of seasonal residents					
Community & institutional structures					
Voluntary associations					
Interest group activity					
Size & structure of local government					
Historical experience with change					
Employment/income characteristics					
Employment equity of disadvantaged groups					
Local/regional/national linkages					
Industrial/commercial diversity					
Presence of planning & zoning					
Political & social resources					
Distribution of power & authority					
Conflict newcomers & old-timers					
Identification of stakeholders					
Interested and affected parties					
Leadership capability & characteristics					
Interorganizational cooperation					
Community and family changes					
Perceptions of risk, health & safety					
Displacement/relocation concerns					
Trust in political & social institutions					
Residential stability					
Density of acquaintanceships					
Attitudes toward proposed action					
Family & friendship networks					
Concerns about social well-being					
Community resources					
Change in community infrastructure					
Indigenous populations					
Changing land use patterns					
Effects on cultural, historical, sacred & archaeological resources					

Figure 25: Example of Social Investigation Variables[201]

Once the planner identifies the specific variables, they can use local research agencies, such as the U.S. Department of the Interior, Census Bureau, local news organizations, Internet research facilities, local law enforcement agencies, and other agencies, to access a wealth of data. Much of this resource information will require collation and possibly modeling to determine the actual effect the data may have in a given situation. Modeling and simulations are excellent analysis tools and are the domain of individuals trained in what is known as operations research

---

[201]   Ibid. pg 243

and systems analysis (ORSA). The modeling and simulations/ORSA domain will be discussed more completely in later chapters.

SOCIAL IMPACT ASSESSMENT MODELS

DELPHI

There is no one singular acceptable model or methodology for conducting a social impact assessment. One frequently used process, however, is the Delphi methodology. Delphi involves the development of structured questionnaires, which are presented in random format/order to a group of individuals that represent a specific study population. The planner gives the questionnaires to the study group several times over a specific period of time, statistically tabulating and examining the results for trends and outliers.

An outlier is a small block of responses that do not seem to fit within the general structure of the responses as a whole. In many statistical studies, these outliers are discarded as anomalies. As cautioned within the U.S. guidelines, however, they may be the more important aspects of the study. The guidelines specifically state,

> Participants are often tempted to dismiss the concerns of others as being merely imagined or perceived. There are two important reasons not to omit such concerns from SIAs and EISs. First, the positions taken by all sides in a given controversy are likely to be shaped by (differing) perceptions of the proposed action. The decision to accept one set of perceptions while excluding another may not be scientifically defensible. Second, if a proponent asserts that their critics are emotional or misinformed, for example, they are guaranteed to raise the level of hostility between themselves and community members and will stand in the way of a successful resolution of the problem.
>
> In summary, some of the most important aspects of social impacts involve not, for example, the physical relocation of human populations, but the meanings or significance attached to these changes.[202]

This does not mean that all outliers are potentially vital. Situations exist where particular individuals, no matter the truth of a situation, will take a position counter to the majority of the population. Such people may represent individuals of interest concerning future disruptive behavior and keep their identification as

---

[202]   Ibid. pg 239

a potential concern discreet to avoid fueling their own belief of self-importance. Such knowledge, however, may enable the security planner to proactively cover a potential source of issues.

The following two examples further show the advantages of cultural evaluation. The first comes from a cultural study review by Yale Law School on risks to democracy. The other example is a declassified report on the potential for the collapse of the Soviet system under Gorbachev written by the CIA in April 1989 and entitled "Rising Political Instability under Gorbachev: Understanding the Problem and Prospects for Resolution."

YALE STUDY

One of the most important aspects of the Yale study is the following statement:

Why, then, should regulatory law afford any weight to the uneducated opinions of ordinary citizens as opposed to the reasoned judgments of politically insulated risk experts? It is the urgency of this question that makes the study of risk perception a policy science of the first order. Employing a diverse array of methods from the social sciences, the field of risk perception seeks to comprehend the diverse processes by which individuals form beliefs about the seriousness of various hazards and the efficacy of measures designed to mitigate them [emphasis added]. Risk perception scholars are not of one mind about the prospects for making public opinion conform to the best available scientific information on risk. But no one who aspires to devise procedures that make democratic policymaking responsive to such information can hope to succeed without availing herself of the insights this field has to offer.[203]

The study continues by stating,

A growing body of work suggests that cultural worldviews permeate all of the mechanisms through which individuals apprehend risk, including their emotional appraisals of putatively dangerous activities, their comprehension and retention of empirical information, and their disposition to trust competing sources of risk information. As a result,

---

[203] Kahan, Dan M., "Fear of Democracy: A Cultural Evaluation of Sunstein on Risk" (2006). *Faculty Scholarship Series.* Paper 104. http://digitalcommons.law.yale.edu/fss_papers/104. pp 1071-1072.

individuals effectively conform their beliefs about risk to their visions of an ideal society. This phenomenon—which we propose to call "cultural cognition"—not only helps explain why members of the public so often disagree with experts about matters as diverse as global warming, gun control, the spread of HIV through casual contact, and the health consequences of obtaining an abortion; it also explains why experts themselves so often disagree about these matters and why political conflict over them is so intense.[204]

This statement lends support to the theory of expectation violation referred to in Chapter 4. A major aspect necessary for determining social risk evaluation entails determining societal expectations from the vision of the population and *not* the political leadership, which often seems significantly out of touch with their constituencies.

CIA SOVIET UNION CULTURAL STUDY

The CIA study on the Soviet Union supports this notion that a government may not fully align or understand the represented populace. This statement from the study foreshadowed the actual political collapse that followed:

Gorbachev's reforms—while yet to remedy existing problems—have caused new challenges to surface. Having seen their quality of life stagnate under Gorbachev, Soviet citizens are becoming increasingly skeptical of reform, seeing it more and more as a threat to the secure existence they recall they enjoyed under Brezhnev. Moreover, the aspects of reform that are potentially most destabilizing are only in their early stages. The political reforms being introduced could further erode central authority and could give disaffected groups new platforms to challenge the regime. Radical economic reform appears further away because the kinds of market-oriented measures required to meet economic objectives would heighten social tensions by raising prices, creating unemployment, and increasing economic inequality. Moreover, such a transition could create a period of economic chaos and a sharp drop in production before the reforms began to yield positive results.[205]

---

[204]   Ibid. pg 1072.

[205]   Directorate of Intelligence, CIA. Rising Political Instability Under Gorbachev: Understanding the Problem and Prospects for Resolution. April 1989. Pg 1. https://www.cia.gov/library/publications/historical-collection-publications/ronald-reagan-intelligence-and-the-end-of-the-cold-war/Reagan%20booklet.pdf

The American social condition, when compared to the Soviet Union via economic activities that demonstrated an increased standard of living for nearly all Americans, was viewed by the Russian population as the answer to social unrest. This resulted in the relatively nonviolent revolution that toppled the government. Ironically, this condition mimicked social unrest that toppled the rein of the Czars a century earlier. Many world national conditions today echo this ignorance or inattention to the social conditions by the old power elite in the Soviet socialist hierarchy. Political unwillingness and/or fear to address a growing unrest in the populace due to concerns of losing standing in the current regime continues to be a challenge and danger for existing governments.

WEIGHTING MODELS

A weighting model is actually quite similar to the Delphi methodology, except that the data source is generally qualitative rather than quantitative. The variables are assigned values or "weights," first associating their importance to the overall assessment regime, then a second set to rank the variable "fit" to this ranking. The two results, multiplied together, provide the overall score. Many of these models use what is known as a Likert scale, from which surveyed individuals will select a common defined value rather than blindly applying their own noncomparable scales.

Most weighting methodologies are statistically complex and are only good for the specific problem statement, assumptions, and conditions. Any change and the results must be reexamined. Additionally, sensitivity testing often demonstrates a degree of reliance upon the weightings rather than the scores associated with the model. To be considered valid, planners must extensively define and correlate factors to the studied conditions.

FOCUS GROUPS

A focus group is a social interview of between ten and twenty individuals with similar background, demographics, and beliefs. The point is to allow the groups to talk within a semistructured environment. The objective of focus groups is to encourage people to talk openly, which limits the outcome to nongeneralized information. Focus groups combine perspectives into a composite picture of a specific set of individuals, but only that set. Therefore, it is a requirement to conduct multiple surveys using different sets of similar individuals, with each set having slightly different constructs.

An Iowa State University brochure on focus group methodologies contains the following statement of caution:

Composing a group with highly different characteristics will decrease the quality of the data. Individuals will tend to censor their ideas in the presence of people who differ greatly from them in power, status, job, income, education, or personal characteristics. To get a cross section of views from a diverse population using focus group method, it is necessary to conduct multiple sessions [sic]. To understand the perspectives of a different group of people, compose multiple focus groups on the same topic.[206]

Because the process produces words and not numbers, the planner must develop a methodology for appropriate evaluation of the information. One approach is the AnSWR tool, developed and used by the U.S. Centers for Disease Control (CDC). AnSWR is the Analysis Software for Word-based Records and is described by the CDC as follows:

AnSWR is a software program for coordinating and implementing large-scale team-based qualitative data analysis. It was developed by the Centers for Disease Control and Prevention as a free (public domain) tool to assist with applied research. Although the program was originally developed to assist with managing and analyzing large multi-site research studies that integrate qualitative and quantitative techniques, it can also effectively be used by a single researcher for more limited research projects.[207]

AnSWR is not a simple tool set requiring thoughtful set up to be effective. Once established, the data development and representation becomes fairly clear and understandable. Information is keyed and sorted based on specific desired filters, including usual important key words and word combinations. These key data elements can be reported in multiple formats and structures, the most useful being the structured quantitative tables. However, graphics such as in Figure 26 are also available and useful.

---

[206] Grudens-Schuck, N., Lundy-Allen, B. and Larson, K. (2004). Focus Group Fundamentals. Pg. 2. Downloaded from http://www.extension.iastate.edu/publications/pm1969b.pdf

[207] McLellan E, Strotman R, MacGregor J, and Dolan D. AnSWR Users Guide. Centers for Disease Control and Prevention, Atlanta, Georgia, U.S.A., 2004. Pg 1.

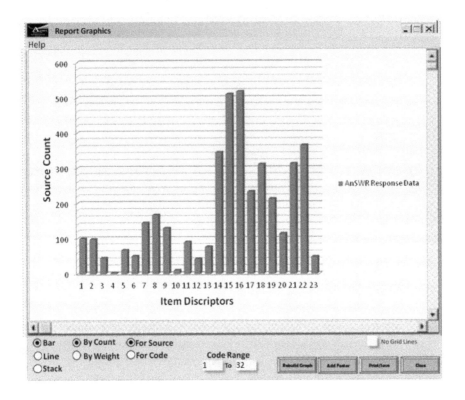

Figure 26: AnSWR Example Report Graphic[208]

AnSWR is available for free download from the CDC website. The download includes a detailed user's manual, but no training per se is available other than a user's manual.

INFORMATION EVALUATION

Once the planner has a valid data set, they must evaluate that information for best use. Joint Publication 2-1.3 defines the information environment as

> the aggregate of individuals, organizations, and systems that collect, process, disseminate, or act on information. It [information evaluation] is made up of three interrelated dimensions: physical, informational, and cognitive. A significant aspect of the information environment is cyberspace, which overlaps the physical and informational dimensions

---

[208] Ibid. pg 86.

of the information environment. It is critical that JIPOE [Joint Intelligence Preparation of the Operational Environment] *analysis of the information environment include support to cyberspace operations and the identification of key individuals and groups having influence among the indigenous population as well as the source of their influence (e.g., social, financial, religious, political).*[209]

Figure 27 depicts the model of this analytical structure as seen by the Department of Defense.

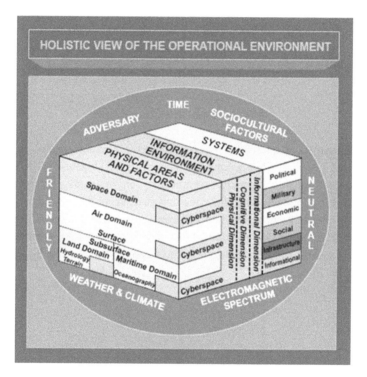

Figure 27: Holistic View of the [Military] Operational Environment[210]

The next question is, "What is intelligence?" Intelligence, for the sake of this text, is processed information. A generally accepted hierarchy of intelligence analysis, developed by Russell Ackoff, includes data, knowledge, information, understanding, and wisdom in progressing order as depicted in Figure 28.

---

[209] Department of Defense Joint Publication 2-1.3 Joint Intelligence Preparation of the Operational Environment. 16 June 2009. Pg I-3.

[210] Ibid

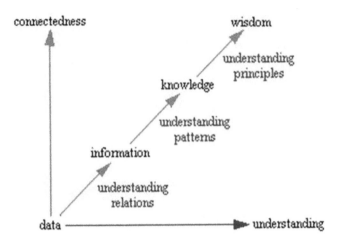

Figure 28: Hierarchy of Knowledge[211]

The hierarchy of knowledge is also called the semantic ladder by Andrew Targowski in his work *From Data to Wisdom*. Targowski states that information that is without quality loses its usefulness.[212] In his work, he develops an operations research approach to defining and structuring the concept of data and information into a recognizable model of cognition.[213] As such, he has developed a pictorial model as shown in Figure 29 that is different and more explanative than the hierarchy shown in Figure 28. Why this is so is discussed in the paragraph following the depiction.

---

[211] Bellinger, G. Data, Information, Knowledge, and Wisdom. Downloaded from http://www.systems-thinking.org/dikw/dikw.htm

[212] Targowski, A. From Data to Wisdom. *Dialogue and Universalism*. No. 5-6/2005. May 1, 2005. Ppg 55-71. Pg 57.

[213] Cognition is the process of acquiring knowledge and understanding thought. Thus a model of cognition is a representation in visual and/or logical form how that process is performed.

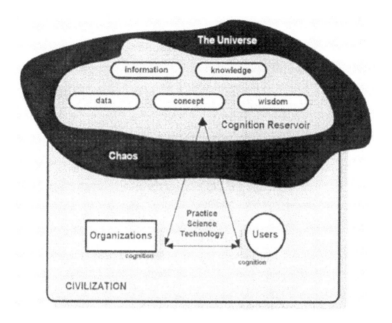

Figure 29: The Cognition Reservoir of Civilization[214]

What this graphic depicts, as related to this text, is that there exists what could be labeled as "integers" within the universe as a whole. These integers are pieces of celestial data waiting for "discovery" through observation. This construct is supported by many renowned physicists. As observations are made, the observer(s) establishes these observations as points of data which implant themselves into the observer's mind or "cognitive reservoir." The mind, in a process as yet unknown, begins to merge or "fuse" these data bits into an acceptable potential picture, which generates information.

As the information quantities grow and link to other sets of information, the observer begins to form a concept of these links and their potential relationship or relativity to all other constructs. In science, this is known as a hypothesis. The mind then constructs, either actively or subconsciously, experiments to test the validity of the information with respect to past experiences, current bias, cognitive expectations, and social culture norms.

At this point, the concept is either accepted or rejected. If accepted, it becomes knowledge and assumes a permanent place of residence within the brain of the observer for use in problem solving and decision making. Once it is used in a decision-making environment and the results of that decision are known and/

---

[214]   Ibid. pg 60.

or experienced, the knowledge, for better or worse, becomes wisdom.[215] Each subsequent use of that knowledge in a decision-making environment increases wisdom. A person evaluates information according to their experiences and application of such knowledge.

> It is in the experiencing of the results of the application of knowledge that information is thereby evaluated.

What, however, is information evaluation? *Army Field Manual 2-0: Intelligence* attempts to define information evaluation through the establishment of characteristics of effective intelligence. The process of the evaluation is undefined in this structure. There are numerous approaches to the evaluation of the effectiveness of the intelligence product, yet not on how to gauge the efficacy of the information used to generate the knowledge that leads to the intelligence product. A 2003 publication from the Joint Military Intelligence College quotes Keith Devlin on this topic, stating, "Intelligence analysis is primarily a thinking process; it depends upon cognitive functions that evolved in humans long before the appearance of language."[216]

The conclusion is that by the act of thinking, information becomes intelligence. Therefore, it is likely that in the formation of intelligence, thinking will determine the applicability of said information. The Swenson document echoes this deduction, stating, "An ordered thinking process requires careful judgments or judicious evaluations leading to defensible conclusions that provide an audit trail."[217] Figure 30 depicts what the Intelligence College considers prerequisite knowledge for successful intelligence analysis. It may also be an appropriate road map for the conduct of information evaluation.

---

[215] Wisdom is generally accepted as being the ability to take experience, thought, and knowledge; and converting it to use in one's life and interactions. One may be able to take data (1+1) and convert it into knowledge (1+1 = 2); yet not be able to see that it applies to any action, process, or thing (2 apples that can then be made into a pie with the addition of flour, sugar, eggs, milk, and baking . . .)

[216] Swenson, R.G. (Editor). *Bringing Intelligence About: Practitioners Reflect on Best Practices.* Center for Strategic Intelligence Research, Joint Military Intelligence College. May 2003. Pg 109.

[217] Ibid. pg 113.

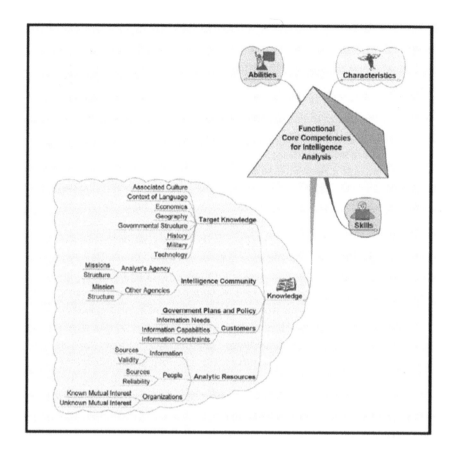

Figure 30: Knowledge Required for Successful Intelligence Analysis[218]

The graphic above depicts what knowledge an analyst needs to produce a successful intelligence product. It also incidentally depicts that if the information does not fit into the puzzle of known information, with respect to all of the other elements shown, it must be considered suspect. Section 3 contains the process of information evaluation, delving further into this concept.

This is only a portion of the information environment. Sir Francis Bacon said that knowledge is power. This is partially true, but it is the use of knowledge in the appropriate way, time, place, and against the correct target that completes the power construct. Simply having knowledge is as useless as having an unloaded weapon, if one is unwilling to exercise the knowledge in the appropriate fashion. Conversely, having knowledge without the cognition of it, possession can be power

---

[218]   Ibid. pg 120.

due to how others who also have the knowledge will react. Such a situation could protect or endanger, without the recognition of possessing individual's awareness, and is the plot of many a mystery movie.

This text has identified the component parts of knowledge, not where it resides. Perform an Internet search on the question "Where does knowledge reside?" and over half a million results come up and approximately as many opinions on the answer to this question. Knowledge exists. It is both tacit, leading to an advantage, and generic, existent as potential in everyday observation. The key is the ability to recognize what contains tacit knowledge, as generic knowledge, though it may become tacit, merely exists and generates little useful value beyond simply being.[219]

Recognition of key tacit knowledge occurs through the application of observation with respect to specific objective requirements. The question remains as to where does knowledge reside. There are only two possible answers outside of the realm of quantum physics: the individual or the organization. Having answered this question, the next important question is how does one recognize knowledge for what it is? This answer requires first recognition that knowledge can exhibit in multiple forms, not the least of which is the most common: written knowledge.

When knowledge leaves the mental confines and enters a recorded medium, it becomes known as written knowledge. This includes formats such as books, reports, pictures, videos, electronic media, etc. The format communicates visually and therefore contains all the wealth and weaknesses of this sensory system, the eyes. For example, the image below is a photograph taken by a high-technology imaging device. What is the subject matter? Notice that there are several very important pieces of information necessary to identify this photograph, which are currently missing. First, what is the type of imaging device? Secondly, what is the focal distance of the object from the lens? Third, what is the scale of the object with respect to the observer or photographer? All of these data pieces are critical to the identification of the object.

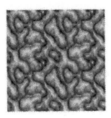

Figure 31: Unreferenced Photo

---

[219] Szulanski G. 1996. Exploring internal stickiness: Impediments to the transfer of best practice within the firm. *Strategic Management Journal*, 17: 27-43.

Add the knowledge that the size of the object is less than one square millimeter in size, and the set of possibilities refines. To even further reduce the possibilities, add that the object is organic and of biological origin. Still, the set remains too large to correctly identify the subject matter. There remain several major pieces of information necessary to recognize and identify this object as a close-up photograph of human skin—from the back of the hand to be precise.

Here is another example. Again, this photograph derives from a high-technology imaging device. Defining the image remains close to impossible without key pieces of information. Notice the structured outlines and internal structures reminiscent of wiring or circuitry. The objects external to the primary outline are of key importance, as is the background. Notice that the external items have what appears to be shadowing.

Figure 32: Second Unreferenced Photo

The observer must consider the source of the shadow. Is this shadowing caused by the camera flash, as the implied circuit board was photographed? If so, what purpose might these outlying structures serve? The reality is that this photograph has nothing to do with circuit boards. Rather, it was an image of an apartment complex roof located in Lawrence, Kansas, taken from a distance above the object of over two hundred miles by an Earth-orbiting satellite.

Figure 33: Referenced Photo Example

Obviously, observation does not equal knowledge. The second key element of knowledge is the ability to intelligently question your observations and understand what the set of possible answers may mean. Since information is available from a variety of sources and those sources may provide incorrect data, it may be disinformation.

The next type of knowledge is often called lore. Lore is audio knowledge in a very real sense. Ages ago, prior to appropriate methods of recording information for ease of transport and long-term storage, humans passed down knowledge verbally from generation to generation. The most common method was usually in song that constructed mental pictures. The song was able to communicate emotion, while the construct of the mental picture through cadence and tune made retention easier for the recipient. The minstrel was a welcome visitor to most areas as both entertainer and conveyor of news. There were also the local lore tellers, tasked with ensuring that appropriate social knowledge was transmitted from generation to generation. These individuals continue to exist in nearly all societies, performing nearly the same function, yet more surreptitiously and often in conjunction with visual and other senses in play.

While not always recognized as a source of knowledge, scent is one of the most important senses. Of all the human and other creature senses, it is the only one that is neurologically wired directly to the reaction and processing centers of the brain. If the reader finds this difficult to believe, the next time you are eating something, have a peeled orange handy, close your eyes, and smell the orange. You will notice that, instead of the flavor of the food you are eating, you will *taste* the orange in your mind.

This may not seem like much of a source of knowledge, yet it is precisely why security professionals use animals in performing various security functions. Dogs, for example, have such a finely developed sense of smell that they are used to locate specific scents that are not noticeable to humans. Another example is that of the shark which can scent a single drop of blood in millions of gallons of seawater and know the direction of the source.

Finally, there is evidential knowledge. Evidential knowledge covers a broad realm of sources and resources from forensic examination to interrogation. It includes scientific data obtained through the gathering of samples. A good example occurred immediately prior to the Normandy invasion. Teams of rangers and commandos were sent on missions into the runnels and gullies that fed the beaches in the Normandy area. The task was to obtain rock samples for analysis of the source of the sand on the beaches.

Samples of the sand itself were inclusive to the question of whether or not the beach was of a sufficient density to support the weight of armored vehicles. Some sand is so fine that it is dusty and a vehicle will quickly sink into it as Rommel and British General Montgomery learned in the Saharan part of North Africa. Other sand is such that a small amount of moisture will solidify it into nearly a concrete-like structure. This is of obvious value to an invading force attempting to move heavy equipment inland where the road network has been either destroyed or is nonexistent due to terrain.

Thus, the type and source of information is critical to understanding the terrain environment of the domain. Evidential knowledge should not be gathered haphazardly to avoid overwhelming the analyst with an abundance of resulting information. The goal is to make information of use to the professional officer both quickly and accurately. The evidence must also key to the structures for which it is descriptive, leading to the next element of the terrain environment, infrastructure.

INFRASTRUCTURE

Infrastructure is a major target for terrorism, one that has already been seriously attacked throughout history. Infrastructure is composed of the basic facilities, services, and installations needed for the functioning of a community or society. Infrastructure ranges from the shelters used to protect the population from the vulgarities of the climate, to the means of collecting and distributing food, water, and clothing, to the ways a society disposes of waste products. Infrastructure includes the transmission of electricity, public transportation, and routes of communications. Department of Homeland Security (DHS) defines critical infrastructure as follows: "systems and assets, whether physical or virtual, so vital to the United States that the incapacity or destruction of such systems and assets would have a debilitating impact on security, national economic security, national public health or safety, or any combination of those matters."[220]

While the DHS-defined items are important in a modern society and critical to modern military operations, individuals can survive without them. Individuals cannot survive, however, without food, clothing, and shelter and will take whatever steps necessary to obtain these essentials first for themselves, then for their families. Altruism rarely exists in a disaster beyond the first few days. The U.S. Army published a handbook, *Handbook No. 1.02: Critical Infrastructure*, which states three specific items of critical infrastructure:[221]

Physical—*Physical assets may include both tangible property (e.g., facilities, components, real estate, animals, and products) and the intangible (e.g., information). Physical protection becomes an even more difficult task when one considers that 85 percent of the nation's critical infrastructures are not federally owned. Proper protection of physical assets requires cooperation between all levels of the government and within the private sector.*

Human—*Human assets include both the employees to be protected and the personnel who may present an insider threat (e.g., due to privileged access to control systems, operations, and sensitive area and information). Those individuals who are identified as critical require protection as well as duplication of knowledge and authority.*

Cyber—*Cyber assets include the information hardware, software, data, and networks that serve the functioning and operation of the asset. Damage to our electronic and computer networks would cause widespread disruption and damage, including casualties. Cyber networks link the United States's energy and the financial and physical securities infrastructures.*

Having identified these structures, the next step is to determine their vulnerability to disruption and the means of that disruption. The objective of this analysis is twofold: first is for self-sustenance, second for use in controlling others, either within and/or outside of the organization. Disruption may come in various forms. The objective of the security professional is to determine both the

---

[220] US Army Deputy Chief of Staff—Intelligence. DCSINT Handbook No. 1.02, Critical Infrastructure Threats and Terrorism 10 August 2006. Pg II-10.

[221] Ibid. Pg I-1/2.

dynamics of the disruption mechanism and the vulnerabilities this mechanism reveals. This is known, within the military, as systems warfare.

The federal government has identified twelve critical infrastructure areas as follows:

a. Agriculture and food production/distribution agencies
b. Water—both consumable and nonpotable, yet critical supplies (e.g., coolant localities and waste facilities)
c. Public health facilities
d. Emergency service organizations
e. Government
f. Defense and defense support organizations/businesses
g. Communications, information, and telecommunications organizations/ facilities
h. Energy industries and energy transportation/distribution materiel/ agencies/facilities
i. Transportation in general
j. Banking and finance institutions and processes
k. Chemical and hazardous materials industries
l. Postal and shipping organizations/industries

To develop support and plans for protection, the August 19, 2005, Department of Defense Directive 3020.40 established the Defense Critical Infrastructure Program (DCIP), shown in Table 6. The directive requires the army to establish, resource, and execute an organizational critical infrastructure program. This directive sets responsibilities for each of the different sectors of the DCIP.[222]

**Table 6: The Defense Critical Infrastructure
Program—Management and Planning Agencies**

DEFENSE SECTOR	LEAD AGENT/AGENCY
Defense Industrial Base (DIB)	Director, Defense Contract Management Agency
Financial Services	Director, Defense Finance & Accounting Services
Global Information Grid (GIG)	Director, Defense Information Systems Agency
Health Affairs	Assistant Secretary of Defense of Health Affairs
Intelligence, Surveillance, and Reconnaissance (ISR)	Director, Defense Intelligence Agency

---

[222] Ibid. pg II-11.

Logistics	Director, Defense Logistics Agency
Personnel	Director, DoD Human Resources Agency
Public Works	Chief, U.S. Army Corps of Engineers
Space	Commander, U.S. Strategic Command
Transportation	Commander, U.S. Transportation Command

Figure 34 depicts the threat assessment methodology in use by the Department of Homeland Security and, by way of the DCIP, the Department of Defense. This methodology ensures that the analyst can visualize the process so that appropriate steps are taken in the appropriate order.

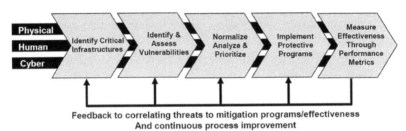

Figure 34: Critical Infrastructure Defense Planning Process[223]

This process is further defined within a structure of risk management and remediation shown in Figure 35. In this graphic, you see the flow-down structure used to assess and respond to risks, whether preemptive or in real time.

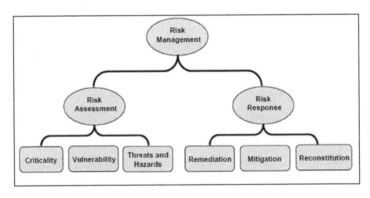

Figure 35: DCIP Risk Management and Remediation Process[224]

---

[223] Ibid. pg. III-3.

[224] Ibid. pg. III-5.

Each domain, physical, human, and cyber, contains its own special issues and means of attack, protection, and reestablishment. It is critical for a security professional to appropriately identify risks, costs, and methods for both protection and recovery prior to the event, as discussed in Section 3 of this text.

PHYSICAL DIMENSIONS

Physical dimensions include geographical terrain, both surface and subsurface, physical constructs (e.g., buildings, transport functionalities, sewers, etc.), aeronautical conditions (e.g., weather, atmospherics, etc.), and nonhuman animal and aquatic life-forms. It is impossible to consider and protect against all aspects within these domains, so the security professional should prioritize and focus on critical elements. This includes having a security process in place for responding to the unusual or the unforeseen, as seen in Figure 3 earlier in this text.

Section 2, Chapter 7 of this text discussed the army process of Intelligence Preparation of the Battlefield. The security professional should perform this level of analysis for the physical dimension, as specific to the nature of the organization, the location, and the criticality of the risks associated. For example, assume the business in question is a hotel located in Anaheim, California.

The potential critical threats from a physical dimension perspective generally do not include rain, although a strong storm may create flooding conditions or even mudslides which, depending on the physical location of the property, might be important. A more potent geographic threat is land movement due to earthquake, carrying with it the related threat to the business via loss of physical structure, access, and personnel—both workers and guests. Though earthquakes cannot be predicted, their conditions and the appropriate response processes can. Proactive protection activities may range from engineering for damage resistance to safety training for personnel. The business can also provide guests with instructions of actions in the event of an earthquake to limit their vulnerability, etc.

As a second example, consider a chemical plant located along the Houston Ship Channel in Houston, Texas. Hundreds of vessels from the world over transit this location monthly. The channel is only a few hundred feet wide and has numerous facilities along its banks, as shown in Figure 36. Notice in the photograph the storage tanks near the channel. These tanks may contain anything from raw petroleum to highly toxic chemical compositions used in manufacturing. It is possible for threats to pinpoint such areas for attack from passing vessels using a variety of resources. Also, notice the terrain in the distance. This is the city of Houston proper, with a population of over eight million. Selecting a day when the prevailing winds are from the south at eight to ten knots and an attack on a chemical plant could produce a highly toxic cloud with little protection for the population.

Figure 36: Houston Ship Channel, Houston, Texas

Following are some photographs from an event that occurred in 1947, just south of the Houston Ship Channel at the Port of Texas City. The Texas City disaster occurred on April 16, 1947, and is a textbook example of the potential danger inherent to areas of industrial concentration.

Figure 37: Texas City (a)

Figure 38: Texas City #2

The event was triggered when a freighter called the *SS Grandcamp* docked at the port and caught fire in the hold. The ship was carrying 2,300 tons of ammonium nitrate, a compound generally used in fertilizer and—unknown at that time—a powerful explosive. The water used by the ship personnel to fight the fire caused a chemical reaction within the cargo, causing the largest nonnuclear detonation to that date. The photo shown in Figure 37 was taken from several miles outside of the town. Figure 38 is what is left of the town out to a distance of over half a mile from ground zero due to the blast effects.

The blast also generated fires and damage in buildings several miles away, as well as a tsunami within Galveston Bay that travelled up the Buffalo Bayou—also known as the Houston Ship Channel today—leaving destruction in its path for many miles. Figure 39 below shows another freighter that was located several hundred yards away from the exploding ship. This freighter was actually destroyed when a second freighter next to the *SS Grandcamp* and carrying a similar cargo exploded in a secondary detonation, demonstrating the force of the explosions and the subsequent tsunami. At least 581 people were recorded as killed in the disaster, but the true number will never be known.

Figure 39: Photograph of the *Wilson B. Keene* Freighter[225]

While the explosion was an accident and could be considered man-made, the deadly tsunami, an event not considered possible except for hurricane storm surges and other natural events, was not. It is important to note that even today, the city of Houston is ill prepared for an event causing such a surge of water, as evidenced during the events of the 2008 Tropical Storm Allison and Hurricane Ike (Figure 40).

---

[225] Information of the disaster is located in the Texas City Disaster museum located within the rebuilt town and port of Texas City, Texas. The photographs were taken by a Mr. J.D. Robinson and are located at both the Houston Fire Memorial and the International Association of Fire Fighters Union website at http://www.local1259iaff.org/texascitydisasterpics.htm

Figure 40: Hurricane Ike in the Gulf of Mexico

Hurricane Ike was a large Category 2 storm. Category 2 is defined by the National Weather Service as having the potential to cause some roofing material, door, and window damage and considerable damage to vegetation, mobile homes, etc. Flooding can also damage piers, and small craft in unprotected moorings may break their moorings. However, this storm became the second worst storm for property damage in the history of the United States, surpassed only by Hurricane Katrina, which hit New Orleans three years earlier.

Earlier, Tropical Storm Allison hit Houston and stayed over the city for a period of several days. According to the National Weather Service, "The storm dropped heavy rainfall along its path, peaking at over 40 inches (1,000 mm) in Texas. The worst flooding occurred in Houston, where most of Allison's damage occurred: 30,000 became homeless after the storm flooded over 70,000 houses and destroyed 2,744 homes. Downtown Houston was inundated with flooding, causing severe damage to hospitals and businesses. Twenty-three people died in Texas."[226] The photo in Figure 41 shows downtown Houston immediately after the storm, which is at forty-three above sea level, unlike New Orleans which lies fifteen feet below sea level. Due to the storm surge blocking river outlets and the significant quantity of rain, the water simply had no outlet.

---

[226] Houston/Galveston National Weather Service (Synoptic Situation) (2006). "Tropical Storm Allison Floods, June 5-9, 2001". Archived from the original on December 14, 2004. http://web.archive.org/web/20041214204857/http://www.srh.noaa.gov/hgx/projects/allison01/synoptic.htm. Retrieved 2012-05-17.

Figure 41: Downtown Houston Following TS Allison[227]

Individuals attempting to leave their downtown buildings tried to exit to the parking garages, which had been protected from rising floodwaters by dam gates, were overtopped, drowned when the elevators taking them to these areas opened fifteen feet underwater.

Interestingly, even with the extensive damage, there was one threat that had not been accurately considered as shown in Figure 42 and Figure 43 below. The creature in Figure 43 was found near the tire shown below.

---

[227] Buffalo Bayou, White Oak Bayou Confluence and Main St.—06/09/01. NOAA Photo Library. Publication of the National Oceanic & Atmospheric Adminstration (NOAA), U.S. Department of Commerce (2002). This photo is the work of a U.S. government agency.

Figure 42: Photo of Hurricane Ike Wreckage on Interstate 45

Figure 43: A Rattlesnake Found in a Boat Marooned on Land by Hurricane Ike[228]

---

[228]   Ibid for photos

The moral here is that terrain assessments for security planning must also include the possible threat of wildlife. The diamondback rattlesnake shown in the image above measured eight feet long and was very upset over the entire ordeal of Hurricane Ike, posing a definite threat to anyone who encountered it. Poisonous snakes were not the only wildlife to consider, as the other boat shown in the images above (beyond the boat in the foreground) had an eight-foot-long alligator trapped underneath.

The Houston populace and those from other coastal areas understand the threat of such storms; however, they do not always accept the full danger. For example, a Category 5 storm impacting the State of Texas with the eye making landfall near Victoria, Texas, would place the "dirty side" of the storm, including the majority of the storm surge, immediately into Galveston Bay (see Figure 44). The graphic shown is of Hurricane Ike, depicting where the eye made landfall to the east of Galveston Bay as a Category 2 storm. This still caused significant damage, considering the impact of a Category 5 storm, which would fill the gulf with the storm surge while releasing the significant quantities of rainfall associated with such storms.

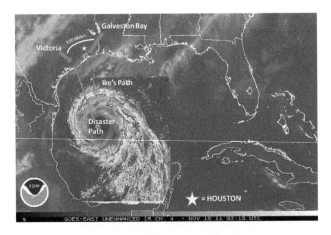

Figure 44: Disaster Potential for Gulf Hurricane

To establish a worst-case scenario, move the storm eye west of Galveston Bay one hundred miles—one of the original tracks for Hurricane Ike—and increase the storm to Category 5.[229] The water entering the bay from the surge would be

---

[229]   To achieve Category 5 level, the wind speeds and barometric pressure are significantly different than a Category 2 storm. Cat 2 winds 96-110 mph, barometric pressure 28.9-28.5 inches, storm surge 4-5 feet ; Cat 5 winds > 156 mph barometric pressure < 27.17 inches, storm surge > 18 feet.

between eighteen and twenty-five feet. On top of this surge would be waves of between twenty and thirty-five or more feet. This makes a surge of approximately thirty-six to sixty feet in depth, entering a narrowing bay like a tsunami. The water will pile up into the north of the bay, increasing the size of the surge to eighty to one hundred feet in depth when it hits the Houston Ship Channel area, creating a water dam of significant height similar to what occurred during Allison. However, this water dam would be three times higher.

What defines the depth of the storm surge is the pressure of the air surrounding the storm in relation to the pressure of the air *inside* the storm. Air has weight. When air pressure outside of a storm is higher, it presses down on the water around the storm, forcing the surface of the water up inside the storm where the pressure is lower. This is highest within the eye of the storm because it is here the pressure is lowest. To visualize this process, picture moving a large sloped-sided box from one room to another and substitute the concept of the box for water. The first room is the ocean, and the second room is the land. The visualization now becomes closer to reality.

Next, add to this scenario the extensive rainfall and run-off amounts generally exceeding six inches an hour, rushing south to meet this saltwater surge moving north. As much of the ground between Galveston, to a distance of one hundred miles inland, is less than sixty feet above sea level, NOAA at one time estimated that the entire area of Houston could potentially be underwater to a depth of forty feet. What this means is that all buildings not more than four stories high could be totally underwater.[230]

The risk intensifies in that all emergency equipment not in a garage above this line would be lost. Water and sanitation facilities would be totally destroyed, as would all electrical, medical, transportation, refinery, etc., facilities. At one time, the City of Houston's plan for emergency equipment was to transport all of it to the garages located at the Hewlett-Packard (at that time Compaq) campus forty miles north of downtown for storage above the suspected water level. This plan was modified on additional study that the roadways would become impassable, making the use of this equipment impossible until the roads were cleared. The City of Houston Hurricane Preparation Timeline document establishes that all departments will relocate emergency equipment outside of expected storm surge areas forty-eight hours prior to landfall.[231] (City of Houson, 2011, pg 4) This means, in our scenario, moving thousands of pieces of emergency equipment over one hundred miles on roads already crowded with fleeing population. The

---

[230] Return to Figure 41 and imagine all of the roadways visible now being under water by approximately 10 additionally feet.

[231] City of Houston, June 2011. *Timeline for Hurricane Preparation; Category 3 and Higher.*

equipment must also be placed in secure covered locations to avoid wind and debris damage compounding the problem, as businesses and individuals will likely be doing the same.

Such a disaster is nearly beyond comprehension. Yet it is why there is such emphasis placed on the physical aspects of the terrain environment. Even given that such a storm would be predicted three to five days prior to landfall, the relocation of tens of millions of individuals from this region is a nearly impossible task. Examine this picture from the evacuation prompted by another Houston area storm, Hurricane Rita. Most of the automobiles in this photo had insufficient fuel to make it out of the county. No plans had been established to account for highway bottlenecks, which slowed vehicle movement to a standstill. This created a perfect storm of traffic, where idling vehicles ran out of gas, clogging the already congested roads.

**Figure 45: Photo of Interstate 45, North in Houston,
During Evacuation Efforts from Hurricane Rita**

Figure 46: Photo of Hurricane Rita Traffic in New Orleans

Many vehicles were still on the road when Hurricane Rita actually hit, which further complicated matters by making the ingress of emergency equipment nearly impossible. In response to the problems faced by evacuees of Hurricane Rita, emergency planners decided to leave the southbound lanes open for emergency traffic in Houston for future storms, such as Ike. However, this only exacerbated the problems of egress for the citizens. However, without the emergency procedures in place, the loss of life might have been significantly greater.

Such emergency procedures are not always possible especially during tornados, where the average warning time is less than fifteen minutes once a funnel cloud actually forms. The saving grace is that a tornado's path is generally not more than a mile wide and less than twenty miles long. A hurricane, however, covers tens of thousands of square miles.

Perhaps, given the grave parameters set in the previous examples, the physical aspects of security planning require a more proactive and pointed approach. However, such modifications to address such worst-case scenarios would likely require measures not likely to be welcomed or applied. Where to draw the line of appropriate planning versus potential calamity is a tightrope walk that all security planners must face, and there are no easy answers. In Section 3, this text examines some of these questions and provides methods for analysis; however, the answers remain conditional.

MANIPULATION OF THE TERRAIN ENVIRONMENT

While the aspects of the terrain environment are at times daunting, it is seldom one needs a plan to such a worst-case scenario depth. This is due primarily to location, the key to any real estate dynamic. Few hurricanes hit Denver, for instance, and there has never been an avalanche in Miami. The security officer for the Exxon refinery in Bay City, Texas, has to consider many of these issues; yet the ARCO refinery security officer in Cleveland, Ohio, does not. Yet in each case, the manipulation of the terrain environment, as we are addressing it in this text, is possible, not by altering the geography per se, but by addressing it up front.

Consider, for example, Seattle, Washington, and the significant threats present there from terrain. Seattle sits inside a funnel defined by the Puget Sound, the Mt. Rainer volcano, and the San Andres Fault line that extends out into the ocean (Figure 47). The San Andres Fault is a zone where one tectonic plate dives under another, creating a "subduction zone," which drags on the ground above it. At a point, the undercurling ground on top of the subduction plate rapidly releases, causing an earthquake; and where the zone is under the water, this triggers a tsunami, as was the case multiple times in Washington state's history and was also the source of the Indian Ocean tsunami of 2004.

Figure 47: Seattle Washington Subduction Zone

The tsunami would rush into Puget Sound, submerging much of Seattle. Tie this in with the fact that subduction zones create volcanoes, such as Mt. Rainier. In a worst-case situation, the earthquake could rupture the geographic plugs that are keeping the mountain quiet, resulting in a massive eruption. The geography of the area from Mt. Rainier to Seattle (Figure 48) is such that a simultaneous earthquake/eruption scenario would create a tsunami meeting a lahoya—a volcanic mud flood—down the river valleys leading to Seattle. This would inundate the entire area in a massive disaster.

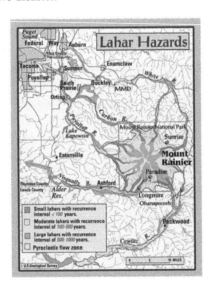

Figure 48: Mt. Rainier Washington Disaster Zones

Manipulation does not necessarily mean changing the physical construct of the terrain, although this is often a starting point when considering such terrain as facilities, buildings, perimeters, and the like. For example, one of the first things a military commander does at every echelon is to ensure that their soldiers have as much clear terrain for use of weapons as possible. They do this by clearing obstacles and removing or mining "dead zones," which are areas where direct observation and direct fire weapons cannot be used. Industrial security planners will implement electronic means of observation and notification in their dead zones. Often, they will use physical barriers, grates, fences, and even moats to limit unwanted access to certain critical areas. All of this falls within the purview of terrain manipulation.

Some facilities use creative landscaping to enhance terrain usability and protection. For example, the planting of thorn thickets creates a nearly impassible barrier for both human and large wildlife while creating escarpments—graded terrain where the critical facilities are raised above surrounding land with highly sloped areas. This makes rapid ingress of specific areas nearly impossible without special bulky equipment that slows infiltrators. The result is more time for both discovery and engagement.

Manipulation can also occur without making a change to the actual physical structures of the terrain. The placement of observation towers in positions that optimize visibility of the surrounding area, as well as the selection of locations where ingress/egress routes are either plentiful or limited based upon need, often does more for operations than extensive landscaping.

In nonmilitary terrains, having areas with assured drainage through both unimpeded water flow and ground absorption, for example, can assist in rapid recovery from flooding conditions. In fact, due to the low elevations in many coastal areas, subdivision developers are grading the access roadways as the drainage media, using the excavated soil to raise the elevation of the homes up to several feet above the roadways, drastically limiting the potential for flood damage. In this way, the developer uses the vastness of the surrounding area as the flood water shed, trading distance for depth, as water spreads over a wider area, lowering the local depth during flood conditions.

Where actual modification of the terrain environment is necessary, the planner needs to take into consideration ecological, safety, OSHA, and other rules and regulations. Egress must not be limited or blocked, while access may be, except in emergency situations. Considerations for disabilities are required under the Americans with Disabilities Act to enable unimpeded access for mobility assistance devices.

There are many stakeholders, rational and irrational, that both believe they are entitled to their input and desire control in any given operation, in spite of the loss of efficiency or increased cost. These individuals may actually denigrate the very concerns they espouse. It is important for the planner to have a detailed understanding of such stakeholder groups, their true goals, and the issues concerning their actions.

IMPLICATIONS TO SECURITY PLANNING AND OPERATIONS

One of the overriding issues in security/intelligence planning and operations is space because space equals time. In military terms, there is an area of interest (AOI) and an area of influence (AOIn). Field Manual 1-2: Operational Terms and Graphics define the area of interest as follows:

> *That area of concern to the commander, including the area of influence, areas adjacent thereto, and extending into enemy territory to the objectives of current or planned operations. This area also includes areas occupied by enemy forces who could jeopardize the accomplishment of the mission.*[232]

This definition means that any area from which a threat is capable of reaching into and impacting operations of the organization being targeted is of concern to a planner. The area of influence is that area over which the targeted organization has the capability of cancelling or limiting the threat's ability to influence operations through either direct action or the threat of direct action. In a military sense, this is usually considered to be through the use of destructive force against the threat. However, force is present in many different forms.

As a famous military leader, Frederick the Great understood that it was not necessary to apply destructive force if through maneuver and position, he could place the enemy at such a disadvantage—of which the enemy is aware—that anything other than capitulation would result in sure and complete annihilation. Luvaas writes of Frederick the Great, saying,

> *It is significant to note that in his Reflections on Projects of Campaign (1775), in which he allowed himself a comfortable margin of superiority in numbers . . . it was not by decisive battle so much as by penetrating into France or Austria and threatening the capital that Frederick expected to persuade the enemy to come to terms.*[233]

The goal in understanding and intelligently using the terrain environment is to place the organization into a position of superiority and control over any threat

---

[232]   US Army September 2004. Operational Terms and Graphics. Pg 1-12.

[233]   Luvaas, J. (1999). *Frederick the Great on the Art of War*. Da Capo Press. New York, NY. Pg 24.

or when the threat is overwhelming, limiting its impact and expediting recovery. Additionally, there is the specter of state and/or militarized planning and control of terrain in extremis.[234] Geslier and Kay wrote,

> *Accommodation and law-and-order have their place in terrains of terror but will be dispensed with if national security is breached or under assault in the judgment of state leaders. Though it would be simplistic to see this progression as iron-clad, it serves as a rough guide to what might trigger the militarization of land use planning. Facilitating conditions are:*
>
> Instability: *radical insurgency challenging existing order;*
>
> Insularity: *property rights create spaces where threats to security can proliferate (e.g., restraint on trespass and free access; the right to use one's owned space to create lethal substances and test them);*
>
> Critical uncertainty: *Law-and-order and accommodation seem to quell only symptoms of a disturbance, precipitating the use of force (e.g., incidents at Waco or Ruby Ridge);*
>
> Ambivalence and ambiguity: *diminished civil liberties tolerated as "cost of survival"*[235]

What are the actual conditions and indicators of such actions as the above occurring? It is not unheard of, even in the United States. During time of extreme national peril or general war, even though such actions on the part of the British Crown led to the Revolutionary War, were sparks leading to American's lasting distrust of a strong military. However, in the interest of public safety and national security, the Model State Emergency Health Powers Act (MSEHPA), which limits

---

[234] This means that the state takes over total control of an area irrespective of legal and/or current ownership.

[235] Geslier, C. and Kay, D. (2007). Land Use Planning and Security in Terrains of Terror. *Conference on the Science and Education of Land Use: A transatlantic, multidisciplinary and comparative approach* (September 24-26, 2007, in Washington, DC, USA). npn.

civil rights during a state of public health emergency, was passed in 2002.[236] Geslier and Kay quote Gostin et al. in the following:

> *A team of legal experts writing in the Journal of the American Medical Association about MSEHPA addressed the powers of sovereign states in light of individual and civil rights (Gostin et al., 2002, 625):*
>
> *Coercive powers are the most controversial aspects of any legal system. Nevertheless, they may be necessary to manage property or protect persons in a public health emergency. There are numerous circumstances that might require management of property in a public health emergency (e.g., shortages of vaccines, medicines, hospital beds, or facilities for disposal of corpses). It may even be necessary to close facilities or destroy property that is contaminated or dangerous . . . There similarly may be a need to exercise powers over individuals to avert a significant threat to the public's health. Vaccination, testing, physical examination, treatment, isolation, and quarantine each may help contain the spread of infectious diseases . . . Provided those powers are bounded by legal safeguards, individuals should be required to yield some of their autonomy, liberty, or property to protect the health and security of the community.[237]*

Even though the concept is justified in the nature of the public good and/or national security, such actions may pose a threat to organizations. This requires the security professional to consider and plan for such possibilities among others. Given the structure of the threat as the subjugation of land and/or property, this threat falls within the boundaries of the terrain environment.

---

[236] The "all hazards" approach has many expressions, including the "Pandemic and All-Hazards Preparedness Act," or "PAHPA," signed into law on December 19, 2006, by President Bush. PAHPA substantially reorganizes federal, state, and local public health efforts across sectors. Ibid.

[237] Ibid. npn

Chapter 8

Cyber Terrain

Cyber terrain is more than just the enterprise information management or IT structures. It includes all aspects of information, communication, technology, and technology personnel and the intellectual property associated with them. This chapter discusses the following:

a. Definitions and Considerations
b. Theories of the Cyber Dimension
c. Pervasiveness of the Cyber Environment
d. Enterprise Security and Risk Management
e. Manipulation of Cybersecurity Dynamics
f. Implications to Security Planning and Operations

Definitions and Considerations

Most texts discuss cybersecurity in terms of information technology. However, as stated in the last chapter, cyber systems,

> Include the information hardware, software, data, and the networks that serve the functioning and operation of the asset. Damage to our electronic and computer networks would cause widespread disruption and damage, including casualties. Cyber networks link the United States's energy, financial and physical securities infrastructures.[238]

---

[238]   Op cit.

Nearly every facet of life in the developed world relies upon cyber systems, from individual life to government infrastructure and security, and this technology is under attack. The U.S. Deputy Chief of Staff for Intelligence provides information that the threat is well identified.

> *Just as the United States has capitalized on the use of computer technology, our enemies have not overlooked the fact that they must also operate in the computer age. As briefed to Congress in July 2003 by the Commander, Joint Task Force-Computer Network Operations, U.S. Strategic Command/Vice Director, Defense Information Systems Agency, the sophisticated threat to our Global Information Grid is extensive and presents a real danger to our national security. This threat includes more than 40 nation-states that have openly declared their intent to develop cyber warfare capabilities. Additionally, it includes transnational and domestic criminal organizations, hacker groups who sympathize with our [U.S.] enemies, terrorist organizations (evidenced by forensic analysis of captured computers) and "insiders" who support our enemies.*[239]

In a recent report to Congress, the Project 2049 Institute, a cybersecurity think tank, identified that a major competitor in the world stage, communist China, unveiled a cyber operations command. According to the report, even though the stated goal of this operation is to protect Chinese cyber systems, there is a threat to the U.S. The institute's report states, "Computer network operations (CNO) in China often are referred to as—network attack and defense [in Chinese: 网络功防], based on the premise that—without understanding how to attack, one will not know how to defend."[240]

Information developed by Symantec, a leading supplier of cybersecurity processes and investigations, resulted in the graph featured in Figure 49, published by Lance Whitney in CNET. Basically, the argument is in terms of how an organization is to determine if an offensive program is successful, unless it is unleashed upon a defended public?

The situation with China becomes more suspicious, considering that a Chinese company now owns a significant portion of this major cybersecurity provider. Huawei, a People's Republic of China telecommunications firm, the second largest in the world, purchased a 49 percent ownership of Symantec Corporation. Here is a country with a stated cyber attack policy now having the

---

[239] Op cit. pg 4.

[240] Stokes, M.A., Lin, J. and Hsaio, L.C.R. (2011). *The Chinese People's Liberation Army Signals Intelligence and Cyber Reconnaissance Infrastructure.* Project 2049 Institute. Washington, D.C. pg 4.

potential for total access to the source code for the world's cybersecurity policy. The concept of the Trojan horse and Troy immediately comes to mind.[241]

Recent news reports also raise concerns regarding cyber attacks of major military institutions globally. Israel has been identified as having successfully launched cyber attacks against Iran. Specific investigations resulted in identification of a systems image to the Stuxnet worm that potentially remains a threat capable of doing significant damage to the systems controlling the nuclear reactors in Iran.[242]

Country of Origin	Percentage of Targeted Attacks	Continent	Percentage of Targeted Attacks
China	28.2%	Asia	46.6%
Romania	21.1%	Europe	37.3%
United States	13.8%	N. America	13.8%
Taiwan	12.9%	Africa	2.4%
United Kingdom	12.0%		
Japan	4.0%		
Cameroon	2.2%		
Korea, Republic of	0.9%		
Russian Federation	0.9%		
OTHER	4.2%		

Figure 49: Origins of Cyber Attacks by IP Address of Originator[243]

Finally, there is the aspect of system manufacturing. The three largest manufacturers of electronic components are China, India, and the United States. These components include silicon electronics known as "chips," which are used

---

[241] Huawei Technologies, the world's No.2 telecoms equipment maker, plans to buy Symantec Corp's 49 percent stake for $530 million in a joint venture between the companies that provides security solutions for corporations. International Business Times Journal. November 14, 2011. http://www.ibtimes.com/articles/249271/20111114/huawei-buys-symantec-stake-jv-530-million.htm

[242] "The particular characteristics of the Stars virus have been discovered," Jalali said. "The virus is congruous and harmonious with the (computer) system and in the initial phase it does minor damage and might be mistaken for some executive files of government organisations." Jalali warned that the Stuxnet worm, discovered in computers at Iran's Bushehr nuclear reactor last year, still posed a potential risk. Some experts described it as the world's first "guided cyber missile," aimed at Iran's atomic program. Mostafavi, R. Iran Says It Has Detected Second Cyber Attack. Reuters News Agency. Mon Apr 25, 2011. http://www.reuters.com/article/2011/04/25/us-iran-computer-virus-idUSTRE73O1OL20110425

[243] Whitney, L. Symantec Finds China Top Source of Malware. CNT. March 26, 2010. http://news.cnet.com/8301-1009_3-20001234-83.html

from cell phones to automobiles to the computers that run aircraft and health instruments. There is the potential for malware introduction at any of these locations by placing these potential passive cyber bombs into the technology for activation at any time. *Time* magazine published an article regarding the concept of an existing "infowar," giving credence to cyber concerns.

> *Infowar evolved with every recent U.S. military foray. In the first day of the Persian Gulf War, Air Force stealth planes armed with precision-guided munitions blinded Saddam by knocking out his communications network and electrical power in Baghdad. The Pentagon launched a sophisticated spy-ops campaign against Haiti's military regime to restore deposed President Jean-Bertrand Aristide. Using market-research surveys, the Army's 4th Psychological Operations Group divided Haiti's population into 20 target groups and bombarded them with hundreds of thousands of pro-Aristide leaflets appealing to their particular affinities. Before U.S. intervention, the CIA made anonymous phone calls to Haitian soldiers, urging them to surrender, and sent ominous E-mail messages to some members of Haiti's oligarchy who had personal computers.*[244]

However, there is another aspect to the concept of the cybersecurity dilemma that the entire process of determining what the threat actually is, and developing theories appropriate to the analysis of appropriate solutions, is more difficult and ethereal than commonly accepted. Bambauer's paper supports this possibility, stating, "Cybersecurity is undertheorized [*sic*]: it is, at best, poorly defined, and it lacks a coherent framework to guide change. Current scholarship on cybersecurity is moored in doctrinal models that both misdiagnose the relevant issues and offer answers that would badly damage the Net's innovative capacity."[245]

Another potential aspect is contained in a report by MITRE Corporation:

> *The challenge in defining a science of cyber-security derives from the peculiar aspects of the field. The "universe" of cyber-security is an artificially constructed environment that is only weakly tied to the physical universe. Therefore, there are few a priori constraints on either the attackers or the defenders. Most importantly, the threats associated with cyber-security are dynamic in that the nature and*

[244]   Waller, D. and Thompson, M., Onward Cyber Warriors. *Time*, 8/21/95, Vol. 146 Issue 8, p38, 7p

[245]   Bambauer, D., Conundrum. Brooklyn Law School Legal Studies, Research Papers, Accepted Paper Series Research Paper No. 227 April 2011. Pg 4.

agenda of adversaries is continually changing and the type of attacks encountered evolve over time, partly in response to defensive actions. For this reason, no one area of science (mathematical, physical, or social) covers all the salient issues.

Given this information, the security professional must be cognizant of the various potentials and consider their impacts to the organization from both physical and electronic attacks. The professional must also consider that what they believe they know about both the structure of the threat, as well as the approaches to ensuring security, may not be accurate or even appropriate. This chapter, therefore, defines the environment rather than simply applying the accepted solutions.

THEORIES OF THE CYBER DIMENSION

What are the theories of the cyber dimension, and why consider them, particularly when the entire environment may be a house of cards? First, cybersecurity and cyber dimension are not all that easy to define. Bambauer recently posted the following in a Harvard Law School blog reviewing a conference on cybersecurity and the law:

Currently, "cybersecurity" is a term that utterly lacks coherence. It encompasses threats including malware, identity theft, hacking, intellectual property infringement, denial of service attacks, espionage, and acts of war by nation-states. It tries to address risks to end users, administrators, ISPs, utility companies, financial institutions, defense contractors, and the government. In short, we're unhelpfully subsuming a congeries of technical and legal policy concerns under a single rubric. They don't fit. Our current conception of cybersecurity hinders us in prioritizing among these issues and then focusing on the most relevant threats.

This is the role of theory: it provides an organizing framework to rank competing concerns, to measure progress in addressing them, and to make and justify the inevitable trade-offs that occur. Theory helps guide policymakers to the most pressing problems, and helps us assess how they're doing at resolving those issues.[246]

---

[246] Bambauer, D. Cybersecurity Theory and Myths. Info/Law Blog. Harvard University. June 8, 2011. http://blogs.law.harvard.edu/infolaw/2011/06/08/cybersecurity-theory-and-myths/

In constructing this section, keep two important observations in mind. The first is that cybersecurity philosophy is not conducted in the same fashion as other scientific thought. For example, in researching for a dissertation, the author identified several appropriate theories of behavior functions that were combined into the structured listing shown in Table 7.

Table 7: Cognitive Behavior Theory Compilation

Theory	Description of theory
Cognitive dissonance	Decisions utilizing approaches which reduce individual discomfort
Consistence theory	Decisions made given the degree to which it satisfies internal alignment to other factors
Commitment	A linkage between a previous public stand forcing a decision path
Certainty effect	The linkage between the level of impact of a decision and the probability of the decision's direct influence on the impact
Confirmation bias	The ability to obtain external support for a particular decision
Scarcity principle	We anticipate regret and so want what is scarce for personal satisfaction
Sunk-cost effect	The degree to which a decision-path is maintained is in proportion to the amount of previous decisions in that direction
Augmentation principle	Decisions are based upon previous, similar correct decisions
Bounded rationality	The utilization of limited logic in decisions
Explanatory coherence	Simple, explainable hypotheses
Filter theory	The use of personal biases to filter information and options to an acceptable conclusion
Multiattribute choice	Utilization of various theories simultaneously or in structured progression
Mere exposure theory	Personal exposure to various issues generates acceptance
Perceptual contrast effect	Utilization of comparisons for determination
Involvement	Desire for increased information being directly related to personal involvement prior to decision making

Each of the above theories, when researched by accessing the founder's writings, are specifically identified and titled as such. For example, Dr. Judee Burgoon, principal author of Expectation Violation Theory, identifies the theory through the following description: "Humans receive a structured set of social communications expectations that, if left unfulfilled, may alter the cognitive reasoning processes of human psychology in ways that affect decision making (Burgoon et al., 2005)."[247]

Few of the cybersecurity sources researched in working on this text are as definitive. For example, one excellent document in terms of the academic and scientific value identifies itself in the following manner: "In this work, we have proposed an interesting evaluation procedure for quantifying cryptographic protocols. Our model has attractive feature [*sic*] since we formalize security in the most general framework [*sic*]. We have also demonstrated [*sic*] that the proposed SA-tool has nice features as well."[248]

With few exceptions, at this point in the study of cybersecurity, the best that one is able to construct is a listing of topics rather than specific theories. It is possible that the reason for this gap is the rapid growth pace of cyber threat development as opposed to the other sciences. Quite literally, information technology systems and processes dramatically outpace other scientific endeavors. By the time a formal theory develops in the IT community, it is out-of-date both technologically and developmentally.

Sankardis et al. state that "one day an intelligent solution is proposed to fix a network vulnerability, and the next day the attackers come up with a smarter way to circumvent the proposed countermeasure." They also state that "the weakness of the traditional network security solutions is that they lack a quantitative decision framework."[249] This then may be a root cause of the lack of structured strategy and approach to cybersecurity efforts.

> By the time a formal theory is developed, it is out-of-date both technologically and developmentally. This then may be a root cause of the lack of structured strategy and approach to cybersecurity efforts.

---

[247] Nimon, H.I. (2008). Relationship of Personality to Virtual Communications Efficacy within a Military Combat Environment. Dissertation. Pg 56.

[248] Source withheld out of respect for the value of the subject matter rather than the inappropriate method of establishing the subject matter as presented.

[249] Sankardas, R., Charles, E., Sajjan, S. Dipankar, D. Vivek, S., Qishi, W. Game Theory as Applied to Network Security. University of Memphis. Pg 1. http://gtcs.cs.memphis.edu/pubs/hicss43.pdf

GAME THEORY OF CYBERSECURITY

Game theory is similar to what the military calls a tactical decision exercise or TDE. The value of the TDE or gaming of cybersecurity is that, whether done on paper or in simulation, the professional can practice visualizing and describing a situation, as well as deciding on a course of action and directing subordinates toward accomplishing the tasks necessary to achieve the desired goals. Additionally, the process can identify weaknesses in the proposed solution set prior to beginning implementation, such that the weaknesses can be countered prior to the expense of building a faulty process.

The process of design and conduct of a TDE is to establish a scenario, create the environment, set a time limit for the decision process, Delphi the decision in an open and facilitated environment, and record and discuss final decisions. There must be a facilitator using Socratic processes to guide discussion, without actually participating in the development of the decisions and critiques. The Socratic process involves questioning a topic in a logical fashion to stimulate alternative neural activity and ideas.

A similar process to gaming is known as red teaming, where a set of individuals act as the threat to challenge "blue team" actions, apply known threat procedures and doctrine, and maintain a counterpressure to the operational development. Nearly all military TDEs use what are known as red, blue, and white cells. The white cell is the controller/facilitator group. Security professionals can conduct TDEs using the following techniques: BOGSAT (bunch of guys sitting around a table), whiteboard, simulation environment, or a mixture of these techniques.

BOGSAT

This is the least expensive process, organized with the least amount of coordination and loss of work time. Its weakness is that it often digresses to other topics and/or results in an Abilene paradox event.[250] The BOGSAT is structured identical to the other processes, with the exception that there are often few to no aids to visualize the scenario, the events, or the dilemma with the exception of one's imagination. Given the inherent issues of the earlier discussed Expectation Violation Theory and Bias Theory, these visualizations are inherently out of synch with each other. Additionally, while the results are recorded, the structure of the BOGSAT cannot provide statistical analysis, as it cannot be exactly replicated.

---

[250] The Abilene Paradox event was discussed in an earlier chapter. Basically, it is where members of a group will agree to a course of action even though all members of the group are aware it is the obviously wrong course of action.

WHITEBOARD

This process is nearly identical to the BOGSAT but uses a visual tool to draw the scenario out using symbols, diagrams, etc. This tool can be a chalkboard, whiteboard, sand table, or other medium. The benefit of this process is that it clarifies the scenario and dilemma into a picture, which each individual may question for better clarity. The weakness is that, as with the BOGSAT, it cannot be exactly replicated for statistical analysis.

SIMULATION ENVIRONMENT

A simulation environment involves the use of some form of automated modeling simulation. The media for the simulation may be anything from a board game with players to a computerized simulation entailing dynamic constructive or virtual experimentation. A constructive simulation is when the model construct runs on its own over a set number of repetitive iterations, with slight changes in the structure of the simulation inputs. The outputs of the iterations are then analyzed statistically. A virtual experiment is where the simulation provides results for specific "play," yet the actual players are all human and not solely machine driven. Section 3 contains a more extensive discussion of this process.

The obvious strength in a simulation environment is that the security professional can use this model to obtain results based upon a specific calculus of predictive dynamics. A good example of predictive calculus is the Lanchester equations. Frederick Lanchester was a British mathematician who applied differential equations to problems of military relevance where there is a predator/prey environment. A differential equation is a mathematical equation for an unknown function of one or more variables that model or simulate the values of the function itself and its derivatives of various orders. Differential equations play a prominent role in operations research, combat simulations and modeling, engineering, physics, economics, and other disciplines.

For example, there is a combat action between two armored vehicles (tanks). Tank A spots Tank B at a range x. The simulation uses various input dynamics (e.g., weather, targeting optics, vegetation, etc.) to determine if Tank A actually "sees" (acquires) Tank B stochastically.[251] If the resulting answer is "yes," a second set of criteria is selected and stochastically determined to see if Tank A "identifies" Tank

---

[251]   A stochastic process is where information on an event is randomly determined or is considered as having a random probability distribution or pattern that may be analyzed statistically but may not be specifically predicted. The event is determined through the generation of a random number that is related to the odds graph (distribution table) to arrive at a 'yes/no' determination.

B as an enemy vehicle that can be engaged. Again, if "yes," Tank A will engage (fire) at Tank B. This sets a third grouping of variables in play to determine if the shot actually "hits" Tank B. If "yes," the simulation examines such things as the type of ammunition, the angle of impact, and the thickness of the armor on Tank B at the spot of impact. Additionally, the hardness of both the ammunition (if kinetic) or penetration power (if chemical/explosive) and the armor arrives at a determination of whether or not the armor of Tank B has been defeated.

If the armor is defeated, the simulation then looks at the "shot line." The shot line is that path beginning at the point of impact and continuing until the energy of the munition is totally expended and the shot ceases its movement. It is possible for a shot to penetrate Tank B from side to side yet do no internal damage because the ammunition does not impact anything critical, explosive, or flammable, nor does the ammunition itself explode. Should the ammunition either impact a critical item inside Tank B or, in the case of a chemical/explosive ammunition, generate sufficient heat energy inside Tank B, Tank B is then damaged and/or destroyed.

All of these calculations require significant input information on probability functions, results data, physical parameters, etc., and a computer to process the calculations. The data must be validated as realistic by an accepted organization to avoid the "garbage-in, garbage-out" dynamic. The strength of the simulation method is that it can be "run" as many times as desired and will differ only in the probabilistic outcomes, creating a normalized distribution of results. The security professional can compare these results mathematically across the different changes in the process analysis.

The weakness of this method is the expense of developing the simulation. Not only must the calculus be codified in a computer, the data must be developed and validated and the scenarios constructed. One individual, using a spreadsheet program such as Microsoft Excel or some other software tool, may build simulations of this type. Most, however, require more variable interactions than can be easily structured in a spreadsheet. Such simulations are akin to the various war games sold for current gaming systems. Section 3 will delve more deeply into the use and structure of simulations.

LIABILITY THEORY

The primary tenant of the liability theory is that the perpetrator of a specific attack is to be found, apprehended, and prosecuted either through criminal and/or civil court proceedings.

Negligence does not require great discussion, but it certainly could be a theory of liability against a computer security publisher. Conspiracy to commit computer fraud and aiding and abetting computer fraud are obvious sources of criminal liability in certain contexts. Certain state computer fraud laws may also implicate computer security publications. Mail fraud and wire fraud may also apply. However, the most important sources of liability are the DMCA and the prospective implementation of the Council of Europe Convention on Cybercrime. Even though the application of the DMCA [Digital Millennium Copyright Act—Author] may not be especially obvious and the Cybercrime Convention may not be especially well-known, both these laws have far-reaching implications for computer security publications.[252]

According to a Department of Justice listing, approximately sixty cybercrimes have been prosecuted between 1998 and 2008. This is a representative sample rather than an exhaustive list.[253] No exact figures on the total amount of cybercrime are available; however, in a 2011 survey by the High Technology Crime Investigation Association (HTCIA), they obtained the responses shown in Figure 50 on specific questions concerning various law enforcement organizations' experiences with cybercrime.

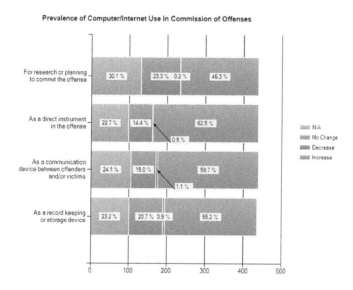

Figure 50: Prevalence of Computer/Internet Use in Commission of Offenses[254]

---

[252] Preston, E. and Lofton, J. Computer Security Publications: Information Economics, Shifting Liability, and the First Amendment. *Whittier Law Review.* Vol 24, 2002, (pp 71-142). Pg. 119.

[253] http://www.cybercrime.gov/cccases.html

[254] HTCIA. 2011. 2011 Report on Cyber Crime Investigation. HTCIA, Inc. Rosedale, CA. pg. 11.

The basic concept for the liability theory is that the Internet service provider, the computer security organization, or other such firms and individuals can be held at fault if there is a breach of current practices. This particularly applies when due to the publication of a specific weakness that can and may be exploited by cyber criminals. The logic appears to be that by making such individuals liable, they will develop the processes and procedures to combat the problem. The Bambauer "Conundrum" paper supports the proposition that such assignment of liability is, at best, fraught with political and constitutional dangers, specifically,

> *Unless carefully managed, liability for computer security publications could seriously distort the market for computer security. Litigation could be used to effectively chill computer security publications, and it is unlikely that the parties bringing suit would have the best interests of the market at heart. In particular, the legal system must account for the possibility that software vendors and computer service providers might use litigation to suppress negative information about their products or services and shift liability for security lapses from themselves. The legal system should only extend liability to computer security publishers with an awareness of the vital role computer security publications play in helping the development of security and providing the market with computer security information.*[255]

This information leads into a second aspect of cybersecurity and new theory, the theory of computer security and information economics.

THEORY OF COMPUTER SECURITY AND INFORMATION ECONOMICS

The Bambauer article raises the computer security and information economics theory, however, does not define it. The best definition is obtained from, of all places, *Wikipedia*, as follows:

> *The economics of information security addresses the economic aspects of privacy and computer security. Economics of information security includes models of the strictly rational "homo economicus" as well as behavioral economics. Economics of security addresses individual and*

---

[255]   Op cit. pg 82.

organizational decisions and behaviors with respect to security and privacy as market decisions.[256]

In this theory, those organizations having the most economic ownership in a given situation will generally be the ones to arrive at a viable and effective solution for the least cost. In the following quote from Anderson (2001):

In a survey of fraud against autoteller machines [4], it was found that patterns of fraud depended on who was liable for them. In the USA, if a customer disputed a transaction, the onus was on the bank to prove that the customer was mistaken or lying; this gave US banks a motive to protect their systems properly. But in Britain, Norway and the Netherlands, the burden of proof lay on the customer: the bank was right unless the customer could prove it wrong. Since this was almost impossible, the banks in these countries became careless. Eventually, epidemics of fraud demolished their complacency. US banks, meanwhile, suffered much less fraud; although they actually spent less money on security than their European counterparts, they spent it more effectively.[257]

Byzantine General Attack Theory

The object of Byzantine fault tolerance is to defend against *Byzantine failures* in which components of a system fail in arbitrary ways (i.e., not just by stopping or crashing, but by processing requests incorrectly, corrupting their local state, and/ or producing incorrect or inconsistent outputs). Correctly functioning components of a Byzantine fault tolerant system will be able to accurately provide the system's service, assuming there are not too many Byzantine faulty components.

A Byzantine fault is an arbitrary fault that occurs during the execution of an algorithm by a distributed system. It encompasses both omission failures (e.g., crash failures, failing to receive a request, or failing to send a response) and commission failures (e.g., processing a request incorrectly, corrupting local state, and/or sending an incorrect or inconsistent response to a request). When a

---

[256] http://en.wikipedia.org/wiki/Economics_of_security. The concept of 'homo economicus' is the concept that when it comes to economic questions, humans are generally rational and will make decisions narrowly and in their own self interest.

[257] Anderson, R. (2001). Why Information Security is Hard—An Economic Perspective. University of Cambridge Computer Laboratory, JJ Thomson Avenue, Cambridge CB3 0FD, UK. Downloaded from http://www.acsac.org/2001/papers/110.pdf

Byzantine failure occurs, the system may respond in any unpredictable way, unless it is designed to have Byzantine fault tolerance.[258]

What this really involves is a set of communications between the system(s) and the control structure(s) in which there is a requirement for agreement. An "invading" or "traitor" construction (e.g., a virus or Trojan horse) tries to either copy or circumvent the agreement to allow it to gain control of the decision processes of the system. The key to the control structure is that a Byzantine Generals solution, or some similar construct, identifies or circumvents the "takeover," maintaining the desired control processes over the system. However, all that a Byzantine Generals solution can do is guarantee that all processors use the same input value. If the input is an important one, then there should be several separate input devices providing redundant values, thus increasing the problem to the invading traitor program.

FORENSICS MODELING

George Santayana said that if we do not learn from the past, we are doomed to repeat it.[259] Forensics modeling is the way a security professional can apply this sage advice as they go about their planning efforts. "It is of the highest importance in the art of detection to be able to recognize out of a number of facts which are incidental and which vital. Otherwise your energy and attention must be dissipated instead of being concentrated."[260]

The historical aspect of forensic analysis is both its strength and its major weakness. The strength derives from the ability of systems to log activities, especially those activities leading to a fault or a failure. It is this very log that is the source of the weakness. The very wealth of data makes it nearly impossible to ascertain with accuracy the causal pathway.

Forensic analysis is the process of understanding, re-creating, and analyzing arbitrary events that have previously occurred. It seeks to answer the questions of how an intrusion occurred and what the attacker did during the intrusion. Forensic analysis also refers to the derivation of information for use in court. That aspect can build on

[258] Lamport, L.; Shostak, R.; Pease, M. (July 1982). "The Byzantine Generals Problem". ACM Transactions on Programming Languages and Systems 4 (3): 382-401. doi:10.1145/357172.357176

[259] Santayana, G. (1905). **Life of Reason, Reason in Common Sense, Scribner's, 1905, p. 284**

[260] Sir Arthur Conan Doyle speaking as Sherlock Holmes, "The Adventure of the Reigate Squire," The Strand Magazine (1893)

*what we describe in this paper, but we focus on the more general notion
of collecting data to reconstruct events and activities.*[261]

Peisert et al. outline a hierarchy of steps they believe necessary as part of the
forensic theory.

a. The ability to log anything
b. A provision for automated metrics, such as path length, and a tuning
   parameter that enables a forensic analyst to decide what to record
c. The ability to log data at multiple levels of abstraction, including those
   not explicitly part of the system being instrumented
d. The ability to place bounds on and gather data about portions of
   previously unknown attacks and attack methods
e. The ability to record information about the conditions both before (cause)
   and after (effect) an event has taken place
f. The ability to model multistage attacks
g. The ability to translate between logged data and the actual event in a
   one-to-one fashion[262]

An article by Kenneth Brancik in the *Information Systems Control Journal*
shows a second model of cybersecurity forensics as seen in Figure 51. This
model links to a structured process of analysis as part of the Homeland Security
cybersecurity process yet is once again presented as a *fait accompli* (or something
that is accomplished and presumably irreversible) rather than a theory for
experimentation.

---

[261] Peisert, S., Bishop, M., Karin, S., and Marzullo, K. (date unknown) *Toward Models
for Forensic Analysis*. University of California San Diego. http://www.cs.ucdavis.
edu/~peisert/research/PBKM-SADFE2007-ForensicModels.pdf. pg 1.
[262] Ibid. pg 4.

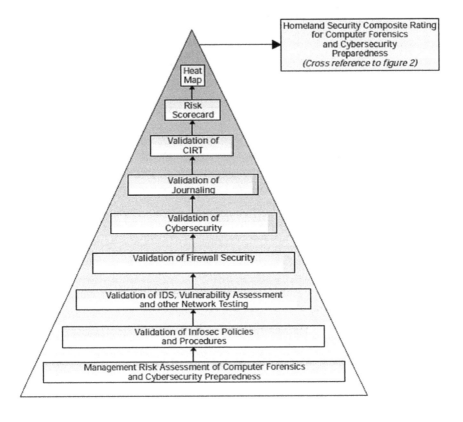

Figure 51: The Computer Forensics and Cybersecurity Governance Model[263]

The security professional needs to remember and focus on the following goal in the forensics modeling process:

> *The goal of the analysis is to determine the appropriate attack graph and the paths in the graph that represent the steps the attacker used. Given the graph, the analyst can ask what changes in the state of the system each attack step introduces. This provides the information needed to analyze the change. This ties forensics to a model of attack, and provides a basis for collecting specific information.[264]*

---

[263] Brancik, K.C. The Computer Forensics and Cybersecurity Governance Model. Information Systems Control Journal. Vol 2. 2003. Pp. 1-8. Downloaded from http://www.isaca.org/Journal/Past-Issues/2003/Volume-2/Pages/The-Computer-Forensics-and-Cybersecurity-Governance-Model.aspx

[264] Peisert, et al. op cit. pg 6.

THREAT ANALYSIS AND QUANTIFICATION METHODOLOGY

The threat analysis and quantification methodology involves probabilistic analysis of resources associated with a threat to the resources available to the protector agency to determine if the structure and resources are available to negate the attack. According to Basagiannis et al., "It is possible to evaluate the level of resource expenditure for the attacker, beyond which the likelihood of widespread attack is reduced and subsequently to compare alternative design considerations for optimal resistance to the analyzed DoS [denial of service] threat."[265] The process is further explained by Symantec Corporation's white paper on cybersecurity threat analysis and quantification, stating,

> One of the greatest challenges facing security organizations today is the ability to efficiently and cost effectively integrate products and services within existing network infrastructures, without disrupting established policies and procedures. The current economic downturn has also put additional emphasis on the cost of integration and the ability to leverage past investments while delivering enhanced security.
>
> Cybersecurity threats aimed at corporations and government organizations arrive faster and are more sophisticated than ever before. Cyber incident identification, analysis, and response are often limited by an organization's view into the global threat landscape and a lack of validated cyber intelligence to substantiate an effective response. This can be exacerbated by the products, services, and resources an organization employs to defend its assets.[266]

In both cases, the objective is the determination of the level of threat involved within a specific attack against which an equal or greater level of response is applied. This, per the methodology, should be sufficient to deter, limit, and/or defeat the attack. The weakness, as in the forensics model, is the potential for the quantity of information to overwhelm the analyst. Additionally, the security professional implements this model, and other models, to overcome current threats. The models are not an experimental theory per se. Thus, there is no current means of validating and verifying the model's functional accuracy or efficacy.

---

[265] Basagiannis, S., Katsaros, P., Pombortsis, A., Alexiou, N. Probabilistic model checking for the quantification of DoS Security Threats. Computers and Security; Sept 2009, Vol. 28, Issue 6, pp 450-465.

[266] Symantec, Inc. Symantec™ Cyber Threat Analysis Program Overview. White Paper: Symantec Security Intelligence Services. Pg 1.

SUPPLY CHAIN SECURITY METHODOLOGY

An excellent model of the cybersecurity supply process was developed in a joint venture between the University of Maryland and the Science Applications International Corporation (SAIC), as seen in Figure 52. The following information from this study establishes a justification for the concept:

> *The cyber supply chain can be described as the mass of IT systems—hardware, software, public, and classified networks—that together enable the uninterrupted operations of government agencies, companies, and international organizations. Attacks on the cyber supply chain can include malware inserted into software or hardware, vulnerabilities found by hackers, as well as compromised systems that are unwittingly brought in house. Tackling the problem of cyber supply chain protection requires new levels of collaboration among security, IT, and supply chain managers, taking into account the roles of developers, vendors, customers, and users.*[267]

The primary thing to remember is that in this chain, as with any chain, the structure is only as strong as its weakest link. Eliyahu M. Goldratt formalized this age-old adage into mathematical certainty in his book *The Goal*. Dr. Goldratt, a physicist turned business guru, focused on quality management. His theory of the quality management chain is possibly the source or concept incentive for the cybersecurity chain model.

Goldratt's theory, known as the theory of constraints, involves examination of the issues of the entire business process to include every aspect that inputs value to the process from agencies downstream—everything/everyone providing input to the build process up to the point being examined are delimiters on the quality of the product at that point. If one is working toward a 100 percent functional product, yet one part of the supply chain is only delivering 79 percent, that one element will drag down the rest of the product, irrespective of its high standard of quality to that 79 percent limit.[268]

---

[267] University of Maryland. http://www.cyber.umd.edu/research/cyber-supply.html

[268] See http://www.goldratt.com/ for information on the Theory of Constraints in quality management.

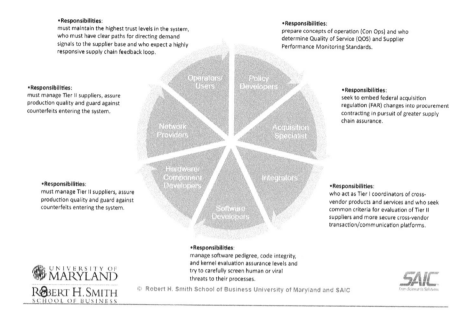

Figure 52: Cybersecurity Supply Chain Actors Model[269]

According to the University of Maryland/SAIC model, the weakest security link in the modeled process also creates the primary source of potential attack. The security professional must coordinate with all elements of the security supply chain to achieve the maximum value of protection, just as in the Goldratt model where one must coordinate with the entire product supply chain. Simply stated, Dilbert says it best.

[269] Boyson, S. and Rossman, H. (2009) Developing A Cyber Supply Chain Assurance Reference Model *A Research Collaboration Between SAIC & The R.H. Smith School of Business University Of Maryland*. Downloaded from http://csrc.nist.gov/groups/ SMA/ispab/documents/minutes/2009-04/ispab_sboyson-hrossman_april2009.pdf and used with the approval of the author.

Figure 53: And So It Begins—Dilbert on Supply Chain Management[270]

While other "theories" may exist and will continue to develop, the one presented here is sufficient to provide the student with an introduction to the structure, depth, and considerations of cybersecurity thought.

PERVASIVENESS OF THE CYBER ENVIRONMENT

The University of Maryland/SAIC study points to the most relevant aspect concerning the cyber environment, namely, that the environment is siloed. In other words, the technical aspects of the domain have become so specialized that organizations have evolved their processes to be within these specific domains and allow, via that specialization, little cross-fertilization of ideas, management, and process, unless deliberately forced to do so. Regarding functional silos, the study specifically states,

> *Functional silos pose a significant threat to cybersecurity. The stovepiped nature of today's cyber supply chains seems to be the single greatest obstacle to cybersecurity assurance. We attribute the entrenched nature of these functional silos to the industry's tendency toward increasing specialization and focus narrowing within each domain—e.g., software, hardware or systems integration. Each specialty area settles into patterns of thought and behavior that become almost like geologic layers over time, patterns often resistant to change.*[271]

---

[270]   Dilbert cartoon published March 14, 2003: http://search.dilbert.com/search?w=and+so +it+begins+just+in+time+inventory&view=list&filter=type%3Acomic

[271]   Ibid. pg 12.

Figure 54 depicts an example of this siloed structure. The labels and identities of the individual departments are unimportant. The graphical representation is.

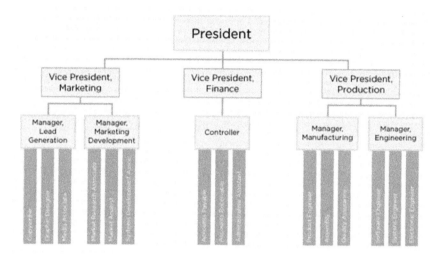

Figure 54: Diagram of a Siloed Business[272]

One need only observe the local coffee shops to understand the depth and breadth of the cyber environment. Each machine in homes, businesses, government, media, etc., is a portal for disruption and attack. The problem is extensive. An article in the *California Management Review* states,

> *Security issues will become increasingly important with wider diffusion of EC [electronic commerce]. Larger and more traditional firms will bring assets, deep pockets, investors, and customers—with all of their attendant expectations—into the wired world. These investors and customers will not be the forgiving, technologically savvy individuals of the early Internet years. If the gap between their expectations and reality is large and if the firm has not exercised due diligence in protecting its information assets, it will encounter significant corporate, and possibly personal, liability. In fact security professionals have cited liability as the number one concern, and a recent report from the National Academy of Science's Computer Science and Telecommunications Board (CSTB) notes that U.S. companies are not using available security measures to protect themselves from cyber*

---

[272] Obtained from http://www.e-myth.com/cs/user/print/post/the-danger-of-silos-in-your-business

attacks. They further note that companies producing unsecure software should be held liable.[273]

The extent of cyber systems extends into every aspect of human life in developed countries. They control the basic requirements of life, from food/water production to sanitation and health management/treatment. The impact of cyber operations is pervasive. The *California Management Review* recognizes this fact and endorses it by stating,

> *While most organizations recognize the need to secure information assets, they have viewed it mainly as a technical problem to be addressed by system managers and/or the IT function, rather than by senior management. This will no longer suffice as projections for the future indicate that blended threats will become more common. Blended threats use multiple methods of propagation, attack multiple points in a system, and require no human action to spread.*[274]

ENTERPRISE SECURITY AND RISK MANAGEMENT

The concept of an enterprise encompasses all aspects of an organization's data and information requirements within a large highly structured environment. Such a structure incorporates all of an organization's processes into a system of systems, providing shared access across all levels and functionalities. The architecture of the security and risk management processes must be just as fully integrated and dynamic. The International Standards Organization (ISO) establishes the requirements for enterprise security and risk management (ESRM) as follows:[275]

a. Security policy
b. Organization of information security
c. Asset management
d. Human resources security
e. Physical and environmental security
f. Communications and operations management
g. Access control
h. Information systems acquisition, development and maintenance

---

[273] Dutta, A. and McCrohan, K. Management's Role in Information Security in a Cyber Economy. *California Management Review.* Vol 45. No.1. Fall 2002. Pp 67-87. Pg. 68-69.

[274] Ibid. pg 69.

[275] ISO 17799. (2005)

    i.   Information security incident management

    j.   Business continuity management

    k.   Compliance

SECURITY POLICY

Policy is developed and enforced at the highest levels of the organization, as those are the locations with the authority and the resources to perform these functions. Management must establish a coordinated program that is understood, approved, and enforced by all aspects of the organization. The signatory must be the highest individual within the structure, and all aspects of enforcement must exist under this individual's purview. The policy should include the specific aspects outlined below.

EXECUTIVE SUMMARY

The executive summary includes the who, what, and how of the policy in summarization and also specifically identifies what the policy does *not* cover. It identifies the authority of the policy with any and all coordinating/supportive policies identified that cover exemptions. The identified exemption policies are to supplement the overall security structure with greater detail on why the exemptions exist and when encountered, what is to occur.

SCOPE AND APPLICABILITY

Identifying the conditions, systems, and individuals covered by the policy ensures a focused and supportable enforcement action when necessary. Again, it is important to identify who and what this section will specifically *not* cover.

GENERAL POLICY

The general policy is the policy itself and must include appropriate definitions for any terms, concepts, and procedures that may be unclear or have multiple potential definitions. Use headings for the various specific groups of equipment (e.g., computers, office equipment, telecommunications, etc.) and personnel (e.g., general employees, IT staff, HR staff, etc.). Each section will identify the specific requirements, rules, and procedures associated with the general grouping, even if this is duplicated between groups. When duplicated, ensure that if a responsibility is vested within a particular group, it is specifically and clearly identified.

ROLES AND RESPONSIBILITIES

There are basically two different types of responsibilities: organizational and functional. Organizational responsibilities are generally for executives and managers who, by way of their organizational position and/or rank, are authorized or required specific activities. Functional responsibilities identify managers and personnel tasked with the actual performance of duties under the security policy.

COMPLIANCE

This section contains the teeth of the security policy. It defines what happens upon violation of specific aspects of the policy and the procedures for investigation, adjudication, and execution of the adjudication. This section must be coordinated with the various laws, regulations, and public enforcement agencies, as many of the policies involved derives from criminal law. Often, organizations choose to omit this section. This is ill advised, however, as such omission can provide judicial notice of a lack of enforcement desire and constancy.

ACCREDITATION OR RISK ASSESSMENT

Accreditation is a process where information pertaining to the security of a company's computer systems, as well as networks and communications systems, is collected, analyzed, and submitted for approval. The information should contain items such as:

a. The type of data processed on the system (company confidential, customer or client information, etc.)
b. Whether or not the system connects to a network (a local area network [LAN] or a wide area network [WAN])
c. Identification of user access to the system
d. System status (e.g., locked down) when not staffed

RISK MANAGEMENT PROCESSES

This section contains the majority of the policy structure. The information that it contains will always be extensive and should include elements such as:[276]

Access controls—Usually descriptions of log-on warning screens on a computer and access lists for dedicated computer rooms, non-disclosure agreements

System backups—By whom, how often, and where stored (off-site is best). The Disaster Recovery Organization recommends that hot or cold sites be established for enterprise-sized organizations. A hot site is an off-site location that duplicates all the functionality of the enterprise and is actively operating in conjunction with the primary production system. A cold site is similar, except that it does not function in active conjunction with the production systems. Rather, it provides office space; and the renting organization supplies the equipment when necessary, pushing periodic updates to keep it synchronized with the primary system. Both sites are *not* generally owned by the organization. Rather, they receive payments for the space to keep organization costs under control.

Incident handling—Information on what should be reported, to whom, what will be the response, and by whom

Virus protection—Mandatory installation, how often updated (automatic or manual), virus incident handling

Unauthorized access—Who is allowed to access the company's computer assets and LAN

Monitoring—Stating who will monitor the network for internal and external intrusions, and users for violations of security policies, who has access to intrusion detection devices, who will review and/or disseminate the logs

Encryption—What is the company standard encryption methodology, when will encryption be used and by whom. The types of encryption structures and information classification codes are also established here.

Digital signatures—What is the company standard, when will digital signatures be used and by whom

Web presence—What is and is not allowed to be placed on a public Web server and who is allowed to publish

---

[276] Patrick, W.F., Creating an Information Systems Security Program. This information was obtained from SANS Institute InfoSec Reading Room at http://www.sans.org/reading_room/whitepapers/policyissues/creating-information-systems-security-policy_534 and modified as necessary to fit the requirements of this text and expand the necessary information.

Disposing of resources—All resources have a specific life span. At the point at which the equipment is no longer economically maintainable, it will be "cleaned" of data and applications and disposed of in a specific manner, usually involving the physical destruction of the storage media.

Passwords—Duration, number of and what type of characters, what individuals must use what kind of passwords, for what and when, how are they created

Use of personal resources within the company—Whether allowed or not allowed, and if so, under what conditions. This includes the use of storage media and identifying what information may be placed on this media.

Inspections and reviews—Covers the conduct of audit and security review of resources, how often, conducted by whom

Entertainment software, games, etc.—Whether these are or are not allowed, and if allowed, when can they be used

Removal media—CDs, floppy disk, for personal or company use and usage marked

Freeware or shareware—Authorized or not, and if authorized, under what conditions. Excellent definitions of both shareware and freeware can be found on the Internet.

Software copyrights and licensing—Software copyright and licensing laws are very stringent. This section identifies who will be liable if a copyright is violated, who is responsible to ensure copyrights are not violated, and how the copyright information will be stored (usually on a special server that is accessed by the application to ensure that licensing and copyrights have not been violated).

Personnel/physical security—This element is generally partitioned into other policy documents, given the extensive nature of the subject. However, having a summary of requirements and reference to the appropriate policies at this point, as well as in the executive summary, is valuable.

Vendor responsibilities—Identifies the rules a vendor will follow when using a company information system asset or when using its own assets on company premises. Again, this should be a separate policy structure constructed and referenced within this location of the developed document.

Public disclosure—Identifies who can release information to the public and under what restrictions, also identifies requirements for nondisclosure agreements for employees and vendors

Computer room facilities/areas—IS Security personnel should be involved in the design stage of new computer room facilities in order in provide safeguards to protect company IS assets.

System configuration change—This structure involves and is usually covered by the organization change management policies and procedures. These are generally changes that alter the security profile (risk) of a company IS asset. They should not be instituted without consulting the IS Security personnel first and generally should involve a specific change management board or committee.

Audit of IS Security compliance—Defines who will audit for compliance and how to conduct the audit. An excellent source for auditing criteria is the Information Systems Audit and Control Association (ISACA). They publish several auditing guidelines, some free for downloading.

Security awareness and training—Establishes the mandates of an IS Security awareness training program, indicating who should attend, how often to conduct, and what to include in the training

Inventory of IS assets—Determines who should keep an inventory of all the company's IS assets, who should have access to that inventory, and if it is available to the risk management/audit teams

Documentation—Defines what documentation is required to support risk management, including what support documentation should be maintained, by whom, and how (e.g., electronically). This includes risk assessment, countermeasures, test results documentation, standard operating procedures (SOPs), and disaster recovery/contingency plans.

ORGANIZATION OF INFORMATION SECURITY

When organizing information security, consider the following: Are the primary aspects of information organization simply the data bits stored on a machine database? Does the organization require more structure to be complete? If so, is it logical to conclude that understanding of that structure is essential to the development of cybersecurity? When one considers the enormity of the problem, the answer becomes obvious. In his book, *The Five Pillars of Knowledge, Information and Data Management*, Dr. H. J. A. Van Kuijk states that there is not only a current, there is also a pending explosion of data/information that makes the current issues of processing and storage insignificant.[277] The graph shown in Figure 55 illustrates this concept.

---

[277] Van Kuijk, H.J.A., (2011), *Five Pillars of Knowledge, Information, and Data Management.* Self-published.

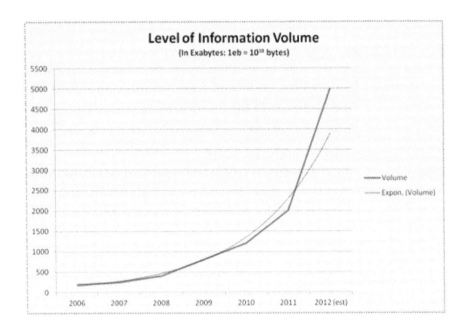

Figure 55: Volumes of Digital Information Created, Captured, and Replicated[278]

Kuijk further states,

> *In most organizations knowledge, information, and data are considered to be separate concepts. Very often, knowledge, information, and data [labeled by Kuijk as "KID"] are managed by different people in separate organizational units. The problem with this approach is that what is data to one person may be information or even knowledge to another. The boundaries between knowledge, information, and data are often blurred . . . People will have to find ways to live with the KID explosion if they want to stay healthy, sane, and productive.[279]*

The security and intelligence professional is a key element in this need for information organization and structure. How to organize this information is a primary concern, but not the only one. There is the additional issue of entropy.

Entropy is defined within the information science discipline as the state within operational environments where data is used actively. The accessibility and

---

[278]   Ibid. pg 3. The data for the years 2006-2011 were obtained from Dr. Van Kuijk's text and projected to 2012 based upon various sources and the estimation of the trend line.

[279]   Ibid. pps 3 and 7.

quality of that data will deteriorate over time unless specific steps are taken to reinforce the data.[280] This is actually part of the second law of thermodynamics. This law basically establishes that within physical systems, energy cannot be transferred from a lower energy state to a higher energy state without the application of external action. Everything that has existence moves to a normal state of equilibrium, and upon reaching that state, it can no longer be used for work. As users access and acquire data, it gives up a part of its nature from the storage medium until it reaches a point where the medium is no longer able to release the "energy" of the data stored. An example of this is the use of magnetic tape or disks. As the disk/tape is accessed (e.g. the magnetic strip on credit cards), the process used to read the data erodes a portion of the media until it reaches the point of being unreadable. Thus, it becomes a part of the tasks of security and intelligence professionals to recognize this need and to assist the appropriate agencies in protecting this valuable asset.

> **It becomes a part of the tasks of security and intelligence professionals to recognize the threat of data entropy and to assist the appropriate agencies in protecting this valuable asset.**

The International Standards Organization (ISO) states that the organization of information security can be thought as having two major directions:

a. That which is directed toward the internal organization, management, and control of information security within the institution; and
b. That which is directed toward maintaining an acceptable level of information security when the institution's information and information processing facilities are accessed, processed, communicated, or managed by external parties.[281]

Loosely interpreted, the organization of information security includes the dynamics of entropy of personnel, of architecture, and of the various management domains and echelons associated with systems, data, storage, and business

---

[280]   Ibid. pg 36.
[281]   ISO 27002, Chapter 6.0. Organization of Information Security. Downloaded from https://wiki.internet2.edu/confluence/display/itsg2/Organization+of+Information+Sec urity+(ISO+6)

continuation. Yet few organizations integrate these functions. The organization process must include the following:[282]

For the internal organization:

a. Management commitment to information security, which includes not only general direction (i.e., implementing a security strategy), allocation of resources, acknowledgment of responsibilities, and other typical management functions, but also institutional governance and oversight of the security function over time

b. Since successful information security programs require good cooperation, information security coordination is another important aspect of internal organization. Thus, the structure of the organization must reflect this dynamic with the full and active support of the highest levels of management.

c. Specific and detailed allocation of information security responsibilities needs to be clearly spelled out as many assets are under the control of widely distributed units throughout the institution. Yet these units must also be informationally coordinated so that efforts on the part of one group are not a surprise to all associated other stakeholders. The military generally handles this dynamic through the institution of liaison personnel with the freedom and authority to be involved in all plans, strategies, and operations that may impact top-level organizations.

d. Internal organization is also responsible for the authorization process for information processing facilities. ISO establishes this requirement as important due to the potential for wide distribution of physical facilities. It should also be considered for the wide distribution of information requirements and data.

e. Stakeholders should identify, execute, enforce, and regularly review requirements for confidentiality agreements or nondisclosure agreements reflecting the organization's needs for the protection of information.

f. The information security organization is responsible for appropriate contact with authorities and special interest groups, as well as the enforcement of breaches and audits of processes and procedures.

g. Periodic independent review of information security is also a responsibility of the information security organization.

Similarly, the general topic of external parties can be assigned:

---

[282] Ibid. These dynamics were obtained and modified from the ISO standard to fit the theme and direction of this text.

a. A primary responsibility is the identification of risks related to external parties.
b. A similar responsibility is addressing security when dealing with "customers" (e.g., students, applicants, alumni, parents).
c. Addressing security in third party agreements to ensure reasonable coverage of all relevant institutional security requirements

Data developed by this process in the cyber realm is known as security patterns. The information found in Figure 56, referenced from a paper by Hafiz, Adamcyzk, and Johnson of the University of Illinois, outlines the security pattern condition. Per this source, once the security organization collects this data, it must be assessed to ensure no duplication of specific data points.

The military has the same requirement referenced as data fusion. Paradis, Breton, and Roy use military command and control as the introduction to the requirement of data fusion in human decision making:

> *Command and control (C2) is defined, by the military community, as the process by which a commanding officer can plan, direct, control and monitor any operation for which he is responsible in order to fulfill his mission. Recently, a new definition has been proposed describing C2 as a dynamic human decision making process that establish the common intent and transform that common intent into a coordinated action.*[283]

---

[283] Paradis, S., Breton, R. and Roy, J. Data Fusion in Support of Dynamic Human Decision Making. Defence Research Establishment. Canada. Pg 1.

How Many Security Patterns?

Yoder and Barcalow wrote the first paper on security patterns[1] in 1997. Others followed it by making security pattern catalogs either individually[2,3,4], or by formal[5] and informal collaboration[6]. Recently, three books on security patterns have been published.

Steel et. al. wrote a book that covers architectural security patterns for J2EE-based applications, Web services and identity management[7]. The book present the fundamentals of Java application security and documents 23 security patterns. It was published in October, 2005.

Markus Schumacher led a working group that produced a book in December, 2005[8]. This book includes 46 security patterns from the domains of enterprise security and risk management, identification and authentication, access control, accounting, firewall architecture, and secure Internet applications.

Microsoft's Patterns and Practices group published a security patterns book[9] accompanying the release of Web Services Enhancement (WSE) 3.0 in March, 2006. The book is a tutorial for using WSE 3.0 in Web services development. It lists 18 patterns that address authentication, message protection, transport and message layer security, resource access, service boundary protection and service deployment. All these patterns are described from the perspective of Microsoft technology.

The patternshare website (www.patternshare.org) is a single repository to describe all kinds of software patterns. One of the goals of patternshare is to develop a uniform vocabulary for practitioners by combining all patterns that differ only by the name into one. The patternshare repository of security patterns summarizes the security patterns from various sources and eliminates overlaps. We are maintaining this repository while the patternshare as a whole is managed by the Hillside Group. In December 2006, the repository contained 90 unique security patterns.

New security vulnerabilities are exposed daily. The problems uncovered by these vulnerabilities and the solutions developed to combat them will add many more security patterns to the arsenal of developers of secure software systems in the years to come.

References

1. J. Yoder and J. Barcalow. Architectural patterns for enabling application security. In Proceedings of the 4th Conference on Patterns Language of Programming (PLoP'97). http://citeseer.ist.psu.edu/yoder98architectural.html, 1997.
2. S. Romanosky. Security design patterns part 1. http://citeseer.ist.psu.edu/575199.html. November, 2001.
3. M. Hafiz. Security Architecture of Mail Transfer Agents. Master's Thesis. University of Illinois at Urbana-Champaign, July 2005.
4. M. Hafiz. A collection of privacy design patterns. In Proceedings of the 13th Conference on Patterns Languages of Programming (PLoP'06), 2006.
5. B. Blakley and C. Heath. Security design patterns technical guide - version 1. Open Group (OG), led by Bob Blakley and Craig Heath. 2004. http://www.opengroup.org/security/gsp.htm.
6. D. M. Kienzle, M. C. Elder, D. Tyree, and J. Edwards-Hewitt. Security patterns repository. 2002.
7. C. Steel, R. Nagappan, and R. Lai. Core security patterns: Best practices and strategies for J2EE(TM), Web services, and identity management. Prentice Hall PTR, October 2005.
8. M. Schumacher, E. Fernandez-Buglioni, D. Hybertson, F. Buschmann, and P. Sommerlad. Security patterns: Integrating security and systems engineering. John Wiley and Sons, December 2005.
9. J. Hogg, D. Smith, F. Chong, D. Taylor, L. Wall, and P. Slater. Web service security: Scenarios, patterns, and implementation guidance for Web Services Enhancements (WSE) 3.0. Microsoft Press, March 2006.

Figure 56: Organizing Security Patterns[284]

---

[284] Hafiz, M., Adamczyk, P. and Johnson, R.E., Towards an Organization of Security Patterns. University of Illinois. Downloaded from http://munawarhafiz.com/research/patterns/haj07-security-patterns.pdf

Webster's defines *data fusion* as the process of synthesizing raw data from several sources to generate more meaningful information, which can be of greater value than single source data. The Data Fusion Lexicon developed by JDL in 1987 defines *data fusion* as:

> *A process dealing with the association, correlation, and combination of data and information from single and multiple sources to achieve refined position and identity estimates, and complete and timely assessments of situations and threats, and their significance. The process is characterized by continuous refinements of its estimates and assessments, and the evaluation of the need for additional sources, or modification of the process itself, to achieve improved results.*[285]

The aspect of data fusion then is to ensure that data containing identical or similar information is considered together rather than separately. A danger in considering the data as separate events is that one reinforces the viability of the other even when such reinforcement is false. Additionally, separate reports from different sources of a similar, yet not identical event, may be viewed as a single event when the separate events reinforce suspect data. An excellent example of this situation occurred on December 7, 1941, when multiple reports of enemy activity were discounted as they were improperly fused into the intelligence of the impending attack.

An important and valuable observation on both the definition of data fusion and the processes that have been designed to answer the problem of the rapidly growing amount of available data from numerous sources is made by Steinberg, Bowman, and White:

> *Automated data fusion processes are generally employed to support human decision-making by refining and reducing the quantity of information that system operators need to examine to achieve timely, robust, and relevant assessments and projections of the situation. Unfortunately, data fusion is a victim of its own popularity: the pervasiveness of data fusion functions has engendered a profusion of overlapping research and development in many applications. A welter*

---

[285] White, F.E. Jr., *Data Fusion Lexicon*, Joint Directors of Laboratories, Technical Panel for C3, Data Fusion Sub-Panel, Naval Ocean Systems Center, San Diego, 1987.

of confusing terminology [Figure 57] obscures the fact that the same ground has been plowed repeatedly.[286]

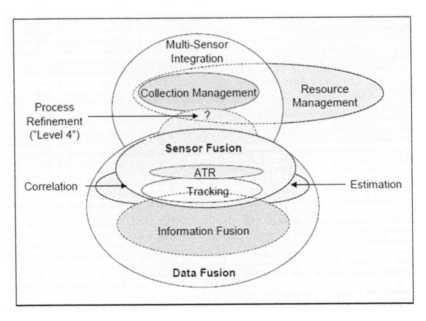

Figure 57: Confusion of Data Fusion Terminology[287]

The goal is to combine data in a format that yields information to:

a. Make the task of analyzing and using the information less taxing on the analyst,
b. Simplify the tasks of combining the data appropriately,
c. Limit instances of redundancy in reports to avoid making events appear more important or factual than they are in reality.

Currently, there have been hundreds of proposed data fusion technology systems developed and proposed. However, none actually performs the tasks with the degree of efficacy necessary to solve the dilemmas of the data overload problems. The best solution remains the appropriate use and training of analysts into the appropriate processes of research and fact-based analysis.

---

[286]   Steinberg, A.N., Bowman, C.L., and White, F.E., (1999). *Revisions to the JDL Data Fusion Model.* ERIM International, Inc. 1101 Wilson Blvd. Arlington, VA 22209. Pg. 2.

[287]   Ibid. pg 3.

Asset Management

For most security managers, asset management involves counting computers and ensuring none of them leave the control of the organization. To this end, the ISO 17799 standard lists three controls: inventory of assets, ownership of assets, and acceptable use of assets. Collectively or individually implemented, these controls enable an organization to maintain appropriate protection of assets.

For intelligence professionals (IPs), as opposed to security professionals, the structure of asset management goes much deeper. The intelligence professional must create what is known as a collection management plan. This plan forces the IP to not only identify what pieces of equipment are available for use. The IP is required to address the skill sets, level of expertise, availability on station (how long an asset is able to perform the assigned function), rotation (moving similar assets in and out of an area to perform the collection process), recovery and maintenance time, and other operational functions.

The IP uses this information to determine how, when, and where to place the assets that are specifically capable of collecting information/data necessary to answer questions concerning operational requirements. These requirements range from determining what a specific threat is both likely and capable of doing, to how friendly operational functions and activities influence progress to a specific objective. Security professionals may construct similar structures for industrial and civil security operations.

When linked to the information organization aspect of the cyber environment, the fusion aspect in particular, asset management establishes the requirement for not only ensuring the proper maintenance and use of current assets but also the appropriate engineering of the entire architecture for optimal use. Steinberg et al. cover this topic of how best to engineer data fusion in the following excerpt:

> The lack of common engineering standards for data fusion systems has been a major impediment to integration and re-use of available technology. This deficiency was revealed in a Correlation Technology Assessment conducted in 1995 for the Defense Airborne Reconnaissance Office (DARO). A survey of over 50 operational and developmental Intelligence Correlation systems found a general lack of standardized—or even well-documented—performance evaluation, system engineering methodologies, architecture paradigms, or multi-spectral models of targets and collection systems. In short, current developments do not lend themselves to objective evaluation, comparison or reuse.[288]

---

[288]   Ibid. pg 15.

Yet given the information in the Human Terrain chapter (Chapter 4), there is insufficient science on how the human brain performs this function. Therefore, how is it possible to establish standards for it? The remaining aspects of the ISO standard guidelines have been or will be discussed in other sections of this text and will not be reiterated here.

Manipulation of Cybersecurity Dynamics

The primary factor of cybersecurity is the codification and encoding of information. It is within this element that the majority of cyber manipulation can and does occur. While physical and electronic means are also available, cipher systems and processes provide the greatest means of security enhancement for the least effort and cost. The principle thing to remember is that anything relating to cybersecurity involves the activities of machine and human interface—recall the Human Terrain chapter of this text for insights into this interaction.

A USAF study conducted by Riechman outlines the problem succinctly: "The dynamics of the IT system interface has created some unique challenges to it because the interface is between a human and a non-human."[289] The system is not the primary target in cyber attacks, such attempts only modify, erase, or rewrite code to achieve a specific function. The true targets in for cyber threats are the humans associated with the system and the value these people place on what the system activity and interface achieves for them.

Granted, the attack may cause disruption in key systems functions and interactions, however, the human always has the ability to override these controls, given a properly engineered architecture. A major weakness develops when the human element lacks sufficient awareness of their system functions to recognize an attack. This is known as IT suspicion.

IT Suspicion

IT suspicion occurs in a user when the system does not operate or respond in an unexpected or unusual manner. There is no specific accepted definition for the term "IT suspicion." Captain M. Olson discusses the reason for this, including a suggested definition, in his thesis proposed during his studies at the U.S. Air Force Institute of Technology:

---

[289] Riechman, D.J., (2010). *Cyber Disrupt and Deny (Cyber D&D)*. United States Air Force Research Laboratory, Sensemaking & Organizational Effectiveness Branch. Wright-Patterson AFB, Ohio. Pg 3.

A unique problem encountered in defining IT suspicion is the sender isn't an individual at all; the sender is the information technology used to pass various services and forms of information to receiver. IT does not have hidden emotional motives as a driver of performance and actions. Actions are driven by design, inputs, physics, and logic. Some inputs, however, do come from other individuals, and real people do design, build, and maintain IT systems. Truthfulness and deception from other definitions of suspicion associated with people become accurateness and corruption of data. Individual motives aren't doubted; IT system designs and policies are doubted. So from this, the following motivational and perceived outcome based definition for IT suspicion emerges: User perceptions that the direction, duration, and intensity of an IT systems behavior will negatively impact their task.[290]

Riechman supports Olson's above conjecture, stating, "IT suspicion can be portioned into an enduring trait characteristic and an induced state characteristic with multiple focuses of the suspicion. The human operator can be suspicious of the IT system and/or the data within the IT system."[291]

This information harkens back to the consideration of bias and expectation violation, addressed in the Olson thesis as a "trust" issue, but likely runs much deeper into the human psyche. The security professional should consider the prospect of using such suspicion as a means of identifying, tracking, and measuring IT security and intelligence fusion dynamics. As this branch of study is fairly recent, it may take time to fully develop.

CRYPTOGRAPHY

Cryptography is the process of hiding information inside of seemingly random or deliberately obfuscating text, pictures, or other media which is decodable by the intended recipient of the information. There are many different forms and types of cryptography.

STEGANOGRAPHY

Steganography is the process of using one message to hide an interior secondary communication to maintain the secrecy of the information. In

---

[290] Olson, M.T. Captain, (2009). The Development of IT Suspicion as a Construct and Subsequent Measure. Master's Thesis. US Air Force Institute of Technology. Wright-Patterson AFB, Ohio. Pg 13.

[291] Ibid.

227

software, there are currently only three effective methods of steganography: least significant bit (LSB) substitution, blocking and palette modification, and network steganography.[292]

LSB involves the bit position in a binary integer which gives the units value. For example, the binary construction for the integer 1 is binary 000001. Add 3 to the integer to sum to 4 and the binary is 000100, changing the least significant bits of 011 (integer 3) to 100 (integer 4). These bits change constantly, while the higher number bits (the leading zeros) do not. A program can therefore use these numbers to do a variety of things to include storing information that, when coupled with a decoding key, hides messages in plain sight.

Blocking uses what is known as discrete cosine transforms (DCTs), which represent certain colors and luminance as shown in Figure 58. Changing these values slightly will not alter a picture's pixel representation to the naked eye but can contain significant amounts of hidden data. Palette modification is similar to blocking in that it uses slight changes in the color palette structure for a given set of bits to transmit the hidden code.

The tree, left, contains the 'Blocked' image, right hidden inside it.

Figure 58: Steganography Blocked Image

Network steganography is a higher tech form of hiding that uses the transfer protocol structures between networks and their basic functionality, which is much more effective and difficult to track. Certain military engineering organizations have used a form of this structure to create a new methodology known as waveforming. A waveform is the structure that an electromagnetic signal takes when transmitted through a medium. Waveforms may take on a variety of shapes as shown in Figure 59.

---

[292] Nabavian, N. (2007). CPSC 350 Data Structures: Image Steganography. Chapman University.   http://www1.chapman.edu/~nabav100/ImgStegano/download/ ImageSteganography.pdf

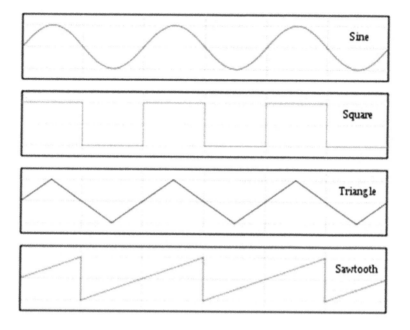

Figure 59: Examples of Electromagnetic Waveforms

Such waveforms are adjusted and overlaid to create a large footprint on the spectrum, with little actual interference from other systems. This allows the system-to-system interface to take place rapidly and securely.

CRYPTOLOGY

Cryptology is the process of changing open information based on a key structure that transforms this information into unreadable numbers, text, and pictures. The incomprehensible symbols require the specific key to unlock this encrypted information. An early example of the use of this kind of technology was the Enigma machine from WWII. This machine used a series of electromechanical wheels to light up a code letter when a specific key was typed and never gave the same code twice.

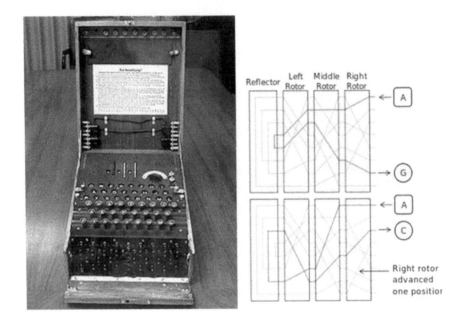

Figure 60: German WWII Enigma Machine

There are many forms of cipher mechanisms and key structures throughout history. For example, Figure 61 shows a DRYAD numeral cipher/authentication code sheet. This sheet contains twenty-five lines or rows indexed by the letters on the left column of the page. The letters are random structures *A* through *Y*. A specific process identifies the starting key for each period of use, enabling anyone with a duplicate cipher pad and knowledge of the key to encrypt/decrypt the specific message.

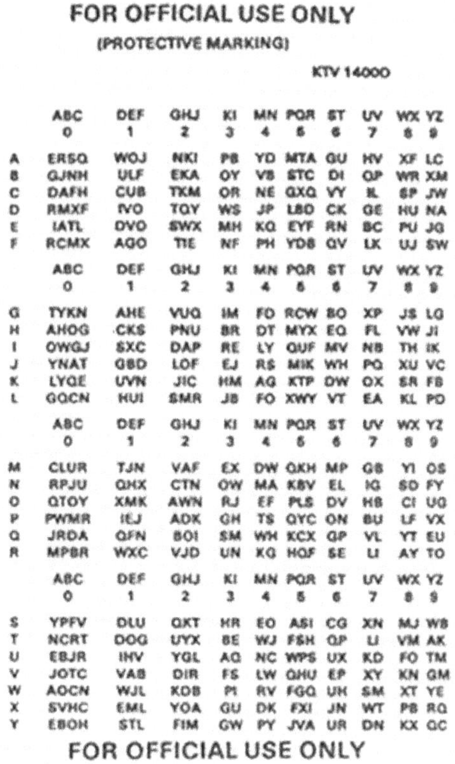

FOR OFFICIAL USE ONLY

(PROTECTIVE MARKING)

KTV 14000

	ABC	DEF	GHJ	KI	MN	PQR	ST	UV	WX	YZ
	0	1	2	3	4	5	6	7	8	9
A	ERSQ	WOJ	NKI	PB	YD	MTA	GU	HV	XF	LC
B	GJNH	ULF	EKA	OY	VB	STC	DI	QP	WR	XM
C	DAFH	CUB	TKM	OR	NE	GXQ	VY	IL	SP	JW
D	RMXF	IVO	TQY	WS	JP	LBO	CK	GE	HU	NA
E	IATL	DVO	SWX	MH	KQ	EYF	RN	BC	PU	JG
F	RCMX	AGO	TIE	NF	PH	YDB	QV	LK	UJ	SW
	ABC	DEF	GHJ	KI	MN	PQR	ST	UV	WX	YZ
	0	1	2	3	4	5	6	7	8	9
G	TYKN	AHE	VUQ	IM	FO	RCW	BO	XP	JS	LG
H	AHOG	CKS	PNU	BR	DT	MYX	EQ	FL	VW	JI
I	OWGJ	SXC	DAP	RE	LY	QUF	MV	NB	TH	IK
J	YNAT	GBD	LOF	EJ	RS	MIK	WH	PQ	XU	VC
K	LYQE	UVN	JIC	HM	AG	KTP	DW	OX	SR	FB
L	GQCN	HUI	SMR	JB	FO	XWY	VT	EA	KL	PO
	ABC	DEF	GHJ	KI	MN	PQR	ST	UV	WX	YZ
	0	1	2	3	4	5	6	7	8	9
M	CLUR	TJN	VAF	EX	DW	QKH	MP	GB	YI	OS
N	RPJU	QHX	CTN	OW	MA	K8V	EL	IQ	SO	FY
O	QTOY	XMK	AWN	RJ	EF	PLS	DV	HB	CI	UQ
P	PWMR	IEJ	ADK	GH	TS	QYC	ON	BU	LF	VX
Q	JRDA	QFN	BOI	SM	WH	KCX	QP	VL	YT	EU
R	MPBR	WXC	VJD	UN	KQ	HQF	SE	LI	AY	TO
	ABC	DEF	GHJ	KI	MN	PQR	ST	UV	WX	YZ
	0	1	2	3	4	5	6	7	8	9
S	YPFV	DLU	QKT	HR	EO	ASI	CG	XN	MJ	W8
T	NCRT	DOG	UYX	BE	WJ	F&H	QP	LI	VM	AK
U	EBJR	IHV	YGL	AQ	NC	WPS	UX	KD	FO	TM
V	JOTC	VAB	DIR	FS	LW	QHU	EP	XY	KN	GM
W	AOCN	WJL	KDB	PI	RV	FGQ	UH	SM	XT	YE
X	SVHC	EML	YOA	GU	DK	FXI	JN	WT	PB	RQ
Y	EBOH	STL	FIM	GW	PY	JVA	UR	DN	KX	QC

FOR OFFICIAL USE ONLY

Figure 61: DRYAD Cipher System

An example of using this system for authentication is for the sending station to say "hotel/whiskey," to which the answering station would respond with the appropriate answer, which is the letter immediately under the *H* row/*W* letter or "hotel" in this instance. Encoding uses a similar, except the letter immediately to the right is the correct answer leading to either the uncoded letter *Y* or number 9, depending on the sent message.

Electronic cipher systems are somewhat similar to this process. *Wikipedia* provides a very good graphic of the electronic cipher process shown in Figure 62. Modern computer scientists consider electronic cipher systems totally secure, and the Germans, Italians, and Japanese believed the same thing when using the Enigma machine prior to and during WWII. However, they were mistaken. This system was partially broken by the Polish just before the German invasion and finished up by Bletchley Park in England to the point that nearly all of Axis communications became an open book.

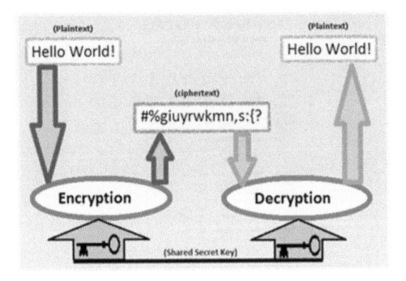

Figure 62: Symmetric-Key Cryptography[293]

Current IT cipher systems operate on a binary bit sequence that, unlike legacy systems, do not manipulate the characters directly. They filter the information via a specific encryption algorithm. A recent process is the Advanced Encryption Standard (AES), developed by the National Bureau of Standards in the Federal Information Processing Standards Publication 197 dated November 26, 2001. This standard was established by the Secretary of Commerce via the IT Reform Act of 1996 (PL 104-106) and the Computer Security Act of 1987 (PL 100-235).

The exact process is complex and too advanced for this text, suffice to state that it involves a series of polynomials that essentially create a Markovian matrix of nearly infinite possible combinations. A Markov matrix is a structure of a probability chain of events where each event leads to a set of other possibilities, each with a specific chance of occurrence. Picture a tree with thousands of branches with an ant at the bottom of the tree. The ant begins to climb the tree. Which leaf will the ant be on when it can no longer continue to climb? At the start, each possible route may have an equal probability. However, as the ant makes a selection, the probabilities change dynamically until there is ultimately only one possible choice left.

From the perspective of the computer cipher, shown in Figure 63, the various choice blocks represent the tree, while the "Kitty Cat" is the ant (i.e., the coded message).

---

[293] Obtained from Wikipedia at http://en.wikipedia.org/wiki/Cryptography

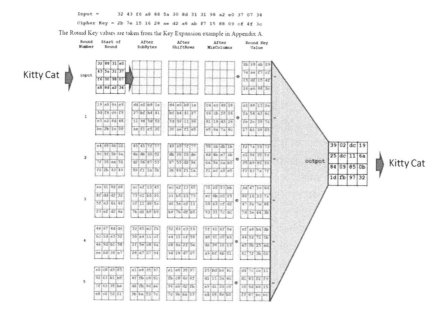

Figure 63: Example Graphical Representation of the Computer Encryption Process

At the start is the input, whether it be an e-mail, an ATM transaction, whatever. The values are placed into the computer as a hexadecimal code.[294] This input value processes through a chain of AES algorithms to achieve a completely random and supposedly unbreakable code structure. Added to this is a packet of code that contains a synchronization key identifier. At the other end, the receiver has either the same key or a related key, which allows that person/agency to identify the encryption key to reverse the process to the specific hexadecimal output. The end result: the machine prints on the screen as "Kitty Cat."

What makes this encryption process so secure is not that it is unbreakable. Nothing made by man is without flaw. One only has to say the word "Titanic" to visualize the fallacy of the concept of unbreakability. Rather, the task requires significant investment in the machinery and programs necessary to perform the billions of trillions of calculations necessary to arrive at an appropriate set

---

[294] Hexadecimal code is a set of values ranging from 0 through 9 (representing the values 0-9) and a-f (representing the values 10-15). Thus, the hexadecimal number 2AF3 is equal to the decimal value 10,995. This is what computers use to communicate as a computer is simply an extremely fast, programmable adding machine.

of potential true values. This was the problem facing the Enigma decoders at Bletchley Park.[295]

SIGNALS INTELLIGENCE AND COMPUTERS

The ultimate manipulation of computer cybersecurity is in the processes of Signals Intelligence of SIGINT. In the United States, this function is conducted by the National Security Agency or NSA located at Ft. Meade, Maryland. This facility is an enormous computer center with gigantic processing capability unmatched anywhere else in the world today. NSA utilizes an unknown number of scientists, programmers, engineers, and technicians whose sole task is the interception, analysis, decryption, and reporting of information gleaned from the electromagnetic spectrum.

Anyone who has watched any of the movies of WWII, such as *Tora, Tora, Tora* or *Bodyguard of Lies*, or any of the others on the secret world of the code breakers can attest to the colossal effort undertaken by these individuals. There have been many excellent documentaries on the efforts by the Enigma code breakers who developed and used the first practical programmable machine to assist in performing the calculations necessary to break the Enigma code. These computers, or "bombes" as they were called then, simply calculated all of the possible permutations of the various individual code letters until a daily key setting was able to be mathematically determined. Once that key setting was determined for that set of Enigma machines, that entire day's transmissions were open to Allied eyes. The trouble was that each major command and many important subordinate commands had their own individual keys.

The Enigma successes were due not just to these scientists and engineers, but also to individuals sent out to combat operations with the specific task of capturing both machines and codebooks. Not only does this capture provide historical knowledge of where the code keys were at a given time, it allows for a process known as traffic analysis (TA).

Specific information on TA is highly classified and, as such, will not be discussed in this text. Suffice to state that knowing who is talking to whom and when is nearly as important as knowing what is being said. The perfect example of this occurred prior to the Battle of Midway in the Pacific Ocean. The partially broken Japanese naval code and the sender-receiver of a specific innocuous piece

---

[295] Bletchley Park was the British code-breaking organization that gave rise to the American National Security Agency. It was here that one of the world's first programmable computers was created to perform the calculations necessary to break the German Enigma coding machine. To learn more, go to http://www.bletchleypark. org.uk/

of untrue information (disinformation) on the status of a saltwater conversion machine identified the Japanese target long enough for the United States Navy to set a trap that cost Japan the initiative in the Pacific and ultimately, the war.

> **For want of a cipher key, the code was lost. For want of the code, secrecy was lost. For want of secrecy, the battle was lost. For want of the battle, the initiative was lost. For want of the initiative, the war was lost!**

IMPLICATIONS TO SECURITY PLANNING AND OPERATIONS

Joyner and Lotrionte provide the best summary for the implications of cybersecurity to security planning and operations, stating,

> *Worldwide interconnectivity through massive computer networks now makes states vulnerable to new threats. Foreign governments can launch computer-based assaults, or acts of information warfare, on another state's domestic systems such as energy grids, telecommunications, and financial facilities that could severely damage or disrupt national defence [sic] or vital social services. Even realizing the new forms of computer-generated weapons and changing concepts of sovereignty and territory brought about by global interdependence, international law is likely to rely on UN Charter principles to define the legal boundaries of cyberspace. While perhaps not armed force literally, resort to cyberforce may be viewed as a form in intervention that can produce harmful or coercive effects, and put at risk the national security of another state.*[296]

The issue involves the threat or use of force by one agency against another, whether they are businesses, nationalities, cyber terrorists, or whatever. At one time, the intelligence and security professional need only be concerned with telecommunications procedures and the possible MIJI—Meaconing, Intrusion, Jamming, and Interference—operations. Now an enemy entity has the potential for electronic invasion of systems with the ability to cause either system disruption, shutdown, or user loss of confidence in the system. This generates human-induced weaknesses and failures, as the system breaks down.

---

[296] Joyner, C.C. and Lotrionte, C. (2001). *Information Warfare as International Coercion: Elements of a Legal Framework*. Institute for Law, Science and Global Security. Georgetown University. Washington, DC. Pg. Abstract.

Human-induced weakness involves the introduction of bias into the processes of decision making. Individual inattention, group-think, preconceived notions, and other aspects come into play either slowing or confusing decision makers, resulting in errors in judgment, delays in reactions, and fear.

One of the most infamous examples of such a failure occurred on December 7, 1941, when two radar technicians reported a flight of several hundred aircraft inbound toward Hawaii from the West. The duty officer in charge had no knowledge or understanding of the system. Since he did not have confidence in the system, he decided that the message meant nothing and should not be reported up the chain for a decision. The flight at that time was approximately one hundred miles away or about twenty minutes at their flight speed. The events of that day at Pearl Harbor could have been quite different had that officer been more educated and confident. Now the important point is to learn from the situation and avoid repeating such breaks in security via appropriate identification and training.

Chapter 9

PERSONNEL TERRAIN

Chapter 4 discussed the human terrain aspects of security and intelligence operations. This chapter deals with the role of human resources (HR), not the company department, rather the operational concept and procedures in security and intelligence operations. The sections herein discuss personnel security policy, procedures, and processes with the objective of examining the various issues and legalities associated with this, the most weakened link of the security and intelligence chain.

DEFINITIONS AND CONSIDERATIONS

Regarding "personnel terrain," a specific definition of *personnel* is, people employed in an organization or engaged in an organized undertaking such as military service. *Terrain* is defined as the geography of an area or rather the nature and relative arrangement of places and physical features. Thus, the definition applied for the purpose of this text is the nature and relative arrangement of people employed in an organization or engaged in an organized undertaking such as military service.

The HR department of most organizations deals with,

> *Recruiting, managing, developing, and motivating people, including providing functional and specialized support and systems for employee engagement and managing systems to foster regulatory compliance with employment and human rights standards.*[297]

---

[297]   Strandberg, C. (2009). *The Role of Human Resource Management in Corporate Social Responsibility: Issue Brief and Roadmap*. Strandberg Consulting. Burnaby, British Columbia. Pg 2.

The United States Office of Personnel Management defines the structure of HR as "a means to integrate decisions about people with decisions about the results an organization is trying to obtain."[298]

In both of these definitions, there is little mention of the HR organization as an advocate for the employee. The primary function of the HR department is to ensure the staffing of the organization with the appropriate level of skilled individuals at the least possible cost, within the guidelines of both law and organized labor contract and associated appropriately to the strategic and operational objectives of the specific levels of the organization.

This primary function does not begin with the specific department or executive over the personnel function. The process begins with the development of a strategic direction, depending on the organization type, as shown in Figure 64.

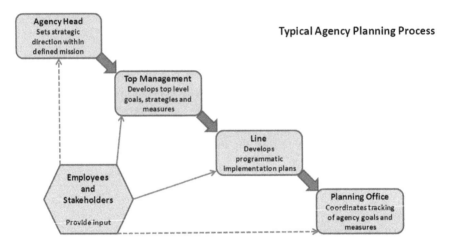

Figure 64: Typical Agency Planning Process[299]

The terrain aspect begins with the appropriate placement of resources (i.e., employees) into specific strategic areas. The mission of the executive/agency head level sets the pace and structure of subordinate organizations from the top down. The more succinct the mission, the greater the limitations placed on individuals below, requiring greater strategic planning. For example, President Roosevelt provided a targeted and succinct strategic mission statement to General Eisenhower prior to the latter's assignment to lead the European Theater of Operations during WWII. That mission was, "You will enter the continent of

---

[298]   US Office of Personnel Management. (1999). *Strategic Human Resources Management: Aligning with the Mission*. Washington, D.C. pg 1.

[299]   Ibid. pg 6.

Europe and, in conjunction with the other United Nations, undertake operations aimed at the heart of Germany and the destruction of her armed forces."[300]

Examine this mission closely and it will demonstrate a focused, measurable, and delimited order. It states the method (enter the continent of Europe), task (undertake operations aimed at the heart of Germany), and the ultimate goal (the destruction of her armed forces). It does not tell Eisenhower how he was to achieve the task of entering Europe, just to do so. It is specific as to what he was to do, which was to undertake operations.

Though Eisenhower was an officer of the U.S. Armed Forces, carrying with the role the implication of military operations, he was not limited to those types of engagement to carry out his mission. His options included diplomatic, surgical, and other means of achieving the final outcome of destroying Germany's armed forces.

The mission likewise did not require Eisenhower to kill all members of the German armed forces for successful operations. The term *destroy* means to put an end to the existence of by damaging or attacking, completely ruining or spoiling the target. If the organization ceased to exist, the entity is destroyed even if all of the humans associated with it remain alive. If the humans no longer have the will to maintain the organization, the organization cannot exist on its own. The human resources necessary to perform the tasks are the organization's life. Remove the supplies needed by people to perform their tasks, remove their will to work, and remove their rewards (both physical and psychological) for performing their work, and the personnel geography will collapse. This is what Eisenhower did.

The actual nature of personnel terrain includes organization strategic and operational objectives. The resources the personnel require to perform the tasks associated with the objectives, the will to perform the tasks through physical and psychological incentives/rewards, and a means of ensuring the personnel can meet their lower basic needs (Maslow's Hierarchy of Needs) so that they can focus on the higher order needs.

PERSONNEL SECURITY AND INTELLIGENCE

Most documents and guidelines handle personnel security only insofar as the access to facilities and information/information systems. Personnel intelligence goes much further. Referring back to Chapter 4, the intelligence community prepares a "Battle Book" on all areas of their concern and oversight. Figure 65 depicts an interesting online depiction of what most military and intelligence organizations worldwide might develop while not being an actual

---

[300] http://www.britannica.com/dday/article-9400217

intelligence-style Battle Book.[301] The one shown is for support to a particular U.S. Army organization, not one that would be used for information on a threat. Notice the pullout of the tabs as areas of focus. The religious support, bioethics, counseling, resource management, and BSRF/Strong Bonds[302] tabs are, with the addition of a personalities tab, the primary elements of the personnel geography. Within these tabs are areas for specific information.

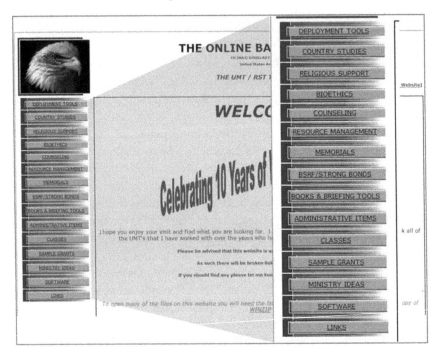

Figure 65: Online Battle Book Example

Private industry has a similar structure known as a Customer Reference Journal (CRJ) or Customer Relationship Management (CRM) system. A CRM system contains intelligence on everything known about an organization's customer base. There are many vender examples of databases, each with their own strengths and weaknesses. Basically, the database will hold any and all information relating to a customer, stakeholder, influencing entity, or vendor. Not just names and contact numbers, but everything that can be discovered and may support or influence decisions, interactions, intentions, market analysis, and sales activities. Some software will have fields for family information (spouse/children

---

[301]   Downloaded from http://dcswift.com/military/index.html

[302]   BSRF = Building Strong and Ready Families

names, birthdays, likes/dislikes, etc.), hobby information, purchase records, negotiation tactics/techniques utilized/preferred, etc. The objective is to have as much information as possible to be able to predict the actions of the person, and by extension, the organization.

Just as your organization is gathering information on allies and actual/ potential opponents, they are doing the same against your organization. Their objective is the same as yours, to gain as much knowledge on your personnel as possible to be able to penetrate your decision cycle. By doing so, they have a negotiating or combat advantage they can use to maneuver around your strengths and exploit your weaknesses. While information may be available from a variety of sources, it does not provide asset allocation or decision making. These areas require human intelligence (HUMINT).

HUMAN INTELLIGENCE

The definition of HUMINT is "a category of intelligence derived from information collected and provided by Human sources."[303] HUMINT is the only technique that exploits the human dimension to determine an adversary's intent for future action. HUMINT derives from interrogations, volunteered information, informants, undercover agents, and recruited/forced agents.

CIA Director William Casey stated the intense need for human intelligence resources before congress in 1981:

> *The wrong picture is not worth a thousand words. No photo, no electronic impulse can substitute for direct on-the scene knowledge of the key factors in a given country or region. No matter how spectacular a photo may be it cannot reveal enough about plans, intentions, internal political dynamics, economics, etc. There are simply too many cases where photos are ambiguous or useless, and electronic intelligence can drown the analyst in partial or conflicting information. Technical collection is of little help in the most difficult problem of all—political intentions. This is where clandestine human intelligence can make a difference.*[304]

What he was stating was that no photograph, no matter how detailed, can see into the minds of the enemy to determine their plans and intents. Only individuals

---

[303] Joint Chiefs of Staff, 8 November 2010. Joint Publication 1-02: Dictionary of Military and Associated Terms. Department of Defense. Washington, D.C.

[304] Pearce, M.W. (2009). *The Evolution of Defense HUMINT Through Post Conflict Iraq.* US Army War College Master's Thesis. Carlisle Barracks, PA. pg 3.

with direct access to such leaders, along with the analysis of personality, history, cause, effect, and capability, can ferret out such information. Such individuals, known colloquially as spies, come in different flavors or types.

During the cold war, the Soviet Union's secret intelligence services listed basically three types of agent: agents of influence, agents of conscious, and agents of opportunity. In each case, an employee of the intelligence service would recruit or coerce an individual within the target organization to provide information on specially targeted areas as a means of gaining detailed cognitive information. Prior to defining these types, examine the definition of an agent.

> *In intelligence usage, one who is authorized and trained to obtain or to assist in obtaining information for intelligence or counterintelligence purposes. (JP 1-02) Also see agent of influence; agent of a foreign entity; asset; foreign intelligence agent.*

> *—Also, a person who engages in clandestine intelligence activities under the direction of an intelligence organization, but is not an officer, employee, or co-opted worker of that organization. (National HUMINT Glossary)*

> *—Also, (1) a person who engages in clandestine intelligence activity under the direction of an intelligence organization but who is not an officer, employee, or co-opted worker of that organization; (2) an individual who acts under the direction of an intelligence agency or security service to obtain, or assist in obtaining, information for intelligence or counterintelligence proposes; [and] (3) one who is authorized or instructed to obtain or assist in obtaining information for intelligence or counterintelligence purposes. (ICS Glossary)*[305]

---

[305] Defense Intelligence Agency. (2 May 2011). *CI Glossary—Terms & Definitions of Interest for DoD CI Professionals*. Pg. GL-4.

> *Typically, the aim of an espionage operation is to recruit an agent [emphasis added], usually a foreign person, to carry out the actual spying. The person who targets, recruits, trains, and runs the agent is, in American parlance, the "case officer."*
>
> —Arthur S. Hulnick, "Espionage: Does It Have a Future in the 21st Century?" *The Brown Journal of World*
>
> *Affairs;* v XI: n 1 (2004).
>
> ---
>
> *Espionage is one of the toughest games played. An agent in the right place is hard to find, but when he is found he should be regarded as a pearl beyond price.*
>
> —David Nelligan, *The Spy in the Castle* (1968)

AGENT OF INFLUENCE

The Defense Intelligence Agency Office of Counterintelligence has published a glossary that contains the following definition of the term *agent of influence*:

> —An agent of some stature who uses his or her position to influence public opinion or decision making to produce results beneficial to the country whose intelligence service operates the agent. (AFOSI Manual 71-142, 9 Jun 2000) [Originally a Soviet term]

> —Also, a person who is directed by an intelligence organization to use his position to influence public opinion or decision-making in a manner that will advance the objective of the country for which that organization operates. (ICS Glossary)

> —Also, an individual who acts in the interest of an adversary without open declaration of allegiance and attempts top exec rise influence covertly, but is not necessarily gathering intelligence or compromising classified material, is known as an agent of influence. (Historical Dictionary of Cold War Counterintelligence, 2007)

> —Also, an agent operating under intelligence instructions who uses his official or public position, and other means, to exert influence on policy, public opinion, the course of particular events, the activity of political organizations and state agencies in target countries. (KGB

Lexicon: The Soviet Intelligence Officer's Handbook, edited by KGB archivist Vasiliy Mitrokhin, 2002).[306]

The important aspect of note of this definition is that the individual may or may not be aware that they are operating in this fashion. If the activity is voluntary and known, it can be considered a significant criminal offense. If without the knowledge of the individual, one could conclude the individual is simply naïve or attempting to use this information for personal benefit.

Rarely is the agent of influence process harmless or to the benefit of the targeted organization. An excellent example of such a situation is the media. Reporters often having little factual information and must rely upon sources for their stories and, by their stories, propel public opinion for or against a topic. Many sources, either deliberately or due to inadequate understanding of the information presented, provide misleading data for which the reporter is insufficiently versed to ascertain. In such situations, an agent who is a celebrity or other popular individual may be inserted to provide slanted and/or misleading data so that the story is focused in a direction that the foreign power desires. The foreign power relies upon the lack of detailed technical knowledge of the reporter, attaining their goal of disinformation. The book *In Denial* uses detailed records from the former Russian secret service (KGB) to drive this point home concerning American historians and other collegiate personnel, many of whom retain their anti-American philosophies regardless of either fact or knowledge that they were to be manipulated (Haynes, 2003).

AGENT OF CONSCIOUS

The agent of conscious is an individual recruited to perform intelligence-gathering functions due to their beliefs and political positions or because of an illegal or immoral activity that the recruiting handler has knowledge of and the agent does not wish to make public. Specific beliefs may be religious, moral, political, ethical, or even psychological (e.g., mental instability). Political positions for such agents generally involve someone already within the party circle who holds a philosophy that does not match the leadership group. Unknown to the rest of the circle, the agent desires to limit or destroy the group's power or influence over the general population involved and is used or directed by the foreign agency to focus on goals beneficial to the foreign power.

Finally, the agent may be the victim of blackmail, where they have or believe they have performed an act which can or will result in criminal prosecution or similar detrimental action to their current lifestyle known by the recruiting foreign

---

[306] Ibid. Pg GL-4/5.

agency. In each of these situations, the agent eventually begins to disobey the controlling agency for any number of reasons, and blackmail is used to maintain control.

AGENT OF OPPORTUNITY

An agent of opportunity is a somewhat mercenary position. It generally involves a person wishing to gain something from their participation in an activity. The gain may be monetary, emotional (e.g., excitement, revenge, etc.), or psychological (e.g., sense of power, sociopathic, etc.). These individuals are often the most damaging and most dangerous, as they are generally the most protected and highly placed individuals recruited. They often are capable of maintaining their position for extended periods due to their high level of intelligence and positions of trust previously held.

OBJECTIVES AND ACTIVITIES

The primary objective of these various agent types is to obtain information not generally available via other means, either due to the protections on this information or the fact that it is not recorded in any fashion and involves close relationships with the target source. The important thing to note is that to be of any value, the individual usually must already be in a position within the target agency or have the ability to gain that access. It is in this nature that the personnel terrain becomes critical.

IMPLICATIONS TO SECURITY PLANNING AND OPERATIONS

The basic nature of counter-HUMINT is counterintelligence (CI), which focuses on background investigations, limitation of access, and periodic reexaminations for the indicators of recruitment or intelligence penetration. Penetration involves the recruitment or infiltration of agents or technical monitoring devices in an organization for the purpose of acquiring information or influencing activities.[307] The best method of determining indications of infiltration is to examine how you would go about getting around your own security defenses. Never rest on the mistaken belief that your defenses are impenetrable and secure—they are not.

---

[307]   Webster's Dictionary

LISTING OF VULNERABILITIES

In a testimony to the U.S. Congress, National Counterintelligence Executive Michelle Van Cleave listed the following vulnerabilities:[308]

a. *Our general culture of openness has provided foreign entities easy access to sophisticated technologies. Each year, for example, we allow tens of thousands of official foreign visitors into U.S. Government-related facilities such as military bases, test centers, and research laboratories. Some of these visitors are dedicated to acquiring U.S. technology and know-how not otherwise available.*

b. *American colleges and universities are centers for high-tech development that employ large numbers of foreign-born faculty and train large numbers of foreign students, many of whom will return to their home countries. For example, an increasing number and proportion (approaching 30 percent) of science and engineering faculty employed at U.S. universities and colleges is foreign-born, according to National Science Foundation statistics. Moreover, the most recent data available indicate that about 40 percent of Ph.D. degrees awarded by U.S. universities in technical sciences and engineering—roughly 8,000 per year—now go to foreign students. The vast majority of these students are legitimately studying and advancing academic pursuits. But some are not.*

c. *Breathtaking advances in information technology have vastly simplified the illegal retrieval, storage, and transportation of massive amounts of information, including trade secrets and proprietary data as well as classified information. Compact storage devices the size of a finger and cell phones with digital photography capability are some of the latest weapons in technology transfer.*

d. *Sophisticated information systems that create, store, process, and transmit sensitive information have become increasingly vulnerable to cyber exploitation. Many nations have formal programs for gathering our network information, and foreign competitors are developing the capability to exploit those vulnerabilities.*

e. *Globalization has mixed foreign and U.S. companies in ways that have made it difficult to protect the technologies these firms develop or acquire, particularly when that technology is required for operations overseas.*

---

[308] Defense Human Resources Activity. Downloaded from http://www.dhra.mil/perserec/adr/counterintelligence/counterintelligenceframeset.htm

LISTING OF INDICATIONS OF INTELLIGENCE PENETRATION

The Cleave testimony also contains the following list of indicators of penetration and/or threat used to initiate investigation into the potential for such security breaches.[309]

INDICATORS OF RECRUITMENT [THE FOLLOWING INFORMATION IS A DIRECT QUOTE FROM THE CONGRESSIONAL TESTIMONY BY CLEAVE]

a. *Close association with an individual who is known or suspected to be associated with a foreign intelligence or security organization.*
b. *Being secretive about contact with any foreign national or visit to a foreign diplomatic facility.*
c. *Failure to report a personal relationship with any foreign national, in situations that require and expect reporting foreign contacts.*
d. *Failure to report an offer of financial assistance for self or family from a foreign national, other than close family.*
e. *Failure to report a request for classified or sensitive unclassified information by a foreign national or any other authorized person.*
f. *Unreported private employment or consulting relationship on the side, separate from one's regular job, with a foreign national or foreign organization.*
g. *Bragging about working for a foreign intelligence service or about selling U.S. technology (such statements should be taken seriously; they indicate at least that the individual is thinking about it, if not doing it).*

INDICATORS OF INFORMATION COLLECTION

a. *Accessing or attempting to access or download unauthorized information.*
b. *Conducting key word searches in a classified database on people, places, or topics about which the individual has no need-to-know.*
c. *Ordering classified or other protected documents or technical manuals not needed for official duties.*
d. *Unusual pattern of computer use (e.g., accessing files for which the individual has no need-to-know) shortly prior to foreign travel.*
e. *Asking others to obtain or facilitate access to classified or unclassified but sensitive information to which the individual does not have authorized access.*

---

[309]   Ibid.

f.   *Unusual inquisitiveness or questioning of coworkers about matters not within the scope of the individual's job or need-to-know.*

g.   *Obtaining or attempting to obtain a witness signature on a classified document destruction record when the witness did not observe the destruction.*

h.   *Copying protected information in other offices when copier equipment is available in the individual's own work area.*

i.   *Intentionally copying classified documents in a manner that covers or removes the classification markings.*

j.   *Extensive use of copy, facsimile, or computer equipment to reproduce classified, sensitive, or proprietary material that may exceed job requirements, especially if done when others are not present.*

k.   *Repeatedly working outside normal duty hours when this is not required and others are not in the office, or visiting classified work areas after normal hours for no logical reason.*

l.   *Repeated volunteering for assignments providing a different or higher access to classified or sensitive information.*

m.   *Bringing an unapproved camera, microphone, or recording device into a classified area.*

n.   *Unauthorized monitoring of electronic communications.*

o.   *Illegal or unauthorized entry into any information technology system.*

p.   *Deliberately creating or allowing any unauthorized entry point or other system vulnerability in an information technology system.*

INDICATORS OF INFORMATION TRANSMITTAL

a.   *Unauthorized removal or attempts to remove classified, export-controlled, proprietary or other protected material from the work area.*

b.   *Storing classified material at home or any other unauthorized place.*

c.   *Taking classified materials home or on trips, purportedly for work reasons, without proper authorization.*

d.   *Retention of classified, export-controlled, proprietary, or other sensitive information obtained at a previous employment without the authorization or the knowledge of that employer.*

e.   *Providing classified or sensitive but unclassified information, including proprietary information, outside official channels to any foreign national or anyone else without authorization or need-to-know.*

f.   *Regularly exchanging information with a foreigner, especially work-related information, whether or not the known information is sensitive.*

g.   *Putting classified information in one's desk or briefcase.*

h.   *Downloading classified material to an unclassified computer or storage device.*

i.   *Communicating electronically or using the Internet in a manner intended to conceal one's identity, e.g., use of "anonymizer" software on one's home computer or use of public computer services at a public library or Internet Café.*

j.   *Excessive and/or unexplained use of e-mail or fax.*

k.   *Short trips to foreign countries or within the United States to cities with foreign diplomatic facilities for unusual or unexplained reasons, or that are inconsistent with one's apparent interests and financial means. This includes a pattern of weekend travel not associated with recreation or family.*

l.   *More than one trip during a two-year period to a country where one has no relatives, no business purpose for the travel, and where the country is not a common location for an annual vacation.*

m.   *Hesitancy or inability by traveler to describe the location reportedly visited.*

n.   *Any attempt to conceal foreign travel.*

o.   *Foreign travel with costs out of proportion to time spent at the foreign location.*

p.   *Frequent foreign travel with costs above the individual's means.*

q.   *Foreign travel not reflected in the individual's passport to countries where entries would normally be stamped.*

r.   *Maintaining ongoing personal contact, without prior approval, with diplomatic or other representatives from countries with which one has ethnic, religious, cultural or other emotional ties or obligations, or with employees of competing companies in those countries.*

s.   *Recurring communication with a person or persons in a foreign country that cannot be explained by known family, work, or other known ties.*

t.   *Illegal or suspicious acquisition, sale, or shipment of sensitive technology.*

u.   *Purchase of high quality international or ham radio-band equipment by other than a known hobbyist.*

INDICATORS OF ILLEGAL INCOME

a.   *Sudden, unusual ability to purchase high-value items, such as real estate, stocks, vehicles, or foreign travel when the source of income for such purchases is unexplained or questionable.*

b.   *When asked about source of money, joking or bragging about working for a foreign intelligence service or having a mysterious source of income.*

c. *Implausible attempts to explain wealth by vague references to some successful business venture, luck in gambling, or an unexplained inheritance; also more explicit explanations of extra income that do not check out when investigated.*

d. *Living style and assets out of line with the individual's known income, especially if this has been preceded by signs of financial distress such as delinquencies or bankruptcy.*

e. *A sudden change in spending habits (e.g., picking up the bar bill for everyone, buying new and expensive clothes, giving expensive jewelry to a girlfriend) all with vague explanation of the source of funds.*

f. *Sudden reversal of a bad financial situation, as shown by repayment of large debts or loans with no credible explanation of the source of funds.*

g. *Extensive or regular gambling losses that do not appear to affect lifestyle or spending habits.*

h. *Display of expensive purchases or large amount of cash shortly after return from leave, especially if the leave involved foreign travel.*

i. *Foreign bank or brokerage account with substantial sums of money, but with no credible explanation for the source of this money or no logical need to maintain funds outside the U.S.*

j. *Large deposits to bank accounts when there is no logical source of income.*

k. *Unexplained receipt of significant funds from outside the U.S.*

l. *Moving funds into or out of the U.S. in amounts or circumstances that are inconsistent with normal business or personal needs. Includes deposit of large sums shortly after return from foreign travel.*

m. *Large currency transactions as noted in Financial Crimes Enforcement Network (FinCEN) reports, unless the transaction was done for one's employer or a volunteer civic organization in which the individual is active.*

n. *Carrying large amounts of cash, when this is inconsistent with normal cash needs or known financial resources.* [end of quote]

INDICATORS OF TERRORIST ACTIVITY

Although a terrorist might also steal information like a spy, the typical terrorist engages in planning, preparing, supporting, or executing some violent action, usually for some political or noncriminal reason or goal. The behaviors that might indicate or reveal terrorist preparations are quite different from those of a spy. Alert employees who recognize and report these clues play a significant role in helping to protect against terrorist attacks and other subversive activities. The following potential indicators show suspicion that an individual may be involved in or planning a terrorist attack. [start of quote from testimony]

a. *Talking knowingly about a future terrorist event, as though the person has inside information about what is going to happen.*

b. *Statement of intent to commit or threatening to commit a terrorist act, whether serious or supposedly as a "joke," and regardless of whether or not it seems likely that the person intends to carry out the action. All threats must be taken seriously.*

c. *Statements about having a bomb or biological or chemical weapon, about having or getting the materials to make such a device, or about learning how to make or use any such device—when this is unrelated to the person's job duties.*

d. *Handling, storing, or tracking hazardous materials in a manner that deliberately puts these materials at risk.*

e. *Collection of unclassified information that might be useful to someone planning a terrorist attack (e.g., pipeline locations, airport control procedures, building plans, etc.) when this is unrelated to the person's job or other known interests.*

f. *Physical surveillance (e.g., photography, videotaping, taking notes on patterns of activity at various times) of any site that is a potential target for terrorist attack. This includes, but is not limited to any building of symbolic importance to the government or economy, large public gathering, transportation center, bridge, power plant or line, communication center, etc.*

g. *Deliberate probing of security responses, such as deliberately causing a false alarm, faked accidental entry to an unauthorized area, or other suspicious activity designed to test security responses without prior authorization.*

h. *Possessing or seeking items that may be useful for a terrorist, but are inconsistent with the person's known hobbies or job requirements, such as explosives, uniforms (i.e., for use to pose as police officer, security guard, airline employee), high-powered weapons, books and literature on how to make explosive, biological, chemical, or nuclear devices.*

i. *Possession of multiple or fraudulent identification documents.* [end of quote]

INDICATORS OF SUPPORT FOR TERRORISM

As compared with espionage, which usually involves individuals working alone, a terrorist attack is frequently a group activity conducted by a small clandestine cell—often loosely associated with a larger network or organized group. Therefore, an individual's associates can indicate support for terrorism (e.g., certain public actions or Internet use, and/or expressed support for a terrorist ideology).

Any support or advocacy of terrorism, or association or sympathy with persons or organizations that are promoting or threatening the use of force or violence, is a concern, even if the individual is not directly involved in planning a terrorist attack. This is especially the case with any expression of militant jihadist ideology but can also include extremist groups. Indicators include the following: [start of quote from Cleave testimony]

    a.   *Membership in, or attempt to conceal membership in, any group which: (1) advocates the use of force or violence to achieve political goals, (2) has been identified as a front group for foreign interests, or (3) advocates loyalty to a foreign interest over loyalty to the U.S. government.*

    b.   *Distribution of publications prepared by a group or organization of the type described above.*

    c.   *Pro-terrorist statements in e-mail or chat rooms, blogs, or elsewhere on the Web. Frequent viewing of websites that promote extremist or violent activity, unless this is part of one's job or academic study.*

    d.   *Financial contribution to a charity or other foreign cause linked to support for a terrorist organization.*

    e.   *Unexplained or inadequately explained travel to an area associated with terrorism or U.S. military action.*

    f.   *Statements of support for the militant jihadist ideology of holy war against the West, such as:*

        1.   *Militant jihad against the West is a religious duty before God and, therefore, necessary for the salvation of one's soul. Peaceful existence with the West is a dangerous illusion. Only two camps exist. There can be no middle ground in an apocalyptic showdown between Islam and the forces of evil.*

        2.   *The separation of church and state is a sin. Democratic laws are illegitimate and sinful, because they are "man-made" laws expressing the will of the electorate rather than God. The only true law is Sharia, the law sent down by God, which governs not only religious rituals but many aspects of day-to-day life.*

        3.   *Muslim governments that cooperate with the West and that have not imposed Sharia law are religiously unacceptable and must be violently overthrown.*

    g.   *Statements of support for suicide bombers, even though they kill innocent bystanders.*

    h.   *Statements of support for violence against U.S. military forces, either at home or deployed abroad.*

i. *Statements of belief that the U.S. government is engaged in a crusade against Islam.*

j. *For U.S. military personnel only: Any action that advises, counsels, urges, or in any manner causes or attempts to cause insubordination, disloyalty, mutiny, or refusal of duty by any member of the armed forces of the U.S.*

k. *Other Behavioral Indicators*

1. *Reporting by any knowledgeable source that an individual may be engaged in espionage or terrorist activities.*

2. *Attempt to conceal any activity covered by one of the other counterintelligence indicators.*

3. *Behavior indicating concern over being investigated or watched, such as actions to detect physical surveillance, searching for listening devices or cameras, and leaving "traps" to detect search of the individual's work area or home.*

4. *Misrepresenting or failing to report use of an alias and/or multiple identities; possession of false identity documents without valid explanation.*

5. *Attempts to place others under obligation through special treatment, favors, gifts, money, or other means.*

6. *Avoiding or declining an assignment that would require a counterintelligence polygraph.*

7. *Withdrawing an application for a security clearance, or resigning from employment, in order to avoid a polygraph examination or other investigative interview.* [end of quote]

RISKS IN PERSONNEL TERRAIN SECURITY DECISIONS

The DHRA website referenced in footnote 308 above also provides a reference source for agency risks when evaluating the possibility of a threat from an individual within the organization or someone attempting to gain a position or increased access to an organization. They list the following two significant issues faced when addressing this requirement:[310]

a. *First, there are practical limits on the number of questions that can be asked during a standard personnel security subject interview, but an almost unlimited number of questions that might be relevant under various combinations of circumstances.*

---

[310] Ibid.

b. *Second, there are practical limits to the amount of counterintelligence knowledge and expertise that can be expected from the average personnel security investigator or adjudicator.*

The Constitution of the United States of America establishes the limits associated with making such interrogation decisions. Associated laws for the interaction of authorities and individuals further define the terms, whether the authorities are intelligence agencies, law enforcement, or corporate security organs. In many cases, the corporate security functions are easier, as a security official may resolve the problem simply by removing the individual under suspicion from employment with the firm without criminal or civil legal action. The situation must always include experts in legal, human resources, financial, and security functions in cooperation and in strict adherence to applicable policy, regulation, and law.

SECTION 3

SECURITY PLANNING
AND MANAGEMENT

Chapter 10

INFORMATION EVALUATION

The term *information evaluation* covers a multitude of sins, ranging from common data input and construction to detailed modeling, simulation, and calculated assessment of facts obtained through stringent academic study and experimentation. It is vital to establish the specific definitions for each of the possible and appropriate levels of the process.

INFORMATION PROCESSING TYPES AND DEFINITIONS

KINDS OF EVALUATION

The National Science Foundation (NSF) identifies the following kinds of evaluation for information processing:

a. Formative Evaluation
b. Summative Evaluation

FORMATIVE EVALUATION

Most dictionaries provide a business or project definition of *formative evaluation*, for example:

a. *Webster's*: A method of judging the worth of a program while the program activities are forming or happening; focuses on the process
b. *Free Dictionary*: Formative evaluation is a type of evaluation which has the purpose of improving programs.

Popham defines *formative evaluation* as "an adjective indicating that whatever noun it modifies is capable of alteration by growth and development."[311] This definition derives from a paper Popham wrote for a seminar on how to evaluate educational programs. The final structure for this paper's definition was: "An assessment is formative to the extent that information from the assessment is used, during the instructional segment in which the assessment occurred, to adjust instruction with the intent of better meeting the needs of the students assessed [*sic*]."[312]

Given the Popham, *Webster's*, and *Free Dictionary* definitions, and for the purpose of this text, an appropriate position on what formative evaluation is may be as follows:

> *Formative evaluation is the use of data to initiate, define, and develop information leading to potential conclusions concerning the existence, negation, and/or determination of effectiveness of programs against an identified threat or potential threat.*

SUMMATIVE EVALUATION

Popham defines *summative evaluation* as "an appraisal of the worth or merit of a mature, essentially final version educational program."[313] The NSF provides the following figure, depicting the relationship between formative and summative evaluation.

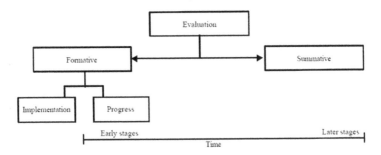

Figure 66: Kinds of Evaluation[314]

---

[311] Popham, W.J. (2006). *Defining and Enhancing Formative Assessment. UCLA.* Pg. 2.

[312] Ibid. pg 3-4.

[313] Ibid. pg 2.

[314] National Science Foundation. (2002). *Evaluation and Types of Evaluation.* Downloaded from http://www.nsf.gov/pubs/2002/nsf02057/nsf02057_2.pdf. pg 8.

TYPES OF EVALUATIONS

As to the types of evaluations, subsets of the kinds of evaluations, what is included depends upon the author. Examination for this text resulted in accepting four major types of evaluations listed below. Establishing a type of evaluation does not indicate the how of the evaluation, only what the ultimate driver(s) for the product(s) is/are.

a. Goal-based evaluation
b. Goal-free evaluation
c. Criteria-based evaluation
d. Mixed-method evaluation

GOAL-BASED EVALUATION

Per Scriven, a goal-based evaluation is "any type of evaluation based on and knowledge of—and referenced to—the goals and objectives of the program, person, or product."[315] A goal-based evaluation involves the extent to which something is meeting predetermined goals or objectives. This is primarily useful in the estimation of the information's ability to fit the situation enough to result in appropriate and accurate conclusions. The design of the evaluation determines both progress toward and achievement of a specific set of goals.

GOAL-FREE EVALUATION

Goal-free evaluation is the opposite of goal-based evaluation. The evaluation takes place without knowledge of the actual goals of the program and focuses on whatever the data actually shows. The strength of this method of evaluation is also its weakness: that one does not relate the information to a specific set of criteria.

CRITERIA-BASED EVALUATION

The *Business Dictionary* begins the definition of *criteria-based evaluation* by defining criterions. A criterion is a benchmark, standard, or yardstick against which accomplishment, conformance, performance, and suitability of an individual, alternative, activity, product, or plan, as well as of risk-reward ratio, measure. The difference between this form and goal-based evaluation is that

---

[315] Scriven, M.S. (1967). The Methodology of Evaluation, in Tyler, R., Gagne, R., and Scriven, M. (eds). *Perspectives of Curriculum Evaluation, (AERA Monograph Series on Curriculum Evaluation)*.Chicago, Il. Rand McNally.

criteria-based evaluation uses measurement elements not based in the organization, that is, they are not specific to a particular organization.

Mixed-Method Evaluation

Mixed-method evaluation basically takes one or more methods and combines their strengths. For example, a security official may evaluate the same data against organization goals to determine how well the process works to achieve these goals, then against benchmarking data to place a ranking with other similar organizations.

Data Development

As there are four main types of evaluation, there are three primary methods of data acquisition:

a. Qualitative
b. Quantitative
c. Mixed Method

Qualitative Methodology

Qualitative research is also known as secondary research. The researcher is not conducting baseline experimentation to develop previously nonexistent data. Instead, they are reviewing the reports, papers, photos, and conclusions of others to glean knowledge rather than developing this from scratch. Additionally, qualitative research focuses primarily on words, pictures, and artifacts as evidence toward a conclusion. A prime example of this type of research is when an individual writes a paper for a college class. The student examines information from a variety of sources and uses their findings to generate supportive conclusions.

Quantitative Methodology

Quantitative research is primary research, as the information gathered generally originates in the process or at least refines to a new degree and/ or methodology for use by the researcher. The quantitative methodology also primarily derives from an experimentation process, usually leading to numerical data, such as specific numbers or statistical values.

Mixed Methodology

A mixed methodology is some combination of quantitative and qualitative methods. The chart in Figure 67 below depicts some of the differences between the two methodologies.

Qualitative	Quantitative
The aim is a complete, detailed description.	The aim is to classify features, count them, and construct statistical models in an attempt to explain what is observed.
Researcher may only know roughly in advance what he/she is looking for.	Researcher knows clearly in advance what he/she is looking for.
Recommended during earlier phases of research projects.	Recommended during latter phases of research projects.
The design emerges as the study unfolds.	All aspects of the study are carefully designed before data is collected.
Researcher is the data gathering instrument.	Researcher uses tools, such as questionnaires or equipment to collect numerical data.
Data is in the form of words, pictures or objects.	Data is in the form of numbers and statistics.
Subjective - individuals interpretation of events is important ,e.g., uses participant observation, in-depth interviews etc.	Objective seeks precise measurement & analysis of target concepts, e.g., uses surveys, questionnaires etc.
Qualitative data is more 'rich', time consuming, and less able to be generalized.	Quantitative data is more efficient, able to test hypotheses, but may miss contextual detail.
Researcher tends to become subjectively immersed in the subject matter.	Researcher tends to remain objectively separated from the subject matter.

Figure 67: Qualitative vice Quantitative Methodologies

The Analytical Process

The most important element of performing any analysis is framing the appropriate question. Psychologically, the establishment of the appropriate question creates the links and expectations of the mind to the achievement of a solution to that specific task. In a commencement speech, Harvard Premier Business Professor Clayton Christensen stated,

> As I participated in the class discussions I would keep noting what questions led to the important insights. I would add them to my list and use them to prepare the next day's case. Sometimes I'd find that a question that had been useful for a specific case rarely was useful on others, so I'd cross it off my list. Over the course of the semester I iterated towards my custom method for thinking through each

category of problem. The valuable skill, I realized, was to ask the right question. That done, getting the right answer was typically quite straightforward.[316]

A text by Palepu, Healy, and Bernard provides an example of the analytical process in which several individuals examine a single corporate financial statement. These individuals, based upon their focus, ask quite different questions, which the single financial statement can provide the data to answer. The following are some of the question types based on the focus of the individuals:

a. A security analyst may be interested in asking, "How well is the firm I am following performing? Did the firm meet my performance expectations? If not, why not? What is the value of the firm's stock given my assessment of the firm's current and future performance?"

b. A loan officer may ask, "What is the credit risk involved in lending a certain amount of money to this firm? How well is the firm managing its liquidity and solvency? What is the firm's business risk? What is the additional risk created by the firm's financing and dividend policies?"

c. A management consultant might ask, "What is the structure of the industry in which the firm operates? What are the strategies pursued by various players in the industry? What is the relative performance of different firms in the industry?"

d. A corporate manager may ask, "Is my firm properly valued by investors? Is our investor communication program adequate to facilitate this process?"

e. A [competing] corporate manager could ask, "Is this firm a potential takeover target? How much value can be added if we acquire this firm? How can we finance the acquisition?"

f. An independent auditor would want to ask, "Are the accounting policies and accrual estimates in this company's financial statements consistent with my understanding of this business and its recent performance? Do these financial reports communicate the current status and significant risks of the business?"[317]

---

[316] Christensen, C.M. (2009). *The Importance of Asking the Right Questions.* Southern New Hampshire University Commencement Speech. Obtained from http://www.claytonchristensen.com/documents/SNHUCommencementtalk-DemocracyCapitalismandReligion.pdf

[317] Palepu, K.G., Healy, P.M., and Bernard, V.I. (2004). *Business Analysis and Valuation: Using Financial Statements, 3e.* Thompson Learning. Mason, Ohio. Pg. 1-1.

Notice that each person's question focuses on different elements of knowledge. Thus, the structure of the approach needs to be different, yet each is performing a qualitative (i.e., the data already exists) analysis.

The questioning is just as important, yet slightly different, when performing a quantitative analysis. Most researchers, to achieve their goals, use the scientific method, as seen in Figure 68, to establish and structure quantitative analysis studies. In business and military organizations, this process is known as operations research (OR). Dominique Heger of Fortuitous Technology defines OR:

> The term Operations Research (OR) describes the discipline that is focused on the application of information technology for informed decision-making. In other words, OR represents the study of optimal resource allocation. The goal of OR is to provide rational bases for decision making by seeking to understand and structure complex situations, and to utilize this understanding to predict system behavior and improve system performance. Much of the actual work is conducted by using analytical and numerical techniques to develop and manipulate mathematical models of organizational systems that are composed of people, machines, and procedures.[318]

Hillier and Lieberman add to this understanding of OR in the following statement:

> The "research" part of the name means that operations research uses an approach that resembles the way research is conducted in established scientific fields. To a considerable extent, the "scientific method" is used to investigate the problem of concern. (In fact, the term "management science" sometimes is used as a synonym for operations research.) In particular, the process begins by carefully observing and formulating the problem, including gathering all relevant data. The next step is to construct a scientific (typically mathematical) model that attempts to abstract the essence of the real problem. It is then hypothesized that this model is a sufficiently precise representation of the essential features of the situation that the conclusions (solutions) obtained from the model are also valid for the real problem. Next, suitable experiments are conducted to test this hypothesis, modify

---

[318] Heger, C. *An Introduction to Operations Research—Benefits, Methods & Application.* Downloaded from http://fortuitous.com/docs/primers/OR-intro.pdf on December 5, 2011.

it (or the model) a needed, and eventually verify some form of the hypothesis.[319]

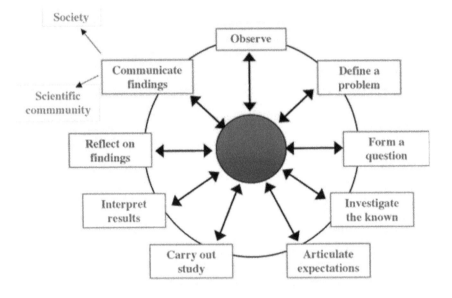

Redrawn from "A Scientific Method Based on Research Scientists' Conceptions of Scientific Inquiry," R. Reiff, W. S. Harwood, T. Phillipson. Proceedings of the 2002 Annual International Conference of the Association for the Education of Teachers in Science.

Figure 68: The Scientific Method[320]

Thoughts of the scientific method can bring to mind a lengthy study involving laboratories, computer models, test tubes, and researchers in lab coats. Yet the majority of humans use this process to assist in daily decision making. The scientific method is the appropriate avenue for information evaluation, though there are those who support other methods of structured thought as either more appropriate or in other ways superior to this processes. For the purpose of this text, the focus will remain on the scientific approach. The point is to use logical analysis.

The challenge in performing information analysis is that it is a word problem from start to finish. It is never as simple as 1 + 1 = 2. Most texts provide the student with a series of steps stating to proceed from questioning to gathering data

---

[319]   Hillier F., and Lieberman G. (2001). *Introduction to Operations Research.* McGraw-Hill. New York, NY. Pg. 2,3.

[320]   Downloaded from http://cires.colorado.edu/education/outreach/rescipe/collection/ inquirystandards.html

to analyzing the data to a conclusion. This is a circular argument in that it states that in order to analyze information, one must perform an analysis, placing the analyst right back where they started, even if the process is exactly that.

Take, for example, the interactions during a criminal trial between a witness on the stand and the defense attorney. The witness performs an information analysis while undergoing a line of questioning by the defense attorney. This information analysis occurs over the course of only a few minutes during courtroom testimony, as the witness is not previously prepared for the line of questioning the defense attorney presents.

The defense attorney asks a series of questions designed to discredit the witness. As the questioning continues, this goal becomes apparent to the witness—this is the observation piece of the scientific method. In response, the witness generates several hypotheses:

H_0: The attorney is not going to a specific point. He is simply asking questions to clarify the situation observed.[321]

H_1: The attorney is attempting to call into question the testimony data, as related to either the timing or ability of the witness to gain information from these data.

H_2: The attorney is attempting to call into question the ability of the witness to logically conclude that the observed data, in fact, leads to the conclusions made by the witness, thus biasing the testimony in an attempt to have it removed from consideration during the trial.

Having mentally formed these three hypotheses, the witness continues to observe the defense attorney's approach, questions, and the responses of the jury at each point of the questioning. The witness rejects H_0, as the attorney would very likely not waste time on asking questions that would not help to his client, nor would the questions involved be viewed favorably by the judge and/or jury. This leaves only H_1 or H_2 as possible hypothesis options.

The witness asks himself several questions concerning the possible lines of logic for each remaining hypothesis. The syllogism for the first (H_1) is as follows:

If the attorney's goal is to prove that the author was not in the proper position to view the crime or was not present at the time of the crime, the questions would center on where the witness stood at a given time, what direction he faced, when he turned to look toward the location/scene of the crime, etc. These were not the types of questions asked. Rather, the attorney asked,

---

[321] NOTE: the 'H' stands for 'Hypothesis.' The zero (0) is used to represent the 'Null Hypothesis.' The null hypothesis that of all observations or data sets, there will be no perceivable difference. All other hypotheses are numbered in order of their development with no specificity to rank or probability of truth.

a. Did you see the defendant holding the weapon identified as the assault weapon?
b. Had the weapon been fired?
c. How were you able to determine that the weapon was fired?
d. Have you ever performed a forensic analysis on either a weapon or victim in the past?

These questions tended to support H_2, which stated the defense attorney was attempting to demonstrate a lack of expertise or capability on the part of the witness's knowledge of weapons.

With this hypothesis in mind, the witness considers several possibilities of action:

a. Allow the questioning to continue in this vein and hope that the jury sees through to the attorney's intended conclusion and that this conclusion is not in line with the facts of the case.
b. Become angry with the attorney and accuse him of trying to use the present line of questioning for discrediting purposes.
c. Simply stop answering the questions, at which point the judge would likely direct the witness to answer or be in contempt of court.

Given these possible steps, the witness runs through a mental experiment to quickly determine the likely outcome for each response to the attorney's line of questioning. For (a), the witness considers how the jury was likely selected by the attorneys to seat individuals who may be open to suggestion, as this is the ideal kind of jury during a trial, enabling the attorneys to convince individuals, even to the point of manipulation of the correctness of their side's argument.

The witness immediately rejects the possible step (b), as confrontation would likely play into the hands of the attorney, making the witness seem emotionally uncontrolled. To a jury, such a witness seems irrational and emotional, incapable of making impartial observations of the crime in question.

Option (c) appears the best possible choice in the witness's observations, but it also comes with certain cautions. The primary consideration is that the witness has sworn before the court and God to provide truthful testimony. Refusing to answer could result in a charge of contempt of court, and the resulting impression on the jury would match that of option (b), discrediting the witness.

Considering this, the witness concludes that a contempt of court charge is a threat to his safety and freedom, as he appears to be in a situation where if he is forced to either answer or refuse to answer, neither option resulting in the full truth he was sworn to provide, due to the attorney's pointed line of questioning. As the witness was sworn to tell "the truth, the whole truth, and nothing but the truth," it was likely his best option to claim that the answer solicited by the defense attorney would result in a violation of the oath.

This conclusion provides a new hypothesis (H_4), requiring a follow-up mental experiment to determine possible outcomes. The result of this analysis is that the witness must phrase his answer in such a way to involve the judge in the adjudication of the legal standing—which is the role of the judge. If the witness provides the judge with a viable legal argument to support the conclusion that the witness cannot answer the final question in compliance with the oath, the judge will have to intervene between the witness and the attorney.

Thus, the witness chooses, as his answer, to invoke his rights under the Fifth Amendment to the Constitution. This immediately gains the judge's, the attorney's, and the jury's attention, as directed to the specific line of questioning. By invoking the Fifth Amendment in this way, the judge is prompted to ask, as the witness expects: "Why do you feel you are in danger of incriminating yourself?" The witness now can answer as he feels will best represent his knowledge of the situation at hand.

The witness is able to state his awareness of the attorney's tactics, which would result in an incomplete representation to the jury. He continues that he can make no answer without sounding either ignorant or dishonest. The witness hopes to communicate several things to the judge, the jury, and the attorneys present:

a. The witness is neither naïve nor incompetent.
b. The witness is capable of observing conditions rapidly and correctly in forming an appropriate course of action to this critical situation.
c. The witness is not easily manipulated and therefore is likely being fully truthful.
d. Further questioning along the attorney's current line will likely result in the witnesses continued invoking of his Fifth Amendment rights. The desired response will either not be obtained or be answered in a manner detrimental to the defense's client (thus confirming option c of refusing to answer any further questions without being shown as combative or incompetent).[322]

Given the above example, the student can perform a quick analysis, return to the diagram of the scientific methodology in Figure 68, and determine if the case study just presented followed that process.

---

[322] Granted, using the word 'Duh!' is not of high academic quality; however it DOES convey a very appropriate message concerning the impact the study had on many very intelligent and detailed-oriented engineers.

ANALYSIS OF INFORMATION IN THE BUSINESS WORLD

The information evaluation analytical process need not involve massive amounts of data, detailed mathematical models, computer processing equipment, and extensive experimentation. But that does not mean the security professional should ignore these tools when needed. For example, a study conducted for a major aircraft manufacturer and given to the U.S. Army involved just such methods leading to what many advanced analysts stated was a "Duh!" solution, yet one that none of these individuals ever considered.

The goal of the study was to conduct a parametric comparison of several particular drone aircraft in a combat situation.[323] With the question properly defined, the team conducted data gathering, constructed the mathematical model, built the computer model, and then ran over one hundred iterations of the study. When the team collected the output data (an important step in quantitative analysis) to determine results, they found a single salient factor suddenly from all of the other parametric items under consideration. The drone model preferred by the army constantly crashed for no apparent reason. This was, of course, a critical observation.

The analysts began to reduce the variables to determine the cause of the constant aircraft failure, removing maintenance issues, enemy fire (there was none), weather factors, etc. As the team was scratching their heads, one analyst joked, "Maybe it's simply running out of gas." This joke led to an epiphany, as the one aircraft was indeed running out of gasoline.

The computer model in use included a feature where, as the analyst added equipment to an aircraft that increased its weight, other less essential items were reduced automatically. One of those items was fuel load. The model design anticipated that the human operators would realize that the aircraft needed additional refuel points if they increased the weight beyond current fuel-carrying capacity. The analysts had not designed the model, however, and did not know about this built-in feature until data review.

ANALYTICAL METHODS (LOGIC)

There are basically two major forms of analytical logic: inductive and deductive. Inductive logic begins with a set of cases or observations, and a

---

[323] NOTE: A parametric comparison or analysis is one where a specific set of items inherent to the object under study receive focus. For example, selecting a proper hair grooming item (comb or brush) would involve looking at the value of teeth over bristles, separation of the teeth/bristles; size (pocket or larger), and likely fit to one's hand. These are the 'parameters' used to make a decision.

conclusion of what caused the observations is made. Inductive logic, or reasoning, does not use the syllogistic method discussed earlier. An individual uses inductive logic when generating hypotheses, formulating theories, and discovering relationships, and it is essential for scientific discovery. Deductive logic is the exact opposite of inductive. In deductive logic, the individual begins with a logically constructed set of prepositions to form a conclusion that derives from the set of premises. For the conclusion to be true and valid, the premises must also be true and valid.

Inductive Reasoning

The following figure shows a test that demonstrates the process of inductive reasoning.[324]

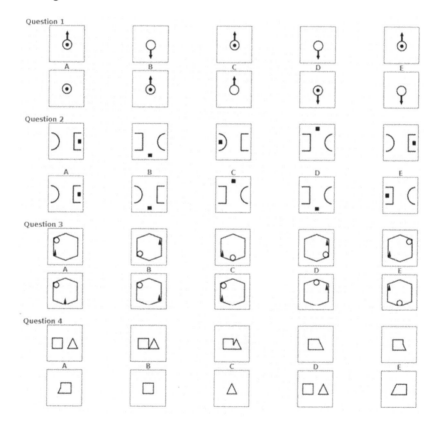

Figure 69: Inductive Logic/Reasoning Test

---

[324] Original is found at www.shl.com

In the above test, the student is instructed to select from the second row of boxes marked with the letters *A* through *E* the box that logically extends the progression of the question row immediately above. To perform this task successfully, the student must examine each individual block to determine what is happening to the various shapes (an observation set). This observation set establishes a pattern that the student uses to complete the next most logical step to the pattern. Is the answer correctly identifying the actual next event? Not really, as the next event may be totally different. Yet from the logic, it is the most likely of the possible next steps.

Answers:

Row 1: The next most likely box is E. Notice that the boxes are toggling between the *circle-dot-up arrow* and the *circle-no-dot-down arrow*. As the last test box is the *circle-dot-up arrow*, the next most logical choice is the *circle-no-dot-down arrow*.

Row 2: Here, both the dot and the shapes are changing position. The dot is moving in a clockwise pattern around the enclosing square. The shapes are exchanging positions with each other. As the final test box has the dot inside the half box, its next position will most likely be at the bottom center of the enclosing square. The half box and the half circle will most likely exchange places in the next iteration. The next most likely answer is D.

Row 3: This one is a bit more difficult, yet also easier, as neither the enclosing square nor the hexagon within the square is changing. The two symbols (black dot and small circle), however, are changing in a precise pattern. The dot is moving from lower left to upper right in a repeating fashion. The circle is moving from one hexagon angle to the next in line in a counterclockwise rotation. The most likely next positions are for the dot to return to the upper right position and the circle to progress to the 12:00 or top center hexagon angle. The most likely next answer then is D.

Row 4: In this question, there is a square and a triangle within the enclosing square. The two shapes are merging with the triangle moving into the square or rather behind it so that triangle is slowing disappearing. As the final box in the question shows the triangle nearly totally gone, the next most likely step places the triangle totally behind or merged with the square. The next most likely answer is B.

Take the test one step further and consider the next three steps of each question as practice. Remember, these are only *likely* answers, as the reality of the situation may completely change. For example, on the question in Row 4, what if the triangle, upon being hidden, was to change direction by ninety degrees? As a ninety change is a positive or clockwise directional change. As such, the next most likely picture would have the crown or point of the triangle emerging partially from the top of the square rather than have a part of the triangle side emerging from the left side of the square. Given that there is no information either supporting or denying this possibility, what is the probability of the next move?

The facts/observations are as follows:

a. The triangle has moved in the same direction for the previous five observations.

b. The sixth observation will most likely show the triangle continuing this direction for a total of six observations.

c. The seventh observation is unknown; however, there is a 6:7 probability that the right-to-left (westward) motion will continue or an 85 percent probability of continued motion to that direction.

d. There are potentially seven additional directions, limiting the set of possible directions to a manageable level, that the triangle can move:
   1. North
   2. South
   3. East (returning the way it came)
   4. Northwest
   5. Northeast
   6. Southwest
   7. Southeast

e. For the remaining 15 percent of the probability set, the probability—all other things being equal—for this movement is 0.47 percent or less than half of a chance in fifteen that the triangle will move outside of its current path.

Notice that in this logic pathway, the caveat of "all other things being equal" provided a delimiter. There are simply too many potential variables to consider. During the course of the movement of the triangle, however, suppose there is a report that there is a round object one-tenth the size of the small square hidden somewhere behind the square. The student now knows that it is there, just not the specific orientation. The report also states that the circle is of sufficient density that it will cause the triangle to rebound, but not shatter, as both the triangle and the circle are of equal mass/density. How would such a report change the probabilities?

First, again using induction, we know that:

a. The size of the triangle makes it impossible to miss the circle once it goes behind the square

b. The observations 1 through 5 do *not* show any deviation in the path of the triangle as it goes behind the square, meaning that the circle cannot be in the right two quadrants of the square or as follows:

c. Thus, the only two possible areas for the circle are quadrants 1 and 3.

d. Given the above, *if* the circle is in quadrant 3, the rebound will make the triangle move, as shown below:

e. If, however, the circle is in quadrant 1, the rebound will be more pronounced, given the greater angle of the strike on a higher portion of the triangle, resulting in the following:

f. Also, now that the vector dynamics (direction of movement forces) are different between D and E, the triangle impacts the dot in D with most of its mass, causing a nearly opposite rebound. However, in E, the dot impact is in the least mass area, creating a fulcrum around which the momentum of the triangle distributes so that it continues forward, but in a modified angle and direction.

So what does this have to do with assessing security and intelligence information, the student may ask. Every observation made concerning a progressing activity will and must result in additional activity unless something occurs to change that progress. This is known as the law of inertia in physics. The *law of inertia* is defined as "an object at rest will stay at rest and an object in motion will stay in motion, unless some other influence causes it to change."

This is true in human activity, with the caveat that the object itself (the human) has the ability to make the energy change through individual will. Once a course of action is decided upon, however, it will generally have a mass and inertia of its own, depending upon the size (energy) of the body performing it. The ability of the security professional to logically deduce the most likely course of action will aid them in meeting threats head-on or potentially prior to implementation.

Take the example of a football play. The players of the offense huddle to decide their course of action. They do this so that all members of the squad know how the leader expects them to perform, when, where, and in what manner. They will only deviate from this course of action if the defending squad performs in a way *not* anticipated by the defensive captain. Most squads in such an event have predetermined safety plays that are subsets of the master play. This enables the leader (quarterback) to know what his teammates will do to achieve the objective of a successful play, given certain courses of action on the part of the opposing team. The larger the body of individuals involved, the more difficult it is to make a major change.

Another excellent example of this prepared action planning took place during WWII during the Battle of the Bulge in Europe. General Patton observed that there were certain events happening on the German side of the battle lines that did not match expectations. Specifically, Patton was nearing German territory and the resistance was reducing rather than increasing, as he expected from an army to protect the homeland. Patton, knowing that it simply was not recent German experience to launch a major winter offensive, deduced that the Germans were pulling forces off of the line to prepare for just this type of attack. With this in mind, several days before the Germans attacked in the Ardennes Forest,[325] Patton ordered his operations people to prepare a plan to rotate his army of some one hundred thousand soldiers and equipment from an eastward attack to a northwestward attack. As written in an official history of the war,

> The Third Army had to stop a full scale attack they had started to the east, pull back the entire army, swing around ninety degrees to the north, and then begin another full scale attack on the southern flank of the German forces. Nothing like that had ever been done in the history of warfare. Everyone thought it was impossible except General Patton. He knew his men could do the impossible.

> It only took three days for the Third army to perform that massive maneuver. Today, military historians readily admit that only Patton's Third Army could have accomplished a maneuver like that and make it look easy. Patton always demanded more from his soldiers than other commanders did and they never let him down.

---

[325] The Ardennes Forest attack became known as The Battle of the Bulge and was the last offensive action undertaken by the German army as they had simply exhausted any offensive capability with this action. From this point, it was only a matter of six months until all German resistance collapsed and the war in Europe ended.

One of the reasons the Third Army performed so well is because they expected the German attack. While Eisenhower and his friends were playing cards in London and the First Army turned part of their area into a R & R (Rest and Recuperation) area, Patton's intelligence officers were hard at work.

The events leading up to the Battle of the Bulge have, like the Falaise Gap and Operation Market-Garden, become controversial issues. Many people believe that Eisenhower's staff at SHAEF made poor decisions when they ignored Third Army reports about a possible German offensive in the Ardennes.

Colonel Oscar Koch, head of Third Army's G-2 Intelligence department, had sent intelligence reports warning SHAEF that the Germans were probably planning a major attack against the First Army's R&R area. His report was ignored. They refused to believe the Germans could collect the mass of weapons, men, and material to launch a large attack. It was a classic case of under-estimating the enemy. At Colonel Koch's suggestion, General Patton gave the order for his staff to design two separate plans in the event of a German attack. General Patton believed Colonel Koch and considered him to be the best G-2 in the European Theater of Operations.

When Patton attended the meeting with the other Allied commanders he told them he could attack in two days with at least two divisions. Everyone thought he was crazy, but he told them that he had already set plans in motion before he left his headquarters. All he had to [do] was place a phone call. When it was finally decided that he should attack as soon as possible, he phoned his headquarters and said, "Nickel." The attack was on.[326]

The difficulty lay not in making the decision of what to do, but in changing the direction of a mass of individuals, equipment, supplies, etc., without causing severe traffic tie-ups as combat units and logistics units strived to orient to a different pathway or route of advance.

---

[326] Province, C.M. *The Third Army in World War II*. Located at http://www.pattonhq.com/textfiles/thirdhst.html

DEDUCTIVE REASONING

Deductive reasoning is the process of creating an argument or developing a conclusion based on a progressive set of premises, moving from a general premise to more specific premises in logical order. Deductive reasoning is sometimes referred to as the "top-down" approach to making a decision. The following are a few examples of deductive reasoning:

All oranges are fruits.
All fruits grow on trees.
Therefore, all oranges grow on trees.

—or—

All bachelors are single.
Johnny is single.
Hence, Johnny is a bachelor.

Sometimes, an individual can establish deductive reasoning without the help of syllogisms, for example:

Every day, I go to work. This journey from my home to my office takes one hour. My office starts at eight o'clock in the morning. Therefore, if I leave my home at seven o'clock in the morning, I will reach the office on time.

Deductive reasoning is also a form of logic lending itself closely to mathematical concepts. It is the primary form of analysis used by the scientific method for this reason. As such, a complete process of analysis formed around this line of reasoning is known as operations research.

OPERATIONS RESEARCH/MANAGEMENT ANALYSIS

A primary goal of the security/intelligence professional is to ascertain when the collection and analysis techniques in use are not providing the information necessary to avoid critical situations. The point is to recognize such threats prior to a serious or catastrophic event. Once the event initiates, it is simply too late to preemptively counter it. Situations rarely occur without some buildup and/ or warning, however, which brings the security planner to the point of statistical analysis.

STATISTICAL ANALYSIS

"Statistical analysis involves the collection, examination, summarization, manipulation, and interpretation of quantitative data to discover underlying causes, patterns, relationships, and trends." (*Webster's*) A simpler definition is that the analyst uses the statistics to determine and separate the possible from the probable in both past and future events. The primary concept is that events of any kind are not random. There exist traceable aspects to the cause of events, which the analyst mathematically determines and then predicts with some measure of certainty. This is the probability of occurrence.

For example, take two six-sided game dice. An individual can roll the dice one thousand times and record the data into a graphical chart known as a scatter chart (Figure 70). The scatter chart is a representation of the results of the rolls over time. If the chart looks as if someone fired a shotgun at it, then you can be fairly certain that the dice are perfectly formed as the results will range from one to twelve in no discernible pattern. However, if the chart has a series of sevens or elevens much more often than any other number, it is now possible that the dice are either improperly balanced or deliberately "loaded" to produce a desired result.

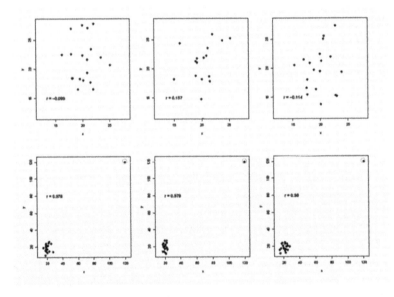

Figure 70: Scatter Chart Examples

Another example of statistical analysis is what is known as standard variation or the bell chart. In Figure 71, there is an example of a bell chart. For this instance, picture a rifle embedded in a stand of concrete, making the weapon immovable. The weapon is intricately sighted on a target exactly one hundred yards away. The rifle should, everything else being perfect, impact only the center of the target with each shot in exactly the same place, except that it doesn't. There are small variations in several influencing aspects: the wind, vibrations in the earth, movements from a passing vehicle, slight imperfections in the bullets, differences in the amount of powder within the cartridge, and many other factors between each shot.

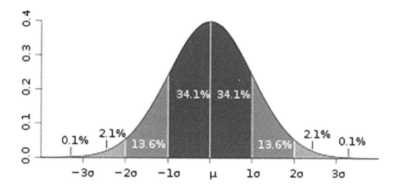

Figure 71: Bell Chart (Standard Variance Graphic)

These variances often occur due to the same kind of minor changes in how, for example, the cartridges were manufactured. The potential for this kind of variation is the basis for the different quality management programs in existence today. The purpose of these programs is not only to reduce the variations as much as possible but also to determine when things like a minor manufacturing inefficiency have become systemic. Taking the rifle-shot example, the majority of the shots will always impact within a specific grouping. That majority constitutes $\pm 1\sigma$ (plus or minus one sigma or standard deviation).[327] As shown in the chart, this constitutes 68.2 percent of the total sample of shots. A second deviation will comprise 95.4 percent of all the shots.

Such knowledge is very useful in statistical evaluation. It permits certain conclusions from various types and amounts of data, which either supports or rejects hypotheses within the boundaries of the collection methodology, the question(s) asked, and the assumptions made.

QUALITY CONTROL STATISTICS

The primary concern of management science is how a business operates and whether or not operations take place in the most efficient, profit-producing manner possible. The concept of quality management was discussed earlier and

---

[327] The sigma (σ) is mathematical notation for a standard deviation or change in the data flow.

mentioned inputs from such experts as Dr. W. E. D. Deming and Dr. I. Goldratt, among others in Chapter 4. Both of these individuals had heavy backgrounds in statistics and developed methodologies that used statistics to predict future events in such a way as to address these events prior to them becoming critical. Examination of this process would take a series of courses all their own. This text will focus on the primary aspects of random sampling and trend dynamics.

RANDOM SAMPLING

Sampling is actually far from random in the statistical world. This text includes random sampling as a topic for two reasons: (a) it is easier to understand and (b) the other forms of sampling require detailed statistical calculations that are unnecessary for this text. The first aspect of a sample process is to understand that a collection population of items is required. Those items need not be homogeneous—all of one "type" of thing—however, having it so makes drawing conclusions from the sample easier.

For example, consider a manager of an automobile production plant in charge of the manufacturing and quality control of pistons. A piston is an integral element in the construction of an engine. The piston *must* be of specific size, density of metal, shape, etc. For the purpose of this example, the text will only consider size.

This particular shop manufactures pistons having a circumference of 100 mm $\pm$ .001 mm. This means that in order to fit into the engine block and function properly, the piston cannot be more than 100.001 mm nor less than 99.999 mm in circumference. Anything more and the piston cannot be placed into the cylinder of the engine block. Anything less and the piston will not compress the fuel/air mix properly for sufficient power to drive the engine, as most of the mixture will seep around the sides of the piston.

The manager's shop produces one hundred thousand pistons per day and must ensure that all of the pistons are within specification, or else he must reject the shipment. The manager has a 0.1 percent reject rate allowed per day. The question is, does the manager sit down or hire enough people to physically measure each and every piston to determine if they are within specifications? The answer is no because (a) it is too costly, (b) it takes too much time, and (c) such a process is unfeasible. So the manager, being a good analyst, knows that a sampling of 10 percent of the pistons will create a probability of 96 percent that all of the pistons in the population are within specification if the 10 percent are found to be within specification.

The pistons are shipped out in separate shipping boxes from eight different production lines. So out of each box, the inspector selects a number of pistons for testing from a random location. Each piston is chosen by pressing a button on a random-number-generating device, and the piston with that number is the one

278

pulled for inspection. The inspector uses the chart found in Figure 72 to plot the test results.

Figure 72: Quality Sampling Chart

In the chart, UCL means the upper control limit. This is the highest level of specification. Anything above this line must be rejected. LCL is the lower control limit. The items that test out smaller than this number must also be rejected. The "X" is the goal "mean" or midline target. Figure 73 shows the results of a set of pulled piston samples.

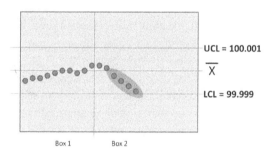

Figure 73: Production Run Samples

Notice that all of the measures are within specification. However, in box 2, there is a disturbing trend showing. Each production machine has variances similar to the earlier example of shots from a concrete-encased rifle. This is simply part of the environment and the machining process. Rises and drops in the measurements are expected. When the inspector sees a situation similar to the one highlighted above, however, it is a red flag. The chart indicates that something is causing the machining process to trend toward producing pistons that will be too small to use, thus unsellable to the customer.

At this point, the manager halts production on that particular line and inspects both the equipment and the workers to find the root of the potential problem before it causes production losses. Upon finding the fault, the manager has it corrected, the line restarted, and production monitored closely to ensure the efficacy of the repair.

The change in the piston circumference from the previous example is termed an "indicator." Analysts use indicators in many different areas, to include intelligence, personnel management, financial management, and just about everything else in the business and government worlds. An indicator is simply a data point that provides potential evidence of a noteworthy occurrence. The definition of the indictor gives value and meaning to the results of a selection of samples, such as those shown in the bell curve from Figure 71.

> **The definition of the indicator is what gives value and meaning to the results of the sample.**

As another example more directly related to security planning, change the definition of the indicator from piston circumference to the number of people visiting a particular important location in a contested area in Afghanistan per minute. Then rather than a box of pistons, group the number of people per minute by the day they visit the site. Now looking back at the Figure 74 findings, with these new label parameters, if the decrease in data trends on a standard business day—and all previous days do not show any such drop in numbers—what does this tell the analyst? It may be an indicator of an approaching event, such as an attack by the insurgency, that the local population is aware of and beginning to avoid.

METRICS

Indicators are simply items of interest, and while the definition is what gives value and meaning to the results of the sampling, it is the sampling that tells a story leading to a conclusion. Metrics are simply a set of measurements. The question becomes how does one develop indicators and metrics? An example process appears in Figure 74. The information/labels in the smaller boxes do not matter as they are expanded upon in later figures. What is important is the format and linkages of the various steps within the process.

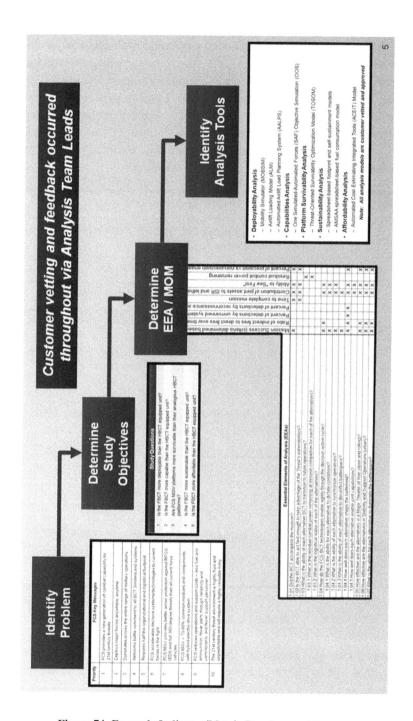

Figure 74: Example Indicator/Metric Development Process

The first step of this process involves the development of the problem or rather determining the right question(s) associated with the analysis. In the current example of visitors to a site, the specific analysis key messages appear in Figure 75 as also shown as the identify problem step in Figure 74: Example Indicator/Metric Development Process. Future Combat Systems (FCS) was an army modernization program terminated in 2011. The key messages in the figure were developed with extensive customer involvement to determine their analysis goal(s). While this study was part of an established business program, similar requirements would apply to other operational situations.

Priority	FCS Key Messages
1	FCS provides a new generation of combat capability for 21st century threats
2	Deploys major forces anywhere, anytime
3	Dominates across the entire range of military operations
4	Networks battle command to all BCT Soldiers and systems
5	Requires half the organizational and logistical footprint
6	FCS accelerates decisive systems/technologies to current forces in the fight
7	FCS MGV provides better armor protection against RPGS, IEDS and full 360-degree threats than all current force vehicles
8	FCS MGV – 70-80% common modules and components with hybrid-electric drive system
9	FCS reduces operations and support costs – *less fuel and ammunition, fewer parts through reliability and commonality, and fewer support personnel*
10	The 21st century threat environment is highly fluid and unpredictable and will require a highly versatile Army

Figure 75: Analysis Key Messages

From these key messages, the analyst developed specific questions to answer, as shown in Figure 76 and is the second step in the metrics process. For this figure, an FBCT is a Future Brigade Combat Team and an HBCT is a Heavy Brigade Combat Team. An HBCT is basically a current armor-heavy combined arms (armor/infantry/artillery/air) organization.

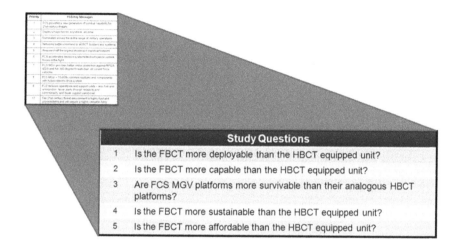

Figure 76: Study Questions from Key Messages

Notice the study questions in the figure above pose specific issues on the performance aspects of the comparison units. From this set of questions, the analyst determines the specific essential elements of analysis (EEAs) and measures of merit (MOMs) as shown in Figure 77.

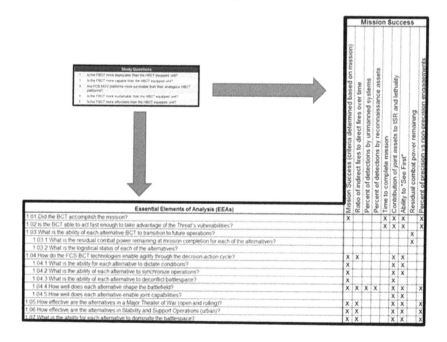

Figure 77: Development of EEAs and MOMs

Notice in the above graphic that the study questions have specific numbers assigned to them. These numbers (e.g., 1.01, 1.02, etc.) relate to established program directives of performance developed by the U.S. Army customer. By linking the EEAs to the contracted guidance document, there is no question as to either the source of the requirement(s) or the relationship of these requirements to the study. Additionally, the "Mission Success" criteria—the specific MOMs for the study—derived from U.S. Army guidance documents and performance specifications. At the juncture point are a series of indicators, or *X*s, that correlate the EEAs to specific MOMs (see Figure 78 for a detailed view). This analysis ensures that all specific requirements have coordinating measurement criteria assigned within the study.

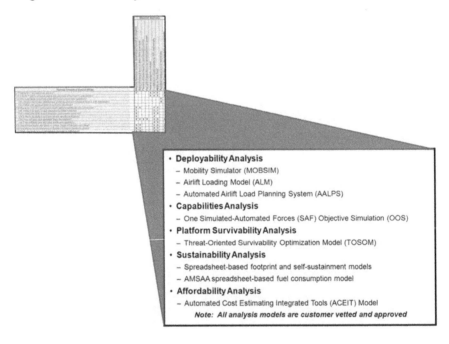

Figure 78: Assignment of Measurement and Analysis Tools to the Study Metrics

The names of the models/simulations here are not important. What is important is that both the analyst and the customer know the models/simulations as capable of rendering in a computer an aspect of the real world, saving resources and potentially human lives. In many business situations, most of the equipment exists only as an expensive prototype. To evaluate prototype systems for effectiveness in a combat environment is both extremely risky and expensive, thus unachievable. However, like the rifle-shot experiment, conducting hundreds of simulation exercises or runs for a known set of scenarios and use options enables metrics, such as those seen in the set of graphics shown in Figure 79.

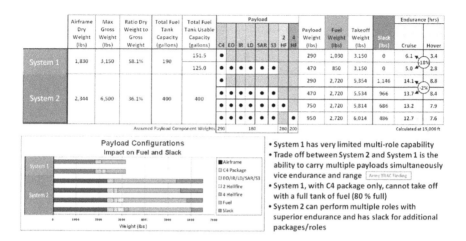

Figure 79: Analytical Structure and Results Example

Such a set of results makes it easy to come to conclusions by generating a picture rather than simply words on a page. As mentioned in Chapter 4, the human mind generally works in pictures and finds such representations easier to store and process. What the above shows is a comparison between the two systems, which enables the viewer to more readily draw conclusions even prior to reading the analytical conclusions located on the bottom right of the graphic. Once the viewer's attention focuses on those conclusions, they serve as a confirmation and reinforce the knowledge gained from the graphic. This makes retention of this information easier, in addition to aiding decision making.

RELATING OPERATIONS RESEARCH TO INTELLIGENCE/ SECURITY PLANNING AND OPERATIONS

STEP 1: DEVELOPMENT OF METRICS

With the right tools, relating OR to the intelligence planning and operations process is fairly simple. The security professional can use the intelligence collection plan, intelligence preparation of the battlespace, and other factors similar to the OR study in the previous example. The first step is to identify the requirements as either key messages or objectives. These derive from the doctrinal guidance publications, such as field manuals, military regulations, joint publications, etc. From these military doctrinal guidelines, the professional develops specific EEAs and end states as shown in Figure 80 below.

	SECURITY		END STATE
Intelligence	• Continue IPB process • Monitor bandit and faction leaders. Determine their intentions • Determine the political ambitions and end states • Conduct reconnaissance (LRSO, SOF, CA, CI, Avn, Inf, Cav)	• Locate weapons, caches, technicals	• Enhanced security • Secure environment for HA operations
Maneuver	• Establish checkpoints and roadblocks • Dismantle "toll" checkpoints • Conduct area and route recons • Secure storage and distribution sites (augment others) • Establish QRF/Reserve	• Conduct convoy security operations • Provide continuous presence • Conduct zone recon to disarm locals • Conduct disarmament/amnesty program • Conduct unit training	• Somalis move freely about their country • Bandits no longer operate
Fire Support	• Provide on-call assets • Provide show of force flyovers	• Develop base camp mortar illum plan • Provide counterfire coverage	• Weapons not visible • Crew-served weapons in storage or confiscated
Mobility Countermobility Survivability	• Provide mine detection and clearing • Establish survivability positions for roadblocks and base camps • Improve ground LOCs to minimum standards	• Maintain ports and airfields • Provide map support and distribution • Provide survey support • Support unit survivability actions	• Open passage along major routes sustained
Combat Service Support	• Support assigned forces • Establish logistical support bases • Secure logistics facilities	• Provide personnel service support	• No technicals[1] • Somali police forces established
C³	• Maintain communications with all sites • Develop command structure prepared to accept coalition forces	• Develop and disseminate ROE • Provide security for contractors and engineers	• UN peacekeeping forces take over security missions
Coordination	• Work with humanitarian agencies • Empower elders • Assist clan leaders in keeping peace • Investigate, adjudicate, and pay foreign claims	• Coordinate with coalition forces • Share routes • Begin transition to UN forces • Provide security for contractors in humanitarian relief sector	
Force Protection	• Provide security for soldiers • Improve base camps • Provide mature medical support for soldiers	• Assist in establishing Somali police force	
Information	• Continue PSYOP themes • Provide credible information systems for the public • Provide public affairs information for each mission		[1]Vehicles with crew-served weapons
Operation System / **Stage of the Operation**	**RELIEF STAGE END STATE** • People live in peace without reliance on their own weapons for protection • Humanitarian agencies operate uninterrupted • Market economy begins		Adapted from a 10th Mountain Division chart used during UNITAF Operations in Somalia (Operation Restore Hope) in 1992-1993

Figure 80: 10th Mountain Division Intelligence Collection Objectives Document

Associating this document to the geographic/terrain environments, the planner can both establish specific tasks and the information required from these tasks, as well as determine the best person(s) to collect against them. The general term for the specific tasks or required information sets is priority intelligence requirements (PIR). These often relate to a named area of interest (NAI) and a targeted area of interest (TAI), which generally are geographic locations but can also mean individuals, facilities, etc. Figure 81 depicts this development process similar to the one depicted in Figure 68.

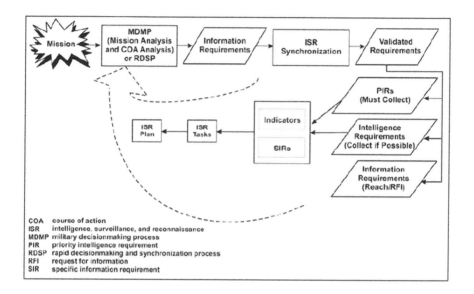

COA   course of action
ISR   intelligence, surveillance, and reconnaissance
MDMP   military decisionmaking process
PIR   priority intelligence requirement
RDSP   rapid decisionmaking and synchronization process
RFI   request for information
SIR   specific information requirement

**Figure 81: Intelligence Requirements Development
and Integration into the ISR Process**[328]

The corporate side of intelligence and security is not that different. Terminology frequently differs. For example, there are no such terms as NAI or PIR, yet the needs for such items remain. The term *key requirements* stands in for PIR in the business domain. For NAI, substitute the terms *business areas of interest* or *measures of performance* (MOPs). Corporate terminology also uses *tiers* rather than the military term of *operational echelons* (see Figure 82).

---

[328]   US Army Field Manual (FM) 2-0 Intelligence dated March 2010. Pg. 4-14.

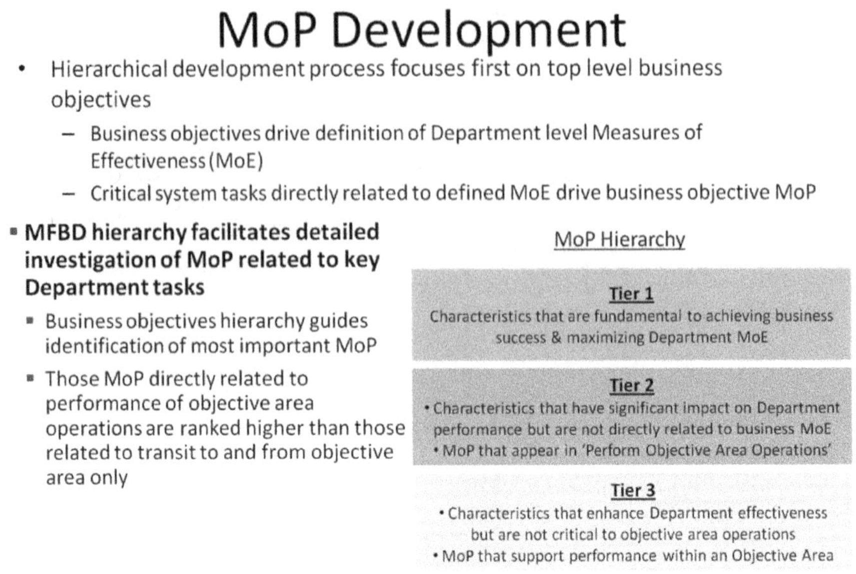

MoP Development

- Hierarchical development process focuses first on top level business objectives
  - Business objectives drive definition of Department level Measures of Effectiveness (MoE)
  - Critical system tasks directly related to defined MoE drive business objective MoP

- **MFBD hierarchy facilitates detailed investigation of MoP related to key Department tasks**
  - Business objectives hierarchy guides identification of most important MoP
  - Those MoP directly related to performance of objective area operations are ranked higher than those related to transit to and from objective area only

MoP Hierarchy

Tier 1
Characteristics that are fundamental to achieving business success & maximizing Department MoE

Tier 2
• Characteristics that have significant impact on Department performance but are not directly related to business MoE
• MoP that appear in 'Perform Objective Area Operations'

Tier 3
• Characteristics that enhance Department effectiveness but are not critical to objective area operations
• MoP that support performance within an Objective Area

Figure 82: Measures of Performance Development and Hierarchy

STEP 2: RELATING METRICS TO TASKS

The second step is to relate the key objectives to the MOEs and MOM/MOPs—establish exact and specific tier-related measures used to develop data and guide analysis. These detailed measures provide the information needed to not only determine the effectiveness of the program but also design and assign tasks for performance. The military intelligence community calls this a collection plan tasking matrix, as seen in Figure 83, but the civilian community calls it a job description.

DTG: ______
MISSION: ______

RECONNAISSANCE AND SURVEILLANCE MATRIX

PRIORITY	NAI	START / STOP	SIR/ INSTRUCTION	RECON	CO A	CO B	CO C	MORTAR	HHC	SNIPERS	FIST	COORDINATION	REMARKS

PIR: Weapons caches

NAI	Priority	Location	Description	Unit	Time	Remarks
6	4	Wardak Province	Hwy A77	Battalion assets	Continuous	Report any movement, attacks, or capture of insurgents moving along highway, direction of movement, etc. using SALUTE format
7	4	Wardak Province	Sar-e Raqowl village	Battalion assets	Random	Report any information on Taliban/Insurgent movement, attacks, kidnappings, or arms discoveries
8	4	Wardak Province	Sheykhabad village and surrounding region; pass through western mountains	CL-IV	During operations	Report any movement, attacks, or capture of insurgents moving along highway, direction of movement, etc. using SALUTE format
9	4	Wardak Province	Sheykhabad village and surrounding region; pass through western mountains	CL-IV	During operations	Report any movement, attacks, or capture of insurgents moving along highway, direction of movement, etc. using SALUTE format

PIR: Preparation of fire support/rocket launching positions

NAI	Priority	Location	Description	Unit	Time	Remarks
6	4	Wardak Province	Hwy A77	Battalion assets	Continuous	Report areas where it appears prepared firing positions are being constructed near known or potential ambush points along highway and major trails
7	4	Wardak Province	Sar-e Raqowl village	Battalion assets	Random	Report locations where bunkers or other potential attack sites are being prepared; identify suspecious digging or emplantation of PVC or other tubing not justified by sanitation or water supply projects.
8	4	Wardak Province	Sheykhabad village and surrounding region; pass through western mountains	CL-IV	During operation	Report locations where bunkers or other potential attack sites are being prepared; identify suspecious digging or emplantation of PVC or other tubing not justified by sanitation or water supply projects.
9	4	Wardak Province	Sheykhabad village and surrounding region; pass through western mountains	CL-IV	During operations	Report any movement, attacks, or capture of insurgents moving along highway, direction of movement, etc. using SALUTE format

PIR: Clearing of civilian population from villages or other populated areas

NAI	Priority	Location	Description	Unit	Time	Remarks
6	4	Wardak Province	Hwy A77	Battalion assets	Continuous	Report any movement, attacks, or capture of insurgents moving along highway, direction of movement, etc. using SALUTE format
7	4	Wardak Province	Sar-e Raqowl village	Battalion assets	Random	Report any information on Taliban/Insurgent movement, attacks, kidnappings, or arms discoveries
8	4	Wardak Province	Sheykhabad village and surrounding region; pass through western mountains	CL-IV	Prior to operation	Establish points of observation and sensors or fields to detect and identify movement into, through, and out of this region. Investigate and service as needed and warranted by ROE
9	4	Wardak Province	Sheykhabad village and surrounding region; pass through western mountains	CL-IV	During operations	Report any movement, attacks, or capture of insurgents moving along highway, direction of movement, etc. using SALUTE format

Figure 83: ISR Tasking Matrix and Orders

Step 3: Fusion, Analysis and Dissemination

The third step in the process is to take the data collected and fuse it into a format that means something. Words in a report are nice and generally convey the information in an understandable manner with few ambiguities. However, such reports take time to absorb, considering the time the user of the information may not have. Think of this as a visual executive summary.

In the past, transmission of information in pictorial format was impossible other than via courier. Now there are networked systems and the Global Information Grid (GIG), which make instantaneous transmission not only possible, but a necessity. The format and style of the representation depend highly on the audience, the information, and the goal of the report, i.e., the intended message.

This is where knowledge of human terrain becomes vital for both information analysis and the dissemination of those results. When the analyst understands human terrain, they are able to:

a. Understand their own bias in the design, construction, and presentation of information, such that these biases are negated in favor of factual logic;
b. Consider how the bias of the target audience may result in a different understanding than the one intended by the analyst;

c. Determine the impact specific terminology will have on the target audience, making factual and logical assessment of actions either more or less likely due to emotional implication and interference;

d. Understand how various graphical and photographic depictions will impact the target audience, both psychologically and emotionally.

A feature article contained in the Military Operations Research Society (MORS) journal discusses some of these issues from the perspective of creating a profile of leaders, specifically as pertains to assessing and profiling threat/enemy leadership. However, having a similar detailed understanding of friendly leadership is equally important in the presentation of analysis. For example, General Douglas MacArthur's staff knew that information provided to him needed to be couched in terms of opportunity rather than serious problems, or they would very likely find themselves in very serious trouble. As per the historian, Nigel Davies,[329]

> *What saved MacArthur was his unrivalled ability with propaganda. He far surpassed his nearest allied military rivals General's Patton and Montgomery. In fact he could be more closely compared to Joseph Goebbels, both in ability, and in veracity. Adolf Hitler and Joseph Stalin would have acknowledged their equals in the ability to tell a big lie. The lengths his propaganda team went to put his earlier fantasies to the pale. The American public were bombarded with stories about valiant defenders, and glorious victories. Not only were the Japanese dying in their thousands, and being shot out of the sky, but their battleships were being sunk apparently at will by MacArthur's vastly outnumbered but indomitable forces. For an American public receiving a steady diet of failure and disaster in the Pacific and Atlantic, MacArthur was presented as a shining beacon of steadfast endurance and indomitable will. What a crock. His troops referred to him as "Dugout Doug."*

Returning to the MORS article,

> *Analysis remains qualitative in scope, as human cognitive behavior is exceedingly difficult, if not impossible, to measure. Even so, behavioral patterns of focused and disciplined adversaries of all stripes can, and*

---

[329] Davies, N. (2010). Rethinking History: General Douglas MacArthur. http://rethinkinghistory.blogspot.com/2010/11/rating-general-douglas-macarthur.html

do, emerge offering insight into the cognitive that may somehow be quantifiable.[330]

McVicar establishes the following elements of a leadership profile. Note how these conditions match the Section 2 terrain discussions:

a. Historical, ideological, and cultural influences
b. Conditions and beliefs
c. Leadership characteristics
d. Decision-making structures and processes
e. Strategy and doctrine
f. Key uncertainties

The process of data fusion can take multiple forms, as discussed earlier in terms of the types and methods of evaluation. The number and types of fusion methodologies are as varied and numbered as the individuals attempting to sell their latest version. Most of these methodologies break down into the basic aspect of comparison of metadata at the basic level. The models look for similarities in time, location, equipment, activity, and other factors, then make a determination of probability as to whether the report addresses the event in question. At this point, some methodologies combine the reports to make the value of "notice" higher or simply annotate that other supporting reports exist.

So what is data fusion expected to do? The model shown in Figure 84 was developed in 1993 at the Joint Directors of Laboratories conference. The idea behind the process was to totally automate the fusion activity due to the massive amounts of information analysts can gather these days.

---

[330] McVicar, M. Profiling Leaders and Analyzing their Motivation. *MORS: Phalanx. Vol 44, No. 4. December 2011.* Pp. 6-8. Pg. 6.

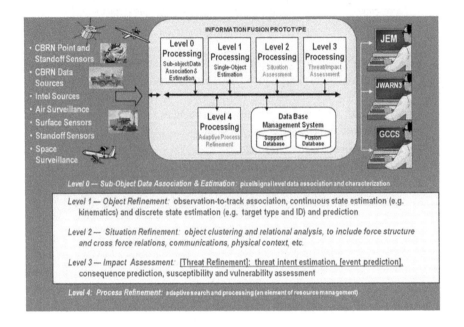

Figure 84: Representation of the JDL Data Fusion Model[331]

The point of the fusion process is to assist the analyst in determining whether or not to include specific information in a particular assessment—if so, to what degree and with what level of importance. Bleiholder and Naumann describe the process as follows:[332]

> *After major technical problems of connecting different data sources on different machines are solved, the biggest challenge remains: overcoming semantic heterogeneity, that is, [sic] overcoming the effect of the same information being stored in different ways. The main problems are the detection of equivalent schema elements in different sources (schema matching) and the detection of equivalent object descriptions (duplicate detection) in different sources to integrate data into one single and consistent representation.*

---

[331]   Llinas, J. (2002). Visualization, Level 2 Fusion, and Homeland Defense. University of Buffalo. NY. Downloaded from ftp://ftp.rta.nato.int/PubFullText/RTO/MP\RTO-MP-HFM-207/\PubFullText/RTO/MP/RTO-MP-IST-040/MP-IST-040-$KN2.pps

[332]   Bleiholder, J. and Naumann, F. Data Fusion. ACM Comput. Surv., 41, 1, Article 1 (December 2008), 41 pages DOI=10.1145/1456650.1456651 http://doi.acm.org/10.1145/1456650.1456651. Pg 1-2.

Whether the process is automated or manual, the data must be collated into a usable format, examined using the logical processes discussed earlier, placed into a recognizable form or format, and disseminated to the user. Otherwise, it will have no value.

Chapter 11

SECURITY PLANNING

As with many other aspects of the security and intelligence professions, there are numerous texts, guides, consultants, and papers on how to do planning. This chapter specifically focuses on providing an introduction to the passive/active aspects of offensive and defensive security and intelligence planning organized as follows:

a. Definitions and considerations
b. Security/intelligence planning involving:
    1. The planning process as established by the Project Management Institute
    2. Planning considerations and how to organize required work
       i. Assets
       ii. Risks
       iii. Costs
       iv. Flow
       v. Stakeholders
       vi. Time
c. Modeling and Simulation
    1. Value in model creation
    2. Value in simulations
    3. Types of simulations
    4. How to use models and simulations in security and intelligence planning
d. Integration of security/intelligence operations
e. How to construct an integrated security/intelligence operations plan

DEFINITIONS AND CONSIDERATIONS

This chapter introduces several new concepts that require definition and additional explanation as the text covers those areas. The definitions, which follow here, are restated and expanded upon in their specific subsections.

Model[333]—A model is a mathematical, logical, or some other structural representation of reality used in the development and analysis of that reality. It operates in a controlled environment with reduced costs and no dangers. Of these, having control over the assignment and modification of variables is nearly as important as the avoidance of dangers associated with reality situations. A computer model, as used in modeling and simulation science, is a mathematical representation of something, whether that is a person, a building, a vehicle, a tree, or any other object. A model also can represent a process, such as a weather pattern, traffic flow, air flowing over a wing, etc.

Simulation[334]—Simulations are also abstractions of reality similar to and often developed from reality situations for investigation and experimentation. Many simulations deliberately emphasize one part of reality at the expense of other parts in order to better understand the hows and whys of the driving conditions and potential results.

Deterministic Modeling[335]—A deterministic model is one in which every set of variable states is uniquely determined by parameters in the model, including sets of previous states of these variables. Therefore, deterministic models perform the same way for a given set of initial conditions each time they are examined or, if digital, run on a computer.

Linear Modeling[336]—Mathematical models are usually composed of variables (i.e., abstractions of quantities of interest in the described systems) and operators that act on these variables—algebraic operators, functions, differential operators, etc. If all the operators in a mathematical model exhibit linearity, the resulting mathematical model is defined as linear. Otherwise, the model is nonlinear.

Static/Dynamic Modeling[337]—A static model does not account for the element of time, while a dynamic model does. Dynamic models typically are represented with difference equations or differential equations.

Probabilistic Stochastic/Monte Carlo Modeling—In a probabilistic or stochastic model, the keys are that selections of values are randomly selected

---

[333] http://www.ist.ucf.edu/background.htm

[334] Ibid

[335] http://en.wikipedia.org/wiki/Mathematical_model

[336] Ibid

[337] Ibid

within proscribed odds and that variable states are not described by unique values, but rather by probability distributions. The simplest form of a probabilistic model is a coin toss. The variable states are heads, tails, and the edge of the coin (not very likely, yet it can happen). The probabilities of each state are heads, $\geq49\%\leq50\%$ (read, greater than or equal to 49 percent yet less than or equal to 50 percent); tails, $\geq49\%\leq50\%$; and the coin edge at $\geq0\%\leq1\%$. Thus, in a probabilistic or stochastic simulation, each toss will result in a value = heads/tails/edge in random fashion.

A Monte Carlo simulation[338] is a class of computational algorithms[339] that rely on repeated random sampling to compute their results. Computer simulations of physical and mathematical systems often use Monte Carlo methods. The name *Monte Carlo* was derived from the games of chance in that mecca of European gambling with very similar dynamics because each pass of the simulation relies upon the roll of the dice for the driving values of the algorithms.

These various types of probabilistic models are well suited to calculation by a computer, especially when it is infeasible to compute an exact result with a deterministic algorithm.[340] The Monte Carlo method is also used to complement the theoretical derivations.[341] It is especially useful for simulating systems with many coupled degrees of freedom, such as fluids, disordered materials, strongly coupled solids, and cellular structures. The resulting programs can model phenomena that have significant uncertainty in their input values, such as the calculation of risk in business or the dynamics of an airplane in flight through different types of air. They are widely used in mathematics, for example, to evaluate multidimensional definite integrals with complicated boundary conditions.[342] When Monte Carlo simulations have been applied in space flight and oil exploration, their predictions

---

[338] http://en.wikipedia.org/wiki/Monte_Carlo_method

[339] An algorithm is not a comment made by former Vice President Al Gore; rather it is an equation representing an event in real life. The equation $1 + 1 = 2$ is NOT an algorithm. The equation $E = MC^2$ is because E = Energy, M = Mass, and C^2 = the velocity of light in centimeters per second squared (multiplied by itself).

[340] A deterministic algorithm is one where the result is always identical given the exact same variable value inputs...it is NOT probabilistic.

[341] A theoretical deviation is simply differences in results that are non-factual. For example, the result of one simulation run (set of coin tosses) are 10 heads, 9 tails, no edges. The second run is 9 heads, 9 tails, 1 edge. Thus the *actual* deviation between the two runs is 1 head, 0 tails, and 1 edge. While coin tosses based upon actual observation, a computer simulation is not and is therefore *theoretical*.

[342] Now, in plain English, to see how an object with a weird shape (like a golf ball) hit with a particular golf club in a specific way will fly once it hits the tree the golfer wasn't aiming at . . . and why.

of failures cost overruns, and schedule overruns are routinely better than human intuition or alternative "soft" methods.[343]

Probability Distribution[344]—The Chapter 10 section on operations research defines *probability distribution* as a statistical function that describes all the possible values and likelihoods that a random variable can take within a given range. This range will be between the minimum and maximum statistically possible values. The location of the possible value on the probability distribution chart depends on a number of factors, including the distribution's mean, standard deviation, skewness, and kurtosis (Figure 85).

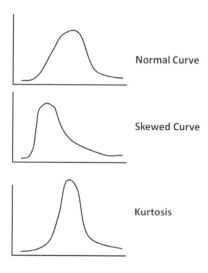

Figure 85: Examples of Curve Types

Agent-based Modeling[345]—An agent-based model (ABM)—also sometimes related to the term *multiagent system* or *multiagent simulation*—is a class of computational models for simulating the actions and interactions of autonomous agents, both for individual and collective entities such as organizations or groups, with a view of assessing their effects on the system as a whole. It combines elements of game theory, complex systems, emergence, computational sociology, multiagent systems, and evolutionary programming. This model includes Monte Carlo methods to introduce randomness. ABMs are also called individual-based models. The models simulate the simultaneous operations and interactions of

---

[343]   A soft method is an expert's guess based on experience.

[344]   http://www.investopedia.com/terms/p/probabilitydistribution.asp#axzz1gCBgrlkh

[345]   Macall, C.M. and North, M.J. Tutorial on agent-based modeling and simulation. Journal of Simulation (2010) 4, No 3. 151-162 Operational Research Society Ltd.

multiple agents in an attempt to recreate and predict the appearance of complex phenomena.

Lanchester Equations—Lanchester's laws are mathematical formulas for calculating the relative strengths of a predator/prey pair. Usually connected with military forces, these are differential equations describing the time dependence of two armies' strengths, A and B, as a function of time, with the function depending only on A and B.

CONSIDERATIONS

The foremost consideration in examining and using simulations and models for planning and evaluating the effectiveness of security and intelligence is the following: *All models of reality are wrong. Some are useful.*[346]

> **The only law of modeling and simulations that is of true value is that all models of reality are wrong; however, some are useful.**

This rule of analysis was first raised by statistician George E. P. Box. What he means by this is that models represent only a portion of reality and will never consider all of reality, nor every possible observation or consideration of that reality. Reality only exists as an observation filtered by individual experiences and biases. As was discussed in Chapter 4, Human Terrain, the brain filters out information that we do not expect to observe and adds information that we do expect to see. Therefore, it is of utmost importance in any form of analysis to understand that both the witness and the analyst will have these biases and to know what they are. Once identified and understood, it is important to include them in the analysis as conditions and/or limitations of the assessment. By culling these out, it is possible to determine how they impact the observations and assessments, improving the probabilities of a correct analysis.

The second important consideration here is that modeling and simulation are best used in the analysis of long-term requirements due to the amount of time they require. While simulations can be invaluable for identifying and assessing resource, funding, and operational concerns, particularly when it requires capital expenditures and functions, they are less accurate than other techniques in short-term considerations. When using these tools, preparatory training and contingency planning are the best options. For planning, situations such as Delphi

[346] Box, G E P, (1976). "Science and statistics", *Journal of the American Statistical Association* 71:791-799

and subject matter expert (SME) evaluation (known in the military as BOGSAT or bunch of guys sitting around a table) are generally of greater value.

SECURITY/INTELLIGENCE PLANNING CONCEPTS

Why plan? What is the point in establishing approaches that may or may not be appropriate or needed? The book *Principles of Security Management* offers the following answer to this question:[347]

> *Planning bridges the gap between where we are now and where we want to be. As pointed out by Korey (1995, 46), "planning includes identifying and solving problems, exploring and determining the best ways and means of attaining established objectives; arranging in sequence and scheduling all significant activities that have to be carried out by the institutions; providing adequate resources, personnel and facilities; maintaining effective coordination, and establishing necessary controls." Planning also means assessing our desired objectives, anticipating problems, and developing solutions. It requires practical thinking in order to "isolate, determine and schedule the actions and achievements required to attain our objectives. It is the formulation and development of the blueprints we expect to follow (Korey 1995, 44)."*

Understanding the planning process means first understanding what type of planning will take place. Some texts immediately delve into the steps of performing structured planning, forgetting to define the different levels and time frames that exist. Conducting an analysis, without first correctly understanding the problem, will likely result in a wrong answer to an improperly prepared question. Therefore, the planner must decide in definitive terms the issue at hand, the level of structure, how much effort or resources to commit to the situation, and most importantly, what condition/risk/threat the solution addresses. Figure 86 is modified from a U.S. Marine Corps planning process and depicts the planner's situation fairly completely.

To understand the differences in the planning process, the planner must first understand the levels of operation. These levels are best labeled in military terminology for clarity of understanding: strategic/global, national, operational, and local/tactical.

---

[347]   Johnson, B.R. (2005). *Principles of Security Management*. Pearson Education, Inc., Upper Saddle River, New Jersey, 07458. Pg 88.

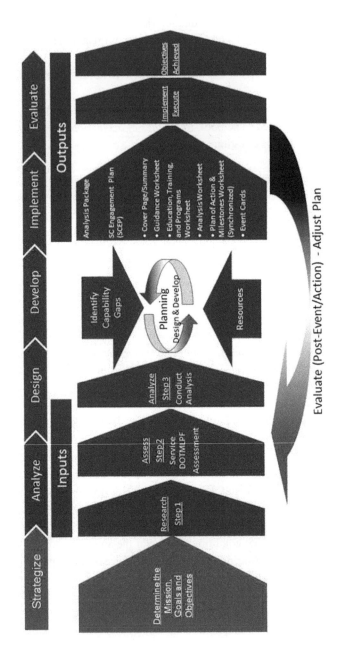

Figure 86: Security/Intelligence Planning Process[348]

---

[348] Obtained from http://www.scetc.usmc.mil/Pages/OT.aspx and modified to fit text subject matter.

STRATEGIC LEVEL CONSIDERATIONS AND CONSTRUCTS

A strategic plan is one that establishes the organization's reason for being in existence. It states unequivocally the who, what, and why of the organization as related to its overall goals. Some authors call this a vision, and vision is definitely a major portion of the strategic plan. Recall the mission President Roosevelt gave to General Eisenhower for the defeat of Nazi Germany. "You will enter the continent of Europe, by force of arms, and destroy the enemy's ability and willingness to continue this war."[349]

Should the student think this was a strategic plan, they would be mistaken. The strategic mission of the American and Allied powers for WWII was the defeat of all warring powers, the return of the world to peace, and the establishment of an international body to ensure that no such future wars could develop. The strategic plan was the defeat of the major threat of Nazi Germany, followed by the subsequent defeat of the Empire of Japan, and the return to stable relations with all nations.

Strategic plans generally have the conditions seen here in Table 8. Note that the geographical element is *not* a specific requirement for strategic planning, only for global. Firms that are local in nature should have strategic plans as part of their overall construct. This ensures focused and successful long-term goals. Do not confuse size with strategic structure, as a business need not be large to be of great impact. The elements, as shown in Table 10, depict the basic nature of national planning

Table 8: Strategic Planning Elements

ELEMENT	CONDITION
Scope	Abstract in nature, general structure with no specifics
Nature	Prescriptive with minimal descriptive elements only when necessary to firmly establish construct
Composition	Simple
Process	Established by the highest-level stakeholders focused on those with the absolute responsibility and authority for both inception and capital funding
Product Description	Simplistic
Time Frame	Five—to ten-year outlook
Resources	Extensive capitalization requirements

---

[349] Op Cit.

Geographic Domain	When considered global, operations will extend to a minimum of two countries and will likely extend onto two or more continents.

NATIONAL-LEVEL PLANNING AND CONSTRUCTS

National-level planning can also be considered strategic in scope if it meets the requirements for the elements from the above (see Table 8), with the exception of the geographic domain. It may also be considered operational, however, given the size and nature of the organization. The major delimiting factors[350] are shown in Table 9.

This level of planning is more in line with the mission General Eisenhower received. Looking back to that mission quote, notice the specific target of the Eisenhower mission was Europe and Nazi Germany and no other location. To achieve this goal, however, Eisenhower was forced to include many other nations in the process such as those in North Africa.

Table 9: National Planning Elements

ELEMENT	CONDITION
Scope	Abstract in nature, general structure with some specifics focusing on those operations and goals considered critical by the governing higher body of executive management
Nature	Prescriptive with moderate descriptive elements to firmly establish construct for the subordinate element being addressed and tasked
Composition	Simple
Process	Established by the highest-level stakeholders as primary objectives for the subordinate body and establishing responsibility and authority for both achievement and capital funding use
Product Description	Simplistic
Time Frame	Two—to five-year outlook
Resources	Extensive capitalization requirements

---

[350] A delimiting factor is something that creates a boundary or 'limit' on how something works or is considered.

Geographic Domain	Involves only a single geographic entity/nation as the target domain, yet may result in the implication of and impact to other areas/ nations in a collateral manner

OPERATIONAL-LEVEL PLANNING AND CONSTRUCTS

Military organizations establish operational-level planning by the size of the units involved and/or the terrain area to be covered. Business texts define operational planning as a subset of the strategic—or national-level plan, containing highly detailed goals and processes. This is similar to the structures and planning associated with the scenario concerning Eisenhower and WWII.

There are, in fact, many levels of operational planning and their associated pieces for the overall strategic objectives. For example, one of the first tasks considered for the Eisenhower strategic objective was how to enter the continent of Europe. Consider that the overall mission had been given to Eisenhower in 1942 and the D-Day invasion did not occur until June 6, 1944. He had to raise forces, then train, equip, and transport them to England where there was housing and other facilities. He still had to determine the proper site for the invasion, have his resources construct the equipment, and include two portable shipping ports because the chosen location had no ports for supply operations.

Each major organization, over three million individuals organized into various-sized functional groups, needed to have their actions coordinated in location, process, and schedule to ensure that everything would be at the proper locations at the exact time needed. This was all while ensuring that the enemy did not discover the truth of where, when, and with what . . . and they were successful, even considering that the weather was not cooperating. All of the men, machinery, supplies, and support absolutely needed to be ashore for the initial phases of the invasion within three days or the invasion would fail.

In the military, organizations are generally identified as units of battalion size to corps. A structure diagram for U.S. Army echelons appears in Figure 87. Corporations have similar, yet more intricate groupings (Figure 88). The delineating criteria shown in Table 9 are for the operational levels of an organization. Note the size structure remains fairly large or involved, yet even firms of fewer than one thousand employees will need to contend with similar requirements, though they often are not appropriately organized to do so.

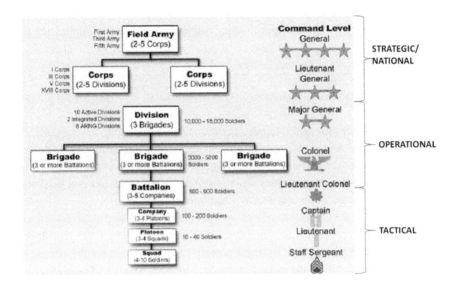

Figure 87: U.S. Army Organization

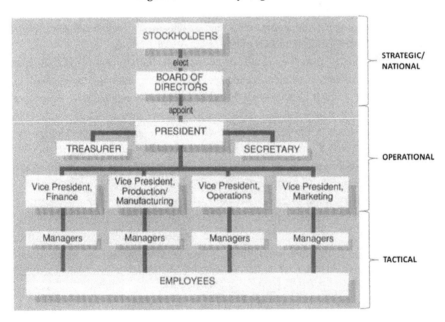

Figure 88: A Typical Corporate Structure

Table 10: Operational Planning Elements

ELEMENT	CONDITION
Scope	Detailed in nature, specifics focusing on those operations and goals decomposed from the higher-level objectives and plans of mid-level executives
Nature	Descriptive with firmly establish constructs for the subordinate elements being addressed and tasked to include definitive schedules, operating specifications, and outcomes
Composition	Complex
Process	Established by second-level executives as primary objectives for subordinate bodies and establishing responsibility and authority for both achievement. Capital funding is provided by higher authority. This level is relegated to managing the expenditures to ensure appropriate utilization of all resources.
Product Description	Complex and detailed documentation to include synchronized schedules, definitive actions/locations, and established outcomes
Time Frame	Six months to two-year outlook
Resources	Limited to those organic to the entity being tasked plus any additional loaned/attached resources provided to support the planning process
Geographic Domain	Involves regional locations generally limited to specific constraints based upon the size of the organizational entity and further disassembled to levels just above the point where individual tasks are assigned

TACTICAL-LEVEL PLANNING AND CONSTRUCTS

Up until this point, most of the planning work has involved establishing strategies and group-level objectives and structures. It is at the tactical level that the specifics become critical, as this is where the work takes place. It is also at this level that management has little control over the resources provided in terms of authorizing an increase to the capabilities or numbers. They can only direct the resources they have in place to achieve their specific tasks. At this level, the tasks are, as defined by the Project Management Institute, actions requiring specific people with specific skill sets (e.g., one to three unique individuals).

The military organization graphic of Figure 87: U.S. Army Organization depicts the lowest unit level as the squad, containing four to ten soldiers. Usually, the squad contains two sections of four soldiers, the squad leader, and his radio/ communications person. There is leadership theory logic for this group size. This logic is known as "span of control." Basically, span of control is the physical/ psychological limit of individuals, activities, entities, organizations that any one individual can efficiently manage without significant degradation in performance.

The *Business Dictionary* defines *span of control* as "the number of subordinates that a manager or supervisor can directly control. This number varies with the type of work: complex, variable work reduces it to six, whereas routine, fixed work increases it to twenty or more." In high-stress conditions, this number is generally reduced to 2 to 3, thus the division of a standard combat squad to two sections, each containing a section leader and three soldiers, plus the communications person and the squad leader. Thus, the squad leader need only directly manage the two section leaders and the radioman.

The individuals within the squad have little to no knowledge of other than their immediate objectives and/or tasks. Often, these tasks are limited to only a few hours or less in duration. Once complete, the section leaders provide subsequent tasks until they reach the immediate operational objectives and realign with their higher controlling units.

Even when the organization is larger, up to one hundred or more individuals, their span of control and tasks remain limited to only a few hours to a few months duration. Table 11 establishes some of the criteria that factors into how to determine the task length.

Table 11: Tactical Planning Elements

ELEMENT	CONDITION
Scope	Extremely detailed and often established within standard operating procedures or task completion instructions
Nature	Very simplistic constructs and set to a highly defined progression of linked tasks to include definitive schedules, operating specifications, and outcomes
Composition	Simplistic instructions linked to standard procedures and/or checklists of steps to perform

ELEMENT	CONDITION
Process	Established by mid—to senior-level managers as primary tasks for subordinate bodies. There is no control over capitalized resources as these are solely provided by higher organizations.
Product Description	Detailed description of how each particular task is to be completed, the schedule for completion, and the specific process to be followed; usually developed as a TTP or SOP. These may also be unwritten yet understood via sand-table drills and other forms of practice runs.
Time Frame	Hours to a few weeks
Resources	Only those provided by higher organizations or organic to the team being assigned the task
Geographic Domain	Area is limited to very small locations, usually a single complex, building, or even point location.

SECURITY/INTELLIGENCE PLANNING

There are basically two ways of developing measures to handle the needs of the organization as stated at the beginning of this text: offensive planning and defensive planning. Both have their strengths and their weaknesses. Both are necessary for an organized and effective force. Neither can take place without some consideration for the other.

OFFENSIVE SECURITY

While there are numerous terms, phrases, and definitions of the words *offensive* and *security*, there are few that combine the terms and fewer still that come close to the meaning applied to them in this text. The best definition available is a fusion of those that derive from information security, the military and financial organizations.

Offensive security planning is the integrated use of assigned and supporting capabilities and activities. These activities are mutually supported by intelligence, analytical processes and tools, and IT operations. The objective is to affect adversary decision makers and achieve or promote specific prevention, protection, and recovery objectives prior to the initiation of action by the adversary. The primary goal is to circumvent or avoid a threat's designed actions intended to increase cost/risk beyond perceived or expected benefit/return. These capabilities and activities include, but are not limited to, operations security, deception, electronic/IT techniques and technology, physical activities and/or actions, and special information operations (e.g., public relations, psychological operations, etc.) and could also include computer network preemptive attacks.

DEFENSIVE SECURITY

Defensive security is the integrated use of assigned and supporting capabilities and activities mutually supported by intelligence and all legal processes to achieve or promote protection during and/or while recovering from an event or series of events. These capabilities and activities include, but are not limited to, disaster recovery; breach of security; electronic and/or physical attacks against facilities, installations, and/or individuals; and destructive events of nature.

What these definitions do not establish is a relationship between offensive/ defensive and proactive/reactive actions. This is because both planning aspects should and must include proactive and reactive considerations. This is due to *risk*, which this text addresses later in this chapter.

PLANNING PROCESS

Figure 89 depicts a model of the planning process discussed in this chapter. There are many such models in existence. This one was constructed as a means of conveying pictorially the underlying structure of this text. The model links the constructs from Sections 1 and 2 to the structure compiled in Section 3. The figure also depicts the need for the different levels of organization consideration in integrated fashion to ensure appropriate resourcing. This consideration also provides links for all levels of operations and objectives from strategic to operation. It associates the entire process to intelligent analysis of alternative approaches to both available assets and needs. The end result is a properly documented and tested approach to the known and suspected risks the organization may face, presented in the most efficient and resource-effective manner.

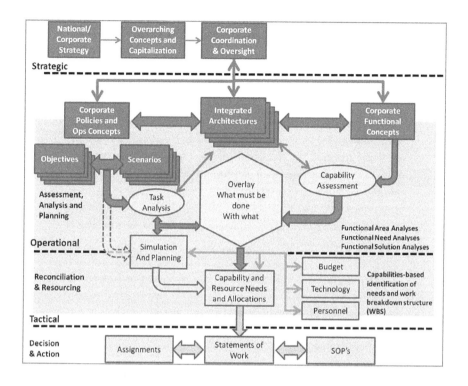

Figure 89: Offensive/Defensive Security Planning Process Model

There are three specific approaches to planning: clinical, research, and design.[351] Achoff breaks these down as follows:[352]

> Clinical Approach—*The clinical approach to planning treats messes and the systems that have them holistically, but, because it does not analyse [sic] them, it deals with no explicit model of their structures. Clinical planners bring together a sample of those preoccupied with different aspects of a mess so they can develop a mutually acceptable formulation and attack on it. Clinical procedures are generally participative with the clinical planner serving primarily as a convener and process consultant. He tries to be nondirective to avoid inserting content into the procedure.*

---

[351] Ackoff, R.L. On the Use of Models in Corporate Planning. *Strategic Management Journal, Vol. 2, 353-359 (1981).*

[352] These definitions are all taken from the above source directly.

Research Approach—*This approach to planning begins by analyzing [sic] a mess so as to identify its parts and their interconnections. It tries to formulate the disassembled plans so that their interconnections are minimal, thereby allowing them to be treated relatively independently of each other. Although stakeholders may be involved in formulating the mess, they are seldom involved in solving the problems it contains because [sic] problem solving requires more technical competence than most stakeholders have. Because the research techniques employed are more applicable to machine-like rather than purposeful behavior [sic], this approach focuses on the technical aspects of socio-technical systems and either ignores the social aspects or leaves it to others to treat as they will. They usually do so clinically. The principal deficiency of the research approach to mess management derives from its almost exclusive reliance on analysis.*

Design Approach—*The design approach to planning is a synthesis of the clinical and research approaches. It tries to adopt their advantages and avoid their weaknesses, and it adds some new ingredients. It involves a concept of planning as a five-phase process:*

    Step 1: Formulating the mess
    Step 2: Ends planning
    Step 3: Means planning
    Step 4: Resource planning
    Step 5: Implementation and control

These steps are embodied in the PMI project planning and management function and begin with what Ackoff calls the identification of the mess (or problem). Irrespective of the label, the development of any plan initiates with a statement of need or, as previously discussed, the mission statement. That statement becomes the master program, which the planner divides into various projects. This structure is often known as a work breakdown structure or WBS.

Any or all of the above approaches may be used, depending upon the level and/or situation the planner requires. The commonality is that in each case, the planner must establish the overall requirements and dissect them into manageable pieces. Figure 90: Automobile WBS Example provides a rendition of the concept in more understandable terms.

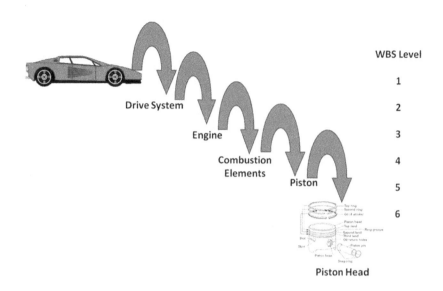

Figure 90: Automobile WBS Example

Note that within the WBS Level 1 "Automobile," there are many level 2 structures such as the drive system, suspension system, body, frame, interior, electronics, etc. Each of these level 2 systems is comprised of subsystems. Take the drive system for example. The component pieces are the engine, transmission, cooling system, power take off, and differentials. Within the engine, the subcomponents include the fuel system, carburetion/injector system, combustion system, etc. Notice that each piece of this process breaks the automobile into smaller, yet more numerous elements until they finally reach the point where one piece (e.g., the piston rings) can be produced by one factory employee to a set tolerance specification. This enables attention to quality and the ability to manage the processes at the point where major problems can arise if the operations planner does not manage specifications correctly.

Imagine an improperly designed/manufactured set of rings on the pistons of the automobile engine. The piston rings are designed to keep the lubrication oil out of the combustion chamber, as this causes damage to the chamber as well as depletes the oil that keeps the engine parts from damage or destruction. Therefore, a small element such as this can result in sufficient damage to require either thousands of dollars of repair or tens of thousands of dollars in new transportation.

"For want of a nail . . ." applies in many such situations and is better known as Murphy's law (If anything can go wrong, it will and at the worst possible time).[353]

What then makes it possible to establish such a breakdown of tasks and the structure to enable the planner to synchronize these tasks? Figure 91: Graphical Depiction of the PMI Project Process helps to detail such a process.

---

[353] As an interesting sideline, the rhyme of 'For want of a nail . . .' is believed to be penned by Benjamin Franklin. The truth is the earliest written version is from John Gower's "Confesio Amantis" dated approximately 1390.

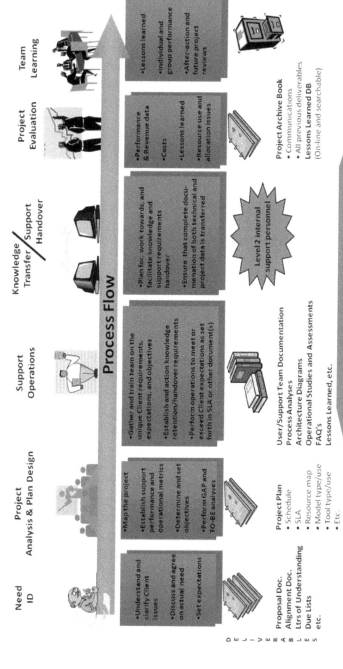

Figure 91: Graphical Depiction of the PMI Project Process

The Project Management Institute (PMI) defines *project* as the following:

> *A project is a temporary endeavor undertaken to create a unique product, service, or result. The temporary nature of projects indicates a definite beginning and end . . . Temporary does not necessarily mean short in duration [and] does not apply to the product, service, or result created by the project; most projects are undertaken to create a lasting outcome . . . Projects can also have social, economic, and environmental impacts that far outlast the projects themselves.*
>
> *A project can create:*
>
> - *A product that can be either a component of another item or an end item in itself,*
> - *A capability to perform a service (e.g., a business function that supports production or distribution), or*
> - *A result such as an outcome or document (e.g., a research project that develops knowledge that can be used to determine whether a trend is present or a new process will benefit society).*[354]

The PMBOK is an international standard for the design, development, and implementation of programs and projects. Membership in the organization requires extensive training, experience in actually performing the tasks of project management, and successful completion of a structured examination. Continued professional membership requires participation in approved and auditable continuing education, expansion of professional knowledge through publication, and continued participation in the profession as a program/project manager. As such, PMBOK criteria are the key for the "what and how" of creating the structures necessary for the development, implementation, and management of security plans.

Intelligence programs, although not formally discussed in this organization, often closely follow the structures and procedures, as the entire science of program/project management was actually developed by the U.S. military to appropriately structure and integrate the myriad of tasks associated with winning World War II. This is why this text includes association of the PMBOK standards and the processes with security planning and management.

---

[354] Project Management Institute. (2010). *Project Management Book of Knowledge (PMBOK)*. PMI, Inc. Newton Square, PA. pg. 5.

Assets

The first process chapter of the PMBOK examines the relationship of assets to the construction of the project and therefore of the planning processes itself. The PMBOK states, "Projects and project management take place in an environment that is broader than that of the project itself [and] Project governance provides a comprehensive, consistent method of controlling the project and ensuring its success."[355] These assets include many of the terrain factors discussed in Section 2 of this text, only adding the need for full integration into all other aspects of the organization's existence. As such, a reexamination of these is unnecessary, with the exception to remind the student that no process of planning can occur without a full understanding of the true nature of what needs to take place, when, and to what extent.

Many organizations fail to establish this critical first step. Take, for example, the impact of two very powerful statements from President John F. Kennedy. "Ask not what your country can do for you. Ask what you can do for your country!" And the second quote,

> *We choose to go to the moon. We choose to go to the moon in this decade and do the other things, not because they are easy, but because they are hard, because that goal will serve to organize and measure the best of our energies and skills, because that challenge is one that we are willing to accept, one we are unwilling to postpone, and one which we intend to win, and the others, too.*[356]

Both of these phrases paved the way for one of the greatest decades in American history. They set the entire tone of both the Kennedy presidency and a mission that propelled the United States to endeavors of which we are still reaping the benefits of in terms of medicine, science, communications, information technology, and millions upon millions of jobs that never existed before these speeches. JFK was the sponsor and driving force for this, even long past his assassination in Dallas on November 22, 1963.

Another speech that established a new endeavor with global impact was delivered at the Berlin Wall in Berlin, Germany, on June 12, 1987, by President

---

[355] Ibid. ppg 15, 20.

[356] The first quote is from President John F. Kennedy's inauguration speech given on the Capital steps in Washington D.C. on January 20, 1961. The second is from his speech outlining the mission to send a man to the moon and return him safely to the earth within the decade of the 1960's given at Rice Stadium in Houston, Texas on September 12, 1962.

Ronald Reagan. He stated, "Mr. Gorbachev, TEAR DOWN THIS WALL!" What these two leaders had in common was the ability to create and sustain a vision that was simple, direct, understandable, and one which established both pride of ownership and challenge. It is that ability that is the foremost challenge to any planner.

> The key to the creation of a workable, acceptable plan of action is the ability to create a simple, direct, understandable vision that communicates pride of ownership and challenge to the populace.

The creation of a clear vision is the first of many important assets. The second is the determination of what can and cannot be accomplished, given the needs of the organization and the available tools/personnel. An asset is any item necessary for the production of work. Assets are skilled and/or trainable people, funding, equipment, facilities, knowledge, and procedures. To be an asset, the person or item must be owned by, employed with, or under the control of the organization involved. They must be available for use and capable of performing the assigned task(s) without damage to the asset or the organization.

The first step in determining what assets are both required and available is to perform the breakdown analysis discussed earlier. The easiest method for this is to start with the primary goal and begin structuring the component elements. This is best performed using a project management tool of which there are several on the market. Figure 92 depicts an example of a type of program-planning structure in extreme draft status.

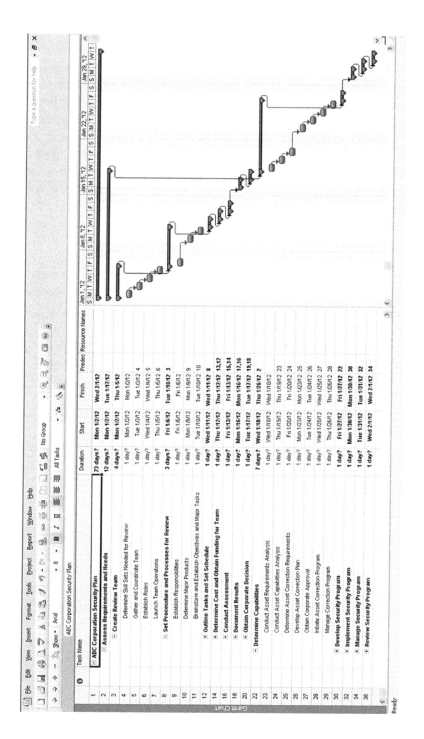

Figure 92: Example Security Program Development Structure

There are several things to notice in this figure. First, there is a WBS indicated by the indented major domains, which break down the major tasks into four distinct areas at this point and are in fact the actual work tasks to be performed. Secondly, there are specific start, finish, and duration times. Third, there are prerequisite elements that must be concluded *before* a new set can begin. For example, the planner must identify the types and skill sets of required employees for a team before hiring them. If a mathematician is needed, it does no good to hire a programmer. Even if their skills are similar, they are not functionally identical. Finally, there is an element available for the identification of nonhuman resources, detailing name, type, and capability. The more complete the structure is, the greater the ability to both manage and cross-level when needed.

RISK ANALYSIS

Risk analysis is the study of what could go wrong and how to mitigate or prevent the risk before it happens. Jon Toigo establishes the need for the risk analysis succinctly in his text as follows:

> *Risk analysis is perhaps the single most misunderstood aspect of disaster recovery planning. To many, the term is vague and mysterious, connoting rarefied techniques and unintelligible calculations known to only a very few privileged practitioners. To others, risk analysis is perceived as an irritating process of formalizing what is self-evident or obvious to anyone with a modicum of horse sense. As one information manager put it, "There is a generally accepted statistic that places the likelihood of a major disaster for any business at right around 1% per year. This is the risk. And when you have a disaster, you either have one or you don't. That's the exposure. That's all the risk analysis that you need. You just prepare for the worst." This is an oversimplification, of course, but the meaning is clear. Risk analysis is a big term for what is essentially a straightforward application of good research and common sense. This is indicated by the three basic objectives of risk analysis:*
>
> *1.   Identify business processes and their associated IT infrastructure resource requirements (that is, the data, applications, systems, and networks that are used in delivering the business process). Prioritize business processes according to time sensitivity and criticality.*
>
> *2.   Identify existing threats to business processes and infrastructure resources.*

3. *Define objectives for strategies to eliminate avoidable risks and to minimize the impact of risks that cannot be eliminated.*[357]

The process of risk analysis begins, not with a guessing game, rather with the detailed determination of what the environment has to offer with respect to the various terrain types identified in Section 2. Again, as Toigo writes,

> *Risk analysis consists of two basic operations: data collection and data analysis. The data collected in risk analysis should include a comprehensive list of business processes and their infrastructure supports, including computer and network hardware and applications, databases, and system software. From these data, business process flow diagrams are created and annotated to show resource requirements. Additionally, planners need to collect information about the amount of activity, traffic, or use of infrastructure resources to deliver each business process during a normal business hour, day, week, or month.*[358]

So once again, the WBS process comes into play. One must not only dissect the major and minor elements of the planning process. One must also dissect the natural processes of a business or organization. This dissection is the beginning of the aspects of offensive and defensive security/intelligence planning, for it this step that identifies and catalogues exploitable vulnerabilities.

> **The dissection of a business or organization's natural processes is the beginning of the offensive/defensive security/intelligence planning process, for it is this step that exploitable vulnerabilities are identified and catalogued.**

There are numerous methods for performing this function. One may establish a questionnaire to present to the users of the end products designed to ascertain which services are used, when, and what their criticality to the continuance of the production process may be. The goal is to obtain both their inputs, processes internal to the specific level being questioned, and their outputs to other entities.

A second method is the Delphi process. Delphi (as discussed starting page 190) is a structured methodology designed to solicit information from experts in a

---

[357] Toigo, J.W. (2003). *Disaster Recovery Planning: Preparing for the Unthinkable.* Prentice-Hall, Inc. Upper Saddle River, New Jersey. Pg. 36.

[358] Ibid. pg. 38.

group setting through a moderated or facilitated structure. The group is provided structured questions to consider, which are refined through stages and the results returned to the group for further consideration. This technique was designed to assist forecasters in making determinations of items, especially those with unknown or uncertain definitive physical, social, or technological facts.

Delphi has three major elements:

a. Facilitation and structuring of the information flow
b. Regular feedback to the participants
c. Anonymity of the participants

Facilitation and a structured information flow are necessary to maintain the process within the boundaries of the question(s) being considered to avoid digression away from the topic into domains where the mind becomes unfocused. The planner also uses group feedback to ascertain the level of confidence in the structure of provided information while enabling deeper assessment into specific areas of concern. Finally, anonymity of the participants avoids process contamination through influence by peers, superiors, or others. During joint or group sessions, individuals will collaborate or "group-think" themselves into an answer or position unsupported by the group as a whole. This is generally due to the belief that a more expert individual may have a greater understanding of the issue; thus, they try to appear to be at a similar level of "expertise" to that of the individual they consider most germane to the question at hand.

A third and generally one of the most accurate methods of risk analysis is benchmarking. Benchmarking involves learning what organizations perform the same or similar functions *and* who are considered to perform these tasks in a manner recognized by a standards organization as being of exceptional quality. Once this is known, the planner creates a relationship with those organization(s) to examine and use their findings as a primary means of determining similar results within the organization. Note that this method does not say to "copy" these systems and procedures, as these will not be identical in risks, assets, and requirements. It is simply a starting point.

The final method of risk analysis for this text is to examine historical information for the planner's organization, should it exist. Knowing what was required and tried in the past, including the results, gives the planner the most accurate information possible. Extrapolations from this baseline provide several benefits:

a. Executive management is already familiar with both the requirements, the costs, and the benefits.

b. This historically demonstrates how changes to current policy/procedure can improve efficacy and at what cost enables rapid decision making and buy-in.

c. Budgeting and staffing, as well as skill set analysis and training, become simpler.

d. Management and measurement criteria and methodologies are usually already in place or less expensive to alter.

Costs Analysis

Almost everything in life and business revolve around the costs. The PMBOK states,

> *Estimate(ing) costs is the process of developing an approximation of the monetary resources needed to complete project activities . . . are a prediction that is based on the information known at a given point in time. It includes the identification and consideration of costing alternatives to initiate and complete the project. Cost trade-offs and risks must be considered, such as make versus buy, buy versus lease, and the sharing of resources in order to achieve optimal costs for the project.*

> *[They] are generally expressed in units of some currency . . . although in some instances other units of measure, such as staff hours or staff days, are used to facilitate comparisons by eliminating the effects of currency fluctuations [and inflation/deflation].*

> *Cost estimates should be refined during the course of the project to reflect additional detail as it becomes available. The accuracy of a project estimate will increase as the project progresses through the project life cycle [Figure 93].*[359]

---

[359] PMBOK, pg. 168.

321

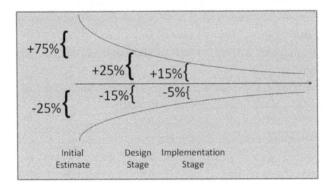

Figure 93: Growth of Cost Estimate Accuracy

As with risk analysis, cost analysis has many different methodologies. Most are similar to those of the risk analysis. Again, the PMBOK and many other texts have extensive instruction on how to perform this work. The WBS continues as a vital part of this process as well, along with the schedule, to determine cost. The planner should seldom perform the analysis on his/her own, instead making use of existing resources, as there are individuals within accounting departments with extensive experience in this kind of assessment. The following are some of the items included in the cost estimate:

a. Machinery/equipment lease amounts
b. Machinery/equipment purchase costs to include such things as maintenance, repair, supplies, etc.
c. Facility lease amounts
d. Facility purchase amounts to include such things as maintenance, repair, etc.
e. Manpower estimates in terms of work hours (converted to currency based upon the actual pay, benefits, tax, and other cost issues as appropriate)
f. Software licensing fees/purchase amounts
g. Disposal fees
h. Vendor estimates

Unmentioned by many planners, the most important cost estimate is time. Most planners consider time to be just an element of schedule, and it is very important to the development of the schedule. PMBOK includes the schedule and the resource calendars as primary inputs, stating, "The type and quantity of resources and the amount of time which those resources are applied to complete the work of the project are major factors in determining the project cost."[360] In each of the following methods of estimating, length of time for the proper completion of the tasks is a vital input value.

The primary tools/methodologies discussed in the PMBOK follow:[361]

a. *Expert judgment—Utilizing individuals or teams who have long-term experience in the performance of the tasks identified in the development of the WBS to provide input on the schedule time and/or associated costs*

b. *Analogous estimating—The use of values of parameters such as scope, cost, budget, and duration or measures of scale such as size, weight, and complexity*

c. *Parametric estimating—Utilization of statistical relationships between historical data and other variables*

d. *Bottom-up estimating—Making cost estimates for the most detailed tasks at the bottom level of the WBS and consolidating up to the top level*

e. *Three-point estimating—Utilization of the most likely estimate, the optimal estimate, and the least likely (pessimistic) in parametric fashion*

Figure 94 is the standard process used in the PMBOK for calculating specific costs. The values are the following:

C_E = Cost Estimate
C_O = Optimal Cost Estimate
C_M = Median Cost (multiplied by 4 due to its more common occurrence)
C_P = Cost Pessimistic (the expected greatest possible cost value)

$$C_E = \frac{C_O + 4C_M + C_P}{6}$$

Where:
E = Estimate
O = Optimal
M = Most Likely
P = Pessimistic

Figure 94: Cost Analysis Algorithm

---

[360] Ibid. pg. 170.
[361] Ibid. ppg. 171-173.

FLOW

Refer back to Figure 92 and notice that to the right of the task information within the WBS section is a block chart with connecting lines. This is known as a Gantt chart. This pictorial reference enables the program personnel to visualize the flow of the program. It contains, when properly used, a wealth of important information. The chart includes the following references:

a. The task box—Which contains an identifier of the specific WBS item, usually in terms of a WBS sequence number/alphanumeric. This identifier directs the manager to the specific task item information of assets, predecessor(s), outputs, costs, criticality, degree of completion, and other important data.

b. The connector graphic—An arrow linking the particular task to its prerequisite and subsequent tasks. The connectors are discussed shortly.

c. Forward start-finish time measured in chronological order

d. Backward finish-start time measured in chronological order

e. Identification of the critical path information and float value

TASK ITEM BOX

The task item box contains the information shown in Figure 95 below.

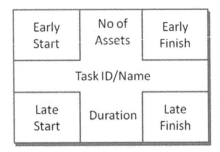

Figure 95: Task Item Box

a. Task ID/Name—The ID is usually an alphanumeric value that relates directly to the WBS and, depending upon the organization, may contain the department or other such information in the identifier. For example, 123A321 could mean "Level three of the WBS (123 value), Accounting (A value), Department 321."

b. Duration—The length of time assigned to the completion of the task, usually expressed in days. For major task items containing multiple subtasks, this is a roll-up of the total durations for all subtasks.

c. Number of Assets—Identifies the specific number of assets that will be employed to the task for the time identified. This item is used only when the task box is a single work element (e.g., assemble infrared sensor device, *not* build and install motion sensor suite, as there are multiple subtasks to this major task item).

d. Early Start—This value is a progressive time period (e.g., date or hours into the project) that this particular task may begin. If this is the very first task within a specific project, the value is usually recorded as "0."

e. Early Finish—This value derives from adding the Early Start time to the duration. This value carries over to the next task box in line of progression plus the addition of "1" value (e.g., day, hour, etc.) as the current task is assumed to require the entire time period to finish. Thus, if the Early Finish for this task is "4," the Early Start for the next progressive task is "5."

f. Late Finish—This value derives from a backward calculation of the time sequence and includes the same one time element difference between boxes as in step *e* above. This process appears in Figure 96.

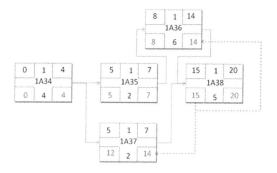

Figure 96: Example of Task Scheduling Calculations

1. Note that the 1A34 task begins and ends with values of zero and four in both sets of schedule data. This is a check that the process was performed correctly.

2. The values in the forward schedule continue to the final finish of twenty periods (e.g., days).

3. At this point, the Late Finish data is entered as the same twenty periods, and the backward calculations is initiated (dashed line) by subtracting the five-period duration of task 1A38 and placing that value in the Late Start data point of this same task.

4. This value of 15 has the one period value subtracted [see step *e* above] and is placed in the Late Finish data point for tasks 1A37 and 1A36.

325

5. Again, the duration is subtracted from the value from substep 4. However, a difference is obtained from the calculation in the Late Start points of these two tasks. The difference is due to the duration periods of the two tasks and indicates a point where "float" exists for one of the tasks (task 1A37 has eight periods of float [see step *h* below] between task 1A34 and task 1A37).

6. Now note that task 1A35 late finish has a value of 7 (from task 1A36), instead of a value of 11 (from task 1A37). This is because the process always takes the *lowest* Late Start value from all of the boxes *and* because while both 1A35 and 1A37 connect to 1A34, *only 1A35 connects to 1A36.*

7. Finally, the beginning task (1A34) receives the Late Start value from task 1A35 to complete the process.

g. Late Start—The late start value is the late finish value *minus* the duration of the specific task. The value in this process is twofold. First, it helps determine what pathway contains the most critical tasks of the program, known as the critical path. Second, it identifies tasks that have float.

h. Float—Float, in project terms, is a task value that allows for a delay in the start of a task for a specific period of time without impacting the overall completion of the program.

i. Critical Path—The progression of tasks that must begin and end at the scheduled periods, or they will cause a delay in the overall program schedule, thus increasing risk and cost.

CONNECTORS

Connectors are the arrows shown in Figure 97. A connector simply shows the point and type of linkage one task item has with others as explained below.

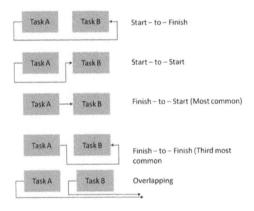

Figure 97: Connector Types for Project Management

a. Start-to-Finish: In the figure above, Task A must start as Task B is finishing, even though it is structured in the WBS as leading Task B. This is an extremely rare situation.

b. Start-to-Start: Both tasks start simultaneously. There may be different reasons for this connection. The most common is the ability to use one set of workers to perform two sets of tasks so similar that the outputs are nearly conjoined.

c. Finish-to-Start: This is the most common connection. As one task ends, it enables the next to begin. For example, from the earlier example of an automobile WBS, one would not install the piston chamber covers until the pistons were actually in place in the engine, as one would not be able to access the chamber with the cover in place. Or said another way, one would not place water on the stove to boil until one had first put the water in a fireproof container.

d. Finish-to-Finish: Both tasks are required to end at the exact same time in order to not delay the continuation of the project.

e. Overlapping: Tasks may start at different times; however, their progress overlaps. One sees this often in construction projects were as one team is constructing the interior walls of a building or home, and another is installing the wiring just as the wall is erected.

The most important thing to realize about flow is that it enables the sensible synchronization of events leading to an efficient project conclusion.

STAKEHOLDERS

The most important consideration in any program planning function is to have an executive champion. This is the most important stakeholder for program continuation and defense from competing programs. The executive champion is the senior manager tasked with the success of the program and who is also a major positive stakeholder. There is only so much capital to go around, no matter what some individuals may believe to the contrary. Keep in mind, however, that the champion rarely can perform this function alone, unless he/she is the CEO/owner.

The PMBOK considers stakeholder identification and management so critical that they devote an entire chapter to the process requirements. Within these standards, there are five basic steps:

a. Identify Stakeholders—Identify all people and/or organizations invested in the project and document relevant information regarding their interests, involvement, and impact on project success.

b. Plan Communications—Determine stakeholder informational needs and define an appropriate approach.

c. Distribute Information—Make relevant information available.
d. Manage Stakeholder Expectations—Communicate and work with stakeholders to meet their needs, addressing issues as they occur
e. Report Performance—Track and evaluate appropriate performance information on both the success of the stakeholder management process and the actions of the stakeholders themselves[362]

While the PMBOK views stakeholders as either positive or, at worst, benign, there are individuals with other intents, thus the need for security and intelligence plans in the first place. Often, these individuals form political influence cells or "cliques" to enhance both their influence and mutual support. Information is valuable, and knowledge of what that information means to the organization is power. When examining things from the political perspective and with the knowledge that resources are limited, competition for resources becomes the norm. When a security professional perceives a threat to one clique's security or objectives, the clique's standard behavior is to protect their domains. Thus, the clique's goal becomes not to appear as a threat or, if that perception is inevitable, to appear as less of a threat than another organization so as to keep attention to where it is most advantageous to your operation.

TIME

Time has been discussed as it relates to scheduling. However, the planner should also consider time in another fashion, that of both requirement and availability as a resource of importance. Consider this classic elementary school math problem. A family begins a trip of one hundred miles. For the first fifty miles, the family averages a speed of twenty-five mph. The math problem asks: how fast does the family need to go to average fifty mph for the entire trip? The answer is that it is impossible for them to make that average. Think about this for a minute. To achieve a fifty mph average for a one-hundred-mile trip, the entire trip must take no longer than two hours to complete. However, the family spent the first fifty miles of the trip averaging twenty-five mph, meaning the two hours are already spent and cannot be reclaimed. Thus, there is no possible way the family can achieve the fifty mph objective. It is a trick question but presents an illustration of an important aspect of time: once spent, it is gone.

What does this mean for planning in a program? If the executives desire to have a ten-month program completed in nine months and two of those months are already gone, there is likely insufficient float in any part to complete the program without removing major elements. Stated another way, concrete requires

---

[362] Ibid. pg. 243.

twenty-four hours per cubic yard to cure and harden. Nothing any engineer can do will speed this process up, as it is a law of physics for the materials that make up concrete. No amount of complaining or threats of repercussions to the employees will make that concrete cure any faster.

MODELING AND SIMULATIONS

It is invaluable to the creation of an effective and efficient plan that the planner be able to visualize the aspects of the program, the problems that will arise, the degree of success a potential solution set may offer, and the impact of various risks to the endeavor. However, does the use of mathematical models and computer simulations result in accurate predictions of the future? How heavily should the planner rely on such tools? The answer to this is contained in the following quote from Niccolo Machiavelli, "Whosoever wishes to foretell the future must consider the past, for human events ever resemble those of preceding times."[363] Friedrich Hegel disputed this concept, however, by saying,

> *What experience and history teach us is this—that peoples and governments never have learned anything from history, or acted on principles deduced from it. Each period is involved in such peculiar circumstances, exhibits a condition of things so strictly idiosyncratic, that its conduct must be regulated by considerations connected with itself, and itself alone. Amid the pressure of great events, a general principle is of no help.*[364]

Actually, both of these individuals are correct. History is the greatest teacher of human nature and how humans will respond to a specific event or set of conditions, showing how those conditions drive and regulate the event. Consider the various battlefields of Europe. How many times over the course of the centuries from Roman times to WWII were the same grounds used in the same ways, only the types and ranges of the weapon systems differed? Often, the same mistakes were made to allow for one side or the other to exploit a fleeting advantage based upon the commander's study of what General So-and-So did at this spot and under what conditions one hundred years previously.

The important point from this study of historical context appears in an article by Len Scott and R. Gerald Hughes, "One lesson of the war on Iraq is

---

[363] Cited in Bernard Crick, 'Introduction' to *Niccolo Machiavelli, The Discourses.* Bernard Crick (ed.), Leslie Walker (trans.), Penguin Publishers, London, 1983. Pg 50.

[364] Georg Wilhelm Friedrich Hegel, (1837) *The Philosophy of History.* Trans. J. Sibree, Dover Publishing. New York (1956). Pg 6.

that [information] needs to be used with precision and circumspection, and with greater acknowledgement of the limitations and contingencies of knowledge."[365] The primary question is: how to achieve this understanding and gain precision and circumspection?

> **One lesson of the war on Iraq is that information needs to be used with precision and circumspection and with greater acknowledgement of the limitations and contingencies of knowledge.**[314]

WHAT IS OPERATIONS RESEARCH

Let us begin this examination with a quote from the United States Undersecretary of Defense, the Honorable David S.C. Chu: "As a decision maker in the challenging international security environment swirling all around us I am, by inclination, experience, and position, more and more reliant upon the application of the science and art of military operations research."[366] Per the MORS reference book, *operations research* is defined as "a scientific method of providing executive departments with a quantitative basis for decisions regarding the operations under their control."[367]

One would add to this definition that operations research also provides a quantitative basis for monitoring, adjusting, and correcting these operations in a near real-time basis, given supportive criteria and appropriately established, tested, and tracked metrics. The MORS guide provides three primary procedures for the conduct of operational analysis:

a. Forming or describing the problem
b. Applying the mechanics of analysis
c. Reporting the results

To achieve the goal of an accurate analysis, MORS establishes specific professional ethics:

---

[365] Scott, L. and Hughes, R.G. (2006). Intelligence, Crises and Security: Lessons from History?, *Intelligence and National Security,* Vol. 21, No. 5, October 2006. Pp. 653-674. Pg. 670.

[366] Loerch, A.G. and Rainey, L.B. (eds). (2007). *Methods for Conducting Military Operational Analysis.* Military Operations Research Society (MORS), Washington, D.C. Pg. Forward.

[367] Ibid. pg 2.

a. Putting aside biases to report objectively
b. Fully explaining assumptions and limitations
c. Correctly selecting methods and tools
d. Objectively presenting results[368]

The process of operations research is not unknown in the corporate world. It is simply referred to by a different name: systems thinking. Charles Cobb, in his text *From Quality to Business Excellence*, outlines the following dynamics that are very similar to the concepts driving military operations research. These dynamics are culled from his writing and not specifically listed in this manner.[369]

a. Business is a complex system that must be considered as a whole environment and not piecemeal, using qualitative values structured into a cross-functional analysis.
b. Standards must be set, information gathered, and metrics applied against these standards to determine the effectiveness and efficiency of the business systems and processes in use.
c. Use of a systems engineering approach that considers all aspects of the organization and not result is localized solutions that adversely impact other areas unintentionally.
d. The use of integrated models providing appropriate views of the business, as relates to specific process maps aligned to strategy and controlled via metric analysis.

HOW OPERATIONS RESEARCH IS USED

Decisions are best made with information that is organized, structured, and logical. The term *logical* does not mean that the data and conclusions remain constant in all situations. It does mean that the data and conclusions for specific situations, with specific assumptions and for a specific stated problem, have their structure within valid syllogisms, forming a true and provable conclusion.

A syllogism is a form of argument that contains a major premise, a minor premise, and a conclusion. The major premise forms the structure of the argument. The minor premise provides information that supports the major premise, leading to the conclusion. There are two aspects of proof within the syllogism: validity and truth. Validity means that the premise does not contain any logical fallacies. Truth is just that, the statement that the premise asserts is factual. It is critical to

---

[368] Ibid. pp. 4-5
[369] Cobb, C.G. (2003). *From Quality to Business Excellence: A Systems Approach to Management.* American Society for Quality, Milwaukee, Ws.

remember, however, that a truthful premise may not make the syllogism valid. For example:

    a.   Cats have four legs with paws, fur, and a tail.
    b.   Benji has four legs with paws, fur, and a tail.
    ∴   (Therefore) Benji is a cat!

Notice that both premises are true, but only up to point. This is the critical aspect. To be truthful, the premise *must* be complete. Thus, a proper syllogism in this situation follows:

    a.   Cats have four legs with paws, fur, and a tail. They belong to the genus *Felis*.
    b.   Benji has four legs with paws, fur, and a tail. They belong to the genus *Canis*.
    ∴   (Therefore) Benji is a dog!

In a situation of planning and decision making, the conditions are similar, though somewhat more involved. Here is an example of an actual situation for a detailed analysis. This problem involved the application of surveillance of a combat area. The question involved which type of overhead surveillance system was the most appropriate and would provide the best coverage of the area. The approach involved the structure of a syllogism with the specific dynamics of value: duration of coverage, completeness of the coverage, and number of significant acquisitions for each option. Figure 98 derives from a portion of the study, detailing the issues.

Study Issues

- Which UAS is more operationally effective?
- Which UAS provides multi-role capability?
- Which UAS is more sustainable?
- Which UAS is more transportable?
- Which UAS is more deployable?
- Which UAS is more affordable?

Figure 98: Unmanned Aerial Vehicle (UAV) Study Criteria

The study involved the design of a specific combat scenario that would test the various conditions (seen in Figure 91) in a certain environment of terrain, threat, weather conditions, and flight dynamics. With this information, the planner created a simulation with the specific attributes involved. The simulation was then run thirty times per UAV/weather/flight situations for a total of ninety runs. The planner compiled the resulting data into the graphics seen in Figure 99 and reported to the customer.

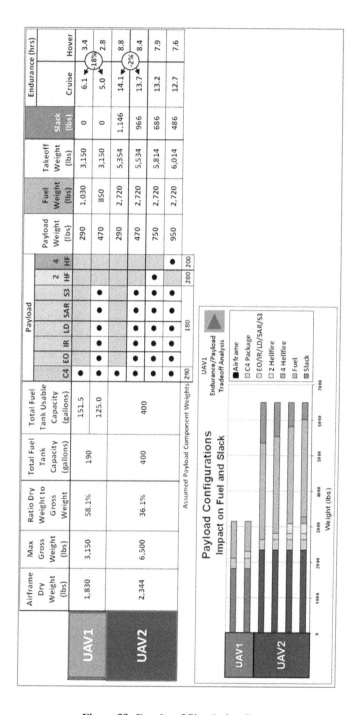

Figure 99: Results of Simulation Runs

In this particular analysis, the customer was a major government organization with concerns that a particular system they were considering for purchase was not going to provide the support needed by their personnel. Upon the conclusion of the study, several experiments were set up where the systems actually flew in conditions similar to those of the simulation. This confirmed the findings. As a result, the agency changed the program.

From the syllogistic perspective, the results were the following:

a. The appropriate unmanned system for the agency is required to perform to the standards set by [specific specifications document].
b. UAV1 performed at a level that was at 85 percent specification for $x,xxx,xxx per copy.
c. UAV2 performed at a level that was at 115 percent specification for $x,xxx,xxx that is 5 percent per copy less than UAV1.
∴ UAV2 is a more appropriate candidate system for the agency.

The point is that planners can use operations research to make decisions, especially when the decisions require high confidence in the results and the risks are moderate to significant.

One of the nation's primary research facilities, Sandia Laboratories, uses operations research to assist in their security planning and operations. Sandia is a government-run experimentation organization consisting of several sites with multiple facilities at widely separated locations. Their security budget is controlled by DoD and is, in fact, limited, particularly where changes to existing facilities are concerned. Therefore, they needed some method of determining where to spend these limited resources.

As with the UAV study above, Sandia had numerous variables, such as the extent and severity of the threat. The questions were: Did they require improvements/upgrades to current system capabilities, or did they require replacement? And to what degree was the risk of damage to national security if a security breach did occur? Add to this the actual costs of performing the upgrade/change in the systems. The goal was to determine where Sandia would have the most value in terms of improved security from the limited capital assets.

The security personnel used a mixture of Delphi and historical analysis to construct a normalized chart of threat, protection value, requirements, and current capabilities. Normalizing is a process whereby items of different type can be provided with a single comparable value. Completing this, the costs for the improvements were applied against a value ratio[370] to arrive at a comparable

---

[370] A value ratio is simply the cost of one item against the cost of the other in a ratio (1.5:1 or 1:3, etc) form.

"degree of goodness." The decision makers could then decide with a great degree of confidence on an appropriate best course of action.

VALUE IN MODEL CREATION

Recall that there is a difference between a *model* and a *simulation*, although the two terms are often used as synonyms. A model is a representation of some reality in microcosm (small scale), while a simulation takes the model and applies dimensions to it (e.g., space, time, activity). The construction of a model, whether on paper, in a computer image, in a sand table, or using other means, is an excellent method for enhancing understanding and visualization.

Referring back to Chapter 4, Human Terrain, the human brain works by creating pictures of the things it wishes to remember. It does this by generating protein chains that stimulate the various aspects of the brain to recreate the experience. A student testing this theory needs simply close their eyes and think of a fond memory. They will *not* see a series of words, rather, they will see a complete picture of the event.

There are numerous texts, writings, and consulting organizations expounding upon the necessity of creating specific types of business models to ensure success. These models establish the mission, the philosophy, the market, and the product(s) of the organization or entity, laying the groundwork within those understanding the model to make it succeed. The concept of neurologic creation (or mind over matter) actually had its beginnings in the shop of a nineteenth century apothecary, Emile Coue.[371]

What Coue actually discovered was a concept now known as the placebo effect, which has surprising ties to the success of a business via a well-thought-out model. The *Webster's Medical Dictionary* defines the *placebo effect* as:

> *A remarkable phenomenon in which a placebo—a fake treatment, an inactive substance like sugar, distilled water, or saline solution—can sometimes improve a patient's condition simply because the person has the expectation that it will be helpful. Expectation too plays a potent role in the placebo effect. The more a person believes they are going to benefit from a treatment, the more likely it is that they will experience a benefit.*

Following this observation, Coue began the study of hypnosis. The aspect of the power of visualization is aptly described in the experiment (both thought and real) as defined by the following:

---

[371] Coué, E: (1922). *Self Mastery Through Conscious Autosuggestion*. Public Domain.

Suppose that we place on the ground a plank 30 feet long by 1 foot wide. It is evident that everybody will be capable of going from one end to the other of this plank without stepping over the edge. But now change the conditions of the experiment, and imagine this plank placed at the height of the towers of a cathedral. Who then will be capable of advancing even a few feet along this narrow path? Could you hear me speak? Probably not. Before you had taken two steps you would begin to tremble, and in spite of every effort of your will [sic] you would be certain to fall to the ground.[372]

Note that if this experiment were tried with the plank only a few feet above the ground, the same effect is experienced. However, when one is firmly convinced of the stability of the plank as well as their own inability to fall, they will perform as if the plank were resting on solid ground. Coue further states from his experimentation and that of other psychologists of his time, something that psychologists today echo (e.g., F. Stetter and S. Kupper.):[373]

Vertigo is entirely caused by the picture we make in our minds that we are going to fall. This picture transforms itself immediately into fact in spite of all the efforts of our will, and the more violent these efforts are, the quicker is the opposite to the desired result brought about.[374]

The formulation of a visual structure of an activity both allows for that activity to be recognized and stored by the human brain. It enhances the activity's success potential.

Value in Simulations

Stated earlier, simulations add dimensional aspects to the model. Dimensional aspects are such things as movement, time, depth, and consequences. A model shows what is at a single given point within the business and/or process. A simulation takes that information, combines it with other values, and moves it along to a logical conclusion based upon the inputs and variables used in its construction. Additionally, depending on the type of simulation used, the results can become fairly close to reality for a given set of circumstances.

---

[372]   Ibid. pg 6.

[373]   Stetter, F. and Kupper S. (2002). Autogenic training: a meta-analysis of clinical outcome studies. *Applied Psychophysiology and Biofeedback, 27 (1), ppg 45-98.*

[374]   Ibid

The UAV study discussed previously is an excellent example of this situation. The simulation was constructed so that a UAV flying specified routes in given conditions would have opportunity to observe an intelligence event occurring randomly along the flight path. Because the intelligence event was random, a single pass by the targeted UAV was unproductive. Given this, to obtain useful data, no valid conclusions could be drawn from the UAV result. However, by conducting both multiple passes and simulation runs, the simulation begins to demonstrate patterns. Multiple runs of the identical scenario results in the appearance of certain averages and distributions of data points that may be statistically evaluated. Once these distributions were established, it becomes possible to validate the simulation through comparison with live data or conduct a set of live experiments to determine analytical matches.

Another example is a simulation that was constructed and run of the WWII Battle of Kursk. In this simulation, the identical location, forces, equipment, numbers, tactics, weather, etc., were created within the simulation. After the simulation, the agency compared the results, which demonstrated a remarkable similarity to those of actual battle in terms of ground gained, losses sustained, enemy killed, and time consumed to attain the final objective.

Business simulations are quite similar. For example, business planners will use value process simulations that examine perturbations within markets and financial structures over a period of time. This process can, for example, determine the impact on the corporate structure's profitability from a set of financial conditions. The models examine a specific set of market, capital, and political situations based on historical data to validate the simulation. Once validated with the historical data, the variables may be adjusted to determine the results of various strategies and/or operations to arrive at a statistical result for these experiments.

Day traders use such simulations constantly. Often, their programs involve specific investment strategies, stock purchases/sales, etc., to determine a means of gaining the most likely success at the greatest rate of return on investment. As with most other simulations, their tools have been validated on historical data keyed to current activities and markets. They also have the same limitations, as they are not able to quantify all the variables that may impact a specific set of circumstances.

The key is that the value of a simulation derives from its ability to copy linear events to arrive at a logical outcome of the input values or make a relationship decision between two related events (Figure 100). What if the events are nonlinear? This question brings up the issue of what linear and nonlinear events represent. A linear event is one that follows another and is caused directly because of the other ($A \rightarrow B \rightarrow C$; $A \neq C$ except that it must pass through B first; e.g., READY $\rightarrow$ AIM $\rightarrow$ FIRE). A nonlinear event may occur outside of this progression and be brought into the calculus at any point ($A \rightarrow B \rightarrow Z \rightarrow C$; e.g.,

READY, AIM, LOAD, FIRE).[375] Often, nonlinear situations appear totally random yet are predictable within the structure of their dynamics (Figure 101).

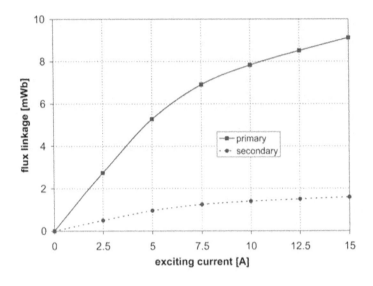

Figure 100: Linear Representation

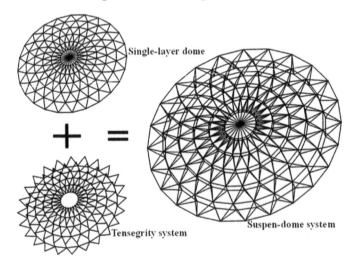

Figure 101: Nonlinear Representation

---

[375] As an aside, this example seems improper, however, when talking about many artillery systems, the weapon is readied first, set into the appropriate aiming, then the ammo or round is loaded into the tube and fired.

While these representations may appear confusing, the right tools and knowledge can unlock their meaning. Those with the appropriate knowledge of both the source dynamics and the application mathematics used can both construct and interpret these data depictions. The value is that enabling a visual representation of the information allows the analyst to rapidly determine the meaning of the data and arrive at conclusions.

Types of Simulations

Earlier in this chapter, the text defined the various types of models. Refer back to these definitions prior to continuing this section. Simulations are generally divided into modes or segments identified by the depth or level of abstraction they examine.

Behavioral simulation

This type of simulation examines each piece of the system as an individual "black box" with specific inputs and outputs that either originate from or feed other "boxes" of the simulation. Prime examples of such a simulation are the highly graphical video games children and many adults play. These simulations must refer to various boxes for each move of the controller. Granted the behavioral level is at a much more detailed level of abstraction, however, this type of game makes the process more understandable.

When the avatar looks to its left, for example, the system must refer to the terrain, facilities, vegetation, line of sight, enemy, and cueing boxes. Each returns a specific value to the main (integrator) application, which compiles the inputs and "paints" them (as required) to the screen. This allows the user to make various decisions (inputs) required, continuing the simulation.

Now add a weapon (rifle for example) and the abstraction becomes more detailed. The player selects to fire the weapon, and a "bullet" releases toward the target. This engages a trajectory or probability of hit (P_H) calculation, likely pulled from the well-known Lanchester equations. This process pulls range, weather dynamics, and other flight characteristics and variables from special tables; applies the probability value; and generates a random number to determine if the bullet hits the target and more specifically, *where* it lands on the target.

At this point, a new set of calculations occur based on the target-bullet-energy relationships. The bullet must have sufficient energy left from its flight to penetrate the various layers of the "skin" of the target, each layer having specific dynamics and energy absorption values. This is known as the shot-line evaluation. As the bullet passes each layer, some of its energy is lost and its ability to continue penetration lowers, particularly when the target has some form of armor.

Now the bullet has passed through the "skin" layers and retains energy to continue moving. The calculations now look at the components of the target lying

339

directly beneath the skin and in direct line of the path the bullet continues to take. Each of these components is a "box" unto itself. Impact by the bullet causes the same penetration calculations; however, an additional calculation of "damage" is applied as the criticality of the component to the "life" of the overall system. For example, if the target is a tank and the first component is a water bottle, the damage to the tank is nearly nonexistent. If, however, the component is a fuel tank, the fuel "ignites," and the tank is destroyed. This process continues until the bullet has lost all of its energy and an output of "killed/damaged/not killed" is returned to the system.

However, it does not stop here, as there are secondary and tertiary effects. The bullet passing through the skin can create heat and spall (flaking) effects. These radiate in a cone out from the point of exit into the interior of the target. Each of these rays, and there may be hundreds of them, requires their own calculations of "damage" and "kill" to report back to the central compiler.

These calculations occur for each observer-target combination involved in the simulation, and the player must complete each and every one prior to the next side of the turn initiating. The military uses such simulations to conduct detailed combat operations analyses, which can consume hundreds of hours of computer run time for each hour of actual playtime. Such simulations are expensive to build, maintain, prepare, and run, let alone the extensive amount of data needed for both inputs and outputs that require examination for accuracy. This leads the analyst to the second type of simulation.

FUNCTIONAL SIMULATIONS

A functional simulation is much closer to the actual processing routines of the standard video game than the behavioral simulation. The nice thing is that a behavioral simulation[376] can be used to generate what are known as probability tables that provide values based on the very detailed structures described above.

---

[376] A behavioral simulation examines the intricate nature and elements of an object with relationship to another in minute detail. For example, the US Army Systems Analysis Agency or AMSAA is tasked with the creation of all such data. One set they develop takes a vehicle system (tank, truck, etc.) and simulates shooting at them from thousands of directions with every possible munition/weapon combination there is. They measure the energy of the munition at impact, the direction of the shot, and follow the shot through the target until the munition runs out of energy. This is known as a shot-line. On the shot line, the analyst looks at what the munition hits during its travel and determines if the damage caused will 'kill' that piece/system/human or cause secondary effects. An example of a secondary effect is the munition penetrating a fuel line or tank and causing a fire or explosion.

Other models can use these tables rather than having to perform the shot-line or line-of-sight calculations themselves. The calculations become simple yes/no values based upon a Monte Carlo draw, a random toss of the dice to determine if the answer is yes or no.

The simulation performs the view changes as before. However, rather than calculating if anything is seen, it *knows* there is a target in the visual field. It determines whether or not to provide this information to the user. This is based on a probability of acquisition (P_A) expressed in terms of a 0 to 1.0 value. The value derives from another simulation "box" obtained from the behavioral simulation that has values for the "seeing" sensor (e.g., naked eyes, binoculars, infrared scope, night-vision scope, etc.) in relation to the target dynamics (e.g., amount visible, camouflage, vegetation, light levels, etc.). If the P_A value is low (0.2 for example), the dice throw must be a 1 or 2 to return a "yes" value. Otherwise, the user does not "see" the target.

If the target is "seen," a similar probability of identification (P_I) value will determine if the user can determine *what* the target is (e.g., tank, truck, person, animal, etc.). This is followed by a probability of recognition (P_R) value (e.g., enemy T-72, friendly M1A1, etc.). This result refers to an enemy/friendly table that returns a yes/no value on engagement. The logic is as follows: If enemy = yes then engage; if not, return to search.

The engagement process uses the same protocol, replacing the acquisition/ identification/ recognition values with the shot/hit/kill probability values discussed earlier. The output of this set of dice rolls determines if the target is undamaged/ damaged, including to what degree, or killed, if shot at with a weapon that can defeat it.

These calculations, because they are using probability values and Monte Carlo rolls, are significantly faster than those conducted during the behavioral simulation, microseconds rather than minutes per shooter/target pair. The outputs are also less cumbersome, although they may remain significant. Additionally, because the calculations are less rigorous than the behavioral simulation, the user must obtain statistical validity by running the functional simulation multiple times to obtain statistical normality, as discussed earlier in this text.

STATIC SIMULATION

Static simulation removes many of the elements of time and movement from the previous two simulation types. The input values are much less demanding and the outputs highly binary (i.e., yes/no). Returning to our simulation example, the "dice roll" reduces to a simple odd/even or specific number value (e.g., if the roll on an 8-sided die is less than 4, the answer is no; otherwise, if 4-8, it is yes). Here, the general assumption is that the user can observe the target and recognize it as an enemy. The dice roll is limited to killed/not killed. Many board games fall into this type of simulation (e.g., Monopoly, Sorry, Aggravation, etc.). Many role-playing games also use this methodology.

LOGIC SIMULATION

Often, this type of simulation is known as a BOGSAT, which the reader will recall stands for a bunch of guys sitting around a table. While humorous, the application is accurate. There are numerous options on how to conduct this type of simulation, such as Delphi or focus-group interactions. In such situations, a given scenario provides the driving conditions for users to run various problems through. The users, who should be known experts in the areas in question, provide interactive inputs to the discussion, which a controller facilitates to keep things on track and curtail arguments and/or disagreements between team members.

The Delphi methodology involves a multiple iteration process where the members are surveyed for their opinions on given topics under a set environment or scenario. The results of the first iteration are made available in summary format for the second run. This repeats for each successive round. At times, the members of the group rotate to obtain a broader range of outputs and/or to strengthen the confidence in the results generated.

Focus groups are conducted in a manner similar to Delphi, except that the results of previous groups are not provided to the new groups and no group is called in for more than one round. Often, the possible responses are limited to achieve specific information results. This does not mean that the results are skewed (although they may be), rather, such a procedure limits the range of responses to a focused domain to avoid digression.

USE OF SIMULATIONS IN SECURITY/INTELLIGENCE PLANNING

Use of simulations as a means to assist planning is not something relegated to the military alone. A prime example appears in a study by the University of North Carolina, concerning the protection of critical infrastructures by identifying potential vulnerabilities and testing various redresses without the need for actual experimentation on the infrastructure itself, an expensive and dangerous process. The authors state,

> *Protecting critical infrastructures, such as electrical power grids, has become a significant concern for many nation states in recent years. Critical infrastructures involve multi-dimensional, highly complex collections of technologies, processes, and people, making them vulnerable to potentially catastrophic failures on many levels.*

Moreover, cross-infrastructure dependencies can lead to cascading and escalating failures across multiple infrastructures.[377]

The model type used is an agent-based model, as shown in Figure 102. Examples of the output graphics from the simulation used for the analysis of disruption impacts appear in Figure 103.[378] Note that the output does not say, "This hospital/police station will be impacted in this particular way." Rather, it shows that there is a zone of impact. The analyst must then delve deeper into what this means, using their experience, research, and other tools to arrive at a full and complete assessment.

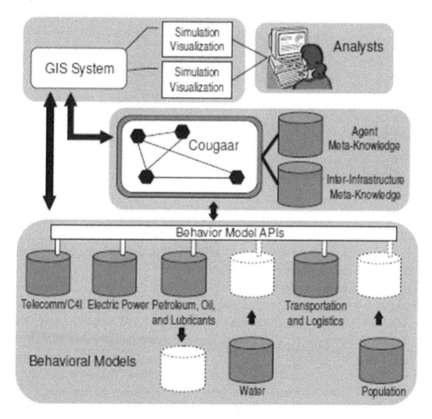

Figure 102: Critical Infrastructure Model/Simulation Architecture

---

[377] Tolone, W.J., Wilson, D., Raja, A., Xiang, W. and Johnson, E.W. (2004). *Applying COUGAAR to Integrated Critical Infrastructure Modeling and Simulation.* University of North Carolina. Charlotte, NC. Pg 1.

[378] Ibid. ppg 5, 6.

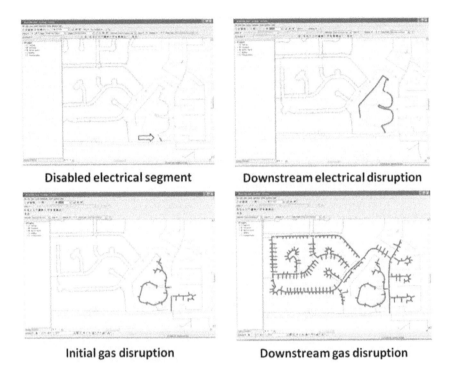

Disabled electrical segment   **Downstream electrical disruption**

Initial gas disruption   **Downstream gas disruption**

Figure 103: Example Output Graphics

Experiments with simulations also have found a way into the cybersecurity domain. An excellent paper on this was developed by several researchers at the University of Memphis, Tennessee. They investigated the use of game-theory architectures as the processing dynamic for assessment of attacker/system administrator interactions to determine appropriate and effective responses, protections, and countermeasures to core security breaches. The paper states,[379]

> *The crux of our holistic security approach is utilization of game theory. Game theory can choose the security measures which make the best tradeoff between the incurred cost and level of security achieved. The cost includes the investment expenditure as well as the performance degradation of the system due to the extra load of the security action. There are two kinds of security decisions—one that is statically chosen*

---

[379] Shiva, S., Roy, S., and Dasgupta, D. (2012). *Game Theory for Cyber Security.* University of Memphis, Memphis, Tn. Pg 2. Downloaded on December 2, 2011, from http://gtcs.cs.memphis.edu/index.php?c=publications

which has an investment cost or performance penalty [defensive] and one which is dynamically selected which causes some performance degradation [offensive].

The experimentation cited in this paper results in several important observations. The most pertinent is the following:[380]

Our observation is that to achieve reliable security we have to consider the interaction of the security decision for one component in the system with the policy taken for others, and as a result, the decision space becomes large. Game theory is a potential tool to model and analyze such an enormous search space involving numerous what-if scenarios. It can also model the inherently selfish and competitive behaviors of the attacker and system administrator and analyze the possible strategies. In addition, game theory has the capability of examining hundreds of thousands of possible scenarios before taking the best action; hence, it can sophisticate the decision process of the network administrator to a large extent.

Most of the experiments in this domain assume perfect knowledge of the targeted system by the system administration team. This is not real world. So the researchers used stochastic modeling techniques, which included various nonzero error probability factors to create false alarms, undetected attacks, and detected attacks that resulted in both a reaction and no reaction. The goal was to avoid what is known as the Nash equilibrium. In game theory, Nash equilibrium (named after John Nash, an accomplished mathematician) is a solution concept of a game involving two or more players in which each player is assumed to know the strategies of the other players, and no player can gain advantage by changing only his own strategy unilaterally.[381] Using a probability-driven stochastic structure, Nash said that equilibrium was not achieved, and other experiments of similar nature were validated. What this means is that the study supports the use of simulation to assist in planning cybersecurity actions as a viable planning tool.

Similarly, such simulations can be and often are used in intelligence planning. One such simulation is the sand table. A sand table is a 3-D construction of the situation, terrain, building, etc., that permits detailed examination of a scenario. The sand tables (Figure 104) used in operations planning and rehearsals are nothing more than one type of model, which becomes a simulation when the

---

[380] Ibid. pg 2.

[381] Nash, J. (1950) "Equilibrium points in n-person games." *Proceedings of the National Academy of Sciences* 36(1):48-49.

players use it to determine move/countermove scenarios. Additionally, there are many computer simulations currently in use by the military for both acquisition and functional analysis and for detailed asset use planning. The point is not the use of simulations, rather how they are used and whether or not they are used correctly.

Figure 104: Sand Table Simulation/Exercise of Forest Firefighters

Sir Arthur Conan Doyle used his fictional character, Sherlock Holmes, to state, "You see but you do not observe. The distinction is clear, [for you see the steps, but not how many nor their condition, leading to the potential for a dangerous fall] . . . It is a capital mistake to theorise [*sic*] before one has data. Insensibly one begins to twist facts to suit theories, instead of theories to suit facts."[382]

The work of intelligence is the collection of data. An analyst establishing a simulation based upon data to answer specific questions (theories) leads to the support/validation or the rejection of all or part of those theories. Again, Doyle's character provides a nugget of wisdom in this area, "When you have eliminated the impossible, whatever remains, *however improbable*, must be the truth."[383] Kristan Wheaton, a noted author, professor, and intelligence officer, states the requirement, "Weathermen, like intelligence analysts, deal daily with complex

---

[382]   Doyle, A.C. (1892). The Adventures of Sherlock Holmes: A Scandal in Bohemia. Harper Publishers, New York, NY. Npn.

[383]   Ibid. The Sign of Four (1890). Pg 92.

data and, again like intelligence analysts, they voice their forecasts in terms of probabilities."[384] This translates to the fact that weathermen and intelligence analysts, due to the high number of variables, cannot be certain of their conclusions, thus use a probability value to state their confidence in the results.

An important point to remember is that there is a difference between intelligence analysis and information retrieval. Koltuksuz and Tekir explain the difference:

> In the first place, intelligence analysis is driven by the question of the policymaker in which there is a formal, explicit question to provide an outcome for. Intelligence analysts do the task of producing the outcome for the intelligence problem at hand. Secondly, information retrieval systems focus on the objective concerns but the person looking for information is of secondary importance. Intelligence analysis systems, on the other hand, try to ease the job of the intelligence analyst by giving access to customizable and automatable analytical and collaboration tools including machine translation, knowledge discovery, trend analysis, and social network analysis tools. In this regard, the intelligence analyst plays a central role and, that is of the primary importance in intelligence analysis.[385]

This difference defines the structure and type of simulations available to the intelligence planner. The analyst focuses on a threat in respect to how known data corresponds to future action in a specific tactical situation. The planner focuses on what measures a threat will take to avoid detection and/or confuse the analyst once detection occurs. As Doyle pointed out in the previous quotes, one must not only see, one must observe and consider the implications of those observations to the task at hand.

The use of both models and simulations in planning basically drives the process of focused logical thought with the inclusion of tools and processes that permit the visualization of data as real objects, whether as a sand table, a rendered terrain graphic, an event flow graphic, or some form of data progression chart/graph. These tools permit the planner to observe the effects changes have on timing, resources, costs, and outcomes, as well as the ability to experiment with alternatives in a safe and inexpensive environment, relative to the real-world costs and risks. The planner should use the developed details in the creation of

---

[384] Wheaton, K. and Chido, D. (2007). Evaluating Intelligence. *Competitive Intelligence Magazine,* Vol 10, No 5. September—October 2007. Ppg 19-23. Pg 20.

[385] Koltuksuz, A. and Tekir, S. (2006). Intelligence Analysis Modeling. *International Conferrence on Hybrid Information Technology/IEEE Computer Society.* Pg 2.

the overall WBS, as the visualization process will likely reveal requirements not considered or hidden through other concerns.

The modeling and simulation events must be planned out using the following steps:

    a.   Determine the target audience/participant requirements.

    b.   Create the objective.

    c.   Create the scenario.

        1.   Design a problem, not a solution.

            i.   Start with a problem in mind.

            ii.   Create uncertainty by leaving certain things to chance or probability.

            iii.   Create friction through refusing to apply a "school solution" based on bias.

        2.   Create the exercise road map and synchronize events.

    d.   Determine the output parameters, metrics, and evaluation processes.

    e.   Determine how the information should be presented to visualize the outcomes.

    f.   Ignore pressure to "fit" conclusions to theories, rather fit theories to the data to arrive at conclusions.

    g.   Design the report format and include all variables, assumptions, limitations, and methodologies, as well as the pre/post-processing data elements and acquisition processes/procedures.

    h.   Review and evaluate the data, outcomes, conclusions, and how the processes contributed to these elements.

    i.   Record and communicate the results and obtain feedback for additional analysis.

INTEGRATION OF OPERATIONS AND PLANNING

> **Integration of security/intelligence operations and planning generally is viewed as the creation of a structure that combines physical security, operational procedures, and monitoring functionality on personnel, information, and physical assets. This is an incomplete view.**

Integration of security/intelligence operations and planning creates a structure that combines physical security, operational procedures, and monitoring functionality on personnel, information, and physical assets. This is an incomplete view, however, as true integration of security/intelligence operations and planning is where the plans and processes for deterrence, detection, delay, response, recovery, and reevaluation are a complete part of the organization/business

OFFENSIVE AND DEFENSIVE SECURITY

enterprise. This includes the measurement of the planning effort's contribution to the bottom-line profitability and/or functionality of the enterprise in total. This is not a simple exercise. However, the need has been identified and codification of the requirement begun as demonstrated in the following text:

> Traditionally, information security and capital planning have been treated as separate activities by security and capital planning practitioners. However, with Federal Information System Management Act (FISMA) legislation, existing federal regulations that charge agencies with integrating the two activities. Additionally, with increased competition for limited federal budgets, agencies must effectively integrate their information security and capital planning processes.[386]

Everything involved in an enterprise has a cost and a return on investment (ROI). Some are simply more difficult to quantify. In most instances, the impact or ROI for an activity is measured negatively, as in the opportunity cost for *not* having the activity already in place. An excellent example of this is the security domain of disaster recovery and business continuation. Organizations that do not have a specific plan in place for continued operations will, once a disaster occurs, be immediately out of business, regardless if their product set is critical to the population.

Examine the differences between Hurricane Ike, which impacted the Texas coast, and Hurricane Katrina, specifically in the area of New Orleans, Louisiana. Damage suffered by the population in both cases was extreme; however, the level of planning and preparation prior to Ike was significantly more advanced. This resulted in many government and business operations recovering in hours to days, instead of years. Significant portions of the New Orleans population remain displaced in 2012, while little of the population of the Houston-to-Beaumont corridor have not either returned or reestablished their lives elsewhere voluntarily.

Specific research on this topic is very limited; however, one report conducted by the Center for Hazards Research and Policy Development placed the unrecovered costs of rebuilding after Hurricane Katrina in excess of $200 billion. The costs for Hurricane Ike were significantly less, a fact owed in no small part to the willingness of the State of Texas to have local logging firms involved in the

---

[386] Bowen, P., Kissel, R. Scholl, M., Robinson, W., Stansfield, J. and Voldish, L. (2009). *NIST Special Publication 800-65 (Rev 1 DRAFT): Recommendation for Integrating Information Security into Capital Planning and Investment Control Process.* US Department of Commerce, Washington, D.C. pg ix.

349

recovery and use of tree blowdown damage, creating a profitable business out of the disaster that created jobs and income used to rebuild.[387]

The difference was the preplanned integration of multiple disciplines and based upon the lessons learned in the failures demonstrated during Hurricane Katrina. Not only did FEMA, TRANSTAR (the Texas Emergency Management Agency), and other officials from various emergency organizations communicate the issues and failures to the general populace of businesses and agencies, these groups began to brainstorm ways to apply their individual strengths to the potential issues. For example, major structural damage to homes was expected, requiring wood and other building materials for repairs. This area of Texas is heavily forested, and past major storms have resulted in extensive tree blowdown.

Federal and state environmental policies and regulations prohibit foresting in various locations, many of which are prime lumber areas. After a major storm, however, there are hundreds, if not thousands, of uprooted and damaged trees that require clearing from land, roadways, and other locations. Previously, the state or FEMA paid for the clearing, and the lumber was wasted. Now there are local companies that clear the trees, transport them to the mills, and turn the lumber into construction boards used in repairs. The companies have the equipment, the state supplies the processed lumber at cost, and the repairs are completed rapidly.

Other infrastructure repairs are completed in the usual manner by the firms responsible for the structures. However, until the roadways and access locations are cleared, the repairs to infrastructure damage cannot begin. The State of Texas collaboration with the lumber industry turned a major stumbling block into a chance for entrepreneurial ingenuity.

Note that the requirement is the ability to conduct cross-functional discussions in an open environment of cooperation of strengths to weaknesses/needs. The organizations must create a community structure that looks to ensure cooperative benefit. This requirement is also true for internal organizational structures. To do this, planners must consider a major distinction, that of the differences between safety and security. Dr. Mary Clifford discusses this in her work:

> *Mary Lynn Garcia . . . notes that safety and security issues are sometimes discussed as if they are the same thing. She cautions people to be aware of the critical distinction between the two: "safety" refers to "abnormal environments," while "security" refers to "malevolent human attacks." Issues such as electrical outages, hurricanes, fires, chemical spills, and other kinds of accidents are safety issues,*

---

[387] Lasley, C.B., Simpson, D.M., Rockaway, T.D., and Weigel, T. (2007). *Understanding Critical Infrastructure Failure: Examining the experience of Bilozi and Gulfport Mississippi after Hurricane Katrina.* University of Louisville, Louisville, Ky.

whereas workplace or school violence is a security issue. Both safety and security issues require response planning. As has been stated throughout this book, security responses should be integrated, and disaster response plans are no exception. The integrated emergency plan or disaster response should be structured and implemented to include everyone in the target environment. In addition to being well educated about a disaster response, people within a target environment need to understand what plan is in place and how they are expected to be involved . . . [388]

The chart in Figure 105 provides some examples of considerations and issues, pertaining to natural disasters and potential impacts to a work environment.

Natural Disaster	Potential Impact on the Workplace
Windstorm (hurricane, tornado)	Damage to structures and equipment; injury due to airborne projectiles, and related storm surge
Earthquake	Damage to structures and equipment; personal injury a hazard as floors and buildings crumble and debris and equipment fall; fire or explosions
Flood (flash flood, storm surge)	Disruption and danger to electrical wiring and gas lines if exposed to flood water; fires
Lightning	Tree falling on facility; fire; damage to equipment; electrocution of individuals
Winter storm	Travel hazards; power outages; roof collapse; frostbite, hypothermia, and death
Heat wave	Heat exhaustion, dehydration, and death

Source: Adapted from S. Wortham, "Expect the Unexpected: How To Protect Your Workers in a Natural Disaster," *Safety and Health* 156, no. 3 (1997): 48–53.

Figure 105: Impact of Natural Disasters on the Workplace

These potential impacts are only starting points. For example, when planning the disaster recovery program for a major computer manufacturing firm, the considerations included the need to feed and protect stay-behind workers and security personnel. The protection requirement was not so much against individuals seeking to loot or steal food, rather to protect them from wildlife displaced by floodwaters and other conditions. During the extensive fires and drought that plagued Texas during the 2011 summer, many different forms of wildlife entered residential areas, searching for water. Many pets were lost to these predators, and some carried significant diseases requiring further protection for citizens.

---

[388]   Clifford, M. (2004). *Identifying and Exploring Security Essentials.* Prentice-Hall, Upper Saddle River, NJ. Pg 289.

Additional problems stem from man-made issues, such as the Occupy movements of the 2011-2012 periods. A lack of preparation for proper hygiene and inadequate consideration for public concerns resulted in the potential for serious health risks. Many of these campsites were overrun with vermin, such as black rats that can carry plague viruses.[389] Other pests showed significant increases, such as raccoons and squirrels, which are known to carry rabies, Lyme's Disease-carrying ticks, and other serious illnesses. The lack of proper coordination and education of both the protestors and the political leadership resulted in the creation of a bill to disallow extermination of these creatures and sanitization of the sites due to misplaced concern for ecology and civil rights.[390]

Returning to the topic of integrated planning, Curtis and McBride define this area of ecological and political preparation as follows:[391]

Planning must be viewed as a continuous process in which an organization analyzes its strengths, weaknesses, and challenges. To conduct planning, the following principles are important:

- *Participation between all ranks of employees and "stakeholders" in the client area;*
- *Open lines of communication for both good and bad news including speaking one's mind without retaliation;*
- *Delegation of authority to employees and field supervisors when appropriate;*
- *Use of appropriate selection processes and compensation packages to attract and retain the best employees;*
- *Use of current technology with an acknowledgment of costs and limitations; and*
- *Identification of support resources and services for dealing with major catastrophic events.*

---

[389] http://www.nbcwashington.com/news/local/Health-Officials-Rats-a-Concern-at-Occupy-DC-Sites-136975513.html

[390] Specific stories on this infestation and resultant call for protection of the rodents were documented in various area news reports to include The Washington Post. Posted at 02:36 PM ET, 01/09/2012 The Washington Post City: *Rat population has 'exploded' around Occupy D.C. camps.* by Annie Gowen. Specific information concerning the proposed and rejected bill is buried in the story.

[391] Curtis, G.E. and McBride, R.B. (2011). *Proactive Security Administration*, Second Edition, by George E. Curtis and R. Bruce McBride. Prentice Hall. New York, NY. Pg 39-40.

There are two main issues here. First, the security service organization must be able to have open lines of internal communication and communication with external ·groups; second, a security service provider must be able to assess the extent to which the service can realistically address and respond to a wide range of potential risks and situations. For example, a city police department may be well prepared to address street crimes that occur in its community but may be totally unprepared to deal with mass casualties and evacuation that might occur if a freight train carrying hazardous materials derails in the center of town. Concurrently, a contract security service that provides access control services may be totally unprepared to provide guard services to a client facing a month-long labor dispute. While most banking institutions can address most frauds, many may be totally unprepared when assets begin disappearing from client accounts because of computer intrusions committed by an overseas competitor.

Curtis and McBride further identify the condition known as the *client area* as "a geographic or agency entity for which services are provided."[392] They also use the term of *resource support network*. This network is specifically the working relationship between organization heads. It is this relationship that becomes critical in the planning and execution stage of the security and intelligence process. At the organization director levels, the main task is politics; that is, forging relationships and understandings that allow for integration of the operations necessary to achieve enterprise goals and objectives both in emergency and nominal operations periods.

This is where the proverbial rubber meets the road in planning. As stated by Diane Ritchey, editor of *Security* magazine, "When all is said and done, security executives and their integrators really can't know enough about each other. The relationship can fail or succeed based on that tried and true fact."[393] While the article is focusing on the relationship between two security personnel, the concept remains true.

CREATING THE ENVIRONMENT FOR INTEGRATION

Returning to Sun Tzu's statement quoted repeatedly in this text, know both yourself and your "enemy." The word *enemy*, traditionally thought of as an opponent, can also simply refer to *another* or an *associate*. Too often in human

---

[392]   Ibid, pg 40.
[393]   Ritchey, D. (ed). (2011). The Security-Integrator Link. *Security*. April, 2011. Ppg. 20-32. Pg 30.

interactions, we view others as competitors. While they can indeed be competitors for resources, especially in business environments, it becomes critical to adopt and use a well-worn West Point philosophy of "cooperate and graduate."

Fantasy/science fiction author, Jim Butcher, established a term in his *Codex Alera* series known as *gedara*.[394] *Gedara*, in his series, is defined as an "honored enemy" or an enemy that is trusted beyond nearly all friends because of their fairness, personal honor, and dedication to what they perceive as "right" and "just," even if it means fighting, but only when there is no other recourse.

A gedara will often work with an enemy to find a way of honor to solve interpersonal and/or intercultural disagreements and conflicts. In the Alera series, two of the main characters are of different species: one human, one a wolflike being. Their cultures are both warlike and focused on the safety and prosperity of their respective societies. They find themselves at war with each other. In the book, the human risks his life and honor to bring the war to a just conclusion so that each side can then face the true enemy to both species, a result that is of maximum benefit to all concerned, whether they accept this or not.

This concept is critical to security/intelligence integration. The integrator must learn the individuals with whom interaction to a mutual end is most advantageous. Toward this end, the security professional must understand the culture(s), behaviors, values, and goals of their potential ally, specifically from the perspective of the other. The goal is to use these perspectives toward a useful and beneficial condition, even if not fully accepted in total. The two sides must mutually agree to the benefit and acceptable return for cost as established and communicated for the relationship. This usually means compromise, but at other times, the security professional may use a quid-pro-quo approach to achieve necessary objectives, even though they appear counter to the objectives of the other group(s).

The two crucial skills necessary to achieve these goals are listening and communicating. Numerous products exist on how to achieve these goals, from *The Seven Habits of Highly Successful People*[395] to *How to Win Friends and Influence People*.[396] These texts, and many others, provide excellent techniques and processes for honing influential skills.

A study conducted by Gollop, Whitby, Buchanon, and Ketley sought the following:

> To explore skepticism [sic] and resistance towards changes in working practice designed to achieve service improvement. Two principal

---

[394] Butcher, J. (2007). *Captain's Furies*. The Berkley Publishing Group, New York, NY.

[395] Covey, S.R. (2004).

[396] Carnegie, D. (1936)

questions were studied: (1) why some people are skeptical or resistant towards improvement programmes and (2) what influences them to change their minds.[397]

Further, this study states:

Managing skepticism and resistance in positive ways is an essential part of the process of gaining support for change. Understanding the psychology of how people are influenced to change, and the stages they pass through during the process, is recognised as being particularly important. Promoting engagement with change by creating attraction and being prepared to explore the rationality of others' points of view is a framework that is also advocated.[398]

The primary obstruction to integration derives from the human terrain environment. The factors associated here range from personal animosity ("not invented here" syndrome or fear of "the new") to simply an inability to subsume personal expectations to a process that requires broadened domains of interaction. The following text will touch on some of these, but there are many reasons not discussed in this text. The integrator must be able to identify the issue, correctly categorize it, and determine how to best reconcile and leverage this knowledge with their own range of issues/observations/beliefs to overcome objections.

RESISTANCE

Resistance has many sources and must be approached from an understanding of these sources. Foremost in this domain is fear, defined as concern for loss. That loss, whatever its source, reveals itself in increased stress, withdrawal from interaction with the perceived source of the loss, lack of concentration, and other physiological functions. It is basic human nature to have protection as an initial burden. However, many individuals elevate their concerns so intelligently and steadfastly that they become quite real. As such, various human reactions such as the fight-or-flight defensive reaction initiate. Identifying the symptoms of the development of these structures and blocks and applying appropriate countermeasures in appropriate strength is a basic requirement to preparing for resistance.

---

[397] Gollop, R., Whitby, E., Buchanon, D., and Ketley, D. (2004). Influencing sceptical staff to become supporters of service improvement: a qualitative study of doctors' and managers' views. Qual Saf Health Care 2004;13:108-114. Pg 108.

[398] Ibid.

The "not invented here" (NIH) syndrome is actually a more difficult issue to overcome. *NIH* is a term used to describe persistent social, corporate, or institutional culture that avoids using or buying already existing products, research, standards, or knowledge because of their external origins. It is normally used in a negative connotation and may be considered an anti-pattern. The reasons for not wanting to use the work of others are varied but can include fear through lack of understanding, unwillingness to recognize/value the work of others, or forming part of a wider "turf war."[399]

From a logic perspective, NIH is an associative fallacy, where the objector establishes a particular connection with some objectionable quality that they inappropriately apply to the condition. The condition often has little or no relationship to the objectionable quality yet causes a neurological relationship that is difficult to overcome without knowledge of the source of the objection. Correction requires the integrator to research where the potential source of the objection lies and how to break the relationship, while maintaining the impression that the individual holding the NIH perception remains of high value. This is better known in the world of education as learning facilitation, perhaps best performed using a type of *compassionate Socratic methodology.*[400]

PERSONAL REASONS FOR RESISTANCE

The least logical and therefore the most difficult source of resistance to overcome is personal resistance. Personal resistance generally develops from fear—fear of a loss of power, loss of prestige, autonomy, and situational control. To battle these conditions, one must discover their source(s) and approach them singularly.

Fear of the loss of power encompasses several other feelings: autonomy, control, and prestige. The term *knowledge is power* is a source of this fear in that when one is in control. Fear is based upon the loss of power; thus loss of control over one's life or a specific situation and the choices that may be made often are overwhelming. Military history holds a multitude of examples. One specific example involves the actions of Major Reno, a subordinate of LTC George Armstrong Custer, while engaged at the battle of the Little Bighorn. Examination of this battle is a good source of education into the extremes of the psychological

---

[399] Webb, N.J., Thoen, C. (2010) The Innovation Playbook: A Revolution in Business Excellence, Nicholas J. Webb, Chris Thoen, John Wiley and Sons, New York, NY. From Wikipedia.

[400] The author defines compassionate Socratic methodology as a questioning process which encourages the learner's evaluation rather than, as some practice, questioning with the goal of emphasizing error or inconsistency.

impacts of fear in this regard. Not only can fear create situations of immobility and outright panic, it can create other disorders.

This fear may be so pervasive that it forms into narcissism. Narcissistic personality disorder is a mental disorder in which people have an inflated sense of their own importance and a deep need for admiration. Those with narcissistic personality disorder believe that they're superior to others and have little regard for other people's feelings. But behind this mask of ultraconfidence lies a fragile self-esteem, vulnerable to the slightest criticism. [401] The structure of overcoming such a condition within a team is to produce a feeling of ownership within the group for the individual simultaneously tempering criticism through positive reinforcement of desired behavior and allowing this type of individual to work low criticality tasks independently.

Maintaining a totally businesslike environment and relationship generally works well, especially when playing to the individual's personality. However, do not become overly fawning, as this will come across as mocking and foster rage in the narcissist. The team lead, in such situations, should maintain proper records of meetings and assignments/solutions and visibly distribute appropriate credit fairly.

The not-invented-here syndrome derives from resistance to externally motivated change. While not much is written on the subject, Hussinger and Wastyn assert that:

> internal resistance is most likely to occur if knowledge is acquired from similar organizations. Individuals and working teams can feel their own expertise threatened when they valuate competitor knowledge and react with resistance against the externally generated knowledge. This hypothesis is supported by our finding that the NIH syndrome occurs when knowledge is acquired from competitors but not if knowledge is acquired from suppliers, customers or universities.[402]

The driving factor for NIH appears to be one of adherence to the norm, while rejecting anything that is outside of the norm due to fear of change. The causes of such fear are varied yet generally appear to stem from a loss of personal control, especially when the driver for change originates with a similar or competing organization (Hussinger and Wastyn, page 2). Individuals within an organization view themselves and their organization as unique, irrespective of the reality of the

---

[401] Definition from Mayo Clinic Diseases and Conditions page. http://www.mayoclinic. com/health/narcissistic-personality-disorder/DS00652

[402] Hussinger, K. and Wastyn, A. (2011). *In Search for the Not-Invented-Here Syndrome: The Role of Knowledge Sources and Firm Success.* Center for European Economic Research. Zurich, Sw. pg 1.

situation. The belief appears to stem from a group-think construct and the need to see value in oneself and one's endeavors. Organizations, to survive, create knowledge and devise routines to support that knowledge. The adherence to routine makes habit, and habit is by its nature resistant to change.

As stated, NIH is a symptom of which fear is the cause. The fearful individual is in need of a reason to reject pending change. Assertions that another's routines are not as good as what currently exists appear to be both logical and acceptable. The individual feels validated by current executive support to his current way of thinking. By raising a question on this support, opposition is often perceived as a challenge to current executives rather than a challenge to change. If the individual were to support change, they would consider this an admission that existing procedures question current operations and their wisdom.

A powerful counter to this fear is always factual education of the specific objection points. For example, the existence of a currently safe pipeline next to the route of a new proposed pipeline that has been both secure and operationally sound is powerful evidence for the security of the system. Yet certain government individuals are stating that there is insufficient evidence for its safety.

A very powerful form of resistance is political. This is because there are few facts and often no evidence supporting political conjectures. The decisions in such situations are frequently in expectation or repayment of individuals for favors and/or donations. Factual presentation of counterarguments has little to no impact on such individuals. The presence of a countermovement of sufficient political support, however, can influence officials. That countermovement need not originate with a political opponent. As the original situation was initiated with donations and favors, others of increased largess will often succeed where accuracy of argument or strong political pressure will not.

A final means of personal resistance that runs counter to logical argument is loss of power. As stated earlier, many consider knowledge as power—and covet it religiously. For these individuals, knowledge is more desirable than cash, and many are willing to pay high prices and grant favors to have information that places them at an advantage over potential competitors. The ability to control the actions of others, especially those outside of organizational or positional hierarchies, is critical to their view of self-worth.

Overcoming resistance from this domain is nearly as difficult as political resistance, in that one needs knowledge to fight knowledge. Only through the application of deduction will a security professional be able to ascertain the general type of information currently used as the coin of the realm. They then must obtain sufficient accurate counterinformation that if freely disseminated, works against such resistance.

PROMOTIONAL RESISTANCE FACTORS

Promotional resistance factors are a group's or individual's negative reaction to the *selling technique* used in an attempt to persuade or change a target group. In this situation, the causes are usually misunderstandings of culture, expectation, and knowledge of the driving factors creating the current conditions/processes. Given that the root cause is misunderstanding, the solution is education on the part of the "sellers." The seller needs to "do their homework" on the "what" and "how" of the selling strategy, with their target audience in mind.

Secondly, the use of a formidable "champion" of sufficient visibility and position to serve as a trendsetter provides sufficient inertia to overcome must promotional factors. A champion, however, is a double-edged sword. The optimum change agent champion is generally also the most active executive in the organization, placing his/her free time at a premium. Such individuals cannot be figureheads as they will be seen as such rapidly by the general populace. Their involvement must be intimate and continuous.

Third, avoid the use of slogans and posters, as these are rapidly ignored by the general population. Dr. E. Deming wrote fourteen points on quality management.[403] Point 10 states that management should eliminate slogans, exhortations, and targets for the workforce. The reason for this is psychological, in that the human brain will ignore what it perceives as superfluous. Some slogans, however, work due to their ingenious presentation and design and particularly because their message resonates within the psyche of the selected audience. A good example would be Super Bowl advertisements. Using posters and slogans to report, for example, the progress of the program are generally well received.

Finally, one must tie the activities to the policies and situations driving them, as well as establish specific measures of merit to ascertain progress toward the coordinating goals. When the *Project Management Book of Knowledge* refers to this requirement, however, it links it solely to planned work performed and the budget through the process of EVM. The EVM determines progress based on the amount of work each task requires, as compared to the actual amount of work spent performing the task. The assumption is the task would not exist unless it was necessary to achieve the project objective. While true, such measures are missing the goals that measures of merit provide.

Given these previous factors, a fully integrated and communicated plan tied to specific requirements and policies is vital in the construction of an efficient and effective security/intelligence program of operation.

---

[403] Dr. W.E.D Deming was the father of the Japanese quality movement. His work led to the creation of The Deming Award for Quality in Japan and the Malcolm Baldridge Quality Award in the United States.

THE PLANNING PROCESS

As stated earlier, there are numerous methods for the creation of an integrated plan. This text presents just one of many ways to go about planning to provide completeness of the topic as a whole. As with any plan, the first and most critical step is the construction of the vision and overall objective. The vision must be complete, depicting the structure of the organization and its means of securing the goals in a single graphic. The Department of Defense calls these graphics operational views or OVs, with the specific primary objective being the OV-1. OVs are numbered.

Figure 107 depicts a sample OV-1 for a DoD program to design a new vertical lift capability.

The Department of Defense systems acquisition process is governed by what is named the Department of Defense Architecture Framework or DoDAF. Within the DoDAF, there are several "products that act as mechanisms for visualizing, understanding, and assimilating the broad scope and complexities of an architecture description through graphic, tabular, or textual means." These products are organized under four views:

- Overarching All View (AV)
- Operational View (OV)
- Systems View (SV)
- Technical Standards View (TV)[404]

The structure of how operational and other views are used within the DoDAF process is shown in Figure 106.

---

[404] Department of Defense Architecture Framework, obtained on October 25, 2012, from http://en.wikipedia.org/wiki/Operational_View and confirmed through examination of the DoDAF.

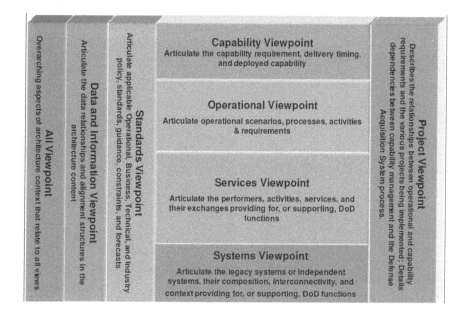

Figure 106: DoDAF Set of Architecture Views[405]

The OV-1 depicts a land and sea basing capability to perform various local and long-distance missions. Each mission, such as combat search and rescue (CSAR), raids, air assaults, and vertical maneuver have specific concepts within military doctrine and operational art. This leads to the next planning element.

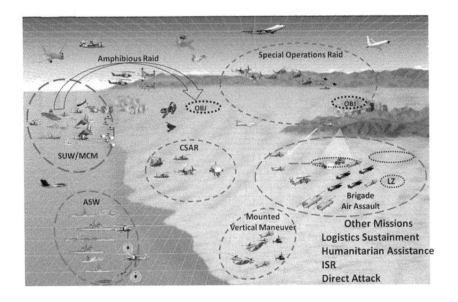

Figure 107: Example OV-1 for Vertical Lift Program

The second element of planning is the identification of needs, roles, assets, requirements, capabilities, and the determination of the best way to respond to these needs via planning and preparation. Figure 108 depicts the initial progression for construction of both an analytical model and a planning model.

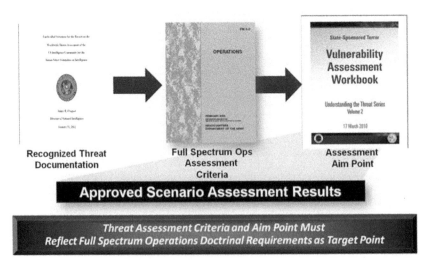

Figure 108: Assessment/Planning Methodology

362

The planning process begins by examining the appropriate documentation used to develop and/or linked to the construct of the OV-1. These documents provide the program's baseline goals, essentially the objectives the group will achieve and how. They provide the "aim point" of the integrated organization, driving the integrated structure of the plan and operational development process.

Given the aim point, the planning professional must establish the specific analytical structures to make operations decisions that can supply analysis data. Figure 109 depicts an example of this process. Note that the idea is to examine current plans and systems against both perceived and realistic threats, as well as other equipment types/organization set capabilities. This data set includes such things as communications pathways/networks, costs, and manpower training/skill set requirements.

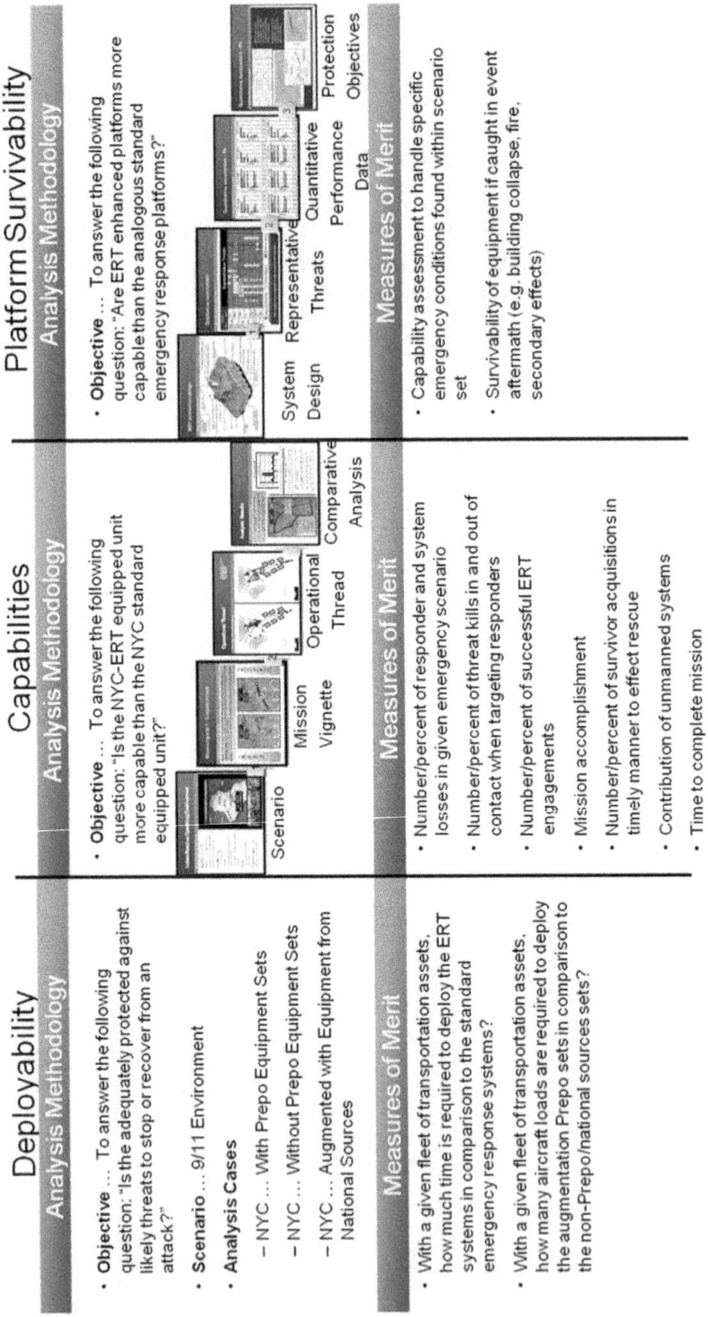

Deployability
Analysis Methodology

- **Objective** ... To answer the following question: "Is the adequately protected against likely threats to stop or recover from an attack?"

- **Scenario** ... 9/11 Environment

- **Analysis Cases**
  - NYC .... With Prepo Equipment Sets
  - NYC .... Without Prepo Equipment Sets
  - NYC .... Augmented with Equipment from National Sources

Measures of Merit

- With a given fleet of transportation assets, how much time is required to deploy the ERT systems in comparison to the standard emergency response systems?

- With a given fleet of transportation assets, how many aircraft loads are required to deploy the augmentation Prepo sets in comparison to the non-Prepo/national sources sets?

Capabilities
Analysis Methodology

- **Objective** ... To answer the following question: "Is the NYC-ERT equipped unit more capable than the NYC standard equipped unit?"

Scenario Mission Operational Comparative
          Vignette Thread   Analysis

Measures of Merit

- Number/percent of responder and system losses in given emergency scenario

- Number/percent of threat kills in and out of contact when targeting responders

- Number/percent of successful ERT engagements

- Mission accomplishment

- Number/percent of survivor acquisitions in timely manner to effect rescue

- Contribution of unmanned systems

- Time to complete mission

Platform Survivability
Analysis Methodology

- **Objective** ... To answer the following question: "Are ERT enhanced platforms more capable than the analogous standard emergency response platforms?"

System Representative Quantitative Protection
Design   Threats   Performance   Objectives
                           Data

Measures of Merit

- Capability assessment to handle specific emergency conditions found within scenario set

- Survivability of equipment if caught in event aftermath (e.g. building collapse, fire, secondary effects)

Figure 109: Capabilities Assessment Model

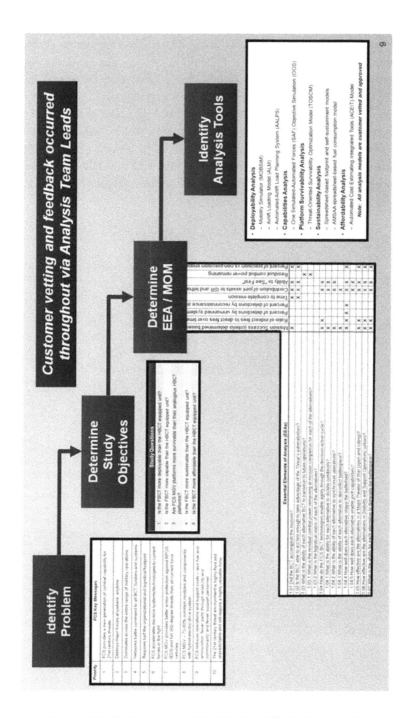

Figure 110: Final Assessment Model of Specific Problem Set(s)

The planner then uses these data points to form the overall detailed assessment model, an example of which appears in Figure 110. The answers to each of the matrixed or connected elements in Figure 111 become the basis for both the master plan and for the WBS, schedule, and performance criteria. Remember to perform each of these steps with the full knowledge and compliance of the adjacent and superior management organizations. This prevents the process from quickly deteriorating into a singular effort with little to no organizational support or compliance. The final results and products of this process are the security/intelligence operations plan, the operational plan and schedule, the operational plan budget, and the change management/feedback plan (Figure 111).

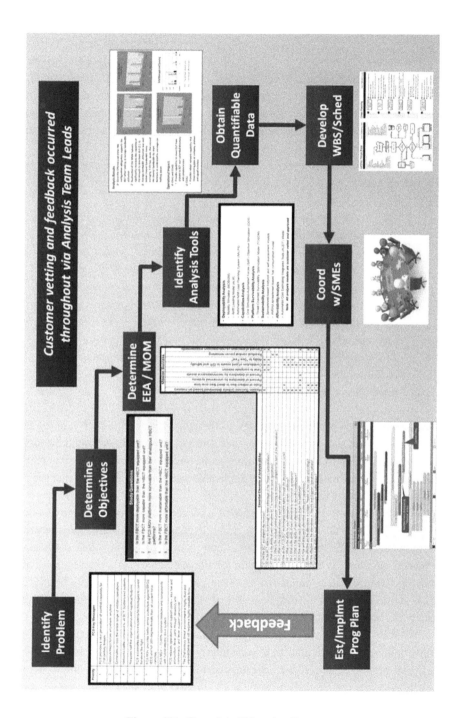

Figure 111: Completed Planning Process

OFFENSIVE-PROACTIVE/DEFENSIVE-REACTIVE PLANNING

The accomplishment of this process is a long-term learning effort. It is not something one picks up in one course, one year, or even one job. Tying this to a concept as complex as offensive/defensive planning requires even more learning and practice. This next section discusses some of the related concepts, as observed by various authors and researchers with some hard-learned examples from the working world experience.

Ackoff uses the term *clinical planning* for defensive-reactive planning. In his text, Ackoff states,

> The clinical approach to planning treats messes and the systems that have them holistically, but, because it does not analyse [sic] them, it deals with no explicit model of their structures. Clinical planners bring together a sample of those preoccupied with different aspects of a mess so they can develop a mutually acceptable formulation and attack on it. Clinical procedures are generally participative with the clinical planner serving primarily as a convener and process consultant. He tries to be nondirective. To avoid inserting content into the procedure. [sic] This approach is used extensively by those who refer to themselves as change agents, process consultants, behavioural [sic] modifiers, action researchers, organizational developers, and so on.[406]

Ackoff is using academic language to basically say that the person doing the research does not want to infect the process with their own ideas. Simultaneously, and somewhat unconsciously, he appears to be saying that clinical studies really have scant basis for making generally applicable conclusions. How is it that such a situation is even possible?

When a laboratory scientist performs an experiment, they currently obtain exact duplicates of the subject of the study. In many medical labs, they actually utilize cloned worms, mice, and other simple subjects to ensure that everything is totally identical, with the exception of the medicine, or whatever, they are studying. Unfortunately, humans cannot be cloned. Nor can humans be placed into a sterile laboratory environment so that each and every one of them receives exactly the same environment, food, care, etc., for the study.

What is done is that the researcher will select a group of subjects of similar nature (all from a particular area, particularly income, etc.). The specific thing that they want to study is then investigated to see what level the thing exists in

---

[406] Ackoff, R. (1981). On the Use of Models in Corporate Planning. *Strategic Management Journal, Vol. 2, 353-359.* Pg 356.

the subject's life. So for example, if out of one thousand subjects, 50 percent had cancer, and 20 percent of those ate sugar, then the research concludes that sugar is 45 percent more likely to cause cancer. This is an extremely overstated example deliberately to emphasize the situation. Examination of statistical processes reveals means and methods of normalizing studies such as these, yet the caution remains valid. There are simply too many variables in the human experience to limit environmental impacts to one or two things.

Ackoff continues his description of clinical planning, stating,

> The advantages of the clinical approach to planning include its willingness to grapple with what is messy, qualitative, value loaded, and unstructured. It tends to generate consensus and commitment to the conclusions reached and to the continuation of planning. Its emphasis on participation often results in an enrichment of work life, and makes the participants feel better about themselves and their condition. The disadvantages of the clinical approach derive from the lack of structure imposed on its output and the absence of explicit criteria with which to evaluate it. What people agree on and feel good about is not necessarily efficient, effective, or even moral.[407]

A second aspect to Ackoff's structure of defensive-reactive planning is what he terms as *research planning*. Research planning is similar in nature to the clinical planning methodology yet incorporates an:

> Approach to planning [that] begins by analysing [sic] a mess so as to identify its parts and their interconnections. It tries to formulate the disassembled pans so that their interconnections are minimal, thereby allowing them to be treated relatively independently of each other . . .
> [408]

The problem with this approach, per Ackoff and many others, is that in decomposing a problem set into subordinate elements, one has lost the view of the systematic whole as explained above. "A system is a whole that cannot be decomposed into independent parts. From this it can be shown that a system always has properties that none of its parts have, and that these are its *essential* properties."[409]

---

[407] Ibid. pg 357.

[408] Ibid.

[409] Ibid. pg 358.

Lastly, Ackoff identifies a means of deliberate planning structured to examine the problem both from its systems perspective and place it into a context whereby the planner incorporates a means of addressing future concerns. To identify these concerns, which have yet to occur, see the _definition of offensive-proactive planning_. Ackoff identifies this as the design approach to planning and establishes five elements to the process:

> *First, formulating the mess. This is done in such a way as to capture and illuminate the essential systemic properties of the mess, not by listing independently formulated threats and opportunities, but by projecting the future that the system would have if it, and its environment, were to continue behaving as they are. The mess that a system currently is in. is the future it will be in, if it does not change its course.*

> *Second, ends planning. Such planning involves selecting the ideals, objectives, and goals to be pursued. This is done by preparing an idealized redesign of the system planned for, a design with which its stakeholders would replace the existing system right now if they were free to replace it with any system they wanted, The differences between the most desired present and the future the organization is headed for, define the gaps to be filled by the remainder of the planning process.*

> *Third, means planning. Here the ways of filling the gaps are selected. These are more likely to require invention than discovery. They too are usually the products of design. Therefore, creativity has at least as large a role to play in selecting means as analytic evaluation.*

> *Fourth, resource planning. Five types of resource are involved: people; facilities and equipment; materials and energy; money; and information, knowledge, and understanding, A determination is made of how much of each type of resource will be required by the means selected, and when these requirements will arise. Then it is necessary to determine whether, and how, these requirements can be met. If they are found to be infeasible, the previously formulated ends or means must be modified and the cycle repeated until a match is obtained between actions to be taken and resources to be available.*

> *Fifth and finally, the design of implementation and control. Decisions are made as to who is to do what, when, and where; and how their*

behavior [sic] and its effects are to be monitored and modified when necessary.[410]

The preceding information is a good description of "the what" of offensive/defensive planning. The how is the illusive aspect. Multiple scenarios exist, giving examples of correct processes. However, most of them confirm the basis of Deming's philosophy: that it is management who has the ability, the resources, and the capability of performing the functions. For example, as we age, we lose certain abilities, both physical and mental. At a point, we can no longer maintain our own homes, finances, etc. In defensive planning, elderly care should reside with any children or relatives willing to take on the load or specific elements of the government Medicare/Medicaid programs. Proactive planning, however, would have each individual take responsibility for making preparations during their youth via insurance, estate planning, annuity, and other savings programs, coupled with living wills describing what to do in the event of specific situations, such as medical or mental impairments.

Taking this a step further, proactive planning would ensure contractual arrangements not only for the types of care, but also the quality of the care. A proactive plan design would need to address possible neglect of the contract terms to ensure arrangements take place, per the agreements and desires of the individual.

One example involved an individual who was a long-term sufferer of Amyotrophic Lateral Sclerosis (ALS), also known as Lou Gehrig's disease. The disease is extremely debilitating, requiring constant protocols for lung, heart, and other functioning. The victim's wife performed nearly all of this care yet was forced for her own health to place him into a care facility specifically designed to assist such patients. He was there for one weekend, during which time he was propped atop a lavatory facility and ignored for over twelve hours. As he was incapable of self-movement and speech, this torture continued until someone found him on the floor where he had fallen and broken his arm in several places. This is obviously not the type of care one would want for a family member or for themselves in a similar situation and is extremely reactive in nature.

A proactive approach to long-term care, for instance, would include a contract with the facility management detailing specific actions at specific times, including established penalties and insurances of performance. Management could be contractually required to maintain specific visual contact with the patient, supplying specific guidance and resources necessary to the staff. The

---

[410]   Ibid. pg 358-360.

design of such resources should address the fact that the staff in such facilities is frequently overwhelmed by both the care requirements and the stress the patient's conditions cause the caregivers. For this example, it is also important to note in the proactive plan that many such facilities have management overwhelmed by government-required reports and other regulatory issues, which add little to the level of care provided for the patient and take away attention to the needs of the staff and patient care.

Another way to look at the idea of proactive planning is through the more general example of the practice of medicine. Today's medical care is the epitome of proactive and reactive security over a highly complex system: the human body. A physical is proactive, especially when conducting an annual health checkup. There are specific protocols of examination of the blood, glands, heart, lungs, bones, and all major organs. The examinations usually find normality. The point is not that the examinations will find any disease. The point is that the examination is a data point in a line of data points. These points will cluster around a consideration of "normality" for each aspect of the body based upon thousands of examinations. Any indication of something out of the "normal" will result in more extensive examination and correction to keep the abnormality from extending into an actual destructive disease.

Should the examination discover a major ailment, however, there are specific protocols in place to address the danger. This proactive approach has been the message throughout this book: know what to look for, have a means of monitoring the indicators, know what a change in the indicators represents, and (most importantly) know what to do about it. Just because the indicators may show a serious situation does not mean the system is in reactive mode. When something unexpected occurs, there are generally additional protocols to assist. This is proactive planning.

Keep in mind, however, that an unexpected event can occur that is totally new and therefore can circumvent well-laid plans. At this point, no specific proven protocol exists. However, a process for examining the situation is put in place that will hopefully result in a healing protocol. This is reactive medicine/ planning. Both types require analysis, observation, knowledge of the threat, a means of gaining additional intelligence when little information is available, and determining a means of combating and correcting the incident.

Returning to the elder care planning example, contracting specific events of management-staff-patient interaction watched over by both family and/or legal representation, the level of care increases dramatically. Publications such as the *Harvard Business Review* support this method, stating: "Human beings adjust behavior based on the metrics they're held against. Anything you measure will impel a person to optimize his score on that metric. What you measure is what you'll get. Period. [*sic*]"[411]

Through the monitoring of the level of management oversight provided to the caregivers, the advocate for the long-term care plan also monitors the level of quality for the care provided. Relying on management policy and protocol to result in the optimal level of care is reactive, resulting in a weak defensive stance should something go wrong. The best approach is to create a means of active measures to ensure appropriate care and responsibility by management personnel. This ensures a proactive environment.

Proactive Examples—Physical Security/Loss Prevention

One may state that the above examples are not security related, yet security includes loss prevention. Losses may originate in theft, both internal and external, damage to property, and lawsuit based upon substandard operations. Linking security, operations, and quality in an integrated fashion with both positive and negative reinforcements, both personnel and management, creates a proactive environment within the organization. Continuing this process to other stakeholders means to identify restrictive and asset-reducing regulations, working with lawmakers to streamline the situations so that the necessary aspects of oversight remain, while overly restrictive regulations and laws are modified to be proactive as well.

Clifford, in her book on security planning, endorses the above as follows:

> *The security objective must include attention to physical security, personnel security, information security, and, where possible, interdepartmental dependencies. These four elements are linked by the important legal and ethical problems that result when the elements are not accurately identified or integrated. In short, the security objective is simple: to develop a seamless, integrated security program that includes all persons involved and results in a stable and predictable environment. Security directors, security consultants, private investigators, security officers, security administrators, company officials, and individual employees all play a part in outlining the overall security objectives and making sure those objectives are maintained.*[412]

---

[411] Ariely, D. (2010). You Are What You Measure. Harvard Business Review, June 2010. Retrieved from http://hbr.org/2010/06/column-you-are-what-you-measure/ar/1

[412] Clifford, M. (2004). *Identifying and Exploring Security Essentials.* Prentice-Hall, Upper Saddle River, NJ. Pg. 115.

Taking this concept and applying it to a specific security/intelligence planning domain, say executive protection, yields the following definition from a specific security organization:

> *Proactive security can best be defined as a security program designed to anticipate and avoid danger. Proactive security suggests a comprehensive approach involving protectee threat analysis, advance planning and training for these threats, logistical sophistication designed to balance the comfort level of an assigned protectee with proper security procedures, and a thorough emergency response/ crisis management plan. Executive protection providers operated most effectively when they understand the risks facing their clients, prepare to reduce or avoid those risks, and have the ability to react properly while maintaining a comfort level suitable to the protectee.*[413]

One example involved a situation concerning a highly classified Defense study where the data in development for the statistical analysis were maintained on what, at the time, was the largest available removable storage media: a 40 MB Bernoulli removable drive cassette. This cassette measured approximately 8 1/2 by 11 by 3/8 inches and contained a magnetic media disk. Data was stored on the disk by way of an armature within the drive that would change the charge of the iron coating on the disk into positive/negative orientations through magnetic influence.

The data was expensive to obtain and highly classified, and as such, the disks were stored inside a special safe requiring two individuals, each with a different combination, to open. This safe was kept within a steel bank-vault type of storage location, also requiring two individuals with different combinations to open. Thus, a total of four separate combination locks. The vault also had a time lock, making it impossible to open with the combinations during specific time periods.

The data placed on the disks were triple-checked for accuracy by three individuals, each person performing their checks three times for a total of nine quality control checks prior to removal from the computer complex and storage in the vault. Even given this level of security, it was found upon reexamining the disks after weekend storage that data had been manipulated on multiple occasions in what appeared to be both random and seriously disruptive manners.

Security examinations of the individuals, the computers, the storage process, and the after-hours protocols revealed nothing. One engineer suggested that the vault be swept for stray microwave emissions which was, at that time, known to

---

be able to cause changes on magnetic disks, figuring either a stray radio emission within the building or a solar radiation as the causes. Having no other ideas at the time, the management agreed to perform the sweep.

From this investigation, the engineers and security personnel learned that there was a directional beam cutting through the metal walls of the vault from a totally unexpected source. Further examination revealed the security issue was not only originating exterior to the building, it was also totally inadvertent. As Figure 112 shows, the real culprit was the Soviet embassy, which was beaming a microwave at the Pentagon in the hopes of using the beam to acquire window vibrations of conversations as an intelligence source. So while not aimed at the analysis firm's offices, it created a security breach and loss of accurate information and work.

The fix was to install microwave-filtering material in the walls of the vault, correcting the problem and preventing future such risks. This is an example of an unanticipated threat, though the location of the embassy and the existence of such beams were known to most DoD-related security personnel in the area. No one had considered, however, if there were any side effects that might impact other operations in the vicinity. To have anticipated this risk would exemplify proactive security and intelligence planning.

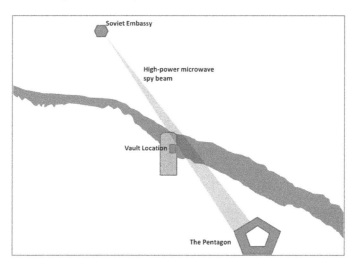

Figure 112: Microwave Security Interference Example

ESTABLISHING THE PLAN FROM THE MODEL

Each of the previous examples, from the ALS care facility to the *leaky vault*, was identifiable, with appropriate preliminary analysis. For example, in the Soviet embassy case, a complete "intelligence preparation of the battlespace" (IPB) construct of the area—considering threats, weapons (i.e., tools available for destructive purposes), and the relationship of known targets to ancillary targets—would have raised a warning.

Consider, for instance, just because an artillery shell or bomb is not specifically targeted against a building, this does not mean that the impact of the detonation will not affect nearby structures adversely—a condition known as collateral damage. In the Soviet microwave beam situation, the physical task of the beam was targeted to read window vibrations at the Pentagon. Every single tool such as this, however, has outlying effects. The security assessment *did* consider that the beam existed; however, it only looked if it could pick up conversations on the building, not other collateral impacts. The vault had no walls on the exterior of the building and no windows; thus, no threat from the beam was considered. This assessment was proven incorrect.

Once a planner has the planning model firmly in mind sufficiently to build a simulation, the very first thing they must remember is that *all models are wrong, some, however, are useful.*[414] This saying is a reminder that any model developed of a system depicts only the aspect of that system observed in a particular way at a particular time, as seen in the vault example. This does *not* make the model useless; it provides the observer with a point of data against which to measure subsequent observations and actions for clarity and efficacy. The planner must not be lulled into the common trap of believing everything the model/simulation structure shows. They must also ask, what is it *not* showing? Such is the source of disinformation or *maskarovka* (Russian for "camouflage").

Planners take mental ownership of their ideas and inventions (see Chapter 4); a human trait that is unavoidable, yet recognizable. Watch for this as a potential flaw and adjust to avoid or at least include the factor in the calculations of what can and cannot occur. Once an individual has assumed full, mental ownership, they are strongly reluctant to consider other options or possibilities. History is rife with examples of this situation. A study of General Robert E. Lee during the Battle of Gettysburg reveals just such a condition and the disastrous result for the Confederacy.

Time available, physical and economic resource limitations and other factors are the reality of incomplete modeling. It is simply not possible to model and then simulate every potential situation. This is why the planner must prioritize potential threats.

---

[414]   Box, G. E. P. and Draper, N. (2007). *Response Surfaces, Mixtures, and Ridge Analyses*, Second Edition [of *Empirical Model-Building and Response Surfaces*, 1987], Wiley.

PROCESS PRIORITIZATION

There are many methods of establishing a prioritization of threats vs. counteraction development. These range from probability calculations to expert opinions to guesses. The one used most often and recommended by this text is the development of a SWOT assessment using probability and subject matter expert (SME) input. A SWOT analysis is simply a method of diagramming strengths, weakness, opportunities, and threats into a read-at-a glance graphic. Numbers are related to each item based on known dynamics transformed into probability values. For example, the three greatest known natural threats in the Texas Gulf Coast region are hurricanes, tornados, and earthquakes.

Hurricanes have been tracked and archived for over a hundred years in the gulf and Caribbean areas. Forecasters predict that this particular area of the coastline will experience a hurricane of "X" strength every "Y" years.[415] Hurricanes follow somewhat predictable paths, as well, given certain atmospheric conditions. These paths refine in probability the closer the storm gets to landfall. Using this data, a security planner can establish a likelihood of occurrence in any individual year and associate the financial risks to this probability using the following formula: financial risk in dollars times (x) probability of occurrence. This results in an estimated dollar risk value for the facility.

The same construct applies to tornados; a much less predictable, yet more frequent concern. Earthquakes are totally unpredictable and, for the area in question, so infrequent as to be virtually nonexistent. From these data points, a planner can construct a relationship between the events as shown in Table 10.

Table 12: Example Risk Quantification Table

EVENT	PROBABILITY	COST	RISK LEVEL	RANK
Earthquake	.00001	$200M damage	$2000	3
Tornado	.20	$5M damage	$1M	2
Hurricane	.1	$20M damage	$2M	1

Based on this analysis, the security planner will focus planning for natural disaster issues on hurricanes as, even though the probability is much less than a tornado. This is because the damage potential and, therefore, the risk level is greater. More to reduce the costs is possible for this risk, given that a hurricane usually has a predicted strike area several days in advance, while tornados are

---

[415] Published by the National Oceanographic and Atmospheric Agency (NOAA), of the United States Government.

predicted only in minutes (usually fifteen to thirty) and earthquakes not at all. There is simply less that can be done for these later risks, with the exception of hardening the site against the potential. Yet how valuable would be hardening the site against an earthquake that *may* result in the greatest damage cost yet has the lowest probability and risk cost—especially when the countermeasures may cost the company $40M or more? The ROI for such a situation would be in terms of twenty thousand years recovery. Few CEOs would ever consider this a viable option. However, were the location changed to Los Angeles, the risk level and costs would rise significantly, likely lowering the ROI to ten to fifteen years—a more acceptable factor.

The planner can apply similar studies to other risks in like manner, risks like physical structure failures, personnel issues, theft, ecological liability, product liability, and so on. As an example, examine a situation that happened at a major computer manufacturer. The office/manufacturing complex was well located for drainage, accessibility, and local physical security. This ignores two major situations, however: microorganisms and utilities. The reader may recall this example from earlier in this text, where pipes were compromised due to bacteria, resulting in major site damage.

Planners had factored only electronic/IT security into their protocols. However, one weekend during nonbusiness hours, a primary development laboratory flooded with water, destroying multiple millions of dollars of sensitive scientific equipment and prototypes. The initial physical security report indicated roof failure, causing a major leak of rainwater into the building and focusing on the laboratory. Management hired a contracting firm to find and repair any and all such actual tasked the facilities department and potential leaks to the buildings. This was a reactive approach estimated to cost at least $30M over a three-year period. The problem with this reactive plan, there had been no rain in the two weeks prior to the event. In other words, the problem was not weather related; and this expensive reactive approach was, therefore, not likely to address the root cause.

Managment halted any contracting for one week to further examine the situation upon this revelation. The facilities personnel began a floor-by-floor examination of the only other possible reason for a significant water leak: the supply pipes, Figure 113. A section of pipe on the main line was found to have what appeared to be a mud wasp nest on it. This nest appears as a tube of mud approximately one inch long and a quarter inch in diameter and is common in the region of the facility. The location of the nest on the pipe, however, was highly questionable.

Figure 113: Iron-Bacteria Encrusted Galvanized Pipe

The facilities engineer had the main line valve closed to shut off additional water pressure and then had the maintenance crew remove the nest. The removal required a pneumatic hammer, which was extremely abnormal for mud wasp nests. Removing what had appeared at first to be a "nest" revealed a one-sixteenth inch diameter hole, which originated from within the pipe.

Research into the construction diagrams and water testing revealed two significant facts. The first was that the pipe was not made of copper, as had been initially specified, due to cost. The pipe was galvanized steel. The second significant fact was that the water in the area contained a benign bacterium that had a voracious appetite for iron. Steel is made of iron. Galvanizing usually protects steel pipe from such dangers as rust, due to electrolysis effects. It does not, however, protect from bacteria, as there are microscopic gaps in the galvanization coating that the bacteria can (a) infiltrate and (b) protect it from the flow of the water, which would wash the bacterial colony out (Figure 113 and Figure 114).

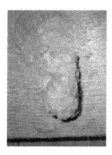

Figure 114: Iron-Bacteria Colony inside Pipe

Figure 115: Iron-Bacteria Colony Restricting Flow

The colony, as it grows, creates a casing based on iron excretions, which is almost as strong as the steel around it. As the bacteria continue to process the iron, it remains strong enough to hold the colony safe from the water pressure, until the hole becomes large enough to release the water into a strong spray. The spray shot 20 feet across the ceiling to collect above the lab, finally causing a collapse in the ceiling and releasing the stored water onto the equipment. Once discovered, the water to the area was shut off, allowing the bacteria to repair their breach enough to make the leak invisible.

With the root cause revealed as the piping, rather than the roofing, management needed to pick a course of action. To replace all of the steel piping in the buildings involved would have cost over $300 million. Thinking outside of the box, the chief engineer discovered that there existed a human-safe water treatment for these bacteria. Adding the treatment process to the water system cost the company $150,000, with an annual supply cost of $30,000. ROI was nearly immediate. Damaged sections of piping still needed replacing, but only those sections showing exterior leakage as the bacteria colonies actually created their own short-term plugs. This was, again, much less costly.

The response to this security issue was reactive, however, it was again preventable in proactive planning, had due diligence in the architectural and construction processes considered the potential threat. The failure was in not including trained security engineers in the facility planning process, as well as in security analysis.

The above example is a good illustration of prioritization gone awry and focusing on the obvious, to the exclusion of the dangerous. The most likely threat or potential cause of concern is not always the real issue. There are several protocols to help with prioritization; one particularly efficient process follows here:

a. Establish a master listing of the concerned topics, usually through a brainstorming process with multiple SMEs and using a single facilitator as referee, as well as a person capable of rapidly recording the ideas expressed in the process.

b. Examine the list, arranging the various items into like topic areas.

c. Using SMEs, historical information, benchmarking, and other tools, ascertain the probabilities and severities of the risk topics within the business environment.

d. Establish an estimated cost to the organization/business, should the event occur in terms of potential for damage and for possible recovery/repair of the damage.

e. Associate cost, recovery potential, and probability of occurrence, as shown in Table 9.

f. Present this listing to senior management for review and recommendations/instructions.

Notice, many of these steps contain the requirement for assessment of individual experiences, specifically where the use of SMEs are concerned. There is a cautionary danger of personal bias that the planner must consider, both for themselves and the SMEs, when doing an assessment. While this danger is significantly discussed in Chapter 4, it is valuable to restate it here, as it relates to judgments of causation and correlation.

CAUSATION AND CORRELATION

The definition of correlation for the purposes of this text is simply that one value enables prediction of another, due to their relationship. The definition of causation is stricter: the value is the driving force of the other value and that value cannot exist without the first. Barnes references "illusory causation" as a major trap in analytical processes. Quoting Chapman and Chapman, Barnes states, "'Illusory correlation' or how one's prior expectation of a relationship between two variables can often lead to perceived correlation when it does not really exist."[416]

Barnes further states,[417]

> *In strategic planning, this problem can be particularly severe in cases where a panel of experts is often used for forecasts. One expert may be reinforced in his observations of illusory correlates by the reports of his colleagues, who themselves may be subject to the same illusion. Such agreement among experts is, unfortunately, often mistaken by planners*

---

[416] Barnes, J.H. (1984). Cognitive Biases and Their Impact on Strategic Planning. *Strategic Management Journal, Vol.5, 129-137.* Pg. 131.

[417] Ibid

as evidence for the truth of the observation. Revenue forecasting has often been undertaken using econometric models. The mathematical elegance of these models often hides the fact that the model really only determines correlation between variables and not necessarily causation (Steiner, 1979; Naylor, 1982). To the manager or planner, the model can and often does create the illusion of cause and effect.

The danger here is that the SME set establish a non-existing causative relationship that skews the analysis, and thus the planning, into a domain that can actually be highly detrimental to the implementation and practice of the plan.

Consider again the example of Pearl Harbor. Evidence had been amassed to include actual combat situations where bomber-launched torpedoes could be very effective against moored ships in shallow anchorages. Yet the "experts" of the time continuously pointed out that all analysis demonstrated that no torpedo could be launched at Pearl Harbor anchorage, as they would plunge into the bottom before achieving enough speed to rise to operating depth. This analysis was obviously demonstrated as devastatingly incorrect.

The way out of the danger is through experimentation; both physical and mental. An interesting digression from this methodology is to include junior individuals who have the training, education, and some experience; yet who lack sufficient long-term experience so as to be "cemented into the box." It has been said that the most productive years of a scientist's career are the first ten to fifteen, when they are still inexperienced enough to "know" that their ideas cannot possibly work. This concept was put into practice in 2011 by the astronaut husband of Arizona State Representative Griffin shortly after her tragic shooting.

Representative Griffin had a significant wound to her head. She was surviving, but with a poor prognosis. Her husband engaged a significantly respected hospital in Houston, Texas, for her rehabilitation, stating that he wanted the youngest team they had, rather than the most experienced and leadership personnel. His stated reason was that they did not yet know that they couldn't save her and return her to close to full functionality. Specifically, "The congresswoman's family wants to ensure she receives the best rehabilitative care possible for her type of serious penetrating brain injury," said Dr. Michael Lemole.[418]

---

[418] Montoya-Brian, S. January 19, 2011, *Associated Press* article. Obtained on October 24, 2012, from http://cnsnews.com/news/article/family-giffords-will-move-houston-rehab-center

Experimentation is what some call the "I'm from Missouri syndrome" or that it will not be believed unless it can be proven.[419] If it cannot be shown to have causative relationship in a representative sampling of environments, then it cannot be causative. The key is to select the environmental set, conditions, and measures that reflect the reality of the threat and/or risk.

COMPLETING THE PLAN

Once the structures of analysis are complete and the tasks/requirements identified, the last step is to compile the actions from the work breakdown structure into a logical progression. Depending on the nature and size of the environment, this structure may be contained in a single or multiple specific projects. A project, as defined by PMI, is a series of tasks having a specific start and finish point. Where multiple projects are required to attain the completed product, a Program is established. A program is simply a set of projects having interrelationships with each other in that the final product cannot be completely finished with them.

The best and simplest example of this is a building, whether a house or larger structure. There are multiple projects that must complete within a set time structure for the final building to exist in a useful fashion. These projects also are *not* always physical. They include financial development, resource acquisition, environmental and governmental standards, training, and others to achieve final implementation and completion. The following, taken from the PMBOK, establishes the range of documentation that the program plan must have. These are considered minimum requirements, many organizations have a more detailed structure.

    a.   Scope Document
        1.   Project authorization
            i.   Charter: includes the why, what, and reason for the project
            ii.   Establishes the vision and strategic need
        2.   Management organization and authority authorization
    b.   Quality Document

---

[419] Named for the famous statement of US Congressman Willard Duncan Vandiver from Missouri: "I'm from Missouri—you'll have to show me." In an 1899 speech, he declared, "I come from a country that raises corn and cotton, cockleburs and Democrats, and frothy eloquence neither convinces nor satisfies me. I'm from Missouri, and you have got to show me." Obtained October 24, 2012, from W. Scott Ingram, Missouri: *The Show-Me State*, Gareth Stevens, 2002, ISBN 0-8368-5309-1 (p. 16).

      1.   Quality standards

      2.   Inspection and correction processes documents

  c. Schedule and Project Management Document

      1.   Work breakdown structure

      2.   Schedule

      3.   Management processes and plan

      4.   Communications plan

      5.   Issue log and reports templates/requirements

      6.   Test and delivery processes, reports, and sign-off documents

  d. Budget and Resource Document

      1.   Resource requirements and identification document

      2.   Resource assignment and authorization documents

      3.   Costs and assigned budget

         i.   Alignment and reallocation process

        ii. Overrun management process

  e. Risk and Risk Management Plan

      1.   Risk analysis document

      2.   Risk avoidance and mitigation plan

         i.   Avoidance and recovery plans

        ii. Cost and cost recovery processes

       iii. Trigger point analysis and determination

       iv. Synchronization matrix and responsibilities assignment

  f. Change Management Document

      1.   Change triggers

      2.   Authorizing processes and authorities

      3.   Reporting and rebase-lining processes/procedures

The conclusion of the program of planning should create, reinforce, and/or support the appropriate structure for successful implementation and management of the security or intelligence plan. Considered pictorially, from the DoDAF again, is the following figure.

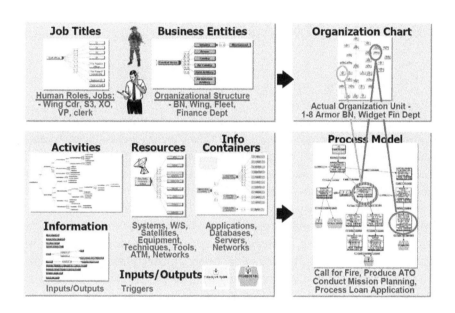

Figure 116: DoDAF Process to Organization Graphic

Chapter 12

SECURITY MANAGEMENT

DEFINITIONS AND CONSIDERATIONS

This chapter is not set up to discuss project management and the techniques for ensuring the appropriate management of the planning and building processes. As stated often in this text, there are many such guides, texts, and books already written that can and do provide excellent lessons on the basics. This chapter examines how these various authors see the processes and the potential pitfalls associated with the primary job of managing the security and intelligence aspects from the perspective of offensive and defensive considerations. This includes issues that result from the processes of security and intelligence operations, as well as proactive management. Because of the nature of management, the requirement to work with humans in a variety of environments and conditions, a review and expansion of neurological functions is necessary. Following this review, the aspects of actual project/program management is presented.

DEFINITIONS

Psychotherapy—A process for delving into the human mind to unlock repressed memories and experiences. The basic tenets of psychoanalysis include the following:

    a.   Human behavior, experience, and cognition are largely determined by irrational drives.

    b.   Those drives are largely unconscious.

    c.   Attempts to bring those drives into awareness meet psychological resistance in the form of defense mechanisms.

d. Beside the inherited constitution of personality, one's development is determined by events in early childhood.

e. Conflicts between conscious view of reality and unconscious (repressed) material can result in mental disturbances such as neurosis, neurotic traits, anxiety, depression, etc.

f. The liberation from the effects of the unconscious material is achieved through bringing this material into the consciousness (e.g., via skilled guidance).

Subconscious/Unconscious—Those areas of the mind which not accessible by the conscious mind. Theory states that this area of the mind includes repressed feelings, automatic skills, unacknowledged perceptions, thoughts, habits and automatic reactions, complexes, hidden phobias and desires. Theory also holds that the conscious mind is often controlled by the unconscious and that the unconscious mind is often the site of extensive psychoanalytical processing that the conscious mind cannot manage, due to the extreme resource requirements necessary to perform the processing. This is similar to a computer program that runs its process in the background while the user continues to work on other applications; but only weakly so.

Eros—Many individuals believe that Freud used this term to identify the sexual identity of the persona. However, the reality is that in psychology it is equivalent to "life force."

> In Plato's work *Symposium*, Plato argues that Eros is initially felt for a person, but that with contemplation it can become an appreciation for the beauty within that person, or even an appreciation for beauty itself in an ideal sense. As Plato expresses it, Eros can help the soul to "remember" Beauty in its pure form. It follows from this, for Plato, Eros can contribute to an understanding of Truth.[420]

Freud explains that the psychoanalytic concept of sexual energy is more in line with the Platonic view of Eros, as expressed in the Symposium, than with the common use of the word *sex* as related primarily to carnal activity.[421] Thus, the psychological concept is a force that encourages the continuation of the species in a form that is more powerful than self.

---

[420] The quote is taken from Wikipedia which references Cobb, William S., "The Symposium" in *The Symposium and the Phaedrus: Plato's Erotic Dialogues*, State Univ of New York Pr (July 1993) as the source.

[421] Freud, S. (1925). "The Resistances to Psycho-Analysis", in *The Collected Papers of Sigmund Freud*, Vol. 5, p.163-74.

Thanatos—Basically, Thanatos is Freud's opposite of Eros. It is the force that is bestial and life taking, enabling the continuation of species over self through the destruction of self. This is not necessarily suicidal, although it does lead to the removal of the individual by removing any inhibitions to danger and self-destruction; particularly in response to extreme stress and/or life-threatening situations. Freud describes it as "a force that is not essential to the life of an organism (unlike an instinct) and tends to denature it or make it behave in ways that are sometimes counter-intuitive."[422]

Id—Freudian subconscious, that aspect of the mind/brain that operates and controls the basic drives and functions of the human.

> *It is the dark, inaccessible part of our personality, what little we know of it we have learned from our study of the Dreamwork and of the construction of neurotic symptoms, and most of that is of a negative character and can be described only as a contrast to the ego. We approach the id with analogies: we call it a chaos, a cauldron full of seething excitations . . . It is filled with energy reaching it from the instincts, but it has no organization, produces no collective will, but only a striving to bring about the satisfaction of the instinctual needs subject to the observance of the pleasure principle.[423]*

Ego—The Freudian term of *ego* is best defined as follows:

> *Ego comprises the organized part of the personality structure that includes defensive, perceptual, intellectual-cognitive, and executive functions. Conscious awareness resides in the ego, although not all of the operations of the ego are conscious. Originally, Freud used the word ego to mean a sense of self, but later revised it to mean a set of psychic functions such as judgment, tolerance, reality testing, control, planning, defence [sic], synthesis of information, intellectual functioning, and memory.[424]*

This is the active, controllable element of the mind/brain. The ego interfaces directly with the external world, processes the aspects of the inputs to arrive at decisions and/or courses of action.

---

[422] Freud, S. (1920) "Beyond the Pleasure Principle" in *On Metapsychology* (Middlesex 1987), pg 275.

[423] Freud, S. (1933). *New Introductory Lectures on Psychoanalysis* (Penguin Freud Library 2) p. 105-6

[424] Snowden, Ruth (2006). Teach Yourself Freud. McGraw-Hill. pp. 105-107.

Superego—The superego is the final Freudian function. "The installation of the super-ego can be described as a successful instance of identification with the parental agency," while as development proceeds "the super-ego also takes on the influence of those who have stepped into the place of parents—educators, teachers, people chosen as ideal models."[425] Freud establishes this aspect of the human experience as that which determines "right and wrong," as established by genetics, culture, training, and experience.

Catecholamines—A neurological/glandular chemical complex released as a set of molecules that have a catechol nucleus consisting of benzene with two hydroxyl side groups and a side-chain amine. They include dopamine, as well as the fight-or-flight hormones adrenaline (a.k.a. epinephrine) and noradrenaline (a.k.a. norepinephrine), released by the adrenal medulla of the adrenal glands in response to stress.

Dopamine—Dopamine plays a major role in the brain system that is responsible for reward-driven learning. Every type of reward that has been studied increases the level of dopamine transmission in the brain. In fact, a variety of highly addictive drugs, including stimulants such as cocaine and methamphetamine, act directly on the dopamine system. There is evidence that people with extraverted (reward-seeking) personality types tend to show higher levels of dopamine activity than people with introverted personalities are.

Several important diseases of the nervous system are associated with dysfunctions of the dopamine system. Parkinson's disease, an age-related degenerative condition causing tremor and motor impairment, is caused by loss of dopamine-secreting neurons in the substantia nigra. Schizophrenia is often associated with elevated levels of dopamine activity in the prefrontal cortex. Attention deficit hyperactivity disorder (ADHD) is also believed to be associated with decreased dopamine activity.

Epinephrine—A hormone and a neurotransmitter, epinephrine increases heart rate, constricts blood vessels, dilates air passages and participates in the fight-or-flight response of the sympathetic nervous system.

Norepinephrine—This chemical plays a significant role in heart rate, blood pressure, and learning. Experiments have shown that this chemical enhances learning, particularly in high stress/danger situations. This "learning" is demonstrated in military operations where experienced soldiers, even if only under fire once, react to incoming munitions instantaneously and unconsciously, while "green" soldiers remain momentarily frozen and usually end up as casualties. The amygdala controls learning in each section of the brain, engaging the instantaneous reaction centers for self-preservation. When surprised or experiencing initial fear,

---

[425] Ibid, Freud, pg 95-96.

norepinephrine is the chemical causing the "jolt" felt in one's chest as the heart kicks into high gear in preparation for immediate action.

Neurotransmitter—Figure 117 depicts a neurotransmitter within a neuron. A neurotransmitter is a chemical "soup" that transmits messages from one neuron to another across the synapse. The extensive nature of the composition and densities of the neurotransmitter and the extensive nature of messages passed stand firmly in opposition to the concept of binary code transmission in computers. Computers operate in linear fashion (one step at a time and no others) using binary code (zeros and ones). Refer back to Chapter 4 for more information on this aspect of Human Terrain.

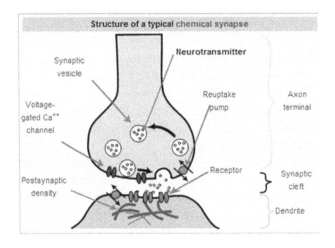

Figure 117: Structure of a Neuron Showing a Neurotransmitter

Cortisol—This chemical is a steroid release that increases the feeling of fear within a human being, as well as most other animals. It also causes increased breathing and enhances oxygen transfer within the body, creating increased transformation of stored energy (i.e., fat) into cell burning sugars.

Amygdala—An almond-sized neuro-mass located in each hemisphere of the brain, the amygdala is considered to control autonomous action that result from external stimuli, based upon both instinctive and learned self-protection behavior.

Axon—One of multiple "arms" of a neuron responsible for the transmission of neuronic chemical structures between neurons. Experiments show that transmission of specific protein-string constructs is responsible for varied responses in lower life-forms. Similar experimentations in humans are ongoing, yet are significantly more complex. This is due to the nature of the human cerebrum, as opposed to the lower life-form cerebellum constructs. To date, there remains no experimentally supported theorem on what this process does or how to produce the level of thought, ideas, and comprehension within the higher life-forms.

EVM—Earned Value Management is a project management process that converts potential work into earned/completed work measurement metrics; usually some form currency. The process first identifies what is the expected value, based on the costs of resources determined by time multiplied by projected cost for a specific task. Upon completion of that task, the actual cost is determined and compared to the projected cost as a means of tracking work performed vs. remaining work to be performed.

EOC—Estimate at Completion is another tool that allows the project manager to determine if the project is trending toward the completion target cost/schedule or, if not, whether there will be an over or under run and why.

CONSIDERATIONS

Stated earlier, this chapter addresses the aspects of plan management not considered by most other sources, thus the focus of the definitions back upon the human aspect. The reason for this centers around the nature of any plan implementation, that of the human resources used to perform the work. The concept of plan implementation for this chapter is better termed as *plan leadership*.

There is a definite difference between leadership and management. Management has often been described as an official position empowering an individual to use resources for the achievement of specific higher authority goals. Leadership is the ability to motivate humans in the attainment of higher authority goals to the greatest level of efficiency and efficacy possible. Leaders may, but do not have to be managers. Managers may, yet often are not leaders.

Individuals who have completed the training for certification and/or identification as project or program managers through industry, academic, or professional organizations generally understand the methodologies of EVM, EOC, and the other tools of managing a project/program. Yet few of these measurements can ascertain either the quality of the product being produced or the relationship of the workers to the culture, their loyalty, their ability to sufficiently work together without significant interpersonal issues, etc.

It is this area of management that this chapter focuses upon. When working in the domain of security, intelligence, or law enforcement, your employees are often armed. Carrying weapons requires training, and there are many texts that discuss appropriate methods of conducting this training. However, few if any of these texts discuss the considerations, issues, and requirements, should these arms be called into use, or how to address the aftermath of an employee having to use arms for enforcement or protection.

Therefore, the question becomes, just what are the issues associated with offensive/defensive security management and how should they be addressed?

ISSUES AND CONSIDERATIONS

NEUROPHYSIOLOGICAL EFFECTS/IMPACTS OF HIGH STRESS

The two highest stress producing non-combat related activities are security/ law enforcement and emergency responding/firefighting. This is because both are life threatening; both from the perspective of losing one's own life and of taking the life of another, either through action or inaction. The reasons for this stress are well known and frequently presented in training scenarios to prepare the professionals to act nearly on autopilot when presented with the situation.

There is a very real human aspect that this training must overcome in order for the professionals' performance to become second nature and automatic. These individuals must train to act counter to their human neurophysical processes for self-preservation—the well-known fight-or-flight instinct. Yet the skeleton in the closet is that very few organizations, to include the military, structure training programs on what to do *after* this instinctive episode when the individuals realize the reality of their actions.

What is it that happens to an individual who finds themselves dealing with the aftermath of a traumatic action? LTC (Ret.) David Grossman research and wrote the book "On Killing" to address such questions, and there are other psychological resources that delve into this area of study, as well. Grossman begins with a description of the physical events associated with post-traumatic conditions, both from an actor and victim perspective, using the graphic shown in Figure 118.[426] Notice the extremes of reaction shown in this chart as heart rate increases. Also notice that there is nothing the individual can do to preclude this automated response. At the point where *fear—or stress-induced heart rate* reaches above around 175 beats per minute, the conscious mind gives over to the animal portion of our brains with one objective: survival. The human body, in fact any animal body, will perform whatever act necessary to survive. To fight this autonomic reaction, the military and other agencies substitute what is known as "operant conditioning" or "brainwashing." This is explained below and is highly effective in the 140-160 bpm range of heart rate activity.

---

[426] Reprinted from Vol. 4, No. 4 of the Post-Traumatic Gazette. © 1998, Patience H. C. Mason.

P O Box 2757, High Springs, FL 32655-2757, 904-454-1651,www.patiencepress.com

You have my permission to reproduce to give away copies as long as this notice is included.

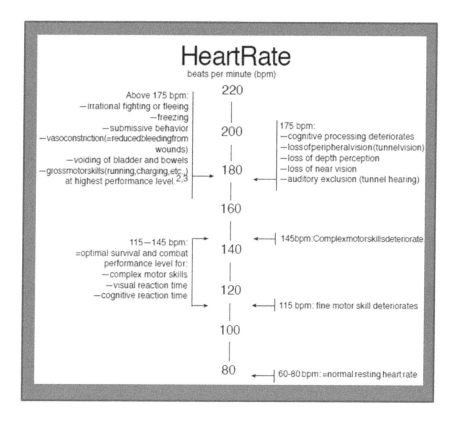

Figure 118: Effects of Hormonal-Induced Heart Rate Increase[427]

OPERANT AND CLASSICAL CONDITIONING

There are basically two types of conditioning: operant and classical. To understand operant and classical, one must first understand what "conditioning" entails. Conditioning is, quite simply, learning. The difference between the two structures or types of conditioning involves the response to a stimulus. A stimulus is basically an event or action that acts as a trigger to initiate some response from the subject, whether it be a dog, such as in the Pavlovian experiments, or a human.[428]

---

[427]   Grossman, D. 1996. *On Killing: The Psychological Cost of Learning to Kill in War and Society.*Self-published. Republished with Permission.

[428]   Specific information on Pavlov's experiments is found at http://www.nobelprize.org/educational/medicine/pavlov/readmore.html

Classical conditioning is where a specific stimulus triggers an involuntary response. Brock provides the following structure of classical conditioning.

Classical Conditioning (Stimulation → Response or [S → R])[429]

The following syllogistic flow explains, in scientific terms, the flow of a stimulus to a response. In normal language, a doctor hits your knee with a rubber hammer and your knee jerks. The subject does not think about it and cannot halt it. Another example is hypnosis . . . where a suggestion is implanted that the subconscious of the subject and the subject reacts to it unwittingly and often with little to no control.

a. *An involuntary response or unconscious response (UCR) is preceded by an unconscious stimuli (UCS), or*
b. *An unconscious stimulus (UCS) automatically triggers an* involuntary *(unconscious) response (UCR)*
c. *A neutral stimulus (NS) associated with UCS automatically triggers a conditioned response.*
d. *The NS becomes a conditioned stimulus (CS)*

In classical conditioning, as demonstrated in Pavlov's experiments, a subject may through repeated reward or punishment processes be made to respond in a particular manner, involuntarily, to a given stimulus. Pavlov established a direct relationship between the ringing of a bell and feeding his dogs so that every time he rang the bell, whether or not food was available, the dogs would respond by salivating. Brock uses the example of a teacher walking to a chalk board while telling the students that those who become and remain quiet will receive reward points toward a prize. After a period of time, just her walking to the board will elicit the response of the students quieting down.

Operant Conditioning (R → SRF)

a. *A voluntary response (R) is followed by a reinforcing stimulus (SRF).*
b. *The voluntary response is more likely to be emitted by the organism.*
c. *A reinforcer is any stimulus that increases the frequency of a behavior.*

---

[429] Brock, S. E. (2012). No Title. Lodi Unified School District. Downloaded on March 13, 2012, from http://www.csus.edu/indiv/b/brocks/Courses/EDS%20240/EDS%20240%20Handouts/Operant%20Conditioning%20O_H%20&%20H_O.pdf

d. *To be a reinforcer, stimuli must immediately follow the response and must be perceived as contingent upon the response.*[430]

Note that in this situation, the response is voluntary and does not necessarily follow from the stimulus; however, there is a strong tendency for the response to occur. This is the type of conditioning present in military and law enforcement weapons training; particularly combat weapons training where various shoot/don't shoot targets are presented and the subject must make an instantaneous decision on whether to fire or not. Samurai Yamamoto Tsunetomo, who lived from 1659 to 1719 and established the code known as *Hagakure*, discusses the requirement for a warrior to make a decision and an action simultaneously, or they are dead.[431]

Various studies have attempted to time the gap between decision and action in various environments and for various stimuli. The problem with doing this is that the actions of deciding is purely cognitive and not open to exact measurement. Neuromapping, using the MRI colored structure of the activation of various parts of the brain, shows that between the instant a stimulus is presented to a subject various areas of the brain become highly active. Depending upon the stimulus (e.g., a picture of a loved one vs. that of an attacking lion), the delay of activation in the reaction centers of the brain may be anywhere from a few nanoseconds to as much as one to two seconds. Converting that neurological response to action then takes additional time for the signal to transmit from the brain to the muscles necessary to carry out the desired response. If one is required to actively think about a proper response, the reaction time may go from microseconds to as much as half a minute or more.

Additionally, there appears to be some form of instinctive resistance to certain acts of violence within the mind of what is considered a normal individual—violence outside of that required for personal survival and the gathering of food. Grossman wrote on Freud that there exists a life instinct that struggles within the individual to control the more animalistic attributes present in the brainstem (Grossman, 2009). Carl Jung supported Freud's concept and applied a more genetic factor establishing that since the more aggressive members of the human ancestry survived to pass on their genes to future generations, there "are deeply ingrained models for behavior called archetypes that exist deep in every human's collective unconscious—an inherited, unconscious reservoir of images

---

[430] Ibid

[431] Tsunetomo, Y. *The Art of the Samurai: Yamamoto Tsunetomo's Hagakure*, Translated by Barry D. Steben, Duncan Baird, September 2008

derived from our ancestors' universal experiences and shared by the whole human race."[432] The graphic in Figure 118 would tend to support this conjecture.

What is also apparent from this discussion is that an individual, to remain useful in such stressful situations, must either (a) retain cognitive control or (b) be so conditioned that they will respond with the appropriate behavior for the situation. As option *b* is nearly impossible to attain for all operant situations, this leaves cognitive control as a viable alternative. Emergency, law enforcement, and military agencies train with this in mind. Additionally, it is well known by these agencies that this level of cognitive control slips as conditions worsen. These agencies have individuals, officers, and other leadership individuals who are able to remain somewhat aloof from the situation and therefore are not placed in the same psychophysiological condition so that they retain more cognitive ability.[433]

The aspect of such military training is operant conditioning. It is the repetitive processes of gunnery, emergency exercises, combat courses, confidence courses, and for the lower ranks, the systematic denigration of self during basic training programs in favor of answering to superior authority without question. And it works almost too well as current levels of post-traumatic stress disorder cases are revealing. The question becomes, why is this necessary, and why does it matter?

WHY IS OPERANT CONDITIONING NECESSARY

Charles Perrow wrote in the book *Normal Accidents* the following:

> We construct an expected world because we can't handle the complexity of the present one, and then process the information that fits the expected world, and find reasons to exclude the information that might contradict it. Unexpected or unlikely interactions are ignored when we make our construction.[434]

The *we* referenced here is all humankind. The reason this happens is that our minds have limited working memory storage and remove unnecessary observations based upon both our historical experiences and expected future. As such, the brain must be restructured to accept and remember the desired actions at a level whereby cognition does not need to be involved.

[432] Grossman. (2009).On Killing. E-Rights/E-Reads, Ltd, New York, NY. Kindle Fire Location 3270 of 5961.

[433] Ibid

[434] Perrow, C. (1999). *Normal Accidents: Living with High Risk Technology.* Princeton University Press. Princeton, NJ copied from Gonzales, L. (2005) *Deep Survival.* Norton and Co. New York, NY.

What occurs during training is that the brain establishes neuropathways or, if you will, bookmarks that are strongest when linked to an emotion. These are known as somatic markers. The reason for this is that logic and reason are much too slow in high-stress situations and are, as Figure 118 shows, disengaged by the brain in these life-or-death conditions. Therefore, the required actions must originate from another location than the reasoning centers—the amygdala.

The amygdala is an almond-sized structure as shown in Figure 119 below. The website, The Brain Connection, gives a good description of the internal neurological processes.[435]

The amygdala is a small, almond-shaped cluster of nuclei set deep in the temporal lobe that seems ideally positioned as the locus of fear learning. It receives input through its lateral nucleus from cortical areas and the thalamus, which is a key sensory relay station within the brain, and it sends output via its central nucleus to a variety of brain regions that are known to mediate fear responses, such as the hypothalamus. In fact, electrical stimulation of the amygdala can cause a previously calm animal to exhibit fearful and/or aggressive behaviors, and humans are not immune to this sort of manipulation. Autopsies of Charles Whitman, the formerly genteel man who carried out a sniper attack from the University Tower at Texas in 1966, showed he had a tumor pressing on his amygdala.

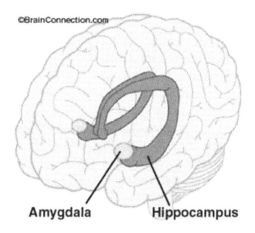

Figure 119: The Amygdala

---

[435] Downloaded on March 16, 2012, from http://brainconnection.positscience.com/topics/?main=fa/fear-conditioning2

Additionally, the amygdala is located very close and is connected to the cerebrum or the "animal brain" element of the human physiology. Both the distances and connections provide rapid reaction to any perceived danger and, once experienced and survived, is usually hard coded and linked to the structure of the brain via emotion (pain/fear) attachments. In training, the strong emotional connections are provided through two very strong mechanisms: peer pressure and fear of failing. Constant repetition provides the reaction pathways that link to the emotion. After training, individuals will perform functions that are often appropriate, even before being aware of any stimulus that would require the response. Again, per Gonzales,[436]

> Most decisions are not made using logic, which we all recognize at least at an unconscious level. LeDoux writes, "Unconscious operations of the brain is . . . the rule rather than the exception throughout the evolutionary history of the animal kingdom" and "include almost everything the brain does."

AND THEN WHAT—AFTER THE AUTONOMIC REACTION

The proactive approach to security planning is to ensure that there are appropriate training programs that enable the individual to react appropriately and quickly to a given set of stimuli. When the task is successfully completed, there is always a backlash. This is when the officer, the security professional, etc., must face the fact that he/she has just performed a function that may have caused the injury or death of another human being; a major neurological taboo inculcated deep into our subconscious. The individual must now face the return to cognition; addressing the numerous questions of could we have done something else? This is registered in the brain as guilt and second-guessing.

The professional has a few approaches of their own to address these feelings. The first way a person may try to deal with these feelings is to bury them beneath the daily pressures of simply living, trying to ignore the event and justify it as necessary for self or other survival. The rationalization may be something like, "It is part of the job that has to be done before they do it to you."

The second coping method is repression. Repression is much more than simply ignoring the even or burying it under life's other pressures. When we bury things and later remember them, the guilt remains and we tell ourselves we will deal with it later; temporarily easing the neurological activities pushing it into conscious thought. Repression, however, is a state of forced subjugation.

---

[436] Gonzales, L. (2005) *Deep Survival*. Norton and Co. New York, NY. Npn.

Subjugation is the forced subordination to another entity or condition. Because it is forced, the brain continues to subconsciously raise the issue requiring more and more energy to keep the memory repressed. The longer this occurs, the greater the amount of energy required to fight the memory, until there is simply an insufficient amount of energy to maintain the repression and a mental breakdown occurs.

The third way to try to deal is to bring the event into the open via group therapy and other such processes. The individual must face the situation and receive some form of absolution for their act, often as a surrogate to the individual harmed. Only through such an exorcism is the individual able to relieve the extreme psychological injuries sustained. This may also occur via societal and peer pressure. Similarly, having someone of respected authority perform a function of approval can result in psychological absolution, which is the primary reason military forces have medals, a means of saying: "You have done well and we accept what you did as right and necessary."

The fourth and most important method is to address the issue prior to the event even occurring. Unfortunately, this is often not done organizations. The reason for this is that it can cause second thoughts in the minds of the performers at a critical moment. Should that occur, the training may fall apart and compromise the task. The danger in failing to provide the pre-event training of psychological need and recovery is that the individual is at risk of unresolved mental unrest, which could threaten their sanity. This may be one of the sources of PTSD.

Freud, per Grossman, established that there exists within each individual, unless there is a physical or psychological defect, a force for life. This is more than the simple aspect of self-preservation; it is species preservation. It is the inherent and incessant drive to protection of the continuation of human life on earth. This drive exists in every creature that exists and is demonstration through the unconscious drive to procreate. This drive exists in the most primitive regions of the brain as demonstrated by species that have little to no conscious thought ability. We call this instinct.

In the human, what we call instinct begins shortly after conception with the development of both the brain and what Freud calls the Id.

> *The id operates entirely out of the unconscious—that is, we have no awareness of its drives, its urges, or its influences over us. The id is closely linked to our biological needs, its main aim being to get food, air, water, sex, or whatever else we need for basic survival. The id grasps and clutches at what it needs without paying any heed to the wants and need of others. It doesn't care about approval, rules, social norms or niceties. It wants what it wants and it wants it now. It has no concept of delayed gratification. It doesn't recognize fear or sense danger; its sole purpose is to reduce the tension built up through*

hunger, thirst, sexual frustration or whatever else our bodies may crave.[437]

This element of our psyche has no restraints over it. That is unacceptable both within society and from nature's perspective. Therefore, the ego steps in to mitigate the id's unrestrained rush toward gratification at any cost, because that cost may put the individual at great risk. As Debnam puts it, the ego is the seat of intellectual processes and problem solving.

The ego in a sense becomes the mediator between the primitive urges of the id and the environment, or context, in which it finds itself. In contrast to the id's pleasure-seeking nature, the ego obeys what Freud describes as the reality principle. Although it gets energy from the id to take action, the ego concerns itself with ensuring the safety and self-preservation of the individual. It has the capacity to distinguish between reality and fantasy, tolerate moderate amounts of tension and engage in rational thought processes to satisfy instinctual needs appropriately without endangering self or others.[438]

Next is what Freud termed the *superego*. Debnam defines the process and use of the superego in Freud's philosophy as follows:

The superego aims to develop a set of values, norms and ethics that are reasonably compatible with the social group the individual finds himself in. Freud's theory suggests that whereas we are born with the id and the ego, we don't develop a superego until we are between three and five years old, when we start to take notice of the messages coming from our parents and teachers about what's right and wrong, good and bad, moral and immoral. To begin with we internalize [sic] or believe only what these significant figures tell us about good and bad behaviour. [sic] We put every effort into living up to the parental ideal, until our world broadens (through school, religion, peer groups) and we begin to absorb and incorporate the rules and norms of a wider group, beyond our family. As we grow we develop a conscience. We subconsciously develop a capacity for guilt, punitive self-evaluation and moral prohibitions when we feel we are not living up to the standards our parents or peer groups set. The "shoulds" and "oughts"

---

[437] Debnam, Susan. (2006). *Mine's Bigger Than Yours*, Marshall Cavendish Limited. London. Pg 38.

[438] Ibid. pg 39.

start to creep in and influence our decisions, without our being aware of them. Because we are not aware of them, we cannot hold them up to the light and scrutinize [sic] them for their relevance and validity in our current context.[439]

These are the underpinnings of the conscience—that part of a person that tells them when they are about to do wrong, are doing wrong, or provides with a sense of guilt of having broken what they know to be acceptable and right. Some individuals and authorities try to maintain that this is an artificial construct that has no bearing on what we do or how we should live our lives. Yet this entity is part of each individual. A person cannot live without it and often have trouble living with it. Within this dichotomy are the roots of proactive management.

> These are the underpinnings of the conscience, that part of use that tells us we are about to do wrong, are doing wrong, or provides us with the guilt of having broken what we know to be acceptable and right. Some individuals and authorities try to maintain that this is an artificial construct that has no bearing on what we do or how we should live our lives. Yet this entity is part of use. We cannot live without it and often have trouble living with it. Within this dichotomy are the roots of proactive management.

Using the Id, the Ego, and the Superego as Management Tools

With so many competing forces, it is easy to see how conflict might arise between the id, ego, and superego. Freud used the term *ego strength* to refer to the ego's ability to function despite these dueling forces. A person with good ego strength is able to effectively manage these pressures, while those with too much or too little ego strength can become too unyielding or disruptive.

According to Freud, the key to a healthy personality is a balance between the id, the ego, and the superego. Maintaining that balance in planning constructs is a proactive measure to ensure individuals perform tasks as needed and that they maintain their grip on both reality and necessity. To achieve this, the manager/leader must first understand the implications, the means of assisting the maintenance of the balance, and the ability to recognize when the balance is slipping.

There are several excellent tools for identifying the basic personality of an individual within specific settings. One of the simplest is the DiSC profile, which stands for dominance, influence, steadiness, and conscientiousness (or caution).

---

[439]   Ibid, pg 40.

The method was developed from the theories of Carl Jung and expanded upon with the work of William Marston.

The primary issue with the use of a personality profile tool is individual resistance. A large number of people believe that such information is highly personal, rejecting attempts at gaining personal information. However, there is nothing illegal or actually sensitive about the DiSC profile, as it is very environmentally dependent and changes based upon this environment. Many major corporations use this approach for project/program management, as it enables more efficient resourcing to task decisions. It is in this aspect that the profile fits into the topic of this text.

The DiSC website provides the following definitions associated with the profile tool:[440]

> The concept of the DiSC assessment is not a new one. First developed by psychologist William Marston in the late 1920s, its benefits to the business world were immediately apparent. By helping to understand a person's behavioral style and preferences, the DiSC assessment made it possible to pinpoint strengths and weaknesses; essentially allowing employers to create a custom tailored workforce. A look at the four areas covered in a DiSC assessment reveals how it could help your company today.

Dominance

How does one handle pressure? Does the individual take control of a project and lead the rest of the way? Or maybe the individual is the low key, cooperative type. Both behavioral styles are important on a team, but an imbalance can create friction in the workplace, or slowing production rates. The ultimate objective of the completion of a non-judgmental DiSC assessment is to help employees capitalize on their individual strengths, leading to a more upbeat, productive work environment.

Influence

Would you have made a great politician? Do others describe your personality as magnetic? Perhaps you're more logical and skeptical—you need to be won over by facts and figures. Again, both types of employees are important to have

---

[440] http://disc-assessment.com/ downloaded March 20, 2012.

402

on board. A DiSC assessment will help determine where on the spectrum you lie, helping to discern which area of the company you will be the most successful in.

Steadiness

Does security rank high on your list of priorities? Are you happy with the status quo? Or are you a restless spirit, constantly seeking a new challenge? It takes risk to secure a new account, and a steady, reliable hand to keep it. A DiSC assessment helps companies maximize effectiveness, and foster an appreciation for different behavior and personality styles.

Compliance

Is the individual all about sticking to the rules? Is their desk organized to within an inch of its life? Or would the individual rather break a rule than adhere to it? Whether individual is a trailblazer or an analyst makes a huge difference in the areas within which they will excel. A DiSC assessment assists in the determination of which managerial or coaching styles will be most effective for the company's staff.

Notice in Figure 120 that the results graphic depicts both a black dot and a green-red-blue-yellow shading.

Figure 120: Sample DiSC Profile Graphic

The dot is indicative of the strength of the individual's mental processes in the specific environmental setting while the shading depicts tendencies within the other domains. The corporation website provides the following description/ explanation of the structure.[441]

Although the circular representation of DiSC is designed to be simple and intuitive, it also conveys a great deal of information about a person's DiSC style at a glance. To start, the angular location of a person's dot indicates the person's primary DiSC style, Figure 121. Many people also lean toward a second DiSC style. For example, in the circle to the right, we have a participant who tends toward the C style, but also has some tendency toward the D style. Most likely, if he had taken the *DiSC Classic* assessment, he would have ended up with a Creative Pattern (composed of the C and D styles) or an Objective Thinker Pattern (composed mostly of the C style.)

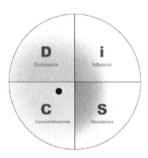

Figure 121: DiSC Profile with Point Identifier

The distance from the dot to the center of the circle also communicates important information about the person's DiSC style. A person whose dot is close to the outer edge of the circle is probably very committed to his or her DiSC style, Figure 122. The shading within the circle reinforces this principle and shows the participant that he has a large amount of the C style and a significant, but slightly less, amount of the D style. The shading also shows that they probably exhibit very little of the S style and even less of the I style. The shading, however, still reinforces that the person has each of these four styles within him. As a result, this participant understands that they probably have some difficulty shifting into an I or S style for long periods of time.

[441] Everything DiSC Application Library. (2011). *How My Graph Became a Dot*. Inscape Publishing, Inc. pg 3. Downloaded on March 2, 2012, from http://www.corexcel.com/ pdf/everything-disc-application-library-research-report.pdf

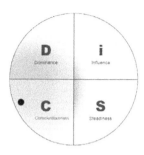

Figure 122: DiSC Point with Adjustment

Figure 121 shows another participant who tends toward CD, but their dot is much closer to the center of the circle than in Figure 122. This person's (Figure 121) CD style will not be as pronounced, and the shading tells them that they will find it easier to shift into the I or S styles without significant stress.

Leaders trained in the use of such tools can determine the processes and considerations of their subordinates and how they interact with others of different personality types. For a given task or set of tasks, the leader can group individuals with the cognitive skills to perform at optimum levels together. To achieve this, the leader must invest the time to ascertain what skills a specific task or set of tasks will require and map these to the available resources. This process is known as skill mapping.

SKILL MAPPING

Per Hiermann and Höfferer, the key factors for the process of skill mapping are as follows:

a. *Finding the right employee(s) for a specific task or project*
b. *Retrieval and assembling of flexible project teams*
c. *Development and updating of employee knowledge and capabilities*
d. *Exploration of future career paths, and*
e. *Accelerate innovation management.*[442]

The dynamics of a skill model appears in Figure 123 from the same publication.

---

[442]   Hiermann, W. and Höfferer, M. (2003). A Practical Knowledge-based Approach to Skill Management and Personal Development. *Journal of Universal Computer Science.* Vol 9. No 12. 1398-1409. pg 1398.

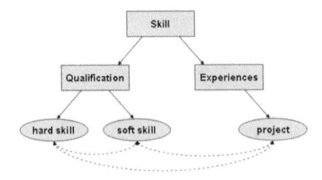

Figure 123: Skill Model

In this process, a skill is made up of both qualifications and experiences. Qualifications derive from "hard" skills (learned technical knowledge and capabilities) and "soft" skills (those related to an individual's sociological or emotional intelligence knowledge). A person's training, education, and personality relationship, essentially; their experiences involving learned behavior based on what has happened during their life up to the point at which the mapping occurs. A simplified process appears in Figure 124.

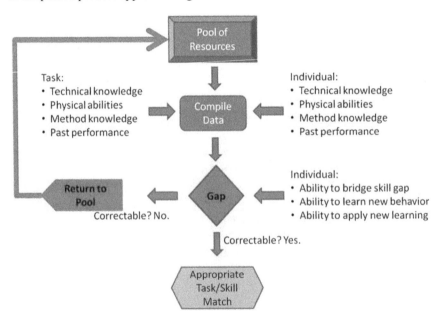

Figure 124: Simplified Skill Mapping Process

A planner determines skill requirements with the requisite knowledge of what is necessary for the particular task at hand. For example, if the task is part of the project of building a house and involves laying the foundation, the requisite skills would likely include: carpentry (measuring, cutting, and constructing the frame, landscaping to prepare the ground, metallurgy to lay and weld the reinforcing steel bars), construction chemistry (to be able to appropriately mix the cement to the proper formula and consistency), and paving (flowing and leveling the cement into the appropriate frame and density). See Chapter 11 for the explanation of the best way for a planner to divide a project into its component elements.

The next step is for the planner to determine the type of individual best suited for the task. If the task or set of tasks associated with this project or repetitive activity requires a specific key performance element, the individual selected must demonstrate that performance where possible. An example is shown in Figure 125 below. However, many of these are cognitive or personality-based aspects that do not lend themselves to either interviewing or short-term/sighted feelings on the matter. It is here that psychological knowledge and evaluation pays dividends.

Use ICT Systems

Entry 1	Entry 2	Entry 3	Level 1	Level 2
1 interact with ICT for a given purpose	1 interact with ICT for a purpose	1a interact with and use an ICT system to meet needs	1a interact with and use ICT systems independently to meet needs	1a select, interact with and use ICT systems independently for a complex task to meet a variety of needs
1.1 use ICT for a given purpose	1.1 use computer hardware	1.1 use correct procedures to start and shut down an ICT system; log in, log out, use shutdown menu	1.1 use correct procedures to start and shut down an ICT system; log in, log out, use shutdown menu	1.1 use correct procedures to start and shut down an ICT system; log in, log out, use shutdown menu
ICT: computer, touch screen, cash-point machine, mobile phone, multi-media devices, on-screen information purpose: find local community information, use learning software		1.2 use input and output devices	1.2 use a communication service to access the internet	1.2 select and use a communication service to access the internet
	keyboard, screen, printer, point and click device, headphones, microphone	keyboard, mouse, touch screen, microphone, printer, headphones	broadband, dial up, network, mobile device	broadband, dial up, network, mobile device
1.2 recognise and use interface features	1.2 use software applications for a purpose; text processing, graphics, web browser, email	1.3 select and use software applications to meet needs and solve problems; word processing, graphics, internet browser, email, audio or video player	1.3 select and use software applications to meet needs and solve given problems; word processing, spreadsheet, graphics, internet browser, email, audio and video software	1.3 select and use software applications to meet needs and solve problems; word processing, spreadsheet, graphics, browser, email, audio and video software
icon, option button, hotspot	1.3 recognise and use interface features	1.4 recognise and use interface features	1.4 recognise and use interface features effectively to meet needs	1.4 select and use interface features and system facilities effectively to meet needs
	icon, option button, hotspot, window menu	icon, option button, hotspot, window, dialogue box, menu, drag and drop	desktop, windows, dialogue box, menu, submenu, toolbar, scrollbar, drag and drop, zoom, minimise, maximise	desktop, windows, dialogue box, menu, submenu, toolbar, scrollbar, drag and drop, zoom, template, wizard

Figure 125: Example of a TYPE Skills Assessment Matrix

The key to the process is the understanding of why. The manager must understand what drives the skill requirement and to what degree will the skill set be important. Individuals who will have constant contact with the public will need to understand how they are viewed and what their actions will communicate to the individuals involved. If a task requires a specific programming language ability, does the person have and demonstrated proficiency with that language and the ability to translate process requirements into code? What are the specific rankings for the structure of the program tasks, as not all skill sets will rank equally across all tasks. These are all questions the manager or planner may need to consider, as tailored to the task at hand.

The issue of ranking is one of the most important yet most neglected aspects of skill/task mapping. An example of this is in Figure 126. The information for this chart was obtained from a survey of various security executives conducted by the Institute of Finance and Management and slightly modified to fit the structure of this text.

Figure 126: Skill Ranking Example[443]

Having such a ranking enables the manager to use a normalization process, which is where the manager evaluates each team member or pool candidate's skills on a numeric scale (known as a Likert scale) of specific values; each value being defined in relationship to the skill. They then multiply the skill rating by the importance ranking to achieve a comparable score. This score is then part of a

---

[443] Data obtained as an example from Institute of Finance and Management. (2011). SDR/ IOMA Guare firm *Ratings & Contracting Security Survey*. Issue 11-02. ppg 1, 11-13.

profile set that includes skill scores, DiSC score, average annual evaluation scores (if known), years of experience in the skill type, and a qualitative ranking from either observation and/or interview to arrive at a final ranking. This process allows for a definitive selection of individuals in a more exact and quantifiable fashion than any unstructured approach.

PROJECT DYNAMICS AND MEASUREMENT

There are many accepted methods of measuring program/project performance. Each has numerous texts associated with how to structure the metrics, develop the information, and assess what that information communicates. Each of these methods, from Earned Value Management (EVM) to Task Completion Analysis (TCA) involves the translation of work to a comparable numeric value, generally money. Each of these processes have the same issue; unless the manager can determine that a task is in trouble before it fails and discerns what to do about it to ensure its success, the process is invalid. The metric must be viewed as an indicator rather than an end in itself.

Using EVM, consider a project, given the following information. Notice that for each task in Figure 127 there is a start date, a finish date, duration, and any task relationships or precedents that may exist. Precedents usually indicate that there are tasks that must be successfully completed prior to the current task beginning. For example, one must install the drainage and supply piping to a property before one lays the concrete foundation or they will have to go back and hammer a hole through the concrete for the pipes.

Using the EVM process, each task has an associated value derived from the resource costs, the hours/days of work necessary, and other incremental aspects. This creates what is called the Budgeted Cost of Work Scheduled (BCWS) for the task (see Figure 128). Should the budgeted cost and the actual cost be identical (accurate), there will exist no cost variance and the BCWP and Actual Cost of Work Performed (ACWP) points will be identical. Additionally, if the scheduled performance period and the actual schedule performance period are likewise equal, there will be no schedule variance in the points.

	❶	Task Name	Duration	Start	Finish	Predec
1		⊟ ABC Corporation Security Plan	99 days?	Tue 1/3/12	Fri 5/18/12	
2		⊟ Assess Requirements and Needs	88 days?	Tue 1/3/12	Thu 5/3/12	
3		⊟ Create Review Team	32 days?	Tue 1/3/12	Wed 2/15/12	
4	▦	Determine Skill Sets Needed for Review	9 days?	Tue 1/3/12	Fri 1/13/12	
5		Gather and Coordinate Team	10 days	Mon 1/16/12	Fri 1/27/12	4
6		Establish Roles	10 days	Mon 1/30/12	Fri 2/10/12	5
7		Launch Team Operations	3 days	Mon 2/13/12	Wed 2/15/12	6
8		⊟ Set Proceudure and Processes for Review	51 days	Thu 2/16/12	Thu 4/26/12	3
9		Establish Responsibilities	6 days	Thu 2/16/12	Thu 2/23/12	
10		Determine Major Products	14 days	Fri 2/24/12	Wed 3/14/12	9
11		Brainstorm and Establish Objectives and Major Tasks	31 days	Thu 3/15/12	Thu 4/26/12	10
12		⊞ Outline Tasks and Set Schedule	1 day?	Fri 4/27/12	Fri 4/27/12	8
14		⊞ Determine Cost and Obtain Funding for Team	1 day?	Mon 4/30/12	Mon 4/30/12	13,12
16		⊞ Conduct Assessment	1 day?	Tue 5/1/12	Tue 5/1/12	15,14
18		⊞ Document Results	1 day?	Wed 5/2/12	Wed 5/2/12	17,16
20		⊞ Obtain Corporate Decision	1 day?	Thu 5/3/12	Thu 5/3/12	19,18
22		⊟ Determine Capabilities	7 days?	Fri 5/4/12	Mon 5/14/12	2
23		Conduct Asset Requirements Analysis	1 day?	Fri 5/4/12	Fri 5/4/12	
24		Conduct Asset Capabilities Analysis	1 day?	Mon 5/7/12	Mon 5/7/12	23
25		Determine Asset Correction Requirements	1 day?	Tue 5/8/12	Tue 5/8/12	24
26		Develop Asset Correction Plan	1 day?	Wed 5/9/12	Wed 5/9/12	25
27		Obtain Corporate Approval	1 day?	Thu 5/10/12	Thu 5/10/12	26
28		Initiate Asset Correction Program	1 day?	Fri 5/11/12	Fri 5/11/12	27
29		Manage Correction Program	1 day?	Mon 5/14/12	Mon 5/14/12	28
30		⊞ Develop Security Program	1 day?	Tue 5/15/12	Tue 5/15/12	22
32		⊞ Implement Security Program	1 day?	Wed 5/16/12	Wed 5/16/12	30
34		⊞ Manage Security Program	1 day?	Thu 5/17/12	Thu 5/17/12	32
36		⊞ Review Security Program	1 day?	Fri 5/18/12	Fri 5/18/12	34

Figure 127: Example Project Tasks

Each differential in the actual-to-budgeted expectations, however, will result in differentials as shown in Figure 128 below. Reading the differentials provides the project manager with information as to the status or health of the project. What it does *not* do is provide the status or health of each task. Therein lays the main problem with the process. While the process is vital for overall project management, there is insufficient visibility at the task level for sufficient proactive control as the metrics used in EVM focus on task completion, rather than intra-task progress. Figure 129 provides a simplistic example of this concept.

PERFORMANCE MEASUREMENT DATA ELEMENTS

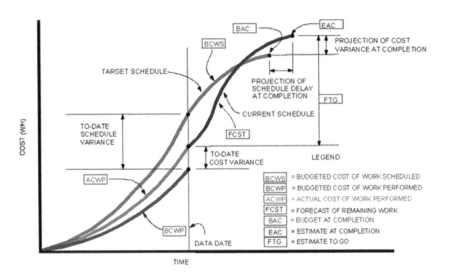

Figure 128: Example EVM Graphic

Notice that a step is not the same thing as a task. Per the PMBOK, a task is a piece of work requiring effort and resources and having a concrete outcome (i.e., a deliverable) that is generally performed by one individual. The following are characteristics of tasks:[444]

a. *A task has a definite beginning and end.*

b. *Tasks are performed in relatively short periods of time. They are usually measured in minutes or hours.*

c. *Tasks are observable. By observing the performance of a jobholder, a definite determination can be made that the task has been performed.*

d. *Each task is independent of other actions. Tasks are not dependent on components of a procedure. A task is performed by an individual for its own sake.*

e. *A task statement is a statement of a highly specific action. It always has a verb and an object. It may have qualifiers, such as "measure distances with a tape measure." A task statement should not be confused with an objective, which has conditions and standards.*

---

[444] Downloaded on March 25, 2012, from http://www.nwlink.com/~donclark/hrd/tasks. html

Steps are the action-by-action instructions for performing the task as shown in the figure below.

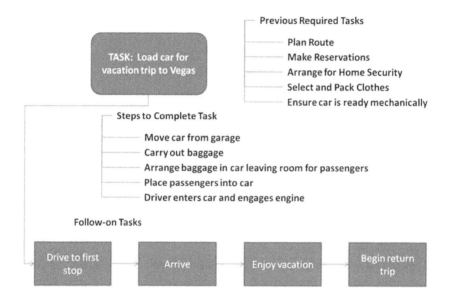

Figure 129: Simplified Task Example

Many texts and project managers will state that reducing any project task to this level is both expensive and counterproductive. There are numerous examples, however, of where it is mandatory that the task refine down to individual steps. This concept depends heavily upon the importance, risks, and concept of the task. For example, if the task is to prepare the surgical tray for open heart surgery, the specific steps become highly important. Similarly, specific steps in the task of preparing an aircraft for takeoff are so critical that checklists are both made and religiously followed. As such, even though the task may only take a few minutes, those performing the tasks may proactively identify a situation critical enough to end the task, thus requiring either restructuring of the task or termination/ rescheduling of the project (e.g., the particular flight on that particular aircraft is delayed or cancelled, pending a new aircraft). The key is to determine which tasks require such expansion and how, and the associated conditions.

Situations involving security operations and/or intelligence tasks fall into this domain. These disciplines provide the knowledge, the conditions, and the protection necessary for the continuation of all other business and other functions. It is important for the planner to consider, diagram, and monitor the steps. Slavish application to the steps without knowledge and appropriate observation of the situations to ensure adjustment as necessary, however, can result in errors.

CONVERSION OF TASKS TO METRICS

Stated earlier in this chapter, the most common method of measuring the completion of tasks is through the conversion of the resource requirements into expected dollars of earnings. A review of Figure 128 provides the various aspects of measurement, such as BCWP, ACWP, BAC, etc. Refer to Figure 128 for a determination of the meanings of these acronyms. Additionally, most project management texts will establish the aspect of quality measurements, where the following calculation provides the end-all of measurement:

Quality = Delivered/Expected

However, when one attempts to apply these basics to various aspects of work producing cognition rather than an actual product, hidden skeletons appear. *CIO Insight* outlined some of the "skeletons" in the EVM closet as follows:[445]

a. Pad the Schedule—*It's the oldest trick in the book. If a project looks like it will take three months, tell management it will take four. If things go wrong, the manager can still beat expectations or at least hide the problems for a while, keeping up appearances.*

b. Push Problem Tasks Forward—*Putting the easiest tasks at the beginning of the project and the hardest tasks at the end can keep a project green for a long time.*

c. Bump the Task Completion Percentages—*What's the difference between a task that's 20 percent complete and one that's 80 percent complete? A project that's red and a project that's green. The longer the task, the larger the "benefit," but changing the completion percentage of any subjective task will help the earned value numbers.*

d. Re-Baseline the Project—*The project manager waits until a scope change or other change request, and uses that as an excuse to redo the project schedule. The project instantly turns green because actual progress now matches expected progress.*

e. Late Integration—*Most problems with IT projects emerge during integration and testing. By putting these tasks at the end and then marking them as partially complete, technical problems were hidden for the entire life of the project.*

---

[445] CIO Ezine. Downloaded March 30, 2012, from http://www.cioinsight.com/c/a/ Past-Opinions/How-to-Lie-with-Earned-Value/

Notice a major issue hidden in item "e" above where *CIO Insight* states, "By putting these tasks at the end and then marking them as partially complete . . ." Here is the major rub in measuring cognitive, security, and intelligence projects using only EVMS. The skeleton here is where and how to mark elements of completion in the manner most appropriate to accuracy and honesty. There are several methods used in IT coding projects that are also used in security/ intelligence projects. The most popular is to record the task as a partial percentage complete at the start, another partial percentage complete when the management believes the coding to be halfway completed, and apply the remaining percentage when the coding is finished but not yet tested. The question is whether EVMS is an accurate method of measuring the progress of the project when the completed code may or may not work. Or should the metric be that only a portion of the work is completed at the completion of the code construction, another portion at successful completion of testing, and the final when the code is promoted to active systems? Whichever pathway is selected, it must be appropriately and clearly defined so that all understand the worth of the information presented.

Nearly all project management texts and websites discuss the process of converting work to financial measures. However, these metrics are likely more appropriate to physical tasks than to cognitive tasks. It is more appropriate to examine the specific steps of the tasks and derive appropriate metrics from these. Returning to Figure 129 and looking at the steps of loading the car, possible metrics could include such things as size of the car vs. cubes of luggage *and* passengers. The auto may be of sufficient size to load all luggage yet leave no room for passengers requiring external storage capability. The external storage could then be a rooftop carrier or a towed carrier, requiring other specifications, such as the ability of the auto design to hold a rooftop carrier of sufficient size or the engine/drive train ability to pull a loaded towed carrier.

Establishing such metrics at the beginning of a project enables the manager to make immediate determinations of trigger points. A trigger point is that time in the project requiring an action to correct potential issues without adversely affecting the project critical path. Notice that such measures are *not* financial conversions, but rather, they are actual specifications. The trigger point is also not translatable to financial values. Rather, it is translatable to time. Time often means money, yet here it means delay if the trigger point passes.

The last consideration for metrics is the aspect of financial values. Work that involves individuals performing a task can, and most often does, convert to a financial value. The basic process is number of work hours to perform the task multiplied by the number of individuals required multiplied by the financial value of their time. There are segues to this, such as if a person is required only part time, or there are different time values. The concept is fairly basic.

Equipment may be financially valued in a similar fashion. This is because a machine employed in one task cannot simultaneously be used on another task.

415

The planner can usually determine value by taking the periodic value of the equipment—the purchase cost divided by its depreciation rate for the period of use, and the cost of operation and required maintenance for the same period. They add this to all other cost factors for the task to arrive at the BCWP. This budgeted cost must also have the potential profit included in the overall value calculation for total accuracy.

DETERMINING PROGRESS

There are basically three methods for determining the actual progress of project tasks: observation, reports, and product delivery. Observation and product delivery are likely the most accurate and easiest to use, as there is physical evidence of the activity. The structure, receipt, and evaluation of reports involve belief in and assessment of the meanings of the reports.

Reports are generated in many forms and templates that relate to the applicable data, the desires of management, and the communication goals of the report. Again, there are courses, texts, and other guides to the development and construction of reports beyond this text that the reader can explore. For the purpose of this text, the following guidelines suffice:[446]

> ***Purpose of a Report: Writing to be Read***
> *A key thing to keep in mind right through your report writing process is that a report is written to be read by someone else. Therefore, the author needs to have in mind the intended audience. Keep the information focused to this audience for effective communication.*
>
> ***Overall Approach: Top-down Outlining***
> *Take a top-down approach to writing the report. This also applies to problem solving in general. This can proceed in roughly three stages of continual refinement of details.*
> 1. *First write the section-level outline*
> 2. *Next the subsection-level outline*
> 3. *Then a paragraph-level outline. The paragraph-level outline would more-or-less be like a presentation with bulleted points. It incorporates the flow of ideas.*

Once the planner develops the paragraph-level flow of ideas, they can easily convert these into a full report by writing out the flow of ideas in full sentences.

---

[446] Downloaded on April 1, 2012, from http://www.cse.iitk.ac.in/users/braman/students/good-report.html

Remember that paragraphs have three to five sentences. Sentence one is the topic of the paragraph and may be a lead in from the previous paragraphs for continuity. Sentences 2-4 provide expansion and/or support information for the topic sentence. The final sentence concludes the thought of the topic and usually provides a lead-in to the next paragraphs for continuity.

Another thing to ascertain while doing the paragraph-level outline is the appropriate terminology. The overall approach also includes multiple stages of refinement and taking feedback from others (peers/advisor/instructor).

Structure of a Report

The following should roughly be the structure of a report. Note that these are just guidelines, not rules. The writer has to use intelligence in structuring the details of the specific writing. Corporate agencies may have standards for such reports, so be sure to determine what these are and how to adapt accordingly for styles and templates. Remember that writing for business is much different than for academic, military, government, or social writing.

Title and Abstract

These are the most-read parts of a report, where the writer attracts attention to the topic at hand. The title should reflect what was done and highlight any eye-catching factor(s) from the data.

The abstract should be short, generally within about two paragraphs (250 words or so total). The abstract should contain the essence of the report, based on which the reader decides whether to go ahead with reading the report in full or not. It can contain the following in varying amounts of detail as is appropriate: main motivation, main design point, essential difference from previous data, methodology, and applicable eye-catching results, if any.

Introduction

Most reports start with an introduction section. This section should answer the following questions (not necessarily in that order, but what is given below is a logical order):

1. What is being addressed in the report in one sentence?
2. Why it is being addressed in no more than two sentences?
3. What is the value of the information to the reader?
4. How should it be used in summary format?

After title/abstract, the introduction and conclusions are the other two most-read parts of a report.

The introduction is nothing but a shorter version of the rest of the report, and in many cases, the rest of the report can also have the same flow. Think of the rest of the report as an expansion of some of the points in the introduction. Which of the above bullets are expanded into separate sections (perhaps even multiple sections) depends very much on the problem topic.

Background

This is expanded upon into a separate section if there is sufficient background that the general reader must understand before knowing the details of the data. It is usual to state that "the reader who knows this background can skip this section" in writing for this section.

Past/Related Data

It is common to have this as a separate section. Here, one must try to think of dimensions of comparison of related elements of data. For instance, one may compare in terms of functionality, in terms of performance, and/or in terms of approach. Even within these, there may be multiple lines of comparison: functionality-1, functionality-2, metric-1, metric-2, etc.

Although not mandatory, it is good presentation style to give the above comparison in terms of a table, where the rows are the various dimensions of comparison and the columns contain the various pieces of related data. Another point is the placement of related data. One possibility is to place it in the beginning of the report, after the intro/background. Another is to place it in the end of the report, just before conclusions. This is a matter of judgment and depends if there is a significant amount of past data related very closely to the current data. If so, then it makes sense to state those differences up front. On the other hand, if current data is substantially different from past data, then it is better to put the related data at the end.

While this conveys a stronger message, it has the risk of the reader wondering all through the report as to how your data is different from some other specific related data. Be sure to clarify this point to keep the report succinct.

Technical Sections

The writer may divide the main body of the report into multiple sections, as the case may be. The author may have different sections delving into different aspects of the problem. The organization of the report here is problem specific. There may also be a separate section for statement of design methodology, or experimental methodology, or proving some dilemmas in the report.

The technical section is the most data specific; hence, it is the least described here. However, it makes sense to mention the following main points:

a. *Outlines/Flow*—For large sections with many subsections, it is appropriate to include a rough outline at the beginning of that section. Make sure to maintain the flow as the reader goes from one section to

418

another. There should be no abrupt jumps in ideas, rather include clear transition statements.

b. *Use of Figures*—Consider the cliché "a picture is worth a thousand words" and spend time thinking about what images or graphics can best support your data. Refer to the figures in text prior to their appearance and, wherever necessary, explain aspects of a figure to avoid leaving the reader wondering about the connection between the figure and the text.

c. *Terminology*—Define each term/symbol before use or right after its first use. Stick to a common terminology and style throughout the report.

Results

This is part of the set of technical sections and is usually a separate section for experimental/design papers. The section must answer the following questions:

a. What aspects of the system or project are being evaluated? That is, what are the questions answered through the evaluations?
b. Why the evaluations being performed?
c. What assumptions, limitations, and constraints are there to the measurements?
d. What are the cases of comparison? What are the performance metrics? Why?
e. What are the parameters of the study?
f. What is the experimental setup? Explain the choice of every parameter value (range) carefully.
g. What are the results?
h. Finally, why do the results look the way they do?

Conclusions

Readers usually read the title, abstract, introduction, and conclusions. In that sense, this section is quite important. The main takeaway points must be stated clearly and can be highlighted in banners or through graphics.

Refinement

No report is perfect, and definitely not on the first version. Well-written reports are those that have gone through multiple rounds of *refinement or proofreading for content*. This refinement may be through self-reading and critical analysis or more effectively through peer feedback (or feedback from mentors/supervisors).

Feedback: Evaluating Someone Else's Report

Writers can self-evaluate their report; however, they may not have the critical eye needed or be too close to the work to recognize issues/errors. Even in a group project, it is not good enough to have one person write the report and the other person read it. This is because all the group members usually know what the project is about and hence cannot critique the paper from the perspective of an external audience.

It is best to take feedback from peers. The feedback procedure is quite simple. The one reading has to be critical and methodical to see if each of the aspects necessary communicates the desired message. It may even help to have a checklist. Although with experience, this becomes unnecessary.

a. Check the structure and approach to ensure it makes sense and is effective/eye catching
b. Ask if all the relevant questions/issues summarized in the introduction
c. Ensure the overall structure of the rest of the section(s) meaningful
d. Look to see if the difference from related/past data is crisp and meaningful
e. Ask if the technical sections understandable. Are the figures/tables explained properly? Is the terminology clear? Are the symbols used defined appropriately
f. Verify the results explained properly. Are the conclusions drawn from the graphs/tables sound? Or are there technical holes/flaws? Do the results show how the data presented is better/worse that the other cases of comparison?

Graphic Construction for Producing a High-Quality Report

There are many sources and structures for guidelines in what an appropriate graphic should contain and depict. The following is an example obtained from a writing guide for a major corporation.[447] Most agencies/companies have similar standards.

---

[447] Obtained from a writing guide constructed by the author for a Boeing Corporation team.

Table 13: Characteristics of High-Quality Graphics

	When to use	Tradeoffs	Tips each type of graphic
Bar chart	Versatile and good for comparisons. Relatively easy to construct.	Y axis units can sometimes be too small to show meaningful differences.	• Position the title directly above the chart or graph • Label the horizontal (x) and vertical (y) axes • Use as few bars or lines as possible (max. 6 bars or 3 lines) • Emphasize one aspect of the data by changing a bar's color or texture
Line graph	Useful to depict trends.	Too many data lines can confuse.	• Move in order across the bar chart from largest to smallest value • To clarify values, add value labels to the top of the bar. • Label lines on line graphs, and if possible, make them different colors. • Draw horizontal lines across the chart, beginning at each interval of the vertical axis
Pie chart	Shows proportions (percentages) well.	Too many categories can mislead. Not ideal for showing trends.	• Use six or fewer slices • Place title above the chart • Use contrasting colors, shades of gray, or simple patterns to increase readability • Label the slices • Emphasize certain piece of data by moving its slice out from the circle (most computer graphing programs, such as Excel, allow you to do this)
Illustrations *Examples:* *Diagrams,* *maps, drawings*	Can convey large amount of information in a small space.	May occupy a large amount of space. Complex illustration may not photocopy well.	• Position title above illustration • Keep the illustration simple. If it needs a lot of explanation, it is probably too complicated for an illustration • Provide ample white space around and within the illustration
Photographs	Can illustrate a technical issue or add a "human face" to the data. Can capture visuals of "before" and "after" a program or intervention.	May be costly. Sometimes difficult to take high-quality photos. Can occupy a large amount of space in a report. May not photocopy well.	• Obtain written permission from subjects (not only to take the picture, but that it can be used as a communication device) • Plan what will and will not be photographed and how the pictures will be used • Use several photographers to capture multiple perspectives

CORRECTING PROBLEM SITUATIONS

The most important aspect to the management of any project is knowing when and how to step in to correct situations before they become major problems. Referring back to Figure 3, it is obvious that there are situations where simply having a good plan for how to determine what the reaction to potential issues is as important as having an actual plan for reaction. Pfeffer and Sutton, in their paper *The Knowing-Doing Gap*, state, "Often we form our impressions of others based on how smart they seem."[448] While not always a good situation, such an individual does instill confidence, and often confidence is all that is necessary to stimulate individuals to move beyond the initial crisis psychology of denial and rapidly into acceptance/doing something.

The best way to establish value, however, is to perform. Too many organizations value intelligence above action, planning above achieving, and talking above performing. Pfeffer and Sutton state,

> *Talk is also valued because, the quantity and "quality" of talk can be assessed immediately, but the quality of leadership or management capability, the ability to get things done, can be assessed only with a greater time lag. Suspending evaluation until more tangible outcomes occur, is difficult for several reasons. First, doing so clashes with the natural human tendency to form impressions quickly, to categorize and stereotype people equally swiftly, and to resist information that contradicts such first impressions. Second, it does not fit within the time scale of the performance appraisal and career progression systems of most organizations.*[449]

Additionally, individuals proceed on what they know from past experience rather than rely upon cognition to guide their steps. This is a natural human reaction, particularly in periods of stress as discussed in Chapter 4. This is why Deming admonishes security professionals to remove fear to achieve quality. Fear leads to stress, which leads to autonomic reaction. Removal of fear allows the engagement of the human intellect when the individual is so inclined. Engaging human intellect enables the individual to consider the issue logically, such that the mind can produce appropriate options for consideration, discussion, and logical selection.

Pfeffer and Sutton go on to state, "It is easier to encourage people to question conventional wisdom and to create dramatic breaks with the past, in an atmosphere of trust and safety. Getting beyond precedent requires having courage. Driving fear out of the organization helps to encourage courageous behavior."[450]

The key to correcting issues then is the ability to devise appropriate measures and metrics to track progress, identify areas of pending problems, communicate

---

[448] Pfeffer, J. and Sutton, R.I (2000). The Knowing-Doing Gap. Harvard Business School Press. Harvard University. Pg 2. Downloaded on April 3, 2012, from http://toolkitforplcs.pbworks.com/w/file/fetch/40397385/The%20Knowing%20Doing%20Gap.pdf

[449] Ibid.

[450] Ibid. pg. 4.

these issues in sufficient time to plan or engage a preplanned reaction, and communicate the success of that action. Pfeffer and Sutton establish the following points in this regard:[451]

> *Measurement practices that help organizations to leverage knowledge effectively typically have the following characteristics:*
> * *The measurements are relatively global in their scope. They focus less on trying to assess individual performance and more on factors critical to organizational success.*
> * *The measures are focused more on processes and means to ends, and less on final outcomes. This focus results in measures that facilitate learning and provide data that can better guide action and decision making.*
> * *They are tied to and reflect the business model, culture and philosophy of the firm. As a result, measurement practices vary from one firm to the other as the business imperatives, cultures, and philosophies vary. And, in measuring things such as adherence to values, recruitment and retention, and working cooperatively with others, the measures depart from conventional accounting-based indicators.*
> * *The measures result from a mindful, ongoing process of learning from experience and experimentation. There is a feeling that the measurement system can always be improved. Because the business environment is likely to change, practices that are effective now, may be ineffective in the future. Measures evolve to serve a fundamental core business and operating philosophy or strategy that is more constant.*
> * *The measurement process uses comparatively few metrics. Although these firms may collect a large amount of data, they focus on a small set of measures that are crucial for supporting the company's business model, philosophy, and culture.*

Conclusion

It is within the structure of knowing, of thinking, and of planning with appropriate means of measuring that the structure of offensive and defensive security and intelligence operations can succeed. It is the processes of knowing what one is doing, why, with what goals/objectives, what outcomes are expected, and how a threat can thwart and/or mimic the desired outcomes to lull the planner

---

[451] Ibid. pg 5-6.

into a false sense of "rightness" that will ignore the developing reality. The goal of this text is to raise the reader's level of awareness rather than cookie-cut a set of solutions.

Remember, when all facts are taken into account and all options that do not fit these facts are removed, what remains, no matter how unlikely, must be the truth.

Bibliography

Ackoff, R. (1981). On the Use of Models in Corporate Planning. *Strategic Management Journal, 2*, 353-359.

Adams, S. (2003, March 14). Dilbert. Retrieved from http://search.dilbert.com/se arch?w=and+so+it+begins+just+in+time+inventory&view=list&filter=type% 3Acomic

Agency, C. I. (n.d.). *Wikipedia/CIA Triad*. Retrieved January 2012, from Wikipedia: http://en.wikipedia.org/wiki/CIA_TRIAD#Key_concepts

Allott, R. (2001). *The Physical Foundation of Language*. Hebeorth, UK: Able Publishers.

Amerman, L. (2008). *The Structure of Jungian Psychology*. Houston, TX: MindStretch.

Anderson, R. (2001). Why Information Security is Hard—An Economic Perspective. Cambridge, UK: University of Cambridge Computer Laboratory. Retrieved from http://www.acsac.org/2001/papers/110.pdf

Anderson, W. a. (2004). Law as a Weapon: How RICO Suberts Liberty and the True Purpose of Law. *The Independent Review, IX*(1), 85-97. Retrieved from http://www.independent.org/pdf/tir/tir_09_1_4_anderson.pdf

Arendt, H. (n.d.). *Encyclopedia of Philosophy*. Retrieved October 14, 2011, from http://www.iep.utm.edu/arendt/#H4

Ariely, D. (2010, June). You Are What You Measure. *Harvard Business Review*. Retrieved January 4, 2012, from http://hbr.org/2010/06/column-you-are-what-you-measure/ar/1

Aunger, R. (2002). *The Electric MEME: A New Theory on How We Think*. New York, NY: The Free Press.

Bambauer, D. (2011, April). Conundrum. *Accepted Paper Series*.

Bambauer, D. (2011, June 8). *Cybersecurity Theory and Myths*. Retrieved September 23, 2011, from Info/Law Blog: http://blogs.law.harvard.edu/infolaw/2011/06/08/cybersecurity-theory-and-myths/

Barnes, J. (1984). Cognitive Biases and Their Impact on Strategic Planning. *Strategic Management Journal*, 129-137.

Basagiannis, S. K. (2009, September). Probabilistic Model Checking for the Quantification of DoS Security Threats. *Computers and Security, 28*(6), 450-465.

BCI. (n.d.). *Glossary of Terms.* Retrieved October 8, 2011, from BCI.org: http://www.thebci.org/Glossary.pdf

Bellinger, G. (n.d.). Retrieved September 1, 2011, from Systems Thinking Organization: http://www.systems-thinking.org/dikw/dikw.htm

Bettinger, R. R. (Vol 50, No 5, October 2009). Rethinking the Origins of Agriculture: Constraints on the Development of Agriculture. *Current Anthropology*, 627-631.

Bleiholder, J. a. (n.d.). *Data Fusion.* doi:1456650.1456651

Blyth, M. (2009). *Business Continuity Management: Building an Effective Incident Management Plan.* Hoboken, NJ: Wiley and Sons.

Bowen, P. K. (2009). *NIST Special Publication 800-65 (Rev 1 DRAFT): Recommendation for Integrating Information Security into Capital Planning and Investment Control Process.* Washington, D.C.: U.S. Department of Commerce.

Box, G. (1976). Science and Statistics. *Journal of the American Statistical Association, 71*(358), 791-799. Retrieved October 30, 2011, from http://links.jstor.org/sici?sici=0162-1459%28197612%2971%3A356%3C791%3ASAS%3E2.0.CO%3B2-W

Box, G. a. (2007). Response Survaces, Mixtures, and Ridge Analysis. In *Empirical Model-Building and Response Surfaces* (2nd ed.). New York, NY: Wiley.

Boyson, S. a. (2009). Developing a Cyber Supply Chain Assurance Reference Model. College Park, Md, USA: The R.H. Smith School of Business University of Maryland. Retrieved from http://www.cyber.umd.edu/research/cyber-supply.html

Brancik, K. (2003). The Computer Forensics and Cybersecurity Governance Model. *Information Systems Control Journal, 2*, 1-8. Retrieved from http://www.isaca.org/Journal/Past-Issues/2003/Volume-2/Pages/The-Computer-Forensics-and-Cybersecurity-Governance-Model.aspx

Brass, C. (2004). *CRS REport to Congress (RL 30795): General Management Laws: A Compendium.* Washington, D.C.: Congressional Report Services.

Brock, S. (2012, March 13). Lodi Unified School District. Sacramento, Ca, United States. Retrieved from http://www.csus.edu/indiv/b/brocks/Courses/EDS%20240/EDS%20240%20Handouts/Operant%20Conditioning%20O_H%20&%20H_O.pdf

Brown, M. (2004). Rapid Knowledge Formation in an Information Rich Environment. *DODCRTS Symposium.* San Diego, CA: Department of Defense.

Bryson, D. (2009, Fall). Personality and Culture, the Social Science Research Council and Liberal Social Engineering. *Journal of the History of the Behavioral Sciences*, 355-386.

Buchanan, J. a. (2000). *Information Overload: A Decision-Making Perspective (MCDM2000)*. Hamilton, New Zealand: Waikato School of Business. Retrieved February 18, 2005, from http://www.mngt.waikato.ac.nz/depts/mnss/john/iomcdm2000_1.pdf

Burgoon, J. a. (1988, No 55). Nonverbal Expectance Violations: Model Elaboration and Application to Immediacy Behavior. *Communication Monographs*, 58-79.

Burgoon, J. a. (1988, No. 55). Nonverbal expectancy Violations: Model Elaboration and Application to Immediacy Behavior. *Communication Monographs*, 58-79.

Burgoon, J. (October 1, 2004). Mindfulness and Interpersonal Communication. *Journal of Social Issues*, 105-128.

Burgoon, M. (1982). The Effects of Communication Context, Source Credibility and Message Valence as Predictors of Perceived Compliance-gaining Message Appropriatenss and Social Influence. *Communication*, 58-77.

Butcher, J. (Captain's Furies). *2007.* New York, NY: The Berkley Publishing Group.

Campo, S. C. (November 11, 2002). Social Norms and Expectancy Violation Theories: Assessing the Effectiveness of Health Communication Campaigns. *American Public Health Association.* Ithaca, NY: American Public Health Association.

Christensen, C. (n.d.). *The Importance of Asking the Right Questions— Commencement Speech.* Southern New Hampshire University. Retrieved from http://www.claytonchristensen.com/documents/SNHUCommencementtalk-DemocracyCapitalismandReligion.pdf

CIO Insight. (2005, October 22). *How to Lie with Earned Value.* Retrieved March 30, 2012, from CIO Insight: http://www.cioinsight.com/c/a/Past-Opinions/How-to-Lie-with-Earned-Value/

Clark, D. (2011, October 18). *Example of EVM.* Retrieved March 1, 2012, from NWLink.com: http://www.nwlink.com/~donclark/hrd/tasks.html

Clavel, J. (. (1983). *The Art of War.* New York, NY: Delecorte Press.

Clifford, M. (2004). *Identifying and Exploring Security Essentials.* Upper Saddle River, NJ: Prentice-Hall.

Cobb, C. (2003). *From Quality to Business Excellence: A Systems Approach to Management.* Milwaukee, Ws: American Society for Quality.

Comadena, M. (1990). Review of the books Nonverbal communications: The unspoken dialogue; Nonverbal communications: Studies and applications (2nd ed.); and the nonverbal communication reader. *Communication Education*, 161-162.

Compliance Department. (n.d.). *IRB Guide.* Retrieved December 19, 2008, from http://compliance.vpr.okstate.edu/irb/documents/IRB_Guide.pdf

Coue, E. (1922). *Self Mastery Through Conscious Autosuggestion.* Public Domain Status.

Crick, B. (1983). Introduction to Niccola Machiavelli: The Discourses. In L. Walker, *Introduction to Niccola Machiavelli: The Discourses.* London, UK: Penguin Publishers.

Curtis, G. a. (2011). *Proactive Security Administration.* Upper Saddle River, NJ: Prentice-Hall.

Curtis, G. a. (2011). *Proactive Security Administration Second Edition.* New York, NY: Prentice-Hall.

Davies, N. (2010, November 2). Rethinking History: General Douglas MacArthur. Melbourne, Australia. Retrieved November 13, 2011, from http://rethinkinghistory.blogspot.com/2010/11/rating-general-douglas-macarthur.html

Davies, R. (Vol 7, 1976). Singulares and Roman Britain. *Britannia*, 134-144. Retrieved October 7, 2011, from JSTOR.org: http://www.jstor.org/pss/525769

Debnam, S. (2006). *Mine's Bigger Than Yours.* London: Marshall Cavendish Limited.

Defense Human Resourses Activity. (2012, 4 4). Adjudicative Desk Reference—Counterintelligence. Washtington, D.C. Retrieved from http://www.dhra.mil/perserec/adr/counterintelligence/counterintelligenceframeset.htm

Defense Intelligence Agency. (2011). *CI Glossary—Terms & Definitions of Interest for DoD CI Professionals.* Washington, D.C.: Defense Intelligence Agancy.

Deming, W. (n.d.). *Deming's 14 Points.* Retrieved January 18, 2008, from http://www.stat.auckland.ac.nz/~mullins/quality/Deming.pdf

Department of Defense. (2009). *Department of Defense Architecture Framework Vol 1: Introduction, Overview, and Concepts—Manager's Guide.* Washington, D.C.: Department of Defense.

Diogenes LLC. (2012, January 21). Basic Executive Protection—Proactive Security. p. (unk). Retrieved from http://diogenesllc.com/executiveprotectionproactivesecurity.pdf

Directorate of Intelligence. (1989). *Rising Political Instability Under Gorbachev: Understanding the Problem and Prospects for Resolution.* Washington, D.C.: Central Intelligence Agency. Retrieved from https://www.cia.gov/library/publications/historical-collection-publications/ronald-reagan-intelligence-and-the-end-of-the-cold-war/Reagan%20booklet.pdf

Disaster Recovery Institute. (n.d.). *Disaster Recovery Process Requirements.* Retrieved October 13, 2011, from Disaster Recovery Institute: www.drii.org/certification/professionalprac.php

DISC Assessment. (n.d.). *Home.* Retrieved March 20, 2012, from DISC Assessment: http://disc-assessment.com/

Donath, J. (2004). Being Real. In K. Goldberg, *The Robot in the Garden: Telerobotics and Telepistemology in the Age of the Internet.* Boston, MA: Massachusetts Institute of Technology Press. Retrieved October 19, 2005, from http://duplox.wz-berlin.de/docs/panel/judith.html

Doyle, A. S. (1890). *The Adventures of Sherlock Holmes: The Sign of Four.* New York, NY: Harper Publishers.

Doyle, A. S. (1892). *The Adventures of Sherlock Holmes: A Scandal in Bohemia.* New York, NY: Harper Publishers.

Doyle, A. S. (1893). Sherlock Holmes: The Adventure of the Reigate Squire. *The Strand Magazine.*

Dutts, A. a. (2002). Management's Role in Information Security in a Cyber Economy. *California Management Review, 45*(1), 67-87.

Duxbury, N. (2001). Signalling [sic] and Social Norms. *Oxford Journal of Legal Studies, 21*(4), 719-736.

Elsea, J. (2004). *CRS RL32567—Lawfulness of Interrogation Techniques Under the Geneva Conventions.* Washington, D.C.: Congressional Research Service—Library of Congress.

Enescu, M. E. (Vol 6(2), 2011). The Specifics of Security management: The functions of Information Security Required by Organizations. *Journal of Economics, Management and Financial Markets*, 201.

Flowe, H. (n.d.). *Psychological Theories of Crime.* Retrieved January 3, 2012, from University of California—San Diego: http://psy2.ucsd.edu/~hflowe/psych.htm

Freud, S. (1061). *The Complete Works of Sigmund Freud (Vol 19).* London, UK: Hogarth.

Freud, S. (1925). The Resistances to Psycho-Analysis. *The Collected Papers of Sigmund Freud, 5*, 163-74.

Freud, S. (1933). *New Introductory Lectures on Psychoanalysis.* Middlesex, UK: Penguin.

Freud, S. (1987). *Beyond the Pleasure Principle—On Metapsychology.* Middlesex, UK: Penguin.

Geslier, C. a. (2007). Land Use Planning and Security in Terrains of Terror. *Conference on the Science and Education of Land use*, (p. npn). Washington, D.C.

Gikas, C. (2010). A General Comparison of FISMA, HIPAA, ISO 27000 and PCI-DSS Standards. *Information Security Journal: A Global Perspective*(19), pp. 132-141. Retrieved October 14, 2012

Glancy, G. a. (2006). The Psychiatric Aspects of Solitary Confinement. *Victims and Offenders*, 361-367.

Goldratt, E. (n.d.). Theory of Constraints in Quality Management. Retrieved from http://www.goldratt.com

Gollop, R. W. (2004). Influencing sceptical staff to become supporters of service improvement: a qualitative study of doctors' and managers' views. *Qual Saf Health Care*(13), 108-114.

Government of Scotland. (n.d.). *Business Continuation Planning.* Retrieved October 8, 2011, from Government of Scotland: http://www.scotland.gov.uk/Publications/2007/06/12094636/36

Grossman, D. (2009). *On Killing.* New York, NY: E-Rights/E-Reads Ltd.

Grudens-Schuck, N. L.-A. (2004). *Focus Group Fundamentals.* Iowa State University. Retrieved from http://www.extension.iastate.edu/publications/pm1969b.pdf

Hafiz, M. A. (n.d.). Towards an Organization of Security Patterns. Retrieved from http://munawarhafiz.com/research/patterns/haj07-security-patterns.pdf

Halloway, S. (n.d.). *Security Model.* Retrieved January 2012, from Bloor Research: http://www.bloorresearch.com/analysis/11624/security-what-security-p1-p1.html

Harris, R. (Vol 50, N. 1 February 1981). The MAGIC Leak of 1941and Japanese-American Relations. *Pacific Historical Review,* 77-96.

Harter, K. (2010). Security and "Gute Policey" in Early Modern Europe:. *Historical Social Research, 35*(4), 41-65.

Hauer, R. (1999). *Psychology of Intelligence Analysis.* Washington, D.C.: Center for the Study of Intelligence.

Haynes, J. a. (2003). *In Denial.* San Francisco, CA, United States: Encounter Books. Retrieved from http://www.encounterbooks.com

Hegel, G. (1837). The Philosophy of History. In J. Sibree, *The Philosophy of History.* New York, NY: Dover Publishing.

Heger, C. (2006). *An Introduction to Operations Research—Benefits, Methods & Application.* Austin, Tx: Fortuitous.com. Retrieved December 5, 2011, from http://fortuitous.com/docs/primers/OR-intro.pdf

Hiermann, W. a. (2003). A Practical Knowledge-based Approach to Skill Management and Personal Development. *Journal of Universal Computer Science,* 1398-1409.

Hillier, F. a. (2001). *Introduction to Operations Researcch.* New York, NY: McGraw-Hill.

Hoffer, E. (n.d.). *Quotes.* Retrieved October 11, 2011, from Eric Hoffer Quotes: www.erichoffer.net/quotes.html

HTCIA. (2011). *2011 Report on Cyber Crime Investigation.* Rosedale, CA: HTCIA.

Hussinger, K. a. (2011). *In Search for the Not-Invented-Here Syndrome: The Role of Knowledge Sources and Firm Success.* Zurich: Center for European Research.

Ingram, W. (2002). *The Show-Me State.* Gareth Stevens.

Inscape Publishing, Inc. (2011). *Everything DiSC Application Library: How My Graph Became a Dot.* Inscape Publishing, Inc. Retrieved from http://www.corexcel.com/pdf/everything-disc-application-library-research-report.pdf

International Standards Organization. (n.d.). ISO 27002—Chapter 6—Organization of Information Security. Retrieved from https://wiki.internet2.edu/confluence/display/itsg2/Organization+of+Information+Security+(ISO+6)

Johnson, B. (2005). *Principles of Security Management.* Upper Saddle River, NJ: Pearson Education Inc.

Joint Chiefs of Staff. (2007). *Joint Publication 3-13.1 Electronic Warfare.* Washington, D.C.: Department of Defense.

Joint Chiefs of Staff. (2009). *Joint Publication 2-1.3—Joint Intelligence Preparation of the Operational Environment.* Washington, D.C.: Department of Defense.

Joint Chiefs of Staff. (2010, November 8). Dictionary of Military and Associated Terms. p. 525. Retrieved May 10, 2012, from http://www.dtic.mil/doctrine/new_pubs/jp1_02.pdf

Joyner, C. a. (2001). *Information Warfare as International Coercion: Elements of a Legal Framework.* Washington, D.C.: Institute for Law, Science and Global Security—Georgetown University.

Jung, C. A. (1968). *The Archetypes and Collective Unconscious.* Princeton, NJ: Princeton University Press.

Kahan, D. (2006). Fear of Democracy: A Cultural Evaluation of Sunstein on Risk. *FAculty Scholarship Series*(104), 1071-1072. Retrieved September 22, 2011, from http://digitalcommons.law.yale.edu/fss_papers/104

Kandel, E. (2001, Vol 294, No 5544). The Molecular Biology of Memory Storage: A Dialogue Between Genes and Synapses. *Science*, 1030-1038.

Kandel, E. S. (2000). *Principles of Neural Science.* New York, NY: McGraw-Hill.

Kimmins, J. D. (Undated). *NIST Special Publication 800-13: Telecommunications Security Guidelines for Telecommunications Management Network.* Washington, D.C.: U.S. Department of Commerce.

Koltuksuz, A. a. (2006). Intelligence Analysis Modeling. *International Conference on Hybrid Information Technology/IEEE Computer Society*, (pp. 1-37). Cheju, Korea. Retrieved from http://doi.ieeecomputersociety.org/10.1109/ICHIT.2006.157

Kraut, A. P. (Vol 3, No 4, Nov 1989). The Role of the Manager: What's Really important in Different Management Jobs. *The Academy of Management Executives*, 286.

Lamport, L. S. (1982). The Byzantine Generals Problem. *ACM Transactions on Programming Languages and Systems, 4*(3), 382-401.

Lasley, C. S. (2007). *Understanding Critical Infrastructure Failure: Examining the experience of Bilozi and Gulfport Mississippi after Hurricane Katrina.* Louisville, Ky: University of Louisville.

Lehman, D. C. (2004). Psychology and Culture. *Annual Review Psychology*(55), 689-714.

Llinas, J. (2002). *Intelligence Fusion.* Retrieved December 1, 2011, from NATO: ftp://ftp.rta.nato.int/PubFullText/RTO/MP\RTO-MP-HFM-207/\/PubFullText/RTO/MP/RTO-MP-IST-040/MP-IST-040-$KN2.pps

Loerch, A. a. (2007). *Methods for Conducting Military Operational Analysis.* Washington, D.C.: Military Operations Research Society (MORS).

Luvaas, J. (1999). *Frederick the Great on the Art of War.* New York, NY: Da Capo Press.

Lynn-Jones, S. (No 4, Summer 1995). Offense-Defense Theory and Its Critics. Security Studies. No 4, Summer 1995. *Security Studies,* 660-691.

Macall, C. a. (2010). Tutorial on Agent-Based Modeling and Simulation. *Journal of Simulation*(4), 151-162.

MacDougall, D. (April 1907). The Soul: Hypothesis Concerning Soul Substance Together with Experimental Evidence of the Existence of Such Substance. *American Medicine,* npn.

Mahoney, M. (2003, January 13). The Subconscious Mind of the Consumer (and How to Reach It). *Harvard Business School Weekly,* p. npn.

Mankiw, N. (2009). *Principles of Economics: 6th Edition.* Mason, Oh: Centgage Learning Products. Retrieved from http://www1.taxfoundation.org/blog/show/1467.html

Markiewicz, A. (2008). The political context of evaluation: what does this mean for independence and objectivity? *Evaluation Journal of Australasia, 8*(2), 35-41.

Maslow, A. (n.d.). *Theories of Personality.* Retrieved October 7, 2011, from About Psychology: http://psychology.about.com/od/theoriesofpersonality/a/hierarchyneeds.htm

Maslow, A. (Vol 50(4), Jul 1943). The Maslow Hierarchy of Needs. *Psychologyical Review,* 370-396.

Mason, P. (1998). Untitled. *Post-Traumatic Gazette, 4*(4).

Massey, D. (2002). A Brief History of Human Society: The Origin and Role of Emotion in Social Life. *American Sociological Review, 67.*

Mather, T. (2011). *RSA Conference Blogs.* Retrieved October 7, 2011, from RSA Conference: https://365.rsaconference.com/blogs/tim-mather/2010/09/29/definition-of-cybersecurity

Mayo Clinic. (2012, January 2). Definition of Diseases and Conditions. Retrieved from http://www.mayoclinic.com/health/narcissistic-personality-disorder/DS00652

Mcavoy, J. a. (2006). Resisting the Change to User Stories: A Trip to Abilene. *International Journal of Information Systems and Change Management,* 48-61.

McClure, S. L. (2004). Neural Correlates of Behavioral Preference for Culturally Familiar Drinks. *Neuron,* 379-387. Retrieved from http://www.hnl.bcm.tmc.edu/articles/Read/McClureLi2004.pdf. pg 384.

McClure, S. L. (2004). *Neuron.* Retrieved March 14, 2005, from http://www.hnl.bcm.tmc.edu/articles/Read/McClureLi2004.pdf

McCrae, R. (2009). Personality Profiles of Cultures: Patterns of Ethos. *European Journal of Personality*(23), 205-227.

McFate, M. (March-April 2005). Anthropology and Counterinsurgency: The Strange Story of Their Curious Relationship. *Military Review*, 24-38.

McLellan, E. S. (2004). *AnSWR Users Guide.* Atlanta, GA: Centers for Disease Control and Prevention.

McVicar, M. (2011, December 4). Profiling Leaders and Analyzing Their Motivation. *MORS: Phalanx, 44*(4), pp. 6-8.

Merabet, L. a.-L. (2010). Neural Reorganization Following Sensory Loss: The Opportunity of Change. *Reviews, 11*, 44-52. Retrieved January 2010

Mifa, K. (2011, November 14). Huawei Technologies Buys Symantec Stake JV $530 Million. *International Business Times Journal*, p. npn. Retrieved from http://www.ibtimes.com/articles/249271/20111114/huawei-buys-symantec-stake-jv-530-million.htm

Moore, D. a. (2003). Bringing intelligence About: Practitioners Reflect on Best Practices. In R. Swenson, *Center for Strategic Intelligence Research* (pp. 95-132). Washington, D.C.: Department of Defense.

Mostifavi, R. (2011, April 25). Iran says it has detected second cyber attack. *Reuters News Agency*. Retrieved from http://www.reuters.com/article/2011/04/25/us-iran-computer-virus-idUSTRE73O1OL20110425

Nabavian, N. (2007). *CPSC 350 Data Structures: Image Steganography.* Chapman University. Retrieved from http://www1.chapman.edu/~nabav100/ImgStegano/download/ImageSteganography.pdf

Nach, J. (1950). Equilibrium Points in N-Person Games. *Proceedings of the National Academy of Sciences, 36*(1), 48-49.

National Science Foundation. (2002). *Evaluation and Types of Evaluation.* Washington, D.C.: National Science Foundation. Retrieved from http://www.nsf.gov/pubs/2002/nsf02057/nsf02057_2.pdf

NBC News. (2012, January 9). Health Officials: Rats a Concern at Occupy DC Sites. *NBC News.* Retrieved March 18, 2012, from http://www.nbcwashington.com/news/local/Health-Officials-Rats-a-Concern-at-Occupy-DC-Sites-136975513.html

Ness, D. a. (1997). *Restoring Justice.* Cincinnati, Oh: Anderson Publishing Co. Retrieved from https://www.ncjrs.gov/App/Publications/abstract.aspx?ID=165803

Newall, P. (2005). Retrieved October 17, 2011, from the Falilean Library: http://www.galilean-library.org/manuscript.php?postid=43792

Nimon, H. (2008). *Relationship of Personality to Virtual Communications Efficacy within a Military Combat Environment.* Houston, TX: University of Phoenix.

Normandeau, A. a. (1998). Restoring Justice (A Book Review). *Canadian Journal of Criminology, 40*(3), 342-345.

Olson, M. (2009). *The Development of IT Suspicion as a Construct and Subsequent Measure.* Wright-Patterson AFB, Oh: U.S. Air Force Institute of Technology.

Palepu, K. H. (2004). *Business Analysis and Valuation: Using Financial Statements* (3rd ed.). Mason, Oh: Thompson Learning.

Paradis, S. B. (No Date). *Data Fusion in support of Dynamic Human Decision Making.* Canada: Defence Research Establishment.

Paterson, M. (2007). *The Secret War: The Inside Story of the Codemakers and Codebreakers of World War II.* Wales, UK: David & Charles, Inc.

Patrick, W. (n.d.). Creating an Informatioin Systems Security Program. Retrieved from http://www.sans.org/reading_room/whitepapers/policyissues/creating-information-systems-security-policy_534

Pearce, M. (2009). *The Evolution of Defense HUMINT Through Post Conflict Iraq.* Carlisle, Pa: U.S. War College.

Peisert, S. B. (Unk). Toward Models for Forensic Analysis. San Diego, Ca, USA. Retrieved from http://www.cs.ucdavis.edu/~peisert/research/PBKM-SADFE2007-ForensicModels.pdf

Perrow, C. (2005). Normal Accidents: Living with High Risk Technology. In L. Gonzales, *Deep Survival.* New York, NY: Norton and Co.

Pfeffer, J. a. (2000). The Knowing-Doing Gap. *Harvard Business School Press*, pp. 1-8. Retrieved April 3, 2012, from http://toolkitforplcs.pbworks.com/w/file/fetch/40397385/The%20Knowing%20Doing%20Gap.pdf

Pictet, J. (1960). *The Geneva Conventions of 12 August 1949. Commentary.* Washington, D.C.: The Library of Congress Research Division.

Planck, M. (1918). *Planck Lecture on Quantum Theory.* Retrieved November 1, 2011, from http://www.nobelprize.org/nobel_prizes/physics/laureates/1918/planck-lecture.html

Popham, W. (2006). *Defining and Enhancing Formative Assessment.* Los Angeles: UCLA.

Pratt, C. (2005). *Quantum Theory Lectures.* Retrieved October 22, 2011, from http://www.pa.msu.edu/courses/2000fall/PHY232/lectures/quantum/quantum_def.html

Preston, E. a. (2002). Computer Security Publications: Information Economics, Shifting Liability, and the First Amendment. *Whittier Law Review*, 71-142.

Project Management Institute. (2010). *Project Management Book of Knowledge.* Newton Square, Pa: PMI, Inc.

Province, C. (n.d.). The Third Army in World War II. Retrieved December 3, 2011, from http://www.pattonhq.com/textfiles/thirdhst.html

R.G., F. (n.d.). *Birth of War.* Retrieved January 2012, from Tennessee Technical University: http://iweb.tntech.edu/kosburn/history-444/birth_of_war.htm

Raman, B. (2004, April). *Report Writing Guidelines.* (Indian Institute of Technology Kanpur) Retrieved April 1, 2012, from How to Write a Good Report: http://www.cse.iitk.ac.in/users/braman/students/good-report.html

Record, J. (2012, January). The Mystery of Pearl Harbor: Why Did Japan Attack the United States Pacific Fleet and Start a War It Could Not Win. *Military History, 28*(5), pp. 28-38.

Riechman, D. (2010). *Cyber Disrupt and Deny.* Wright-Patterson AFB, Oh: U.S. Air Force Research Laboratory.

Ritchey, D. (2011, April). The Security-Integrator Link. *Security*, 20-32.

Roosevelt, F. (1942). Quote: Mission Statement to General D.W. Eisenhower. Washington, D.C. Retrieved October 12, 2011, from http://www.britannica.com/dday/article-9400217

Rosner, C. (2010 Vol 90, Issue 4). Isolation. *Canada's History.*

Sankardas, R. C. (n.d.). *Game Theory as Applied to Network Security.* Retrieved December 2, 2011, from University of Memphis: http://gtcs.cs.memphis.edu/pubs/hicss43.pdf

Santayana, G. (1905). Life of Reason, Reason in Common Sense.

Schwartz, J. a. (2002). *The Mind and the Brain: Neuroplasticity and the Power of Mental Force.* New York, NY: HarperCollins Publishers.

Scott, L. a. (2006, October 5). Intelligence, Crises and Security: Lessons from History? *Intelligence and National Security, 21*(5), 653-674. Retrieved October 11, 2011

Scott, R. (2000). The Limites of Behavioral Theories of Law and Social Norms. *Virginia Law Review*, 1603.

Scriven, M. (1967). The Methodology of Evaluation. In R. G. Tyler, *Perspectives of Curriculum Evaluation (AERA Mongraph Series on Curriculum Evaluation.* Chicago, Il: Rand-McNally.

SDR/IOMA. (2011). Institute of Finance and Management. *Ratings & contracting Security Survey*(11-02), 11-13.

Sears, S. (2011, October 7). *Gettysburg.* Retrieved October 7, 2011, from The Brothers War: http://www.brotherswar.com/Gettysburg-3q.htm

Sherman, D. (1975). *Sherman75.pdf.* Retrieved March 14, 2005, from University of Pennsylvania: http://www.ling.upenn.edu/~beatrice/300/pdf/ sherman75.pdf

Shiraev, E. a. (2010). *Cross-Cultural Psychology: Critical Thinking and Contemporary Applications (3rd Edition).* Boston: Allyn and Bacon.

Shiraev, E. a. (2010). *Cross-Cultural Psychology: Critical Thinking and Contemporary Applications (4th Ed).* Boston, MA: Allen and Bacon.

Shiva, S. R. (2010, May). *Game Inspired Cyber Security.* Retrieved December 2, 2011, from Department of Computer Science University of Memphis: http://gtcs.cs.memphis.edu/index.php?c=publications

Simon Fraser University. (n.d.). *History of Mathematics: The Brahmagupta.* Retrieved October 21, 2011, from Mathematics Department: http://www.math.sfu.ca/histmath/India/7thCenturyAD/brahmagupta.html

Smith, B. F. (Vol 17, Issue 1). Impacts from Repeated Mass Media Campaigns to Promote Sun Protection in Australia. *Oxford Journals: Health Promotion International*, 51-60.

Smith, M. (2009). *Rybollov Seccurity Model*. Retrieved December 2011, from http://www.guerilla-ciso.com/archives/1406

Snowden, R. (2006). *Teach Yourself Freud*. New York, NY: McGraw-Hill.

Sontag, S. D. (1998). *Blind Man's Bluff: The Untold Story of American Submarine Espionage*. New York, NY: Harper_Collins.

South Carolina University. (n.d.). *Business Ethics History*. Retrieved October 13, 2011, from Ethics: http://www.scu.edu/ethics/practicing/focusareas/business/conference/presentations/business-ethics-history.html

Steinberg, A. B. (1999). *Revisions to the JDL Data Fusion Model*. Arlington, VA: ERIM International Inc.

Stetter, F. a. (2002). Autogenic Training: A Meta-Analysis of Clinical Outcome Studies. *Applied Psychophysiology and Biofeedback, 27*(1), 45-98.

Stokes, M. L. (2011). *The Chinese People's Liberation Army Signals Intelligence and Cyber Reconnaissance Infrastructure*. Washington, D.C.: Project 2049 Institute.

Strandberg, C. (2009). *The Role of Human Resource Management in Corporate Social Responsibility: Issue Grief and Roadmap*. Burnaby, BC, Canada: Strandberg Consulting.

Swidler, A. (1986). Culture in Action: Symbols and Strategies. *American Sociological Review, 51*, 273-286.

Swift.com. (n.d.). Figure: Intelligence Battle Book. Retrieved December 28, 2011, from http://dcswift.com/military/index.html

Symantec Inc. (No Date). *Symantec Cyber Threat Analysis Program Overview White Paper*. Symantic Security Intelligence Services.

Szulanski, G. (1996). Exploring Internal Stickiness: Impediments to the Transfer of Best Practice within the Firm. *Strategic Management Journal*(17), 27-43.

Targowski, A. (2005, May 1). From Data to Wisdom. *Dialogue and Universalism*(5-6), 55-71.

Thompson, I. (October 17, 1990). *Quantum Mechanics and Consciousness: A Causal Correspondence Theory*. Retrieved October 23, 2011, from Generative Science Organization: http://www.generativescience.org/ps-papers/qmc1i.pdf

Toigo, J. (2003). *Disaster Recovery Planning: Preparing for the Unthinkable*. Upper Saddle River, NJ: Prentice-Hall, Inc.

Tolone, W. W. (2004). *Applying COUGAAR to Integrated Critical Infrastructure Modeling and Simulation*. Charlotte, NC: University of North Carolina.

Tsunetomo, Y. (2008, September). *The Art of the Samurai: Yamamoto Tsunstomo's Hagakure*. (B. Steben, Trans.) Duncan Baird.

U.S. Army. (1988). *Army Regulation 380-67*. U.S. Army.

U.S. Army. (1991). *Army Regulation 190-13*.

U.S. Army. (1992). *Army Regulation 190-16.*

U.S. Army. (1997). *Field Manual 101-5-1: Operational Terms and Graphics.* Washington, D.C.: U.S. Army.

U.S. Army. (2000). *Army Regulation 380-5 Information Security.*

U.S. Army. (2006). *DCSINT Handbook No. 1.02—Critical Infrastructure Threats and Terrorism.* Washington, D.C.: U.S. Army.

U.S. Army. (2007). *Army Regulation 530-1: Operations Security.* Washington, D.C.: U.S. Army.

U.S. Army. (2009). *Field Manual 2-01.3—Intelligence Preparation of the Battlefield.* Washington, D.C.: U.S. Army.

U.S. Army. (2010). *Field Manual 2-0: Intelligence.* Washington, D.C.: U.S. Army.

U.S. Army. (2010). *Field Manual 3-90.15—Site Exploitation.* Washington, D.C.: U.S. Army.

U.S. Army. (2010). *TRADOC Pamphlet 525-7-8 Cyberspace Operations concept Capability Plan 2016-2028.* U.S. Army.

U.S. Congress. (2004, January 19). United States Code, 3 USC 19. Washington, D.C., United States: U.S. Congress.

U.S. Continental Congress. (1788, September 13). Constitution of the United States of America. Philidelphia, PA, United States: United States Congress.

U.S. Department of Commerce. (2002). *NIST FIPS 140-2.3.* Washington, D.C.: U.S. Department of Commerce.

U.S. Department of Commerce. (2003). *Impact Assessment and Project Appraisal.* Washington, D.C.: U.S. Department of Commerce. Retrieved September 27, 2011, from http://www.nmfs.noaa.gov/sfa/reg_svcs/social%20guid&pri.pdf

U.S. Department of Commerce. (n.d.). *Hyatt Regency Walkway Collapse.* Retrieved October 12, 2011, from Wikipedia: http://fire.nist.gov/bfrlpubs/build82/PDF/b82002.pdf

U.S. Department of Homeland Security. (2012). *Department of Homeland Security.* Retrieved May 3, 2012, from http://www.dhs.gov/files/prepresprecovery.shtm

U.S. Department of Transportation. (n.d.). Retrieved October 23, 2011, from http://www4.uwm.edu/cuts/bench/change.htm#resist

U.S. Office of Personnel Management. (1999). *Strategic Human Resources Management: Aligning with the Mission.* Washington, D.C.: U.S. Office of Personnel Management.

Ulrich, T. (1999). *Computer Mediated Communications and Group Decision Making.* Milwaukee, WI: University of Wisconsin.

University of Maryland & SAIC, Inc. (n.d.). Cybersecurity Supply Model. (U. o. Maryland, Ed.) College Park, MD, USA. Retrieved from http://www.cyber.umd.edu/research/cyber-supply.html

UNK. (n.d.). *Brain Parts.* Retrieved October 17, 2011, from Brain Health Puzzles: www.brainhealthandpuzzles.com

UNK. (n.d.). *Science Fair Projects*. Retrieved October 11, 2011, from Science Buddies.org: http://www.sciencebuddies.org/science-fair-projects/project_scientific_method.shtml

Unk. (n.d.). *Security History*. Retrieved October 7, 2011, from http://www.hsmc-ul.com/customer-info/security-history

Unk. (n.d.). The Amygdala. Retrieved March 16, 2012, from http://brainconnection.positscience.com/topics/?main=fa/fear-conditioning2

UNK. (n.d.). *Workplace Health Safety and Security*. Retrieved October 13, 2011, from Allbusiness.com: http://www.allbusiness.com/human-resources/workplace-health-safety-security/479512-1.html#ixzz1ag2zwZYb

Van Kuijk, H. (2011). *Five Pillars of Knowledge*. Houston: Self.

Waller, D. a. (1995, August 21). Onward Cyber Warriors. *Time, 146*(8), pp. 38-45.

Walthall, J. (1980). *Prehistoric Indians of the Southeast: Archeology of Alabama and the Middle South*. Huntsville, Alabama: University of Alabama.

Warner, N. a. (2004). Structural Model of Team Collaboration. DODCRTS.

Webb, N. a. (2010). *The Innovation Playbook: A Revolution in Business Excellence*. New York, NY: John Wiley and Sons.

Weber, M. G. (1948). *Max Weber: Essays in Sociology*. Oxford, UK: Routledge.

Wheaton, K. a. (2007, September—October). Evaluating Intelligence. *Competitive Intelligence Magazine, 10*(5), 19-23.

White House Council of Economic Advisors. (2002). *Almanac of Policy Issues*. Retrieved December 10, 2011, from http://www.policyalmanac.org/economic/archive/torts.shtml

White, F. J. (1987). *Data Fusion Lexicon*. San Diego, CA: Joint Directors of Laboratories—Naval Ocean Systems Center.

Whitney, L. (2010, March 26). Symantec finds China top source of malware. *CNET*. Retrieved from http://news.cnet.com/8301-1009_3-20001234-83.html

Yoogalingam, R. (2003). Retrieved January 8, 2005, from http://www.schulich.yorku.ca/ssb-extra/phd.nsf/0/ 3751c20e40c86f4c85256b200072e586?OpenDocument

Young, M. (Vol 22:1, 2011). Electronic Surveillance in the Era of Modern Technology and Evolving Threats to National Security. *Stanford Law & Policy Review*, 11-39.

Zaltman, G. (2005). *How Customers Think: Essential Insights into the Mind of the Market*. Boston, MA: Harvard Business School Press.

Zimbardo, P. (1972). On the Ethics of Intevention in Human Psychological Research: With Special Referrence to the Stanford Prison Experiment. *Cognition 2(2)*, 243-256.

Index

U

V

W

Lightning Source UK Ltd.
Milton Keynes UK
UKHW03f1830270318
320138UK00001B/112/P